Computer Law and Software Protection

Computer Law and Software Protection

A Bibliography of Crime, Liability, Abuse and Security, 1984 through 1992

compiled by
REBA A. BEST *and*
D. CHERYN PICQUET

McFarland & Company, Inc., Publishers
Jefferson, North Carolina, and London

British Library Cataloguing-in-Publication data are available

Library of Congress Cataloguing-in-Publication Data

Best, Reba A.
    Computer law and software protection : a bibliography of crime,
liability, abuse and security, 1984 through 1992 / compiled by Reba
A. Best and D. Cheryn Picquet.
       p.   cm.
    Continuation of : Computer crime, abuse, liability and security,
published in 1985.
    Includes indexes.
    ISBN 0-89950-840-5 (sewn softcover : 50# alk. paper) ∞
    1. Computers—Law and legislation—Bibliography.   2. Computer
crimes—Bibliography.   3. Data protection—Law and legislation—
Bibliography.   4. Software protection—Law and legislation—
Bibliography.   I. Picquet, D. Cheryn.   II. Best, Reba A.   Computer
crime, abuse, liability and security.   III. Title.
K564.C6A154   1993
016.343099'9—dc20
[016.3423999]   92-56631
                                                                      CIP

Manufactured in the United States of America

McFarland & Company, Inc., Publishers
  Box 611, Jefferson, North Carolina 28640

Dedicated to the memory of John W. Best and
with gratitude to Margaret Cassell Picquet

Table of Contents

Acknowledgments

The authors gratefully acknowledge the assistance of
Tonya R. Wheat, Kelly L. McCarter, and Wendy Waterworth
in the preparation of this manuscript.

Introduction

Computer Crime, Abuse, Liability and Security: A Comprehensive Bibliography, 1970–1984, the predecessor of this volume, was published in 1985. This volume picks up where that one ends.

At the time of the earlier publication, terms such as bits and bytes, ROMs and RAMs, and CPUs and chips were being introduced into the everyday vocabulary of many Americans, particularly through their workplaces. An era which had become known as the "computer age" had come into its own, bringing with it a new language, new sociological trends, and new perspectives on data storage and information retrieval. As emphasized in that earlier research guide, society had, as a consequence, been introduced to a world of criminal activity which had previously been technologically impossible. Logic bombs and salami techniques, piggybacking and superzapping, and data diddling and hacking were new concepts in the realm of technological crime and abuse.

With this new style of abusiveness had come unexpected needs for innovative security, criminal investigation and detection, and trial technique, especially in the areas of evidence and discovery. Legislators had begun to hear the societal demands for statutory response, and the courts were beginning to hear cases without precedent. This so-called computer age had caught the legal system with its briefs down. Issues ranging from privacy to freedom of information access, from financial management systems to EFTs and credit cards, and from intellectual property to trade regulation had failed to escape invasive permeation by the computer age.

The earlier guide covered the 14-year period from 1970 through mid-1984. During the eight years since that time, introduction and change have given way to evolution and development. The types and prevalence of computer crime have mushroomed. The legal system, especially in the form of legislative developments, has moved so rapidly into these diverse fields that it can now purport to being in touch with the technological times.

Concerns about legal protections such as copyright, patents, privacy, and consumer rights and issues, including antitrust and trade secrets and practices have reached international proportions. (The 1970–1984 guide included 114 entries—or 6.6 percent of its total—dealing with copyright issues; while the current volume includes 626 copyright entries, or 20.8 percent of its total.)

At least 49 of the 50 states in the United States (along with the District of Columbia) now have legislation governing computer-related crime. Newly introduced forms of abuse are also obviously on the rise: the earlier volume contained no entries involving viruses, whereas this volume includes more than 380 entries regarding viruses.

As a result of this highly accelerated activity, the expansion of the subsequent body of literature has proven phenomenal in similar proportions. In 1984 only 1704 entries and 200 resultant subject index terms were actually available to represent a fairly comprehensive sweep of the computer law and crime literature. That bibliography covered almost twice as many years as this volume, which presents to the researcher access to 3304 title entries through approximately 400 subject index terms (almost twice as many entries and terms overall). Demands for such a guide at this time far surpass the demands experienced in 1984.

Scope

The material in this book covers the years from mid–1984 through 1992, making it a continuation or chronological companion volume of *Computer Crime, Abuse, Liability, and Security: A Comprehensive Bibliography, 1970–1984* (Best and Picquet, 1985, published by McFarland). The 1984 date was chosen so that there would be neither gaps nor overlaps in the time coverage. Entries of newly published materials were added to the manuscript as late as April 1993. These publications bear 1992 copyright dates, but they were not available until 1993. Materials published prior to mid–1984 are not included in this volume, and materials published after 1992 are likewise not included.

Topic

Topical coverage includes literature on computer crime, abuse, liability, security, and other issues of direct relevance such as privacy, patents, copyright, and antitrust and trade practices. As the index topics demonstrate, subject matter runs from the general to the specific—from law and legislation in general to the Semiconductor Chip Protection Extension Act of 1987; from banks and banking to electronic fund transfers. Relative but separate issues, such as admissibility of computer-generated evidence, are included only if the discussion is based on direct relevance to a computer crime topic. To insure accessibility of materials cited, non–English language entries and local newspaper articles have been omitted.

Sources

Titles cited in this bibliography have been gleaned from the widest variety of sources available: legal, technical, business, and popular indexing; government publications (both agency and Congressional materials); and footnotes, citations, and bibliographies appearing in monographic treatises, series, and periodicals. Unlike the earlier bibliography, this one does not attempt to index *Computer World* and similar newspaper-style publications on current awareness "notices" as opposed to more in-depth or academic analyses. (Such publications are usually self-indexed. When they are not, they tend not to be storehoused as faithfully by libraries, diminishing substantially their accessibility.) Every title included has been examined in order to determine appropriateness and subject, and to ensure relative accessibility.

Through its design, scope, and coverage, this bibliography is intended to guide various types of researchers, from the student to the professional, through their respective research projects. For the reader who is simply interested in a general view of legal aspects of the impact of computers on society, this bibliography should prove equally beneficial.

Format

This book contains four sections: a bibliography of books, a bibliography of articles, a coauthor index, and a subject index. The books and articles sections are individually arranged in alphabetical order by author name or by title for those publications listing no author. The entries are numbered continuously throughout these two sections.

The subject index contains approximately 400 terms by which both books and articles are indexed. Because books usually treat a wide array of topics within a general subject area, they are frequently indexed via the more general index terms.

The coauthor index is a listing of joint secondary authors of both books and articles. Convenient access to these authors' works would not be possible without this index.

There exist, therefore, three means of access to this bibliography: by author through the alphabetical arrangements in the books and articles sections; by author through the coauthor index; and by subject through the subject index. A number of "see" and "see also" references appear throughout the subject index for the convenience of the user.

Bibliography — Books

1 Abrams, Howard B. *The Law of Copyright.* 2 vols. (looseleaf) New York: Clark Boardman, 1991-.

2 Abrams, Marshall D., and Harold J. Podell. *Tutorial Computer and Network Security.* Washington, D.C.: IEEE Computer Society Press, 1987.

3 *Advanced Claim Drafting and Amendment Writing Workshop.* (Patents, Copyrights, Trademarks, and Literary Property Course Handbook Series, no. 327) New York: Practising Law Institute, 1991.

4 *Advanced Workshop on Copyright Law.* (Patents, Copyrights, Trademarks, and Literary Property Course Handbook Series, no. 312) New York: Practising Law Institute, 1991.

5 *Advising and Representing Computer and High Technology Clients.* [Virginia]: Virginia Law Foundation, 1987.

6 *Amongst Friends in Computers and Law: A Collection of Essays in Remembrance of Guy Vandenberghe.* Boston: Kluwer Law and Taxation Publishers, 1990.

7 Anchordoguy, Marie. *Computers Inc.: Japan's Challenge to IBM.* Cambridge, Mass.: Council on East Asian Studies, Harvard University, 1989.

8 Ansell, Edward O. *Intellectual Property in Academe: A Legal Compendium.* Washington, D.C.: National Association of College and University Attorneys, 1991.

9 *Applications of Computer Card Technology 1990.* Washington, D.C.: G.P.O., 1990.

10 Aufrichtig, Peter D. "Copyright Protection for Computer Programs in Read Only Memory Chips." In *Copyright Law Symposium: Number Thirty-Two.* New York: Columbia University Press, 1986.

11 Australia. Attorney-General's Department. *Review of Commonwealth Criminal Law: Interim Report — Computer Crime, November 1988.* Canberra: Australian Government Publishing Service, 1988.

12 Bainbridge, David I. *Computers and the Law.* London: Pitman Publishing, 1990.

1

13 Baker, Donald I., and Roland E. Brandel. *The Law of Electronic Fund Transfer Systems.* 2nd ed. Boston: Warren, Gorham and Lamont, 1988.

14 Baker, Richard H. *Computer Security Handbook.* 2nd ed. Blue Ridge Summit, Penn.: TAB Professional and Reference Books, 1991.

15 Bale, Harvey E., Jr. "A Computer and Electronics Industry Perspective." In *Intellectual Property Rights and Capital Formation in the Next Decade.* Eds. Charls E. Walker and Mark A. Bloomfield. Lanham, Md.: University Press of America, 1988.

16 Barker, Joe F. "Copyright for Integrated Circuit Designs: Will the 1976 Act Protect Against Chip Pirates?" In *Copyright Law Symposium: Number Thirty-Three.* New York: Columbia University Press, 1987.

17 *Barriers to Domestic Technology Transfers: Hearing Before the Subcommittee on Oversight and Investigations of the Committee on Energy and Commerce, House of Representatives, One Hundred Second Congress, First Session, July 25, 1991.* Washington, D.C.: G.P.O., 1992.

18 *Basics of Computer Law, May 10-11, 1991, Boston, Massachusetts: ALI-ABA Course of Study Materials.* Philadelphia: American Law Institute–American Bar Association Committee on Continuing Professional Education, 1991.

19 Baum, Michael S., and Henry H. Perritt, Jr. *Electronic Contracting, Publishing and EDI Law.* New York: John Wiley and Sons, 1991.

20 Baumgarten, Jon A. *'Fact' and Data Protection After Feist.* Englewood Cliffs, N.J.: Prentice-Hall Law and Business, 1991.

21 Becker, Stephen A. *Patent Applications Handbook.* Deerfield, Ill.: Clark Boardman Callaghan, 1992.

22 Bender, David. *Computer Law.* (looseleaf) New York: Matthew Bender, 1978-.

23 Bennett, Colin J. *Regulating Privacy: Data Protection and Public Policy in Europe and the United States.* Ithaca, N.Y.: Cornell University Press, 1992.

24 Bequai, August. *Computers + Business = Liabilities: A Preventive Guide for Management.* Washington, D.C.: Washington Legal Foundation, 1984.

25 Bequai, August. *Technocrimes.* Lexington, Mass.: D. C. Heath and Co., 1987.

26 Berenbeim, Ronald E. *Safeguarding Intellectual Property.* New York: Conference Board, [1989].

27 Bernacchi, Richard L., Peter B. Frank, and Norman Statland. *Bernacchi on Computer Law: A Guide to the Legal and Management Aspects of Computer Technology.* (looseleaf) Boston: Little Brown and Co., 1986-.

28 *Berne Convention Implementation Act of 1987: Hearings Before the Subcommittee on Courts, Civil Liberties, and the Administration of Justice of the*

Committee on the Judiciary, House of Representatives, One Hundredth Congress, First and Second Sessions, June 17, July 23, September 16 and 30, 1987, February 9 and 10, 1988. Washington, D.C.: G.P.O., 1988.

29 *Berne Convention Implementation Act of 1988: Report of the Committee on the Judiciary, House of Representatives, (to Accompany H.R. 4262) May 6, 1988.* Washington, D.C.: G.P.O., 1988.

30 Besek, June M. "Copyright Protection for Computer Software and Databases: An Overview." In *How to Handle Basic Copyright and Trademark Problems 1992.* (Patents, Copyrights, Trademarks, and Literary Property Course Handbook Series, no. 337) New York: Practising Law Institute, 1992.

31 Beutel, Richard Armstrong. *Contracting for Computer Systems Integration: Legal, Business and Programmatic Strategies to Mitigate Risk.* Charlottesville, Va.: Michie Co., 1991.

32 Bigelow, Robert P. *Computer Contracts: Negotiating and Drafting Guide.* (looseleaf) New York: Matthew Bender, 1987-.

33 Bitter, Gary G. *Computers in Today's World.* New York: John Wiley and Sons, 1984.

34 BloomBecker, Buck. *Spectacular Computer Crimes: What They Are and How They Cost American Business Half a Billion Dollars a Year!.* Homewood, Ill.: Dow Jones-Irwin, 1990.

35 BloomBecker, Jay, ed. *Computer Crime, Computer Security, Computer Ethics.* Los Angeles: National Center for Computer Crime Data, 1986.

36 BloomBecker, Jay, ed. *Introduction to Computer Crime.* Los Angeles: National Center for Computer Crime Data, 1985.

37 Blume, P., M. B. Andersen, H. Bender, J. Bing, M. Borjesson, J. Kiuru, A. Saarenpaa, P. Seipel, and L. Skuterud. *Nordic Studies in Information Technology and Law.* Boston: Kluwer Law and Taxation Publishers, 1991.

38 Bonser, David W. "Preemption of 'Shrink-Wrap' Legislation by the Copyright Act." In *Copyright Law Symposium: Number Thirty-Seven.* New York: Columbia University Press, 1990.

39 Borking, John J. *Third Party Protection of Software and Firmware: Direct Protection of Zeros and Ones.* Amsterdam: Elsevier Science Publishers, 1985.

40 Bowers, Dan M. *Access Control and Personal Identification Systems.* Boston: Butterworths, 1988.

41 Brandon, George, and John K. Halvey. *Data Processing Contracts: Structure, Contents, and Negotiation.* 3rd ed. New York: Van Nostrand Reinhold, 1990.

42 Brickman, Bruce K. *Legal Aspects: Acquiring and Protecting Software.* (looseleaf) Madison, N.J.: Carnegie Press, 1984.

43 Brown, Geoffrey. *The Information Game: Ethical Issues in a Microchip World.* Atlantic Highlands, N.J.: Humanities Press International, 1990.

44 Buck, Edward R., III. *Introduction to Data Security and Controls.* 2nd ed. Boston: QED Technical Publishing Group, 1991.

45 *Bugs in the Program: Problems in Federal Government Computer Software Development and Regulation: Staff Study by the Subcommittee on Investigations and Oversight Transmitted to the Committee on Science, Space, and Technology, U.S. House of Representatives, One Hundredth First Congress, First Session, September 1989.* Washington, D.C.: G.P.O., 1989.

46 Burger, Ralf. *Computer Viruses: A High-Tech Disease.* 2nd ed. Grand Rapids, Mich.: Abacus, 1988.

47 Burger, Ralf. *Computer Viruses and Data Protection.* Grand Rapids, Mich.: Abacus, 1991.

48 Caelli, William, Dennis Longley, and Michael Shain. *Information Security for Managers.* New York: Stockton Press, 1989.

49 Callahan, Joseph F. *Personal Computer Security.* Boston: Executive Information Network, 1988.

50 Campbell, Duncan, and Steve Connor. *On the Record: Surveillance, Computers and Privacy — The Inside Story.* London: Michael Joseph, 1986.

51 Carr, Henry. *Computer Software: Legal Protection in the United Kingdom.* Oxford: ESC Publishing, 1987.

52 Carr, Henry, and Richard Arnold. *Computer Software: Legal Protection in the United Kingdom.* 2nd ed. London: Sweet and Maxwell, 1992.

53 Carroll, John M. *Computer Security.* 2nd ed. Boston: Butterworths, 1987.

54 Carroll, John M. "Computer Security." In *Handbook of Loss Prevention and Crime Prevention.* 2nd ed. Ed. Lawrence J. Fennelly. Boston: Butterworths, 1989.

55 Carroll, John M. *Confidential Information Sources: Public and Private.* 2nd ed. Stoneham, Mass.: Butterworth-Heinemann, 1991.

56 Chalton, Simon, and Shelagh Gaskill. *Data Protection Law.* London: Sweet and Maxwell, 1988.

57 Chalton, Simon, Shelagh Gaskill, and J. A. L. Sterling, eds. *Encyclopedia of Data Protection.* (looseleaf) London: Sweet and Maxwell, 1988-.

58 Chantico Publishing Company, Inc. *Combating Computer Crime: Prevention, Detection, Investigation.* New York: McGraw-Hill, 1992.

59 Cherry, Don T. *Total Facility Control.* Boston: Butterworths, 1986.

60 Chisum, Donald S., and Maxim H. Waldbaum. *Acquiring and Protecting Intellectual Property Rights.* (looseleaf) New York: Matthew Bender, 1985-.

61 Chorafas, Dimitris N. *Electronic Funds Transfer.* London: Butterworths, 1988.

62 Chu, John T. "Computer Crime and Victim Justice." In *To Be a Victim: Encounters with Crime and Injustice.* Eds. Diane Sank and David I. Caplan. New York: Plenum Press, 1991.

63 Clapes, Anthony Lawrence. *Software, Copyright, and Competition: The "Look and Feel" of the Law.* Westport, Conn.: Quorum Books, 1989.

64 Clark, Robert. *Data Protection Law in Ireland.* Dublin, Ireland: The Round Hall Press, 1990.

65 Cohen, Frederick B. *A Short Course on Computer Viruses.* Pittsburgh, Penn.: ASP Press, 1990.

66 Comer, Michael J. *Corporate Fraud.* 2nd ed. London: McGraw-Hill, 1985.

67 *Communications and Computers in the 21st Century: Hearing Before the Technology Policy Task Force of the Committee on Science, Space, and Technology, House of Representatives, One Hundredth Congress, First Session, June 25, 1987.* Washington, D.C.: G.P.O., 1987.

68 *Compendium of State Privacy and Security Legislation: 1987 Overview.* Washington, D.C.: Bureau of Justice Statistics, U.S. Dept. of Justice, 1988.

69 *Competitiveness of the U.S. Software Industry: Hearing Before the Committee on Commerce, Science, and Transportation, United States Senate, One Hundred Second Congress, First Session, November 13, 1991.* Washington, D.C.: G.P.O., 1992.

70 *The Computer Abuse Amendments Act of 1990: Hearing Before the Subcommittee on Technology and the Law of the Committee on the Judiciary, United States Senate, One Hundred First Congress, Second Session, on S. 2476...July 31, 1990.* Washington, D.C.: G.P.O., 1991.

71 *The Computer Abuse Amendments Act of 1990: Report of the Committee on the Judiciary, United States Senate, (to Accompany S. 2476) October 19, 1990.* Washington, D.C.: G.P.O., 1990.

72 *Computer and Communications Law: A Conference and Workshop on the Emerging Legal Issues Resulting from the Convergence of the Computer and Communications Industries and Recent Regulatory Changes Relating to Telecommunications, Jan. 14-16, 1985.* [Tempe, Ariz.]: Arizona Law and Technology Institute and the Arizona State University Center for the Study of Law, Science and Technology, 1985.

73 *Computer and Communications Security and Privacy: Hearing Before the Subcommittee on Transportation, Aviation and Materials of the Commit-*

tee on Science and Technology, U.S. House of Representatives, Ninety-Eighth Congress, Second Session, September 24, 1984. Washington, D.C.: G.P.O., 1985.

74 *Computer and Communications Security and Privacy: Hearings Before the Subcommittee on Transportation, Aviation and Materials of the Committee on Science and Technology, U.S. House of Representatives, Ninety-Eighth Congress, First Session, Sept. 26; Oct. 17, 24, 1983.* Washington, D.C.: G.P.O., 1984.

75 *Computer and Communications Security and Privacy: Report Prepared by the Subcommittee on Transportation, Aviation and Materials Transmitted to the Committee on Science and Technology, U.S. House of Representatives, Ninety-Eighth Congress, Second Session, Apr. 1984.* Washington, D.C.: G.P.O., 1984.

76 *Computer Contracts in a Changing Environment: The 11th Annual New England Computer Law Institute, Jointly Sponsored with ALI-ABA.* Boston: Massachusetts Continuing Legal Education, 1991.

77 *Computer Crime.* Edinburgh: Scottish Law Commission, 1986.

78 *Computer Crime: Electronic Fund Transfer Systems Fraud.* Washington, D.C.: Bureau of Justice Statistics, U.S. Dept. of Justice, 1985.

79 *Computer Crime and Computer Security: Hearing Before the Subcommittee on Crime of the Committee on the Judiciary, House of Representatives, Ninety-Ninth Congress, First Session, on H.R. 1001 and H.R. 930...May 23, 1985.* Washington, D.C.: G.P.O., 1986.

80 *Computer Crimes: High-Tech Theft.* Boulder, Colo.: Paladin Press, 1990.

81 *Computer Data Security: A Practical and Legal Guide to Liability, Loss Prevention, and Criminal and Civil Remedies.* Washington, D.C.: BNA, 1989.

82 *Computer Fraud and Abuse Act of 1986.* (Public Law 99- 474, 100 Stat. 1213) Washington, D.C.: G.P.O., Oct. 16, 1986.

83 *The Computer Fraud and Abuse Act of 1986: Hearing Before the Committee on the Judiciary, United States Senate, Ninety-Ninth Congress, Second Session, on S. 2281...April 16, 1986.* Washington, D.C.: G.P.O., 1986.

84 *Computer Fraud and Abuse Act of 1986: Report of the Committee on the Judiciary, House of Representatives, (to Accompany H.R. 4718) May 22, 1986.* Washington, D.C.: G.P.O., 1986.

85 *Computer Fraud and Abuse Act of 1986: Report Together with Additional Views of the Committee on the Judiciary, United States Senate, (to Accompany S. 2281, as Amended) September 3, 1986.* Washington, D.C.: G.P.O., 1986.

86 *Computer Fraud Legislation: Hearing Before the Subcommittee on Criminal Law of the Committee on the Judiciary, United States Senate, Ninety-Ninth Congress, First Session, on S. 440...and S. 1678...October 30, 1985.* Washington, D.C.: G.P.O., 1986.

87 *Computer Fraud Survey.* London: HMSO, 1985.

88 *Computer Law: Current Trends and Developments, a Satellite Program.* (Patents, Copyrights, Trademarks and Literary Property Course Handbook Series, no. 272) New York: Practising Law Institute, 1989.

89 *Computer Law: Practical Approaches to the Acquisition and Marketing of Computer Goods and Services.* [Albany, N.Y.]: New York State Bar Association, 1988.

90 *Computer Law: Program Materials, 1988.* Athens, Ga.: The Institute of Continuing Legal Education in Georgia, 1988.

91 *Computer Law Developments: 1984.* Washington, D.C.: Computer Law Reporter, 1985.

92 *Computer Law Developments: 1985.* Washington, D.C.: Computer Law Reporter, 1986.

93 *Computer Law Developments: 1986.* Washington, D.C.: Computer Law Reporter, 1987.

94 *Computer Law Developments: 1987.* Washington, D.C.: Computer Law Reporter, 1988.

95 *Computer Law Fundamentals: Program Materials 1989.* Athens, Ga.: Institute of Continuing Legal Education in Georgia, 1989.

96 *Computer Law Institute 1984.* (Patents, Copyrights, Trademarks, and Literary Property Course Handbook Series, no. 191) New York: Practising Law Institute, 1984.

97 *Computer Law Institute 1985.* (Patents, Copyrights, Trademarks, and Literary Property Course Handbook Series, no. 209) New York: Practising Law Institute, 1985.

98 *Computer Law Institute 1986.* (Patents, Copyrights, Trademarks, and Literary Property Course Handbook Series, no. 230) New York: Practising Law Institute, 1986.

99 *Computer Law, 1984.* Indianapolis: Indiana Continuing Legal Education Forum, 1984.

100 *Computer Law 1988.* Indianapolis: Indiana Continuing Legal Education Forum, 1988.

101 *Computer Law 1988: Contracts, Litigation, and Software Protection.* Harrisburg, Penn.: Pennsylvania Bar Institute, 1988.

102 *Computer Litigation 1985: Trial Tactics and Techniques.* (Litigation Course Handbook Series, no. 280) New York: Practising Law Institute, 1985.

103 *Computer Matching: Taxpayer Records: Hearing Before the Subcommittee on Oversight of Government Management of the Committee on Governmental Affairs, United States Senate, Ninety-Eighth Congress, Second Session, June 6, 1984.* Washington, D.C.: G.P.O., 1984.

104 *Computer Matching and Privacy Protection Act Amendments of 1989.* (Public Law 101-56, 103 Stat. 149) Washington, D.C.: G.P.O., July 19, 1988.

105 *Computer Matching and Privacy Protection Act of 1986: Hearing Before the Subcommittee on Oversight of Government Management of the Committee on Governmental Affairs, United States Senate, Ninety-Ninth Congress, Second Session, on S. 2756...September 16, 1986.* Washington, D.C.: G.P.O., 1986.

106 *Computer Matching and Privacy Protection Act of 1987: Hearing Before a Subcommittee of the Committee on Government Operations, House of Representatives, One Hundredth Congress, First Session, on S. 496... June 23, 1987.* Washington, D.C.: G.P.O., 1987.

107 *The Computer Matching and Privacy Protection Act of 1987: Report of the Committee on Governmental Affairs, United States Senate (to Accompany S. 496) (To Amend Title 5 of the United States Code...), September 15, 1988.* Washington, D.C.: G.P.O., 1988.

108 *Computer Matching and Privacy Protection Act of 1988.* (Public Law 100-503, 102 Stat. 2507) Washington, D.C.: G.P.O., Oct. 18, 1988.

109 *Computer Matching and Privacy Protection Act of 1988: Report of the Committee on Government Operations, House of Representatives, (to Accompany H.R. 4699) July 27, 1988.* Washington, D.C.: G.P.O., 1988.

110 *Computer Matching and Privacy Protection Amendments of 1990: Hearing Before the Government Information, Justice, and Agriculture Subcommittee of the Committee on Government Operations, House of Representatives, One Hundred First Congress, Second Session, September 11, 1990.* Washington, D.C.: G.P.O., 1991.

111 *Computer Matching and Privacy Protection Amendments of 1990: Report of the Committee on Government Operations, House of Representatives, (to Accompany H.R. 5450) September 27, 1990.* Washington, D.C.: G.P.O., 1990.

112 *Computer Pornograph[y] and Child Exploitation Prevention Act: Hearing Before the Subcommittee on Juvenile Justice of the Committee on the Judiciary, United States Senate, Ninety-Ninth Congress, First Session, on S. 1305, A Bill to Amend Title 18...October 1, 1985.* Washington, D.C.: G.P.O., 1986.

113 *Computer-Related Crime.* (Field Circular, U.S. Army Military Police School, 19-146) Port Townsend, Wash.: Loompanics Unlimited, 1990.

114 *Computer-Related Crime: Analysis of Legal Policy.* Paris: Organisation for Economic Co-operation and Development, 1986.

115 *Computer-Related Crime: Recommendation No. R (89) 9 on Computer-Related Crime and Final Report of the European Committee on Crime Problems.* Strasbourg: Council of Europe, 1990.

116 *Computer Security.* (Understanding Computers) Alexandria, Va.: Time-Life Books, 1990.

117 *Computer Security: Hearing Before the Subcommittee on Technology and Competitiveness of the Committee on Science, Space, and Technology, U.S. House of Representatives, One Hundred Second Congress, First Session, June 27, 1991.* Washington, D.C.: G.P.O., 1991.

118 *Computer Security Act of 1986: Report Together with Additional and Dissenting Views (to Accompany H.R. 2889 Which...Was Referred Jointly to the Committee on Science and Technology and the Committee on Government Operations) (Including Cost Estimate of the Congressional Budget Office) August 6, 1986.* [Washington, D.C.: G.P.O., 1986].

119 *Computer Security Act of 1987.* (Public Law 100-235, 101 Stat. 1727) Washington, D.C.: G.P.O., Jan. 8, 1988.

120 *The Computer Security Act of 1987: Hearing Before the Subcommittee on Science, Research and Technology and the Subcommittee on Transportation, Aviation and Materials of the Committee on Science, Space, and Technology, House of Representatives, One Hundredth Congress, First Session, February 26, 1987.* Washington, D.C.: G.P.O., 1987.

121 *Computer Security Act of 1987 — Part 1: Report of the Committee on Government Operation, House of Representatives, (to Accompany H.R. 145...) June 11, 1987.* Washington, D.C.: G.P.O., 1987.

122 *Computer Security Act of 1987 — Part 2: Report of the Committee on Government Operation, House of Representatives, (to Accompany H.R. 145...) June 11, 1987.* Washington, D.C.: G.P.O., 1987.

123 *Computer Security Act of 1987: Report Prepared by the Subcommittee on Technology and Competitiveness Transmitted to the Committee on Science, Space, and Technology, House of Representatives, One Hundred Second Congress, Second Session, July 1992.* Washington, D.C.: G.P.O., 1992.

124 *Computer Security Applications Conference.* (annual) Los Alamitos, Calif.: IEEE Computer Society Press, 1990-. (Previously the *Aerospace Computer Security Applications Conference*)

125 *Computer Security Handbook: The Practitioner's "Bible."* 4th ed. Northborough, Mass.: Computer Security Institute, 1987.

126 *Computer Security in the Age of Information: Proceedings of the Fifth IFIP International Conference on Computer Security, IFIP/Sec '88 Gold Coast, Queensland, Australia, 19-21 May, 1988.* Amsterdam: Elsevier Science Publishers, 1989.

127 *Computer Security Policies: Hearing Before the Subcommittee on Transportation, Aviation, and Materials of the Committee on Science and Technology, House of Representatives, Ninety-Ninth Congress, First Session, June 27, 1985.* Washington, D.C.: G.P.O., 1985.

128 *Computer Security Requirements: Guidance for Applying the Department of Defense Trusted Computer System Evaluation Criteria in Specific Environments.* [Ft. Meade, Md.?]: DoD Computer Security Center, 1985.

129 *Computer Security Research and Training Act of 1985: Hearing Before a Subcommittee of the Committee on Government Operations, House of Representatives, Ninety-Ninth Congress, First Session, on H.R. 2889... September 18, 1985.* Washington, D.C.: G.P.O., 1985.

130 *Computer Software and Chips: Protection and Marketing 1985.* (Patents, Copyrights, Trademarks, and Literary Property Course Handbook Series, nos. 201 and 202) New York: Practising Law Institute, 1985.

131 *Computer Software and Chips 1986: Protection and Marketing.* (Patents, Copyrights, Trademarks, and Literary Property Course Handbook Series, nos. 225 and 226) New York: Practising Law Institute, 1986.

132 *Computer Software and Intellectual Property: Background Paper.* Washington, D.C.: G.P.O., 1990.

133 *Computer Software 1988: Protection and Marketing.* (Patents, Copyrights, Trademarks, and Literary Property Course Handbook Series, no. 255) New York: Practising Law Institute, 1988.

134 *Computer Software 1989: Protection and Marketing.* (Patents, Copyrights, Trademarks, and Literary Property Course Handbook Series, nos. 275 and 276) New York: Practising Law Institute, 1989.

135 *Computer Software 1990: Protection and Marketing.* (Patents, Copyrights, Trademarks, and Literary Property Course Handbook Series, no. 298) New York: Practising Law Institute, 1990.

136 *Computer Software Rental Amendments Act: Hearing Before the Subcommittee on Courts, Intellectual Property, and the Administration of Justice of the Committee on the Judiciary, House of Representatives, One Hundred First Congress, Second Session, on H.R. 2740, S. 198, and H.R. 5297...July 30, 1990.* Washington, D.C.: G.P.O., 1990.

137 *The Computer Software Rental Amendments Act of 1988: Hearing Before the Subcommittee on Patents, Copyrights and Trademarks of the Committee on the Judiciary, United States Senate, One Hundredth Congress, Second Session, on S. 2727...August 24, 1988.* Washington, D.C.: G.P.O., 1989.

138 *Computer Software Rental Amendments Act of 1989: Hearing Before the Subcommittee on Patents, Copyrights and Trademarks of the Committee on the Judiciary, United States Senate, One Hundred First Congress, First Session, on S. 198...April 19, 1989.* Washington, D.C.: G.P.O., 1990.

139 "Computer Technology and Informational Privacy." In *Genetic Witness: Forensic Uses of DNA Tests.* Washington, D.C.: G.P.O., 1990.

140 *Computer Virus Legislation: Hearing Before the Subcommittee on Criminal Justice of the Committee on the Judiciary, House of Representatives, One Hundred First Congress, First Session, on H.R. 55 and H.R. 287... November 8, 1989.* Washington, D.C.: G.P.O., 1990.

141 *Computer Viruses: Hearing Before the Subcommittee on Technology and the Law of the Committee on the Judiciary, United States Senate, One Hundred First Congress, First Session, on the Impact of Computer Viruses..., May 15, 1989.* Washington, D.C.: G.P.O., 1991.

142 *Computer Viruses: Hearing Before the Subcommittee on Telecommunications and Finance of the Committee on Energy and Commerce, House of Representatives, One Hundred First Congress, First Session, July 20, 1989.* Washington, D.C.: G.P.O., 1989.

143 *Computer Viruses (Part 2): Hearing Before the Subcommittee on Telecommunications and Finance of the Committee on Energy and Commerce, House of Representatives, One Hundred First Congress, Second Session, February 21, 1990.* Washington, D.C.: G.P.O., 1990.

144 *Computer Viruses: Legal and Policy Issues Facing Colleges and Universities.* Chevy Chase, Md.: United Educators Insurance Risk Retention Group, 1989.

145 *Computer Viruses: Myths, Realities and Safeguards.* Wellesley Hills, Mass.: Management Advisory Publications, 1990.

146 *Computer Viruses: Proceedings of an Invitational Symposium, October 10-11, 1988.* New York: Deloitte Haskins and Sells, 1989.

147 *Computers: Crimes, Clues and Control: A Management Guide.* [Washington, D.C.: G.P.O.], 1986.

148 *Computers and Intellectual Property: Hearings Before the Subcommittee on Courts, Intellectual Property, and the Administration of Justice of the Committee on the Judiciary, House of Representatives, One Hundred First Congress, First and Second Sessions, November 8, 1989; and March 7, 1990.* Washington, D.C.: G.P.O., 1991.

149 *Computers and Law Institute — 1988.* Vancouver: Continuing Legal Education Society of British Columbia, 1988.

150 *Computers at Risk: Safe Computing in the Information Age.* Washington, D.C.: National Academy Press, 1991.

151 Conly, Catherine H. *Organizing for Computer Crime Investigation and Prosecution.* Washington, D.C.: National Institute of Justice, U.S. Dept. of Justice, 1989.

152 Cooper, Frederick L., III. *Law and the Software Marketer.* Englewood Cliffs, N.J.: Prentice-Hall, 1988.

153 Cooper, Frederick L., III, ed. *Protection, Marketing, and Distribution of Computer/Communications Technology.* 1990 ed. Winston-Salem, N.C.: Wake Forest CLE, [1990].

154 Cooper, James Arlin. *Computer and Communications Security: Strategies for the 1990s.* New York: McGraw-Hill, 1989.

155 Cooper, James Arlin. *Computer-Security Technology.* Lexington, Mass.: Lexington Books, 1984.

156 "Copyright." In *1984 Entertainment Publishing and the Arts Handbook.* Eds. Michael Meyer and John David Viera. New York: Clark Boardman Co., 1984.

157 *The Copyright Clarification Act: Hearing Before the Subcommittee on Patents, Copyrights and Trademarks of the Committee on the Judiciary, United States Senate, One Hundred First Congress, First Session, on S. 497, May 17, 1989.* Washington, D.C.: G.P.O., 1990.

158 *Copyright Protection for Computer Software to Enhance Technology Transfer: Hearing Before the Subcommittee on Technology and Competitiveness of the Committee on Science, Space, and Technology, U.S. House of Representatives, One Hundred Second Congress, First Session, July 18, 1991.* Washington, D.C.: G.P.O., 1991.

159 *Copyright Protection for Intellectual Property to Enhance Technology Transfer: Hearing Before the Subcommittee on Science, Research and Technology of the Committee on Science, Space, and Technology, U.S. House of Representatives, One Hundred First Congress, Second Session, April 26, 1990.* Washington, D.C.: G.P.O., 1990.

160 "Copyright Registration for Computer Programs—Circular 61." In *How to Handle Basic Copyright and Trademark Problems 1991.* (Patents, Copyrights, Trademarks, and Literary Property Course Handbook Series, no. 314) New York: Practising Law Institute, 1991. Also appears in no. 316, same series.

161 Cornwall, Hugo. *Datatheft: Computer Fraud, Industrial Espionage and Information Crime.* London: Heinemann Professional Publishing, 1987.

162 Cornwell, Roger, and Marie Staunton. *Data Protection: Putting the Record Straight: The NCCL Guide to the Data Protection Act.* London: National Council for Civil Liberties, 1985.

163 The Council of Better Business Bureaus. *How to Protect Your Business.* Elmsford, N. Y.: The Benjamin Co., 1985.

164 *Counterfeit Access Device and Computer Fraud and Abuse Act: Hearings Before the Subcommittee on Crime of the Committee on the Judiciary, House of Representatives, Ninety-Eighth Congress, First and Second Session, on H.R. 3181, H.R. 3570, and H.R. 5112 . . . September 29, November 10, 1983; and March 28, 1984.* Washington, D.C.: G.P.O., 1984.

165 *Counterfeit Access Device and Computer Fraud and Abuse Act of 1984: Report of the Committee on the Judiciary, House of Representatives, (to Accompany H.R. 5616) July 24, 1984.* Washington, D.C.: G.P.O., 1984.

166 *Criminal History Record Information: Compendium of State Privacy and Security Legislation, 1992.* Washington, D. C.: U.S. Dept. of Justice, Office of Justice Programs, Bureau of Justice Statistics, 1992.

167 *Criminal Justice Information Policy: Strategies for Improving Data Quality.* Washington, D.C.: U.S. Dept. of Justice, Office of Justice Programs, Bureau of Justice Statistics, 1988.

168 *Criminal Sanctions for Violation of Software Copyrights: Report of the Committee on the Judiciary, United States Senate, (to Accompany S. 893) April 7, 1992.* Washington, D.C.: G.P.O., 1992.

169 *Critical Connections: Communication for the Future.* Washington, D.C.: G.P.O., 1990.

170 Cronin, Daniel J. *Microcomputer Data Security: Issues and Strategies.* New York: Prentice-Hall Press, 1986.

171 *Current Developments in Computer Software Protection 1991.* (Patents, Copyrights, Trademarks, and Literary Property Course Handbook Series, no. 315) New York: Practising Law Institute, 1991.

172 Czarnota, Bridget, and Robert J. Hart. *Legal Protection of Computer Programs in Europe - A Guide to the EC Directive.* London: Butterworths, 1991.

173 *Data Protection, Computers, and Changing Information Practices: Hearing Before the Government Information, Justice, and Agriculture Subcommittee of the Committee on Government Operations, House of Representatives, One Hundred First Congress, Second Session, May 16, 1990.* Washington, D.C.: G.P.O., 1991.

174 *Datapro Reports on Information Security.* 3 vols. (looseleaf) New York: McGraw-Hill, 1985?-.

175 Davidson, Duncan M., and Jean A. Davidson. *Advanced Legal Strategies for Buying and Selling Computers and Software.* New York: John Wiley and Sons, 1986.

176 Davis, G. Gervaise, III. *Software Protection: Practical and Legal Steps to Protect and Market Computer Programs.* New York: Van Nostrand Reinhold, 1985.

177 *Decline of U.S. Semiconductor Infrastructure: Hearing Before the Subcommittee on Commerce, Consumer Protection, and Competitiveness of the Committee on Energy and Commerce, House of Representatives, One Hundred First Congress, Second Session, May 9, 1990.* Washington, D.C.: G.P.O., 1990.

178 *Defending Secrets, Sharing Data: New Locks and Keys for Electronic Information.* Washington, D.C.: G.P.O., 1987.

179 Denning, Peter J. *Computer Viruses.* [Moffett Field, Calif.]: Research Institute for Advanced Computer Science, 1988.

180 Denning, Peter J., ed. *Computers Under Attack: Intruders, Worms, and Viruses.* New York: Addison-Wesley Publishing Co., 1990.

181 *Department of Justice Computer Security: Neglect Leads to High Risk: Tenth Report by the Committee on Government Operations, House of Representatives, One Hundred Second Congress, First Session, December 5, 1991.* Washington, D.C.: G.P.O., 1991.

182 *Department of Justice Computer Security, Bureau of Prison's Sentry System: Hearing Before the Government Information, Justice, and Agriculture Subcommittee of the Committee on Government Operations, House of Representatives, One Hundred Second Congress, First Session, September 11, 1991.* Washington, D.C.: G.P.O., 1992.

183 *Department of Justice Security Problems: The Sale of Surplus Computer Equipment Containing Sensitive Information: Hearing Before the Government Information, Justice, and Agriculture Subcommittee of the Committee on Government Operations, House of Representatives, One Hundred Second Congress, First Session, March 21, 1991.* Washington, D.C.: G.P.O., 1991.

184 Deutsch, Dennis S. *Protect Yourself: The Guide to Understanding and Negotiating Contracts for Business Computers.* New York: John Wiley and Sons, 1984.

185 *Domestic and International Data Protection Issues: Hearings Before the Government Information, Justice, and Agriculture Subcommittee of the Committee on Government Operations, House of Representatives, One Hundred Second Congress, First Session, April 10, and October 17, 1991.* Washington, D.C.: G.P.O., 1992.

186 Dordick, H. S. "Intellectual Property: Protecting Rights and Privileges in an Electronic Age." In *1986 Entertainment, Publishing and the Arts Handbook.* Eds. John David Viera and Robert Thorne. New York: Clark Boardman, 1986.

187 Dorr, Robert C., and Christopher H. Munch. *Protecting Trade Secrets, Patents, Copyrights, and Trademarks.* New York: Wiley Law Publications, 1990.

188 Doswell, R., and G. L. Simons. *Fraud and Abuse of IT Systems*. Manchester, England: The National Computing Centre, 1986.

189 Drumm, Harold E. "Copyrighting Computer Programs." In *1984 Entertainment, Publishing and the Arts Handbook*. Eds. Michael Meyer and John David Viera. New York: Clark Boardman, 1984.

190 *EDP Engagement: Assisting Clients in Software Contract Negotiations.* (Management Advisory Services Practice Aids: Series; no. 5) New York: American Institute of Certified Public Accountants, 1984.

191 *Effects of Information Technology on Financial Services Systems: Hearing Before the Committee on Banking, Finance and Urban Affairs, House of Representatives, Ninety-Eighth Congress, Second Session, September 12, 1984.* Washington, D.C.: G.P.O., 1984.

192 *85th Annual Report of the Register of Copyrights for the Fiscal Year Ending September 30, 1982.* Washington, D.C.: G.P.O., 1983.

193 *86th Annual Report of the Register of Copyrights for the Fiscal Year Ending September 30, 1983.* Washington, D.C.: G.P.O., 1984.

194 *87th Annual Report of the Register of Copyrights for the Fiscal Year Ending September 30, 1984.* Washington, D.C.: G.P.O., 1985.

195 *88th Annual Report of the Register of Copyrights for the Fiscal Year Ending September 30, 1985.* Washington, D.C.: Library of Congress, 1986.

196 Einhorn, David. "The Scope of Computer Software Copyright." In *Copyright Law Symposium: Number Thirty-Five*. New York: Columbia University Press, 1989.

197 *Electronic and Computer Patent Law.* (Patents, Copyrights, Trademarks, and Literary Property Course Handbook Series, no. 292) New York: Practising Law Institute, 1990.

198 *Electronic Collection and Dissemination of Information by Federal Agencies: A Policy Overview: Twenty-Eighth Report by the Committee on Government Operations.* Washington, D.C.: G.P.O., 1986.

199 *Electronic Communication Privacy: Hearing Before the Subcommittee on Patents, Copyrights and Trademarks of the Committee on the Judiciary, United States Senate, Ninety-Ninth Congress, First Session, on S. 1667 . . . November 13, 1985.* Washington, D.C.: G.P.O., 1987.

200 *Electronic Information Publishing: Old Issues in a New Industry.* (Patents, Copyrights, Trademarks and Literary Property Course Handbook Series, no. 187) New York: Practising Law Institute, 1984.

201 *The Electronic Supervisor: New Technology, New Tensions.* Washington, D.C.: Congress of the United States, Office of Technology Assessment, 1987.

202 *11th Annual Computer Law Institute.* (Patents, Copyrights, Trademarks, and Literary Property Course Handbook Series, no. 279) New York: Practising Law Institute, 1989.

203 Ellis, David R. *A Computer Law Primer.* Largo, Fla.: Sudavel Publishing, 1986.

204 *Encyclopedia of Information Technology Law.* (looseleaf) London: Sweet and Maxwell, 1990-.

205 Ermann, M. David, Mary B. Williams, and Claudio Gutierrez. *Computers, Ethics, and Society.* New York: Oxford University Press, 1990.

206 Evans, Alastair. *The Data Protection Act.* London: Institute of Personnel Management, 1984.

207 Evans, Alastair. *Data Protection Policies and Practice.* London: Institute of Personnel Management, 1987.

208 *Federal Computers and Telecommunications: Security and Reliability Considerations and Computer Crime Legislative Options: A Final Report for the Office of Technology Assessment.* [Washington, D.C.]: G.P.O., 1985.

209 *Federal Government Computer Security: Hearings Before the Subcommittee on Transportation, Aviation, and Materials and the Subcommittee on Science, Research and Technology of the Committee on Science and Technology, House of Representatives, Ninety-Ninth Congress, First Session, October 29, 30, 1985.* Washington, D.C.: G.P.O., 1986.

210 *Federal Government Information Technology: Electronic Record Systems and Individual Privacy.* Washington, D.C.: Office of Technology Assessment, 1986.

211 *Federal Government Information Technology: Electronic Surveillance and Civil Liberties.* Washington, D.C.: Office of Technology Assessment, 1985.

212 *Federal Research Policy and the American Semiconductor Industry: Hearing Before the Subcommittee on Transportation, Aviation and Materials and the Subcommittee on Science, Research and Technology of the Committee on Science, Space, and Technology, U.S. House of Representatives, One Hundred First Congress, First Session, November 8, 1989.* Washington, D.C.: G.P.O., 1990.

213 *The Federal Research Policy for Semiconductors: Hearing Before the Subcommittee on Science, Research and Technology of the Committee on Science, Space, and Technology, U.S. House of Representatives, One Hundred First Congress, Second Session, March 29, 1990.* Washington, D.C.: G.P.O., 1990.

214 *The Federal Reserve Bank of New York Discount Window Advance of $22.6 Billion Extended to the Bank of New York: Hearing Before the Subcom-*

mittee on Domestic Monetary Policy of the Committee on Banking, Finance and Urban Affairs, House of Representatives, Ninety-Ninth Congress, First Session, December 12, 1985. Washington, D.C.: G.P.O., 1986.

215 Fetterman, Daniel J. "The Scope of Copyright Protection for Computer Software: Exploring the Idea/Expression Dichotomy." In *Copyright Law Symposium: Number Thirty-Six.* New York: Columbia University Press, 1990.

216 *5th Annual Computer Law Institute: Program Materials 1990.* Athens, Ga.: Institute of Continuing Legal Education in Georgia, 1990.

217 Finch, James H., and E. Graham Dougall. *Computer Security: A Global Challenge.* Amsterdam: Elsevier Science Publishers, 1984.

218 *Finding a Balance: Computer Software, Intellectual Property and the Challenge of Technological Change.* Washington, D.C.: G.P.O., 1992.

219 Finkel, LeRoy. *Software Copyright Interpretation.* Syracuse, N.Y.: ERIC Clearinghouse on Information Resources, 1985.

220 Fisher, Bruce D., and Michael J. Phillips. "Protection of Business Ideas." In *The Legal, Ethical and Regulatory Environment of Business.* 4th ed. St. Paul, Minn.: West Publishing Co., 1992.

221 Fisher, Royal P. *Information Systems Security.* Englewood Cliffs, N.J.: Prentice-Hall, 1984.

222 Fishman, Stephen. "Adaptations and Compilations." In *The Copyright Handbook: How to Protect and Use Written Works.* Berkeley, Calif.: Nolo Press, 1992.

223 Fites, Philip, Peter Johnston, and Martin Kratz. *The Computer Virus Crisis.* New York: Van Nostrand Reinhold, 1989.

224 Fites, Philip E., Martin P. J. Kratz, and Alan F. Brebner. *Control and Security of Computer Information Systems.* Rockville, Md.: Computer Science Press, 1989.

225 FitzGerald, Jerry. "Network Security and Control." In *Business Data Communications: Basic Concepts, Security, and Design.* 3rd ed. New York: John Wiley and Sons, 1990.

226 Flaherty, David H. *Data Protection and Privacy: Comparative Policies: A Report to the Government Information Technology Project, Office of Technology Assessment, U.S. Congress.* London, Canada: The Privacy Project, University of Western Ontario, 1985.

227 Flaherty, David H. *Protecting Privacy in Surveillance Societies: The Federal Republic of Germany, Sweden, France, Canada, and the United States.* Chapel Hill, N.C.: The University of North Carolina Press, 1989.

228 *Forensic DNA Analysis: Joint Hearing Before the Subcommittee on Civil and Constitutional Rights of the House Committee on the Judiciary and*

the Subcommittee on the Constitution of the Senate Committee on the Judiciary, One Hundred Second Congress, First Session, June 13, 1991. Washington, D.C.: G.P.O., 1992.

229 Forester, Tom, ed. *Computers in the Human Context: Information Technology, Productivity and People.* Oxford: Basil Blackwell, 1989.

230 *14th Annual Computer Law Institute.* (Patents, Copyrights, Trademarks, and Literary Property Course Handbook Series, nos. 344 and 345) New York: Practising Law Institute, 1992.

231 Frank, Lars. *EDP-Security.* Amsterdam: Elsevier Science Publishers, 1992.

232 Freedman, Warren. *The Right of Privacy in the Computer Age.* New York: Quorum Books, 1987.

233 *Freedom of Data Flows and EEC Law: Proceedings of 2nd CELIM Conference.* Boston: Kluwer and Taxation Publishers, 1988.

234 Friedman, Aryeh S. *The Law of High Technology Innovation.* (looseleaf) Salem, N.H.: Butterworth Legal Publishers, 1992-.

235 *GAO Survey, Federal Government Computer Security: Hearing Before the Subcommittee on Transportation, Aviation and Materials of the Committee on Science, Space, and Technology, House of Representatives, One Hundredth Congress, First Session, May 19, 1987.* Washington, D.C.: G.P.O., 1987.

236 Gadbaw, R. Michael, and Timothy J. Richards. *Intellectual Property Rights: Global Consensus, Global Conflict?* Boulder, Colo.: Westview Press, 1988.

237 Garvey, Christi E., ed. *Security and Privacy: Volume I: Proceedings of the First Five Symposia 1980-1984.* Los Alamitos, Calif.: IEEE Computer Society Press, 1990.

238 Garvey, Christi E., ed. *Security and Privacy: Volume II: Proceedings of the 6th, 7th, and 8th Symposia 1985-1987.* Los Alamitos, Calif.: IEEE Computer Society Press, 1990.

239 Gasser, Morrie. *Building a Secure Computer System.* New York: Van Nostrand Reinhold, 1988.

240 Gaze, Beth. *Copyright Protection of Computer Programs.* Annandale: Federation Press, 1989.

241 Gemignani, Michael C. *Computer Law.* (updated by supplements) Rochester, N.Y.: The Lawyers Co-operative Publishing Co., 1985-.

242 Gemignani, Michael C. *A Legal Guide to EDP Management.* Westport, Conn.: Quorum Books, 1989.

243 General Accounting Office. *Information Systems: Agencies Overlook Security Controls During Development.* Washington, D.C.: G.P.O., 1988.

244 Gilburne, Miles R., Ronald L. Johnston, and Allen R. Grogan, eds. *The Computer Law Annual 1985.* New York: Law and Business, Inc./Harcourt Brace Jovanovich, 1985.

245 Goldscheider, Robert. "Computer Software." In *Technology Management: Law/Tactics/Forms.* (looseleaf) New York: Clark Boardman, 1988-.

246 Goldstein, Paul. *Copyright: Principles, Law and Practice.* 3 vols. (updated by supplements) Boston: Little, Brown and Co., 1989-.

247 Gordon, Mark L. *Computer Software: Contracting for Development and Distribution.* New York: John Wiley and Sons, 1986.

248 Gorman, Robert A. *Copyright Law.* Washington, D.C.: Federal Judicial Center, 1991.

249 Great Britain. Law Commission. *Computer Misuse.* London: HMSO, 1988.

250 Green, Gion. "Computer Security." In *Introduction to Security.* 4th ed. Boston: Butterworths, 1987.

251 Greenia, Mark W. *Computer Security Information Sourcebook: A Guide for Managers, Attorneys and Other Concerned Professionals.* Sacramento, Calif.: Lexikon Library Services, 1991.

252 Grimson, Jane B., and Hans-Jurgen Kugler. *Computer Security: The Practical Issues in a Troubled World.* Amsterdam: Elsevier Science Publishers, 1985.

253 Grissonnanche, Andre, ed. *Security and Protection in Information Systems: Proceedings of the Fourth IFIP TC 11 International Conference on Computer Security, IFIP/Sec '86 Monte Carlo, Monaco, 2-4 Dec., 1986.* New York: Elsevier Science Publishers, 1989.

254 Grover, Derrick, ed. *The Protection of Computer Software - Its Technology and Applications.* New York: Cambridge University Press, 1989.

255 *Guide to Computer Law.* 2 vols. (looseleaf) Chicago: Commerce Clearing House, 1989-. (Case materials cumulated in *Computer Cases,* v. 1-.)

256 *Guide to the Prosecution of Telecommunication Fraud by the Use of Computer Crime Statutes.* Chicago: ABA, 1989.

257 Gulleford, Kenneth. *Data Protection in Practice.* London: Butterworths, 1986.

258 Hafner, Katie, and John Markoff. *Cyberpunk: Outlaws and Hackers on the Computer Frontier.* New York: Simon and Schuster, 1991.

259 Hagelshaw, R. Lee. *The Computer User's Legal Guide.* Radnor, Pa.: Chilton Book Co., 1985.

260 Halvey, John K. "A Rose by Any Other Name: Computer Programs and the Idea-Expression Distinction." In *Copyright Law Symposium: Number Thirty-Five.* New York: Columbia University Press, 1988.

261 Hancock, William A., ed. *Data Processing Agreements.* 2nd ed. (looseleaf) Chesterland, Ohio: Business Laws, Inc., 1990-.

262 Hanneman, H. W. A. M. *The Patentability of Computer Software: An International Guide to the Protection of Computer-Related Inventions.* Boston: Kluwer Law and Taxation Publishers, 1985.

263 Hansen, Hugh C. "Copyright Protection for Computer Programs in the EEC and Europe." In *Global Intellectual Property Series: Political Strategies - Trademark and Copyright.* (Patents, Copyrights, Trademarks, and Literary Property Course Handbook Series, no. 318) New York: Practising Law Institute, 1991.

264 Harris, Thorne D., III. *The Legal Guide to Computer Software Protection: A Practical Handbook on Copyrights, Trademarks, Publishing, and Trade Secrets.* Englewood Cliffs, N.J.: Prentice-Hall, 1985.

265 Harry, M. *The Computer Underground: Computer Hacking, Crashing, Pirating and Phreaking.* Port Townsend, Wash.: Loompanics Unlimited, 1985.

266 Hart, William M. "Current Developments in Copyright Computer Software." In *Current Developments in Copyright Law 1990.* (Patents, Copyrights, Trademarks, and Literary Property Course Handbook Series, no. 296) New York: Practising Law Institute, 1990.

267 Haynes, Colin. *The Computer Virus Protection Handbook.* Alameda, Calif.: Sybex, 1990.

268 Hazard, John W., Jr. *Copyright Law in Business and Practice.* New York: Prentice-Hall/Rosenfeld Launer Publications, 1989.

269 Helfant, Robert, and Glenn J. McLoughlin. *Computer Viruses: Technical Overview and Policy Considerations.* [Washington, D.C.]: Congressional Research Service, Library of Congress, 1988.

270 Heller, James S., and Sarah K. Wiant. "Computers and Copyright." In *Copyright Handbook.* (AALL Publications Series, no. 23) Littleton, Colo.: Fred B. Rothman and Co., 1984.

271 Helsing, Cheryl, Marianne Swanson, and Mary Anne Todd. *Computer User's Guide to the Protection of Information Resources.* Gaithersburg, Md.: National Computer Systems Laboratory, National Institute of Standards and Technology, 1989.

272 Henn, Harry G. *Copyright Law: A Practitioner's Guide.* 2nd ed. New York: Practising Law Institute, 1988.

273 Henn, Harry G. *Henn on Copyright Law: A Practitioner's Guide.* 3rd ed. New York: Practising Law Institute, 1991.

274 Hershey, John E., and R. K. Rao Yarlagadda. *Data Transportation and Protection.* New York: Plenum Press, 1986.

275 Hicks, Jack B. "Copyright and Computer Databases: Is Traditional Compila-
     tion Law Adequate?" In *Copyright Law Symposium: Number Thirty-
     Seven*. New York: Columbia University Press, 1990.

276 Highland, Harold Joseph. *Computer Virus Handbook*. Oxford: Elsevier
     Science Publishers, 1990.

277 Hoffman, Lance J., ed. *Rogue Programs: Viruses, Worms, and Trojan
     Horses*. New York: Van Nostrand Reinhold, 1990.

278 Hoffman, Paul S., ed. *Software Contract Forms: 1992 Collection*. Chicago:
     ABA, 1992. (Continues *Software Contract Forms: 1987 Collection*.
     Chicago: ABA, 1987.)

279 Hollander, Patricia A. *Computers in Education: Legal Liabilities and Ethical
     Issues Concerning Their Use and Misuse*. Asheville, N.C.: College Ad-
     ministration Publications, 1986.

280 Houpt, James E. *Access to Electronic Records: A Guide to Reporting on State
     and Local Government in the Computer Age*. Washington, D.C.: The
     Reporters Committee for Freedom of the Press, 1990.

281 Hruska, Jan. *Computer Viruses and Anti-Virus Warfare*. New York: Ellis
     Horwood, 1990.

282 Hruska, Jan, and Keith M. Jackson. *Computer Security Solutions*. Boston:
     CRC Press, 1990.

283 Huband, Frank L., and R. D. Shelton, eds. *Protection of Computer Systems
     and Software: New Approaches for Combating Theft of Software and
     Unauthorized Intrusion*. Clifton, N.J.: Law and Business, 1986.

284 Hughes, Gordon, ed. *Essays on Computer Law*. Melbourne, Australia:
     Longman Cheshire, 1990.

285 Hutt, Arthur E., Seymour Bosworth, and Douglas B. Hoyt, eds. *Computer
     Security Handbook*. 2nd ed. New York: Macmillan Publishing Co., 1988.

286 *Implementation of the Computer Security Act: Hearing Before the Subcom-
     mittee on Transportation, Aviation and Materials and the Subcommittee
     on Science, Research and Technology of the Committee on Science,
     Space, and Technology, U.S. House of Representatives, One Hundred
     First Congress, First Session, March 21, 1989*. Washington, D.C.: G.P.O.,
     1989.

287 *Implementation of the Computer Security Act: Hearing Before the Subcom-
     mittee on Transportation, Aviation and Materials of the Committee on
     Science, Space, and Technology, House of Representatives, One Hun-
     dredth Congress, Second Session, September 22, 1988*. Washington,
     D.C.: G.P.O., 1989.

288 *Implementation of the Computer Security Act (Public Law 100-235): Hear-
     ing Before the Subcommittee on Transportation, Aviation and Materials*

of the Committee on Science, Space, and Technology, U.S. House of Representatives, One Hundred First Congress, Second Session, July 10, 1990. Washington, D.C.: G.P.O., 1990.

289 *Informatics Trade Problems with Brazil: Hearing Before the Subcommittee on Commerce, Consumer Protection, and Competitiveness of the Committee on Energy and Commerce, House of Representatives, One Hundredth Congress, First Session, July 15, 1987.* Washington, D.C.: G.P.O., 1988.

290 *The Intellectual Property Antitrust Protection Act of 1988: Report of the Committee on the Judiciary, (to Accompany S. 438, as amended) August 25, 1988.* Washington, D.C.: G.P.O., 1988.

291 *Intellectual Property Antitrust Protection Act of 1989: Hearing Before the Subcommittee on Economic and Commercial Law of the Committee on the Judiciary, House of Representatives, One Hundred First Congress, Second Session, on H.R. 469...February 8, 1990.* Washington, D.C.: G.P.O., 1991.

292 *Intellectual Property Issues in Software.* Washington, D.C.: National Academy Press, 1991.

293 *Intellectual Property Rights: Hearing Before the Subcommittee on International Trade of the Committee on Finance, United States Senate, Ninety-Ninth Congress, Second Session, on S. 1860 and S. 1869, May 14, 1986.* Washington, D.C.: G.P.O., 1986.

294 *Intellectual Property Rights in an Age of Electronics and Information.* Washington, D.C.: G.P.O., 1986.

295 *International Computer Law: A Practical Guide to the International Distribution and Protection of Software and Integrated Circuits.* (looseleaf) New York: Matthew Bender, 1988-.

296 *Introduction to Computer Law.* (Patents, Copyrights, Trademarks, and Literary Property Course Handbook Series, no. 195) New York: Practising Law Institute, 1985.

297 *Issues Confronting the Semiconductor Industry: Hearings Before the Subcommittee on Technology and the Law of the Committee on the Judiciary, United States Senate, One Hundredth Congress, First Session, on S. 442...February 26; and March 3, 1987.* Washington, D.C.: G.P.O., 1987.

298 JJ & J Consultants. *Legal Protection of Computer Hardware and Software Marketed in Europe.* Sudbury, Mass.: Technology and Business Communications, 1986.

299 Jacobson, Robert V. *The PC Virus Control Handbook: A Technical Guide to Detection, Identification, Disinfection, and Investigation.* 2nd ed. San Francisco, Calif.: Miller Freeman Publications, 1990.

300 Jager, Melvin F. "Trade Secret Protection for Computer Programs." In *1984 Trade Secrets Law Handbook.* New York: Clark Boardman, 1984.

301 Jager, Melvin F. "Trade Secret Protection for Computer Technology." In *Trade Secrets Law,* Vol. 2. (looseleaf) Deerfield, Ill.: Clark Boardman Callaghan, 1985-.

302 Johnson, Deborah G. *Computer Ethics.* Englewood Cliffs, N.J.: Prentice-Hall, 1985.

303 Johnson, Deborah G., and John W. Snapper. *Ethical Issues in the Use of Computers.* Belmont, Calif.: Wadsworth Publishing Co., 1985.

304 Johnson, Douglas W. *Computer Ethics: A Guide for a New Age.* Elgin, Ill.: The Brethren Press, 1984.

305 Joseph, Bruce G. "Computers and Compilations." In *Advanced Seminar on Copyright Law 1992.* (Patents, Copyrights, Trademarks, and Literary Property Course Handbook Series, no. 336) New York: Practising Law Institute, 1992.

306 Jussawalla, Meheroo. *The Economics of Intellectual Property in a World Without Frontiers: A Study of Computer Software.* (Contributions in Economics and Economic History, no. 131) Westport, Conn.: Greenwood Press, 1992.

307 Kane, Pamela. *V. I. R. U. S. Protection: Vital Information Resources Under Siege.* New York: Bantam Books, 1989.

308 Katsh, M. Ethan. *The Electronic Media and the Transformation of Law.* New York: Oxford University Press, 1989.

309 Katzke, Stuart W. *A Small Business Guide to Computer Security.* Washington, D.C.: U.S. Small Business Administration, [1987?].

310 Keet, Ernest E. *Preventing Piracy: A Business Guide to Software Protection.* Reading, Mass.: Addison-Wesley Publishing Co., 1985.

311 Kellogg, Michael K., John Thorne, and Peter W. Huber. *Federal Telecommunications Law.* Boston: Little, Brown and Company, 1992.

312 Kenny, J. J. P., ed. *Data Privacy and Security.* Oxford: Pergamon Infotech, 1985.

313 Knight, Peter, and James Fitzsimons. *The Legal Environment of Computing.* Sydney: Addison-Wesley Publishing Co., 1990.

314 Kramsky, Elliott N. "New Protection for the Semiconductor Chip: A 1984 Federal Law Gives Exclusive Rights and Related Remedies to 'Mask Work' Owners." In *1985 Entertainment, Publishing and the Arts Handbook.* Ed. John David Viera. New York: Clark Boardman, 1985.

315 Kuong, Javier F. *Computer Auditing, Security, and Internal Control Manual.* Englewood Cliffs, N.J.: Prentice-Hall, 1987.

316 Kuong, Javier F., Gerald I. Isaacson, and Chester M. Winters. *Microcomputer Security, Auditability and Controls.* Wellesley Hills, Mass.: Management Advisory Publications, 1985.

317 Kusic, Jane Y. *White-Collar Crime 101 Prevention Handbook.* Vienna, Va.: White-Collar Crime 101, 1989.

318 Kutten, L. J. *Computer Software: Protection, Liability, Law, Forms.* (looseleaf) New York: Clark Boardman, 1987-.

319 Kutten, L. J., Bernard D. Reams, and Allen E. Strehler. *Electronic Contracting Law: EDI and Business Transactions.* New York: Clark Boardman, 1991.

320 Kutten, L. J., and James Talbott. *Sales and Use Taxation of Computer Software.* (looseleaf) Wayne, Penn.: Kutish Publications, 1992-.

321 Ladd, David, David E. Leibowitz, and Bruce G. Joseph. *Protection for Semiconductor Chip Masks in the United States: Analysis of the Semiconductor Chip Protection Act of 1984.* Munich, Germany: The Max Planck Institute for Foreign and International Patent, Copyright, and Competition Law, 1986.

322 Landreth, Bill. *Out of the Inner Circle: A Hacker's Guide to Computer Security.* Bellevue, Wash.: Microsoft Press, 1985.

323 Landwehr, Carl E., ed. *Database Security: Status and Prospects: Results of the IFIP WG 11.3 Initial Meeting Annapolis, Maryland, U.S.A., October 1987.* Amsterdam: Elsevier Science Publishers, 1988.

324 Lane, V. P. *Security of Computer Based Information Systems.* London: Macmillian Education, 1985.

325 Laudon, Kenneth C. *Dossier Society: Value Choices in the Design of National Information Systems.* New York: Columbia University Press, 1986.

326 Lautsch, John C. *American Standard Handbook of Software Business Law.* Reston, Va.: Reston Publishing Co., 1985.

327 Laver, Murray. *Information Technology: Agent of Change.* New York: Cambridge University Press, 1989.

328 *Lawyers On Line: Ethical Perspectives in the Use of Telecomputer Communication.* Chicago: ABA, 1986.

329 Leaffer, Marshall A. *Understanding Copyright Law.* New York: Matthew Bender, 1989.

330 *Legal and Business Aspects of Periodical and Electronic Publishing.* (Patents, Copyrights, Trademarks and Literary Property Course Handbook Series, no. 273) New York: Practising Law Institute, 1989.

331 *A Lesson of the Gulf War: National Security Requires Computer Security: Hearing Before the Subcommittee on Government Information and*

Regulation of the Committee on Governmental Affairs, United States Senate, One Hundred Second Congress, First Session, June 19, 1991. Washington, D.C.: G.P.O., 1992.

332 Lever, Jack Q., ed. *U.S. Intellectual Property Legislative Review: An Annual Survey.* New York: Clark Boardman, 1991-.

333 Levin, Richard B. *The Computer Virus Handbook.* Berkeley, Calif.: Osborne McGraw-Hill, 1990.

334 Levy, Steven. *Hackers: Heroes of the Computer Revolution.* Garden City, N.Y.: Anchor Press/Doubleday, 1984.

335 Lindey, Alexander. "Computers." In *Lindey on Entertainment Publishing and the Arts: Agreements and the Law.* Vol. 3. 2nd ed. Ed. Michael Landau. Deerfield, Ill.: Clark Boardman Callaghan, 1980-.

336 Linowes, David F. *Privacy in America: Is Your Private Life in the Public Eye?* Chicago: University of Illinois Press, 1989.

337 Lipner, Seth E., and Stephen Kalman. *Computer Law: Cases and Materials.* Columbus, Ohio: Merrill Publishing Co., 1989.

338 Lobel, Jerome. *Foiling the System Breakers: Computer Security and Access Control.* New York: McGraw-Hill, 1986.

339 Longley, Dennis, and Michael Shain. *Data and Computer Security: Dictionary of Standards, Concepts and Terms.* New York: Stockton Press, 1987.

340 Ludwig, Mark A. *The Little Black Book of Computer Viruses: Volume One: The Basic Technology.* Tuscon, Ariz.: American Eagle Publications, 1991.

341 Lundell, Allan. *Virus: The Secret World of Computer Invaders That Breed and Destroy.* Chicago: Contemporary Books, 1989.

342 McAfee, John, and Colin Haynes. *Computer Viruses, Worms, Data Diddlers, Killer Programs and Other Threats to Your System: What They Are, How They Work, and How to Defend Your PC, Mac, or Mainframe.* New York: St. Martin's Press, 1989.

343 McCarthy, J. Thomas. *McCarthy's Desk Encyclopedia of Intellectual Property.* Washington, D.C.: BNA, 1991.

344 McEwen, J. Thomas. *Dedicated Computer Crime Units.* Washington, D.C.: National Institute of Justice, U.S. Dept. of Justice, 1989.

345 McIntosh, Toby J. *Federal Information in the Electronic Age: Policy Issues for the 1990s.* Washington, D.C.: BNA, 1990.

346 Maggs, Peter B., and James A. Sprowl. *Computer Applications in the Law.* St. Paul, Minn.: West Publishing Co., 1987.

347 Maggs, Peter B., John T. Soma, and James A. Sprowl. *Computer Law: Cases—Comments—Questions.* St. Paul, Minn.: West Publishing Co., 1992.

348 Mann, J. Fraser. *Computer Technology and the Law in Canada.* Toronto: Carswell, 1987.

349 *Markup of Bills H.R. 191 and H.R. 2941: Markup Sessions Before the Subcommittee on Technology and Competitiveness and the Full Committee on Science, Space, and Technology, U.S. House of Representatives, One Hundred Second Congress, First Session, November 7, 22, 1991.* Washington, D.C.: G.P.O., 1992.

350 Marzouk, Tobey B. *Protecting Your Proprietary Rights in the Computer and High Technology Industries.* Washington, D.C.: Computer Society Press, 1988.

351 Mawrey, Richard B., and Keith J. Salmon. *Computers and the Law.* Oxford: BSP Professional Books, 1988.

352 Mayo, Jonathan L. *Computer Viruses: What They Are, How They Work, How to Avoid Them.* Blue Ridge Summit, Pa.: Windcrest Books, 1990.

353 Meijboom, A. P., and C. Prins, eds. *The Law of Information Technology in Europe 1992.* (Computer Law Series, 9) Boston: Kluwer Law and Taxation Publishers, 1991.

354 Mick, Stephen R. "Applying the Merger Doctrine to the Copyright of Computer Software." In *Copyright Law Symposium: Number Thirty-Seven.* New York: Columbia University Press, 1990.

355 *Microcomputer Security.* (Management Advisory Services Practice Aids, no. 13) New York: American Institute of Certified Public Accountants, 1990.

356 Milgram, Roger M., ed. *Milgram on Trade Secrets.* 4 vols. (looseleaf) New York: Matthew Bender, 1967-.

357 *Military and Civilian Control of Computer Security Issues: Hearing Before the Legislation and National Security Subcommittee of the Committee on Government Operations, House of Representatives, One Hundred First Congress, First Session, May 4, 1989.* Washington, D.C.: G.P.O., 1989.

358 Millard, Christopher J. *Legal Protection of Computer Programs and Data.* Toronto: Carswell, 1985.

359 Millen, Jonathan K. "Models of Multilevel Computer Security." In *Advances in Computers,* Vol. 29. Ed. Marshall C. Yovits. New York: Academic Press, 1989.

360 Moeller, Robert R. *Computer Audit, Control, and Security.* New York: John Wiley and Sons, 1989.

361 *Moral Rights in Our Copyright Laws: Hearings Before the Subcommittee on Patents, Copyrights and Trademarks of the Committee on the Judiciary, United States Senate, One Hundred First Congress, First Session, on S. 1198...and S. 1253...June 20, September 20, and October 24, 1989.* Washington, D.C.: G.P.O., 1990.

362 Motyka, Carol. "U.S. Participation in the Berne Convention and High Technolgy." In *Copyright Law Symposium: Number Thirty-Nine.* New York: Columbia University Press, 1992.

363 Moulton, Rolf T. *Computer Security Handbook: Strategies and Techniques for Preventing Data Loss or Theft.* Englewood Cliffs, N.J.: Prentice-Hall, 1986.

364 Muftic, Sead. *Security in IBM Systems.* Holtsville, N.Y.: Computer Technology Research Corp., 1990.

365 Mylott, Thomas R., III. *Computer Law for Computer Professionals.* Englewood Cliffs, N.J.: Prentice-Hall, 1984.

366 National Advisory Committee on Semiconductors. *Attaining Preeminence in Semiconductors: Third Annual Report to the President and the Congress.* Arlington, Va.: The Committee, 1992.

367 National Advisory Committee on Semiconductors. *Capital Investment in Semiconductors: The Lifeblood of the U.S. Semiconductor Industry.* Arlington, Va.: The Committee, 1990.

368 National Advisory Committee on Semiconductors. *A National Strategy for Semiconductors: An Agenda for the President, the Congress, and the Industry.* Arlington, Va.: The Committee, 1992.

369 National Advisory Committee on Semiconductors. *Preserving the Vital Base: America's Semiconductor Materials and Equipment Industry.* Arlington, Va.: The Committee, 1990.

370 National Audit Office. *Computer Security in Government Departments: Report by the Comptroller and Auditor General.* London: HMSO, 1987.

371 National Computer Security Center. *Computer Security Subsystem Interpretation of the Trusted Computer Evaluation Criteria.* [Washington, D.C.: G.P.O., 1988].

372 National Computer Security Center. *Personal Computer Security Considerations.* Washington, D.C.: G.P.O., 1985.

373 *National High-Performance Computer Technolgy Act of 1989: Hearings Before the Subcommittee on Science, Technology, and Space of the Committee on Commerce, Science, and Transportation, United States Senate, One Hundred First Congress, First Session, on S. 1067. . .June 21, July 26, and September 15, 1989.* Washington, D.C.: G.P.O., 1989.

374 National Research Council. Computer Science and Telecommunications Board. System Security Study Committee. *Computers at Risk: Safe Computing in the Information Age.* Washington, D.C.: National Academy Press, 1991.

375 National Research Council. *Intellectual Property Issues in Software.* Washington, D.C.: National Academy Press, 1991.

376 *Negotiating Computer Contracts.* Clifton, N.J.: Law and Business, 1985.

377 Neitzke, Frederic William. *A Software Law Primer.* New York: Van Nostrand Reinhold, 1984.

378 Neugent, William, John Gilligan, Lance Hoffman, and Zella G. Ruthberg. *Technology Assessment: Methods for Measuring the Level of Computer Security.* Gaithersburg, Md.: Institute for Computer Sciences and Technology, National Bureau of Standards, 1985.

379 Niblett, Bryan. *Data Protection Act 1984.* London: Oyez Longman Publishing, 1984.

380 Nimmer, Raymond T. *The Law of Computer Technology.* Boston: Warren, Gorham and Lamont, 1985.

381 Nimmer, Raymond T. *The Law of Computer Technology.* 2nd ed. (looseleaf) Boston: Warren, Gorham and Lamont, 1992-.

382 *1984: Civil Liberties and the National Security State: Hearings Before the Subcommittee on Courts, Civil Liberties, and the Administration of Justice of the Committee on the Judiciary, House of Representatives, Ninety-Eighth Congress, First and Second Sessions, November 2, 3, 1983, and January 24, April 5, and September 26, 1984.* Washington, D.C.: G.P.O., 1985.

383 *1989 Computer Security and Privacy Plans (CSPP) Review Project: A First-Year Federal Response to the Computer Security Act of 1987 (Final Report).* [Washington, D.C.]: U.S. Department of Commerce, National Institute of Standards and Technology, 1990.

384 *90th Annual Report of the Register of Copyrights for the Fiscal Year Ending September 30, 1987.* Washington, D.C.: Library of Congress, 1988.

385 *Ninth Annual Computer Law Institute.* (Patents, Copyrights, Trademarks, and Literary Property Course Handbook Series, no.239) New York: Practising Law Institute, 1987.

386 Nugter, A. C. M. *Transborder Flow of Personal Data Within the EC: A Comparative Analysis of the Privacy Statutes of the Federal Republic of Germany, France, the United Kingdom and the Netherlands and Their Impact on the Private Sector.* (Computer/Law Series, 6) Boston: Kluwer Law and Taxation Publishers, 1990.

387 Office of Technology Assessment. *Federal Government Information Technology: Electronic Record Systems and Individual Privacy.* Washington, D.C.: G.P.O., 1986.

388 Okimoto, Daniel I., Henry S. Rowen, and Michael J. Dahl. *The Semiconductor Competition and National Security.* Stanford, Calif.: Stanford University, 1987.

389 *Oversight on Communications Privacy: Hearing Before the Subcommittee on Patents, Copyrights and Trademarks of the Committee on the Judiciary, United States Senate, Ninety-Eighth Congress, Second Session on Privacy in Electronic Communications, September 12, 1984.* Washington, D.C.: G.P.O., 1985.

390 Palmer, I. C., and G. A. Potter. *Computer Security Risk Management.* New York: Van Nostrand Reinhold, 1989.

391 Parker, Donn B. *Computer Crime: Criminal Justice Resource Manual.* 2nd ed. (Issues and Practices in Criminal Justice) Washington, D.C.: U.S. Department of Justice, 1989.

392 Parker, Donn B., Susan Swope, and Bruce N. Baker. *Ethical Conflicts in Information and Computer Science, Technology, and Business.* Wellesley, Mass.: QED Information Sciences, 1990.

393 Paul, Philip F. "Product Liability in Computer Products." In *Swartz Proof of Product Defect.* Ed. Edward M. Swartz. Rochester, N.Y.: Lawyers Cooperative Publishing Co., 1985.

394 Pearson, Hilary E. *Computer Contracts: An International Guide to Agreements and Software Protection.* New York: Chapman and Hall, 1984.

395 Perelman, Bruce. "Proving Copyright Infringement of Computer Software: An Analytical Framework." In *Copyright Law Symposium: Number Thirty-Four.* New York: Columbia University Press, 1987.

396 Perry, William E. *Management Strategies for Computer Security.* Boston: Butterworths, 1985.

397 Pfleeger, Charles P. *Security in Computing.* Englewood Cliffs, N.J.: Prentice-Hall, 1989.

398 Pilarski, John H. "User Interfaces and the Idea-Expression Dichotomy, Or Are the Copyright Laws User Friendly?" In *Copyright Law Symposium: Number Thirty-Seven.* New York: Columbia University Press, 1990.

399 *A Practical Guide to the Cable Communications Policy Act of 1984.* (Patents, Copyrights, Trademarks, and Literary Property Course Handbook Series, no. 200) New York: Practising Law Institute, 1985.

400 President's Council on Integrity and Efficiency. *Computers: Crimes, Clues and Controls: A Management Guide.* [Washington, D. C.: G.P.O.], 1986.

401 *Prevention and Prosecution of Computer and High Technology Crime.* (looseleaf) New York: Matthew Bender, 1988-.

402 *Privacy and 1984: Public Opinions on Privacy Issues: Hearing Before a Subcommittee of the Committee on Government Operations, House of Representatives, Ninety-Eighth Congress, First Session, April 4, 1984.* Washington, D.C.: G.P.O., 1985.

403 *Privacy of Social Security Records: Hearing Before the Subcommittee on Social Security and Family Policy of the Committee on Finance, United States Senate, One Hundred Second Congress, Second Session, February 28, 1992.* Washington, D.C.: G.P.O., 1992.

404 Probert, John. "Investigating Computer-Related Crimes Involving Small Computer Systems." In *Critical Issues in Criminal Investigation.* 2nd ed. Ed. Michael J. Palmiotto. [Cincinnati, Ohio]: Anderson Publishing Co., 1988.

405 *Proceedings: the Computer Security Foundations Workshop III, June 12-14, 1990, The Franconia Inn, Franconia, New Hampshire.* Los Alamitos, Calif.: IEEE Computer Society Press, 1990.

406 *Proceedings of the Computer Security Foundations Workshop II.* Washington, D.C.: IEEE Computer Society Press, 1989.

407 *Proceedings of the Congressional Copyright and Technology Symposium: Prepared at the Request of the Subcommittee on Patents, Copyrights and Trademarks for Use of the Committee on the Judiciary, United States Senate, July 1985.* Washington, D.C.: G.P.O., 1985.

408 *Prospects for a New United States–Japan Semiconductor Agreement: Hearing Before the Subcommittee on International Economic Policy and Trade of the Committee on Foreign Affairs, House of Representatives, One Hundred Second Congress, First Session, March 20, 1991.* Washington, D.C.: G.P.O., 1991.

409 *Protecting Computer Technology: Europe and Asia Pacific.* Chicago: Longman Professional, 1985.

410 *Protecting Computer Technology: The Americas.* Chicago: Longman Professional, 1985.

411 *Protecting Trade Secrets 1989.* (Patents, Copyrights, Trademarks and Literary Property Course Handbook Series, no. 269) New York: Practising Law Institute, 1989.

412 *Protective Orders for Semiconductor Chip Products: Report of the Committee on the Judiciary, House of Representatives, (to Accompany H.R. 1951) October 21, 1987.* Washington, D.C.: G.P.O., 1987.

413 Quirk, W. J., ed. *Safety of Computer Control Systems 1986 (Safecomp '86) — Trends in Safe Real Time Computer Systems: Proceedings of the Fifth IFAC Workshop, Sarlat, France, 14-17 October 1986.* New York: Pergamon Press, 1986.

414 Raymond, Eric S., ed. *The New Hacker's Dictionary.* Cambridge, Mass.: The MIT Press, 1991.

415 Reed, Chris, ed. *Computer Law.* London: Blackstone Press, 1990.

416 Remer, Daniel, and Stephen Elias. *Legal Care for Your Software: A Step-by-Step Guide for Computer Software Writers and Publishers.* 3rd ed. Berkeley, Calif.: Nolo Press, 1987.

417 *Renewal of the United States-Japan Semiconductor Agreement: Hearing Before the Subcommittee on International Trade of the Committee on Finance, United States Senate, One Hundred Second Congress, First Session, March 22, 1991.* Washington, D.C.: G.P.O., 1991.

418 Rennie, M.-T. Michele. *Computer Contracts Handbook: Precedents of Contracts for the Sale, Purchase, Support, Distribution and Licence of Computers and Computer Software.* London: Sweet and Maxwell, 1985.

419 Rennie, M.-T. Michele. *Further Computer Contracts: Precedents of Contract for the Sales, Purchase, Licence, Distribution, Development, Support, Escrow and Protection of Computers and Computer Software.* London: Sweet and Maxwell, 1989.

420 *Report of the Data Protection Registrar.* (annual) London: HMSO, 1985-.

421 *[Reports Prepared for the Office of Technology Assessment* (Su. Doc. Y3.72/2:2C73/10/v. 1, v. 2, v. 3), volumes 1-3.] (No Collective Author/Title Information on Publications) Washington, D.C.: Office of Technology Assessment, [1983-85].

422 Ridley, Clarence H., Peter C. Quittmeyer, and John Matuszeski. *Computer Software Agreements: Forms and Commentary.* (updated by cumulative supplements) Boston: Warren, Gorham and Lamont, 1987-.

423 Roberts, Ralph. *COMPUTE!'s Computer Viruses.* Greensboro, N.C.: COMPUTE! Books, 1988.

424 Robertson, Ranald. *Legal Protection of Computer Software.* 1st ed. London: Longman Group UK, 1990.

425 Rose, Lance, and Jonathan Wallace. *Syslaw.* 2nd ed. Winona, Minn.: PC Information Group, Inc., 1992.

426 Rosenberg, John, and J. Leslie Keedy, eds. *Security and Persistence: Proceedings of the International Workshop on Computer Architectures to Support Security and Persistence of Information, 8-11 May 1990, Bremen, West Germany.* New York: Springer-Verlag, 1990.

427 Rostoker, Michael D., and Robert H. Rines. *Computer Jurisprudence: Legal Responses to the Information Revolution.* New York: Oceana Publications, 1986.

428 Rothfeder, Jeffrey. *Privacy for Sale: How Computerization Has Made Everyone's Private Life an Open Secret.* New York: Simon and Schuster, 1992.

429 Rubin, Michael Rogers. *Private Rights, Public Wrongs: The Computer and Personal Privacy.* Norwood, N.J.: Ablex Publishing Corporation, 1988.

430 Russell, Deborah, and G. T. Gangemi, Sr. *Computer Security Basics.* Sebastopol, Calif.: O'Reilly and Associates, 1991.

431 *S. 1920, Small Business Computer Crime Prevention Act: Hearing Before the Committee on Small Business, United States Senate, Ninety-Eighth Congress, Second Session, on S. 1920...March 7, 1984.* Washington, D.C.: G.P.O., 1984.

432 Sackman, Harold, ed. *Comparative Worldwide National Computer Policies.* Amsterdam: Elsevier Science Publishers, 1985.

433 Salone, M. J. *How to Copyright Software.* Ed. Stephen Elias. 3rd ed. Berkeley, Calif.: Nolo Press, 1989.

434 Sand, Leonard B., John S. Siffert, Walter P. Loughlin, and Steven A. Reiss. *Modern Federal Jury Instructions,* Vol. 1A. (looseleaf) New York: Matthew Bender, 1984-.

435 Sandler, Corey, Tom Badgett, and Larry Lefkowitz. *VAX Security: Protecting the System and the Data.* New York: John Wiley and Sons, 1991.

436 Sauvant, Karl P. *International Transactions in Services: The Politics of Transborder Data Flows.* London: Westview Press, 1986.

437 Schroeder, Dirk. *Computer Software Protection and Semiconductor Chips.* (Current EC Legal Developments Series) London: Butterworths, 1990.

438 Schwartz, Laurens R. *Computer Law Forms Handbook: A Legal Guide to Drafting and Negotiating.* (annual) New York: Clark Boardman, 1986-.

439 Schweitzer, James A. *Computer Crime and Business Information: A Practical Guide for Managers.* Amsterdam: Elsevier Science Publishing Co., 1986.

440 Schweitzer, James A. *Computers, Business, and Security: The New Role for Security.* Boston: Butterworths, 1987.

441 Schweitzer, James A. *Managing Information Security: Administrative, Electronic, and Legal Measures to Protect Business Information.* 2nd ed. Boston: Butterworths, 1990.

442 Schweitzer, James A. *Protecting Information on Local Area Networks.* Boston: Butterworths, 1988.

443 *Science, Technology and the First Amendment: Special Report.* Washington, D.C.: G.P.O., 1988.

444 Scott, Michael D. *Scott on Computer Law.* 2nd ed. (looseleaf) Englewood Cliffs, N.J.: Prentice-Hall Law and Business, 1991-.

445 Seberry, Jennifer, and Josef Pieprzyk. *Cryptography: An Introduction to Computer Security.* New York: Prentice-Hall, 1989.

446 *Security Evaluation for Small Computer Centers.* Wellesley, Mass.: QED Information Sciences, 1985.

447 Seipel, P., ed. *From Data Protection to Knowledge Machines: The Study of Law and Informatics.* Boston: Kluwer Law and Taxation Publishers, 1990.

448 *The Semiconductor Chip Protection Act Extension of 1987: Report of the Committee on the Judiciary, United States Senate, (to Accompany S. 442) June 9, 1987.* Washington, D.C.: G.P.O., 1987.

449 *The Semiconductor Chip Protection Act of 1983: Hearing Before the Subcommittee on Patents, Copyrights and Trademarks of the Committee on the Judiciary, United States Senate, Ninety-Eighth Congress, First Session, on S. 1201, A Bill to Amend Title 17...May 19, 1983.* Washington, D.C.: G.P.O., 1984.

450 *The Semiconductor Chip Protection Act of 1984.* New York: Law and Business, 1984.

451 *Semiconductor Chip Protection Act of 1984: Report from the Committee on the Judiciary, House of Representatives, (to Accompany H. R. 5525) (Including Cost Estimate of the Congressional Budget Office), May 15, 1984.* Washington, D.C.: G.P.O., 1984.

452 *The Semiconductor Chip Protection Act of 1984: Report of the Committee on the Judiciary, United States Senate, (to Accompany S. 1201) May 2, 1984.* Washington, D.C.: G.P.O., 1984.

453 *Semiconductor Chip Protection Extension.* (Public Law 100-159, 101 Stat. 899) Washington, D.C.: G.P.O., Nov. 9, 1987.

454 *Semiconductor International Protection Extension Act of 1991: Hearing Before the Subcommittee on Intellectual Property and Judicial Administration of the Committee on the Judiciary, House of Representatives, One Hundred Second Congress, First Session, on H. R. 1998 and H. R. 1999...May 1, 1991.* Washington, D.C.: G.P.O., 1992.

455 *Semiconductor International Protection Extension Act of 1991: Report of the Committee on the Judiciary, House of Representatives, (to Accompany H.R. 1998) June 21, 1991.* Washington, D.C.: G.P.O., 1991.

456 *The Semiconductor International Protection Extension Act of 1991: Report of the Committee on the Judiciary, United States Senate, (to Accompany S. 909) June 11, 1991.* Washington, D.C.: G.P.O., 1991.

457 Sheldon, Jeffrey G. *How to Write a Patent Application.* New York: PLI, 1992.

458 Sherman, Cary H., Hamish R. Sandison, and Marc D. Guren. *Computer Software Protection Law.* (looseleaf) Washington, D.C.: BNA, 1989-.

459 Shue, Virginia V., and James V. Vergari. *State Computer Law: Commentary, Cases and Statutes.* Deerfield, Ill.: Clark Boardman Callaghan, 1992.

460 Sieber, Ulrich. *The International Handbook on Computer Crime: Computer-Related Economic Crime and the Infringements of Privacy.* New York: John Wiley and Sons, 1986.

461 Simon, David F. *Computer Law Handbook: Software Protection, Contracts, Litigation, Forms.* Philadelphia: ALI-ABA, 1990.

462 Sivin, Jay P., and Ellen R. Bialo. *Ethical Use of Information Technologies in Education: Important Issues for America's Schools.* Washington, D.C.: U.S. Department of Justice, Office of Justice Programs, National Institute of Justice, 1992.

463 Sizer, Richard, and Philip Newman. *The Data Protection Act: A Practical Guide.* Brookfield, Vt.: Gower Publishing Co., 1984.

464 Sloan, Irving J., ed. *The Computer and the Law.* (Legal Alamanac Series, no. 83) New York: Oceana Publications, 1984.

465 Sloan, Irving J., ed. *Law of Privacy Rights in a Technological Society.* Dobbs Ferry, N.Y.: Oceana Publications, 1986.

466 *Small Business and Computer Crime: Hearing Before the Subcommittee on Regulation and Business Opportunities of the Committee on Small Business, House of Representatives, One Hundredth Congress, First Session, November 16, 1987.* Washington, D.C.: G.P.O., 1988.

467 *Small Business Computer Security and Education Act of 1984.* (Public Law 98-362, 98 Stat. 431) Washington, D.C.: G.P.O., July 16, 1984.

468 *Small Business Computer Security and Education Act of 1984: Report of the Committee on Small Business, United States Senate, (to Accompany H.R. 3075) May 10, 1984.* Washington, D.C.: G.P.O., 1984.

469 *Software Protection: The U.S. Copyright Office Speaks on the Computer/ Copyright Interface.* New York: Law and Business/ Harcourt Brace Jovanovich, 1984.

470 Sookman, Barry B. *Sookman Computer Law: Acquiring and Protecting Information Technology.* (looseleaf) Toronto: Carswell, 1989-.

471 Spafford, Eugene H., Kathleen A. Heaphy, and David J. Ferbrache. *Computer Viruses: Dealing with Electronic Vandalism and Programmed Threats.* Arlington, Va.: ADAPSO, 1989.

472 Steinauer, Dennis D. *Security of Personal Computer Systems: A Management Guide.* Washington, D.C.: Institute for Computer Sciences and Technology, National Bureau of Standards, 1985.

473 Sterling, Bruce. *The Hacker Crackdown: Law and Disorder on the Electronic Frontier.* New York: Bantam Books, 1992.

474 Sterling, J. A. L. *The Data Protection Act 1984: A Guide to the New Legislation.* Bicester, Oxfordshire: Commerce Clearing House Editions, 1985.

475 Stern, Richard H. *Semiconductor Chip Protection.* New York: Law and Business, 1986.

476 Stoll, Clifford. *The Cuckoo's Egg: Tracking a Spy Through the Maze of Computer Espionage.* New York: Doubleday, 1989.

477 *Symposium: Intellectual Property Protection of Computer Technology.* (Michigan Yearbook of International Legal Studies, Vol. VIII, 1987). Ann Arbor, Mich.: Michigan Yearbook of International Legal Studies, 1988.

478 Talbot, J. R. *Management Guide to Computer Security.* Ed. D. M. Powell. Revised and reprinted 1985. Hants, England: Gower Publishing Co., 1985, c1981.

479 Tapper, Colin. *Computer Law.* 4th ed. London: Longman Group UK, 1989.

480 *Technology Licensing and Litigation.* (Patents, Copyrights, Trademarks, and Literary Property Course Handbook Series, no. 287) New York: Practising Law Institute, 1990.

481 *Technology Licensing and Litigation 1991.* (Patents, Copyrights, Trademarks, and Literary Property Course Handbook Series, no. 308) New York: Practising Law Institute, 1991.

482 *Technology Licensing and Litigation 1992.* (Patents, Copyrights, Trademarks, and Literary Property Course Handbook Series, no. 334) New York: Practising Law Institute, 1992.

483 *Technology Transfer from Federal Laboratories and Universities: Report Prepared by the Subcommittee on Technology and Competitiveness Transmitted to the Committee on Science, Space, and Technology, House of Representatives, One Hundred Second Congress, Second Session, July 1992.* Washington, D.C.: G.P.O., 1992.

484 *Technology Transfer Improvements Act of 1991: Report of the Committee on Science, Space, and Technology, House of Representatives, (to Accompany H.R. 191...) December 6, 1991.* Washington, D.C.: G.P.O., 1991.

485 *Technology Transfer Improvements Act of 1991: Report of the Senate Committee on Commerce, Science, and Transportation, United States Senate, One Hundred Second Congress, First Session, on S. 1581...November 27, 1991.* Washington, D.C.: G.P.O., 1991.

486 *Tenth Annual Computer Law Institute.* (Patents, Copyrights, Trademarks, and Literary Property Course Handbook Series, no. 259) New York: Practising Law Institute, 1988.

487 *Thirteenth Annual Computer Law Institute.* (Patents, Copyrights, Trademarks, and Literary Property Course Handbook Series, no. 322) New York: Practising Law Institute, 1991.

488 Thompson, Howard. *The Manager's Guide to Computer Security: A Eurostudy Special Report.* London: Eurostudy Publishing Co., 1990.

489 Tien, James M., Thomas F. Rich, and Michael F. Cahn. *Electronic Fund Transfer Systems Fraud: Computer Crime.* Washington, D.C.: U.S. Department of Justice, 1985.

490 Tinto, Mario. *Computer Viruses: Prevention, Detection, and Treatment.* [Ft. George G. Mead, Md.]: National Computer Security Center, [1990].

491 *To Allow Railroad and College Police Access to Federal Criminal Records: Hearing Before the Subcommittee on Criminal Law of the Committee on the Judiciary, United States Senate, Ninety-Ninth Congress, Second Session, on S. 1203...January 22, 1986.* Washington, D.C.: G.P.O., 1986.

492 Toedt, D. C., III., ed. *The Law and Business of Computer Software.* (looseleaf) New York: Clark Boardman, 1989-.

493 *Transborder Data Flows: Proceedings of an OECD Conference Held December 1983.* Amsterdam: Elsevier Science Publishers, 1985.

494 Tunick, David C. *Computers and the Law.* Houston, Tex.: John Marshall Publishing Co., 1991.

495 *12th Annual Computer Law Institute.* (Patents, Copyrights, Trademarks, and Literary Property Course Handbook Series, no. 301) New York: Practising Law Institute, 1990.

496 *Unfair Foreign Trade Practices (Part 4): Hearings Before the Subcommittee on Oversight and Investigations of the Committee on Energy and Commerce, House of Representatives, Ninety-Eighth Congress, Second Session, on Customs Enforcement Program, July 26, August 6, and September 20, 1984.* Washington, D.C.: G.P.O., 1985.

497 U.S. Congress, Office of Technology Assessment. *Computer Software and Intellectual Property: Background Paper.* Washington, D.C.: G.P.O., 1990.

498 U.S. Congress, Office of Technology Assessment. *Federal Government Information Technology: Management, Security, and Congressional Oversight.* Washington, D.C.: G.P.O., 1986.

499 U.S. Department of Justice. Justice Management Division. *Basic Considerations in Investigating and Proving Computer-Related Federal Crimes.* Washington, D.C.: G.P.O., 1988.

500 United States General Accounting Office. *Computers and Privacy: How the Government Obtains, Verifies, Uses, and Protects Personal Data; Briefing Report to the Chairman, Subcommittee on Telecommunications and Finance, Committee on Energy and Commerce, House of Representatives.* Washington, D.C.: GAO, 1990.

501 University of Southern California. Law Center. *Annual Computer Law Institute.* Los Angeles: University of Southern California Law Center, 1980-.

502 *The Use of Computers to Transmit Material Inciting Crime: Hearing Before the Subcommittee on Security and Terrorism of the Committee on the Judiciary, United States Senate, Ninety-Ninth Congress, First Session, on the Use of Computers...June 11, 1985.* Washington, D.C.: G.P.O., 1985.

503 *A User's Guide to Computer Contracting: Forms, Techniques and Strategies.* (looseleaf) Englewood Cliffs, N.J.: Prentice-Hall Law and Business, 1984-.

504 Vallabhaneni, S. Rao. *Auditing Computer Security: A Manual with Case Studies.* New York: John Wiley and Sons, 1989.

505 Van der Merwe, D. P. *Computers and the Law.* Johannesburg: Juta and Co., 1986.

506 Van Duyn, J. *The Human Factor in Computer Crime.* Princeton, N.J.: Petrocelli Books, 1985.

507 Van Tol, Joan E., ed. *College and University Student Records: A Legal Compendium.* Washington, D.C.: National Association of College and University Attorneys, 1989.

508 Vandenberghe, G. P. V., ed. *Advanced Topics of Law and Information Technology.* Boston: Kluwer Law and Taxation Publishers, 1989.

509 Vergari, James V., and Virginia V. Shue. *Fundamentals of Computer-High Technology Law.* Philadelphia: ALI-ABA, 1991.

510 Wacks, Raymond. *Personal Information: Privacy and the Law.* Oxford: Clarendon Press, 1989.

511 Waldron, Joseph, Betty Archambeault, William Archambeault, Louis Carsone, James Conser, and Carol Sutton. *Microcomputers in Criminal Justice: Current Issues and Applications.* Cincinnati, Ohio: Anderson Publishing Co., 1987.

512 Walker, Charls E., and Mark A. Bloomfield, eds. *Intellectual Property Rights and Capital Formation in the Next Decade.* Lanham, Md.: University Press of America, 1988.

513 Wallace, Jonathan D. *Understanding Software Law.* Sherman Oaks, Calif.: Alfred Publishing Co., 1984.

514 Ware, Willis H. *Computer Security Policy Issues: From Past Toward the Future.* Santa Monica, Calif.: RAND Corporation, 1987.

515 Warren, Jim, Jay Thorwaldson, and Bruce Koball, eds. *Computers, Freedom and Privacy: A Comprehensive, Edited Transcript of the First Conference on Computers, Freedom and Privacy Held March 26-28, 1991 in Burlingame, California.* Los Alamitos, Calif.: IEEE Computer Society Press, 1991.

516 Wasik, Martin. *Crime and the Computer.* Oxford: Clarendon Press, 1991.

517 Waterman, David. "Electronic Media and the Economics of the First Sale Doctrine." In *1987 Entertainment, Publishing and the Arts Handbook.* Eds. Robert Thorne and John David Viera. New York: Clark Boardman, 1987.

518 Waters, Gil, ed. *Computer Communication Networks.* London: McGraw-Hill Book Co., 1991.

519 Weil, Vivian, and John W. Snapper, eds. *Owning Scientific and Technical Information: Value and Ethical Issues.* London: Rutgers University Press, 1989.

520 Weisburd, David, Stanton Wheeler, Elin Waring, and Nancy Bode. *Crimes of the Middle Classes: White-Collar Offenders in the Federal Courts.* New Haven, Conn.: Yale University Press, 1991.

521 Will, Yanush. *Computer Fraud and Collusion in Customer Service and Billing Systems.* Infracombe, Great Britain: Arthur H. Stockwell, 1987.

522 Williams, John J. *Absolute Computer File Security.* Alamogordo, N. Mex.: Consumertronics Co., 1986.

523 Wiltbank, J. Kelley, ed. *The Practical Aspects of Technology Transfer: A Legal Compendium.* Washington, D.C.: National Association of College and University Attorneys, 1990.

524 Wold, Geoffrey H., and Robert F. Shriver. *Computer Crime Techniques Prevention.* Rolling Meadows, Ill.: Bankers Publishing Co., 1989.

525 Wold, Geoffrey H., and Robert F. Shriver. *Disaster Proof Your Business: A Planning Manual for Protecting a Company's Computer, Communications and Records Systems and Facilities.* Chicago: Probus Publishing Co., 1991.

526 Wolk, Stuart R., and William J. Luddy, Jr. *Legal Aspects of Computer Use.* Englewood Cliffs, N.J.: Prentice-Hall, 1986.

527 Wood, Charles Cresson, William W. Banks, Sergio B. Guarro, Abel A. Garcia, Viktor E. Hampel, and Henry P. Sartorio. *Computer Security: A Comprehensive Controls Checklist.* Ed. Abel A. Garcia. New York: John Wiley and Sons, 1987.

528 Wrenn, Gregory J. "Federal Intellectual Property Protection for Computer Software Audiovisual Look and Feel: The Lanham, Copyright, and Patent Acts." In *Copyright Law Symposium: Number Thirty-Nine.* New York: Columbia University Press, 1992.

529 Wright, Benjamin. *The Law of Electronic Commerce, EDI, FAX, and E-Mail: Technology, Proof, and Liability.* (updated by supplements) Boston: Little, Brown and Co., 1991-.

530 *Yearbook of Law, Computers, and Technology.* (annual) Leicestershire, England: Leicester Polytechnic School of Law, 1984-.

531 Zamore, Joseph D., ed. *Business Torts,* 4 vols. (looseleaf) New York: Matthew Bender, 1989-.

Bibliography—Articles

532 "ADAPSO Receives Justice Department Approval for Software Protection Device." *Software Protection*, 4, no. 8 (Jan. 1986), pp. 1-2.

533 "ADP Consents to Quotron's Demand for Injunctive Relief." *The Computer Lawyer*, 9, no. 6 (June 1992), p. 36.

534 "ALN Associates' Injunction Dissolved." *The Computer Lawyer*, 9, no. 11 (Nov. 1992), p. 25.

535 "AMD Denied Summary Judgment Motion in 287 Action." *The Computer Lawyer*, 9, no. 6 (June 1992), pp. 33-34.

536 "AMD's JNOV Denied, Copyright Action Stayed, Special Verdict Upheld." *The Computer Lawyer*, 9, no. 12 (Dec. 1992), p. 33.

537 Aaland, Mikkel. "Preventing Computer Disaster." *Working Woman*, 13, no. 11 (Nov. 1988), pp. 88-92.

538 Abrams, Hugh A. "Copyright/Computer Programs." *Illinois Bar Journal*, 72, no. 9-11 (May-July 1984), pp. 486-91.

539 Abrams, Idelle R. "Statutory Protection of the Algorithm in a Computer Program: A Comparison of the Copyright and Patent Laws." *Computer/Law Journal*, 9, no. 2 (Spring 1989), pp. 125-44.

540 Abramson, Ronald. "*Atari v. Nintendo*: Another Collision of Patent and Antitrust Policies." *The Computer Lawyer*, 6, no. 4 (Apr. 1989), pp. 24-31.

541 Abramson, Ronald. "Database Protection and New Storage Technologies: An Update." *Software Protection*, 5, no. 3 (Aug. 1986), pp. 5-12.

542 Abramson, Ronald. "'Look and Feel' of Computer Software." *Case and Comment*, 95, no. 1 (Jan.-Feb. 1990), pp. 3-8.

543 Abramson, Ronald. "Why *Lotus-Paperback* Uses the Wrong Test and What the New Software Protection Legislation Should Look Like." *The Computer Lawyer*, 7, no. 8 (Aug. 1990), pp. 6-11.

544 Abromats, Philip. "Anticompetitive Software Licensing Restrictions as Copyright Misuse (Part I)." *Software Protection*, 10, no. 4 (Sept. 1991), pp. 3-13.

545 Abromats, Philip. "Anticompetitive Software Licensing Restrictions as Copyright Misuse (Part II)." *Software Protection*, 10, no. 5 (Oct. 1991), pp. 3-15.

546 Abromats, Philip. "Copyright Misuse and Anticompetitive Software Licensing Restrictions: *Lasercomb America, Inc. v. Reynolds.*" *University of Pittsburgh Law Review*, 52, no. 3 (Spring 1991), pp. 629-67.

547 Abromats, Philip. "Nondisclosure of Preexisting Works in Software Copyright Registrations: Inequitable Conduct in Need of a Remedy." *Jurimetrics Journal*, 32, no. 4 (Summer 1992), pp. 571-600.

548 "Abstractions Test to Follow Similarity Analysis." *The Computer Lawyer*, 9, no. 9 (Sept. 1992), pp. 32-33.

549 "The Accom[m]odation of Intellectual Property Law to Technological Change: Implications for Policy." *Software Protection*, 5, no. 4 (Sept. 1986), pp. 11-16.

550 "Accord on Computer Security." *The New York Times*, 138, no. 47822 (27 Mar. 1989), p. B13.

551 Adamo, Kenneth R. "Problems Connected with Acquisition, Licensing and Enforcement of Intellectual Property." *Albany Law Review*, 50, no. 2 (Winter 1986), pp. 475-94.

552 "Addressing Computer Crime in Massachusetts: The Problems with Comprehensive New Criminal Statutes—The Advantages to a Multifaceted Approach." *New England Law Review*, 21, no. 4 (1985-86), pp. 759-77.

553 "Addressing the New Hazards of the High Technology Workplace." *Harvard Law Review*, 104, no. 8 (June 1991), pp. 1898-916.

554 Adney, William M., and Douglas E. Kavanagh. "The Data Bandits." *Byte*, 14, no. 1 (Jan. 1989), pp. 267-70.

555 "Against Software Patents: The League for Programming Freedom." *Comm/Ent*, 14, no. 2 (Winter 1992), pp. 297-314.

556 Agranoff, Michael H. "Curb on Technology: Liability for Failure to Protect Computerized Data Against Unauthorized Access." *Santa Clara Computer and High Technology Law Journal*, 5 (1989), pp. 263-320.

557 Aguilar, J. Arnold. "Proprietary Protection of Computer Software in the United States and Brazil." *Texas International Law Journal*, 19, no. 3 (Summer 1984), pp. 643-73.

558 Ahituv, Niv, Yeheskel Lapid, and Seev Neumann. "Protecting Statistical Databases Against Retrieval of Private Information." *Computers and Security*, 7, no. 1 (Feb. 1988), pp. 59-63.

559 Ahl, David H. "Employee Computer Crime on the Rise." *Creative Computing*, 11, no. 6 (June 1985), p. 6.

560 Ahl, David H. "The Problem of Being Popular." *Creative Computing*, 10, no. 3 (Mar. 1984), p. 45.

561 Alagar, Vangalur S. "A Human Approach to the Technological Challenges in Data Security." *Computers and Security*, 5 (1986), pp. 328-35.

562 Albanese, Jay S. "Tomorrow's Thieves." *Current Municipal Problems*, 15 (1988-89), pp. 453-60. (First published in *The Futurist*, 22, no. 5 [Sept.-Oct. 1988], pp. 24-28.)

563 Albano, Tin. "Michelangelo Strikes: Beware the 6th of March." *PC Magazine*, 11, no. 6 (31 Mar. 1992), pp. 30-31.

564 Albert, Mark. "Business-Minded Professor." *Fortune*, 119, no. 9 (24 Apr. 1989), p. 319.

565 Albinger, Lisa Anne. "Personal Information in Government Agency Records: Toward an Informational Right to Privacy." *1986 Annual Survey of American Law*, 2 (1986), pp. 625-43.

566 Al-Dossary, Ghannam M. "Computer Virus Prevention and Containment on Mainframes." *Computers and Security*, 9, no. 2 (Apr. 1990), pp. 131-37.

567 "Alleged Derivative Software Not Within Scope of Injunction." *The Computer Lawyer*, 9, no. 9 (Sept. 1992), p. 36.

568 Allen, Lynne B. "The Patentability of Computer Programs: Merrill Lynch's Patent for a Financial Services System." *Indiana Law Journal*, 59, no. 4 (1983-84), pp. 633-57.

569 Allman, William F. "Computer Hacking Goes on Trial." *U.S. News and World Report*, 108, no. 3 (22 Jan. 1990), p. 25.

570 Allred, William S. "Criminal Law—Connecticut Adopts Comprehensive Computer Crime Legislation: Public Act 84-206." *Western New England Law Review*, 7, no. 3 (1985), pp. 807-22.

571 Alter, Scott M. "Selecting Protection for Computer Programs: Know Your Options." *Federal Bar News and Journal*, 39, no. 4 (May 1992), pp. 264-68.

572 "An Alternative Approach to Computer Pirating Disputes, the Mnookin-Jones Settlement: *IBM v. Fujitsu.*" *Temple International and Comparative Law Journal*, 3, no. 1 (Spring 1989), pp. 113-28.

573 Altman, James S. "Copyright Protection of Computer Software." *Computer/Law Journal*, 5, no. 3 (Winter 1985), pp. 413-32.

574 "Ambiguous Protection." *Scientific American*, 251, no. 3 (Sept. 1984), pp. 87-88.

575 Ambrosio, Christina, and Roni Schneider. "Copyright Misuse...Getting Defensive: *Lasercomb America, Inc. v. Reynolds.*" *St. John's Journal of Legal Commentary*, 6, no. 1 (1990), pp. 181-99.

576 "Amended Proposal for a Council Directive on the Legal Protection of Computer Programs." *Software Protection*, 9, no. 5 (Oct. 1990), pp. 2-16.

577 "Amendments to Technical Data Rights FAR Proposed." *The Computer Lawyer*, 8, no. 1 (Jan. 1991), pp. 40-41.

578 American Bar Association: Section of Patent, Trademark and Copyright Law. "Model Software Licensing Provisions." *The Computer Lawyer*, 8, no. 2 (Feb. 1991), pp. 16-33.

579 Amsel, Ellen. "Network Security and Access Controls." *Computers and Security*, 7, no. 1 (Feb. 1988), pp. 53-57.

580 Anacker, Paul C. "For Your Eyes Only: Computer Security Products Can Help Keep Client Files Confidential." *California Lawyer*, 8, no. 3 (Apr. 1988), pp. 62-64.

581 Anawalt, Howard. "To License or Not—A Proposal to Improve Patent Law." *Santa Clara Computer and High Technology Law Journal*, 5, no. 2 (1989), pp. 199-209.

582 Anderson, Alisa E. "The Future of Software Copyright Protection: Arbitration v. Litigation." *Comm/Ent*, 12, no. 1 (Fall 1989), pp. 1-32.

583 Anderson, Charles. "Using Technology." *Wilson Library Bulletin*, 65, no. 6 (Feb. 1991), pp. 112-13, 152-53.

584 Anderson, Eric R. "How Secure Is Your Credit Data?" *Business Credit*, 93, no.1 (Jan. 1991), pp. 11-13.

585 Anderson, G. Christopher. "Hacker Trial Under Way." *Nature*, 343, no. 6255 (18 Jan. 1990), p. 200.

586 Andewelt, Roger. "Recent Revolutionary Changes in Intellectual Property Protection and the Future Prospects." *Albany Law Review*, 50, no. 2 (Winter 1986), pp. 509-21.

587 "Another 'Look and Feel' Lawsuit." *The Computer Lawyer*, 4, no. 5 (May 1987), p. 37.

588 Anthony, William L., Jr., and Robert C. Colwell. "Litigating the Validity and Infringement on Software Patents." *Washington and Lee Law Review*, 41, no. 4 (Fall 1984), pp. 1307-34.

589 Antonoff, Michael. "The Decline of Copy Protection." *Personal Computing*, 11, no. 5 (May 1987), pp. 155-57.

590 Antton, D. Lee, and Brett N. Dorny. "How Copyrightability Trivialized Substantial Similarity: The Significance of *Lotus v. Borland*." *The Computer Lawyer*, 9, no. 10 (Oct. 1992), pp. 6-11.

591 Antton, D. Lee, and Gary M. Hoffman. "Copyright Protection and Innovation: The Impact of *Lotus Development v. Paperback Software*." *The Computer Lawyer*, 7, no. 8 (Aug. 1990), pp. 1-5.

592 "Appellate Briefs from Whelan v. Jaslow Laboratories, Inc." *Software Protection*, 4, no. 10-11 (Mar.-Apr. 1986), pp. 1-29.

593 "Apple and Franklin Settle — Who Really Won?" *Software Protection*, 2, no. 5 (Jan. 1984), pp. 1-2.

594 "*Apple v. Microsoft and H-P* Developments." *The Computer Lawyer*, 8, no. 9 (Sept. 1991), pp. 29-30.

595 Arckens, Ingrid M. "Obtaining International Copyright Protection for Software: National Laws and International Copyright Conventions." *Federal Communications Law Journal*, 38, no. 2 (Aug. 1986), pp. 283-300.

596 Armbruster, William. "Database Flushes Fraud Suspects." *The Journal of Commerce and Commercial*, 384, no. 27259 (28 June 1990), p. 8B.

597 Armstrong, Larry. "This Could Be the Key to Keeping Computer Intruders Out." *Business Week*, no. 3117 (31 July 1989), p. 54.

598 Armstrong, Stephen. "License Restrictions Are Costly to Users, Software Industry." *PC Week*, 8, no. 41 (14 Oct. 1991), p. 85.

599 "Army to Award Contract for Studying Potential of Computer Viruses as Electronic Countermeasure." *Aviation Week and Space Technology*, 132, no. 20 (14 May 1990), p. 38.

600 Arnheim, Michael. "Computer Software and the Law." *Solicitors' Journal*, 132, no. 19 (13 May 1988), pp. 674-78.

601 Arnold, Tom, Michael G. Fletcher, and Robert J. McAughan, Jr. "Managing Patent Disputes Through Arbitration." *Arbitration Journal*, 46, no. 3 (Sept. 1991), pp. 5-12.

602 Aronovitz, Cory. "To Start, Press the Flashing Button: The Legalization of Video Gambling Devices." *Software Law Journal*, 5, no. 4 (Dec. 1992), pp. 771-96.

603 "Asset Transfer Extinguished Seller's Preexisting Copyright Infringement Claims Against Asset Purchaser." *The Computer Lawyer*, 8, no. 2 (Feb. 1991), pp. 34-35.

604 Assia, Naomi. "Legislation Relating to Software in the Common (Single) Market — 1992." *Software Protection*, 9, no. 11 (Apr. 1991), pp. 8-11.

605 "At Last, Chips Get Copyright Protection." *Physics Today*, 38, no. 3 (Mar. 1985), p. 66.

606 "At the Wire: U.S. Marshals Help Microsoft Seize Software." *PC Week*, 8, no. 35 (2 Sept. 1991), p. 99.

607 Atchison, Sandra D. "Electronic Data Could Make Trouble for the Law." *Business Week*, no. 2970 (27 Oct. 1986), pp. 128, 132, 134.

608 Athanasiou, Tom. "Encryption — Technology, Privacy, and National Security." *Technology Review*, 89, no. 6 (Aug.-Sept. 1986), pp. 56-66.

609 "Attorneys' Fees Recoverable for Derivative Work." *The Computer Lawyer,* 9, no. 7 (July 1992), pp. 37.

610 August, Raymond S. "Turning the Computer Into a Criminal." *Advocate,* 27, no. 4-7 (Apr.-July 1984), pp. 20-22.

611 Austin, R. C. "The Data Protection Act 1984: The Public Law Implications." *Public Law,* 1984 (Winter 1984), pp. 618-34.

612 "Australian Appellate Court Finds Software Copyrightable." *Software Protection,* 3, no. 1 (June 1984), pp. 1-4.

613 Aylward, Sean Michael. "Copyright Law: The Fourth Circuit's Extension of the Misuse Doctrine to the Area of Copyright: A Misuse of the Misuse Doctrine? — *Lasercomb America, Inc. v. Reynolds,* 911 F.2d 970 (4th Cir. 1990)." *University of Dayton Law Review,* 17, no. 2 (Winter 1992), pp. 661-95.

614 "BCS Response to the Government's White Paper Entitled 'Intellectual Property and Innovation' (Cmnd 9712)." *Software Protection,* 5, no. 6 (Nov. 1986), pp. 13-16.

615 Bacal, Glenn Spencer. "Computer Software and Service Contracts: Anticipating Vendor and User Bankruptcy." *The Journal of Law and Technology,* 2, no. 1 (Winter 1987), pp. 183-208.

616 Badenhorst, K. P., and Jan H. P. Eloff. "Framework of a Methodology for the Life Cycle of Computer Security in an Organization." *Computers and Security,* 8, no. 5 (Aug. 1989), pp. 433-42.

617 Bagai, Eric. "Give Hackers Honorable Mention: Most Computer Hobbyists Are Content to Tinker." *Los Angeles Times,* (21 Jan. 1989), p. II-8.

618 Bahr, Susan J. "The Canadian Computer Software Copyright Law: One Small Step for U.S. Software Vendors." *Rutgers Computer and Technology Law Journal,* 17, no. 1 (1991), pp. 139-76.

619 Baig, Edward C. "Storing Computer Data Far from the Office." *Fortune,* 113, no. 7 (31 Mar. 1986), pp. 65-66.

620 Bailey, James M. "Effective Information Networks Combine Flexibility with Security." *The CPA Journal,* 59, no. 1 (Jan. 1989), pp. 60-62.

621 Bainbridge, D. I. "Computer-Aided Diagnosis and Negligence." *Medicine, Science and the Law,* 31, no. 2 (Apr. 1991), pp. 127-36.

622 Bainbridge, David I. "Computer Misuse: What Should the Law Do?" *Solicitors Journal,* 133, no. 15 (14 Apr. 1989), pp. 466, 68.

623 Bainbridge, David I. "Computers and Copyright." *Modern Law Review,* 50, no. 2 (Mar. 1987), pp. 202-16.

624 Bainbridge, David I. "The Copyright (Computer Software) Amendment Act (1985)." *Modern Law Review,* 49, no. 2 (Mar. 1986), pp. 214-24.

625 Bainbridge, David I. "Hacking—The Unauthorised Access of Computer Systems; the Legal Implications." *Modern Law Review,* 52, no. 2 (Mar. 1989), pp. 236-45.

626 Bainbridge, David I. "The Scope of Copyright Protection for Computer Programs." *Modern Law Review,* 54 (Sept. 1991), pp. 643-63.

627 Baird, Bruce J., Lindsay L. Baird, Jr., and Ronald P. Ranauro. "The Moral Cracker?" *Computers and Security,* 6 (1987), pp. 471-78.

628 Baker, Richard F. "Avoiding Virus Infections." *California Lawyer,* 12, no. 6 (June 1992), pp. 45-46.

629 Baker, Steven J. "Criminal Liability for the Misappropriation of Computer Software Trade Secrets." *University of Detroit Law Review,* 63, no. 3 (Spring 1986), pp. 481-98.

630 Bakst, Shelley. "Beware of Potholes on the Path to PC Security." *The Office,* 111, no. 6 (June 1990), pp. 44-45.

631 Balding, Robert G. "A Socratic Approach to Understanding the Limits (If Any) of Software Copyright Protection." *Jurimetrics Journal,* 28, no. 2 (Winter 1988), pp. 153-59.

632 Baldy, Anderson L., III. "Computer Copyright Law: An Emerging Form of Protection for Object Code Software After *Apple v. Franklin.*" *Computer/ Law Journal,* 5, no. 2 (Fall 1984), pp. 233-55.

633 Band, Jonathan, and Laura F. H. McDonald. "The Proposal EC Database Directive: The 'Reversal' of *Feist v. Rural Telephone.*" *The Computer Lawyer,* 9, no. 6 (June 1992), pp. 19-21.

634 Bandman, Marc B. "Balancing the Risks in Computer Contracts." *Commercial Law Journal,* 92, no. 4 (Winter 1987), pp. 384-85.

635 Bangsberg, P. T. "Hong Kong Software Pirates Face Crackdown." *The Journal of Commerce and Commercial,* 389, no. 27571 (26 Sept. 1991), pp. 1A-2A.

636 Banham, Russ. "Computer Viruses Mushroom: But Insurance Is Rarely Used to Cover Damage." *The Journal of Commerce and Commercial,* 388, no. 27490 (3 June 1991), pp. 7A-9A.

637 Banham, Russ. "Surprise! Companies Are Covered for 'Viruses.'" *The Journal of Commerce and Commercial,* 384, no. 27218 (1 May 1990), pp. 9A-11A.

638 Barger, Robert W. "Arbitration of Computer Disputes in the United States: A Status Report." *Arbitration Journal,* 43, no. 1 (Mar. 1988), pp. 55-58.

639 Barkume, Anthony R. "Proprietary Protection of Computer User Interfaces." *St. John's Law Review,* 64, no. 3 (Spring-Summer 1990), pp. 559-85.

640 Barlow, John Perry. "The Law Comes to Cyberspace." *Byte,* 16, no. 10 (Oct. 1991), p. 332.

641 Barnes, Roger. "Expert Offers Computer Virus Primer." *National Underwriter-Property and Casualty/Risk and Benefits Management Edition,* 93, no. 13 (27 Mar. 1989), pp. 32-33.

642 Barr, Robert, and Susan Hollander. "Design Patents Revisited: Icons as Statutory Subject Matter." *The Computer Lawyer,* 9, no. 6 (June 1992), pp. 13-18.

643 Barrett, Lee E. "Patentable Subject Matter: Mathematical Algorithms and Computer Programs." *Software Protection,* 8, no. 5 (Oct. 1989), pp. 6-16.

644 Barrett, Lee E. "Report on Patentable Subject Matter: Mathematical Algorithms and Computer Programs." *The Computer Lawyer,* 6, no. 10 (Oct. 1989), pp. 18-26.

645 Barrett, William P. "Does the FBI Have a File on You?" *Forbes,* 142, no. 7 (3 Oct. 1988), p. 184.

646 Barrett, William P. "'We're Basically Insurance!'" *Forbes,* 150, no. 11 (9 Nov. 1992), pp. 196, 201.

647 Barry, Marcia C. "Computer Viruses: Interview with Frederick Cohen." *Special Libraries,* 81, no. 4 (Fall 1990), pp. 365-67.

648 Barthel, Matt. "Vendor Countersues EDS, Claiming Software Piracy." *American Banker,* 157, no. 21 (31 Jan. 1992), p. 3.

649 Bartz, Philip D., and Jonathan Band. "*Feist v. Rural Telephone*: The Beginning of the End of Software Overprotection?" *The Computer Lawyer,* 8, no. 7 (July 1991), pp. 10-12.

650 Basch, Kenneth D., and Anton H. van Schijndel. "The Brazilian Software Law of 1987." *The International Lawyer,* 23, no. 1 (Spring 1989), pp. 281-86.

651 "A Battle Over a User-Friendly Computer." *Newsweek,* 114, no. 26 (25 Dec. 1989), p. 59.

652 "A Battle Over the Macintosh 'Look.'" *Newsweek,* 111, no. 13 (28 Mar. 1988), p. 51.

653 Baumgarten, Jon A. "Copyright Protection of Computer Programs." *Federal Bar News and Journal,* 32, no. 5 (June 1985), pp. 220-25.

654 Beale, Ian. "Computer Eavesdropping—Fact or Fantasy." *The EDP Auditor Journal,* 3 (1988), pp. 39-42.

655 Beall, Robert. "Developing a Coherent Approach to the Regulation of Computer Bulletin Boards." *Computer/Law Journal,* 7, no.4 (Fall 1987), pp. 499-516.

656 Beck, Henry. "Copyright Protection for Compilations and Databases After *Feist." The Computer Lawyer*, 8, no. 7 (July 1991), pp. 1-9.

657 Beck, Patrick Edward. "Patent Policy + Protection of Inventor's Rights = The Patentability of Mathematical Algorithms." *Dayton Law Review*, 17, no. 1 (Fall 1991), pp. 181-206.

658 Becker, Loftus E., Jr. "The Liability of Computer Bulletin Board Operators for Defamation Posted by Others." *Connecticut Law Review*, 22, no. 1 (Fall 1989), pp. 203-38.

659 Becker, Lynn. "Electronic Publishing: First Amendment Issues in the Twenty-First Century." *Fordham Urban Law Journal*, 13 (1984-85), pp. 801-68.

660 Becker, Stephen A. "Drafting Patent Applications on Computer-Implemented Inventions." *Harvard Journal of Law and Technology*, 4 (Spring 1991), pp. 237-56.

661 Becker, Stephen A. "Legal Protection of Semiconductor Mask Works in the United States." *Computer/Law Journal*, 6, no. 4 (Spring 1986), pp. 589-605.

662 Beckett, J. Thomas. "Computer Law." *1984 Annual Survey of American Law*, 2 (1984), pp. 787-809.

663 Beckstrand, Shelley M. "Experiences Prosecuting Sof[t]ware Related Patent Applications." *Idea*, 31, no. 3 (1991), pp. 207-21.

664 Beercheck, Dick. "Developing a Vaccine for Computer Viruses." *Machine Design*, 61, no. 2 (26 Jan. 1989), p. 4.

665 Begun, Daniel A. "Protecting Your E-Mail Privacy." *PC Magazine*, 12, no. 1 (12 Jan. 1993), p. 32.

666 Behar, Richard. "Psst, Secrets for Sale: Shady Dealers Are Doing a Brisk Trade in IRS, FBI and Other Federal Data." *Time*, 139, no. 8 (24 Feb. 1992), p. 42.

667 Behar, Richard. "Surfing Off the Edge." *Time*, 141, no. 6 (8 Feb. 1993), pp. 62-63.

668 Beierwaltes, William T. "Safeguarding Records in a Microcomputer." *Journal of the American Society of CLU*, 40, no. 5 (Sept. 1986), pp. 86-91.

669 Bell, Trudy. "How to Market and Protect the Software You Write." *Personal Computing*, 8, no. 1 (Jan. 1984), pp. 221-27.

670 Bellegarde, Esther Donio. "Legal Regulations for Software in Brazil." *Software Protection*, 6, no. 9 (Feb. 1988), pp. 1-4.

671 Belsie, Laurent. "Bulgarian 'Dark Avenger' Part of East-Bloc Legacy." *The Christian Science Monitor*, 84, no. 122 (19 May 1992), p. 8.

672 Belvis, Glen P. "Computers, Copyright and Tying Agreements: An Argument for the Abandonment of the Presumption of Market Power." *Boston College Law Review*, 28, no. 2 (Mar. 1987), pp. 265-96.

673 Bendekgey, Lee. "Copyright Protection for Computer Software Visual Displays: Protecting a Program's Look and Feel." *Software Protection*, 6, no. 8 (Jan. 1988), pp. 1-7.

674 Bendekgey, Lee. "International Trademark Protection for Computer Products: How to Make a Mark in Foreign Markets." *Santa Clara Computer and High-Technology Law Journal*, 3, no. 1 (Jan. 1987), pp. 73-85.

675 Bendekgey, Lee, Caroline H. Mead, and Shigeru Miki. "The Rights of Computer Program Users Under Japanese and United States Copyright Laws." *UCLA Pacific Basin Law Journal*, 9, no. 1-2 (Spring 1991), pp. 1-16.

676 Bender, David. "*Computer Associates v. Altai*: Rationality Prevails." *The Computer Lawyer*, 9, no. 8 (Aug. 1992), pp. 1-9.

677 Bender, David. "The More Things Change, the More They Stay the Same: An Unhurried Reflection on Software Protection Over the Years." *Rutgers Computer and Technology Law Journal*, 16, no. 2 (1990), pp. 309-21.

678 Bender, David. "Protecting Computer Software: New Twist in Intellectual Property Litigation." *Trial*, 26, no. 6 (June 1990), pp. 58-61.

679 Bender, David. "Protection of Computer Programs: The Copyright/Trade Secret Interface." *Intellectual Property Law Review*, 19 (1987), pp. 485-536. (First published in *University of Pittsburgh Law Review*, 47, no. 4 (Summer 1986), pp. 907-58.)

680 Bender, David. "The Renaissance of the 'Software Patent.'" *Hamline Law Review*, 13, no. 2 (Spring 1990), pp. 205-20.

681 Bender, David. "Software Copyright: 'Look and Feel' Issues." *Software Protection*, 8, no. 6 (Nov. 1989), pp. 1-10.

682 Bender, David, and Anthony R. Barkume. "Disclosure Requirements for Software-Related Patents." *The Computer Lawyer*, 8, no. 10 (Oct. 1991), pp. 1-7.

683 Bender, David, and Anthony R. Barkume. "Patents for Software- Related Inventions." *Software Law Journal*, 5, no. 2 (Apr. 1992), pp. 279-98.

684 Benjamin, Louise M. "Privacy, Computers, and Personal Information: Toward Equality and Equity in an Information Age." *Communications and the Law*, 13, no. 2 (June 1991), pp. 3-16.

685 Bennett, Colin J. "Regulating the Computer: Comparing Policy Instruments in Europe and the United States." *European Journal of Political Research*, 16 (1988), pp. 437-66.

686 Benson, Jeffrey R. "Copyright Protection for Computer Screen Displays." *Minnesota Law Review*, 72, no. 5 (May 1988), pp. 1123-58.

687 Bequai, August. "Computer Crime: What Can Be Done About It?" *The Office*, 104, no. 4 (Oct. 1986), p. 132.

688 Bequai, August. "The Rise of Cashless Crimes." *USA Today*, 114, no. 2488 (Jan. 1986), pp. 83-85.

689 Bequai, August. "Using Confidentiality Agreements to Secure Micros." *Journal of Accountancy*, 166, no. 4 (Oct. 1988), pp. 136-38.

690 Bequai, August. "What To Do About Crime in the Electronic Office." *The Office*, 101, no. 1 (Jan. 1985), pp. 101, 104.

691 Berke, Stephen P. "Ownership of Intellectual Property Rights in Development Agreements." *The Computer Lawyer*, 6, no. 6 (June 1989), pp. 18-23.

692 Berkowitz, Jeffrey A. "Computer Software Copyright Infringement: The Second Generation." *Touro Law Review*, 4, no. 1 (Fall 1987), pp. 97-132.

693 Berman, Jerry J. "National Security vs. Access to Computer Databases: A New Threat to Freedom of Information." *Software Law Journal*, 2, no. 1 (Winter 1987), pp. 1-15.

694 Berman, Jerry J. "The Right to Know: Public Access to Electronic Public Information." *Software Law Journal*, 3, no. 3 (Summer 1989), pp. 491-530.

695 Berney, Karen. "The Cutting Edge." *Nation's Business*, 74, no. 4 (Apr. 1986), p. 57.

696 Bernstein, Paul. "Telecommunications Use Raises Security Concerns." *New York Law Journal*, 194, no. 59 (23 Sept. 1985), pp. 31-32.

697 Bertrand, Andre. "Legal Issues Arising from Adapting Software to a Foreign Language." *Software Protection*, 10, no. 3 (Aug. 1991), pp. 1-3.

698 Bertrand, Andre. "The Legal Protection of Computer Software in France: 1984 Developments." *Software Protection*, 3, no. 4 (Sept. 1984), pp. 1-13.

699 Bertrand, Andre R. "Copyright Protection for Computer Software in Civil Law Countries." *Software Protection*, 4, no. 5 (Oct. 1985), pp. 9-14.

700 Bertrand, Andre R. "Copyright Protection for Computer Software in France Under the Law of July 3, 1985." *Software Protection*, 4, no. 3 (Aug. 1985), pp. 5-9.

701 Bertrand, Andre R. "French Supreme Court Declares Software and Video Games 'Original Works of Authorship' Under the 1957 Copyright Act." *Software Protection*, 4, no. 9 (Feb. 1986), pp. 14-15.

702 Bertrand, Andre R. "Legal Aspects of Bad Quality in Software." *Software Protection*, 7, no. 6-7 (Nov.-Dec. 1988), pp. 10-13.

703 Bertrand, Andre R. "Legal Protection of Computer Software in the Ivory Coast: Rational and Methodology (and Questions Concerning Protection of American Software)." *Software Protection*, 7, no. 3 (Aug. 1988), pp. 3-5.

704 Bertrand, Andre R. "Software Protection in France: 1990/1991 Developments." *Software Protection,* 10, no. 4 (Sept. 1991), pp. 1-2.

705 Bertrand, Andre R. "Source Code Escrow, Protection for Software Developers and Users: The French Experience." *Software Protection,* 4, no. 8 (Jan. 1986), pp. 14-15.

706 Bertrand, Andre R., and Marina Couste. "Current Issues Concerning French Software Protection." *Software Protection,* 6, no. 12 (May 1988), pp. 1-6.

707 Betten, Jurgen. "The Legal Protection of Computer Software in West Germany." *Software Protection,* 5, no. 2 (July 1986), pp. 1-6.

708 Betten, Jurgen. "New Decision of the German Federal Supreme Court Concerning Copyright Protection of Computer Programs." *Software Protection,* 9, no. 6-7 (Nov.-Dec. 1990), pp. 10-17.

709 Betten, Jurgen. "New Decisions of the European Patent Office Concerning Patent Protection for Computer Software." *Software Protection,* 8, no. 4 (Sept. 1989), pp. 7-18.

710 Betten, Jurgen. "Patent Protection of Computer Programs by the EPO." *Software Protection,* 5, no. 7 (Dec. 1986), pp. 1-7.

711 Betten, Jurgen. "Semiconductor Products Protection Act in the Federal Republic of Germany." *Software Protection,* 6, no. 12 (May 1988), pp. 11-16.

712 Beutel, Richard Armstrong. "Copyright Infringement and Derivative Software: Proving the Substantial Similarity of Data Base Products." *The Computer Lawyer,* 4, no. 3 (Mar. 1987), pp. 12-19.

713 Beutel, Richard Armstrong. "Software Engineering Practices and the Idea/Expression Dichotomy: Can Structured Design Methodologies Define the Scope of Software Copyright?" *Jurimetrics Journal,* 32, no. 1 (Fall 1991), pp. 1-32.

714 Beutel, Richard Armstrong. "Trade Dress Protection for the 'Look and Feel' of Software: The Lanham Act as an Emerging Source of Proprietary Rights Protection for Software Developers." *Journal of the Patent and Trademark Office Society,* 71, no. 12 (Dec. 1989), pp. 974-88.

715 "Beware of 'Snuffware.'" *Personal Computing,* 10, no. 2 (Feb. 1986), p. 85.

716 "Beware, Virus Due on Ides of March." *PC Week,* 9, no. 8 (24 Feb. 1992), p. 172.

717 Bhojwani, Ashok. "Copyright Laws and the Nature of Computer Software." *Software Protection,* 9, no. 1 (June 1990), pp. 1-11.

718 Bidgoli, Hossein, and Reza Azarmsa. "Computer Security: New Managerial Concern for the 1980s and Beyond." *Journal of Systems Management,* 40, no. 10 (Oct. 1989), pp. 21-27.

719 Bierman, Bruce. "Does Your Computer Need 'Debugging?'" *Byte,* 9, no. 1 (Jan. 1984), p. 102.

720 Bierman, Ellen M. "It Walks Like a Duck, Talks Like a Duck,...But Is It a Duck? Making Sense of Substantial Similarity Law as It Applies to User Interfaces." *University of Puget Sound Law Review,* 16, no. 1 (Fall 1992), pp. 319-71.

721 Bigelow, Robert P. "The Challenge of Computer Law." *Western New England Law Review,* 7, no. 3 (1985), pp. 397-404.

722 Bigelow, Robert P. "Computer Security Crime and Privacy." *The Computer Lawyer,* 6, no. 2 (Feb. 1989), pp. 10-19.

723 Bigley, Tom. "Keep Your PC All Safe with XTree's AllSafe." *InfoWorld,* 14, no. 16 (20 Apr. 1992), p. 101.

724 Bikoff, James L., Jon L. Roberts, and David I. Wilson. "Intellectual Property Protection." *The Washington Lawyer,* 6, no. 4 (Mar.-Apr. 1992), pp. 36-40.

725 "Bill Would Permit Government Agencies to Copyright Software Prepared Under Cooperative R & D Agreements." *The Computer Lawyer,* 8, no. 3 (Mar. 1991), p. 36.

726 Bing, Jon. "Amendments to the Norwegian Copyright Law." *Software Protection,* 9, no. 11 (Apr. 1991), pp. 6-8.

727 Bing, Jon. "Look and Feel the Norwegian Way." *Software Protection,* 8, no. 7 (Dec. 1989), pp. 1-4.

728 Birnbaum, L. Nancy. "Strict Products Liability and Computer Software." *Computer/Law Journal,* 8, no. 2 (Spring 1988), pp. 135-56.

729 Biskup, Joachim, and Hans Hermann Bruggemann. "The Personal Model of Data: Towards a Privacy-Oriented Information System." *Computers and Security,* 7, no. 6 (Dec. 1988), pp. 575-97.

730 Bixby, Michael B. "Synthesis and Originality in Computer Screen Displays and User Interfaces: The 'Look and Feel' Cases." *Willamette Law Review,* 27, no. 1 (Winter 1991), pp. 31-50.

731 Black, George. "Update on Open Systems Security." *Computers and Security,* 11, no. 8 (Dec. 1992), pp. 699-702.

732 Black, John, and Fred M. Greguras. "Impact of Recent Changes to the Export Administration Regulations on Software Exporters." *Software Protection,* 9, no. 4 (Sept. 1990), pp. 8-18.

733 Blanden, Michael. "Plagiarism, Piracy and Profit." *The Banker,* 141, no. 787 (Sept. 1991), pp. 41-42.

734 Blank, Sally J. "Taking a Byte Out of Crime: Some Guidelines on Computer Theft Prevention." *Management Review,* 75, no. 1 (Jan. 1986), pp. 28-29.

735 Blanton, J. Ellis, and Joann Rosenberger. "Determining Your Information System's Vulnerability to Viruses." *Journal of Systems Management,* 42, no. 5 (May 1991), pp. 10-12, 24-27.

736 Bliss, Daniel H. "Intellectual Property: Patents, Trademarks, and Copyrights; Copyrights." *Detroit College of Law Review,* 1991, no. 2 (Summer 1991), pp. 735-43.

737 Bloch, Marla R. "The Expansion of the Berne Convention and the Universal Copyright Convention to Protect Computer Software and Future Intellectual Property." *Brooklyn Journal of International Law,* 11, no. 2 (Spring 1985), pp. 283-323.

738 Blodgett, Nancy. "Computer Law Quicksand: Pioneers in Burgeoning Field Have Little to Guide Them." *ABA Journal,* 70, no. 11 (Nov. 1984), pp. 32-33.

739 Blodgett, Nancy. "Will Bills Hack It? Computer Mail Privacy Urged." *ABA Journal,* 72, no. 3 (1 Mar. 1986), p. 28.

740 BloomBecker, Buck. "Computer Crime: How California Penal Code Section 502 Helps—and Hinders—Prosecutions." *Los Angeles Lawyer,* 12, no. 4 (June 1989), pp. 34-42, 63-65.

741 BloomBecker, J. J. "Short-Circuiting Computer Crime." *Datamation,* 35, no. 19 (1 Oct. 1989), pp. 71-72.

742 BloomBecker, Jay. "Computer Crime Update." *The Prosecutor,* 19, no. 3 (Winter 1986), pp. 15-23, 26-28.

743 BloomBecker, Jay. "Computer Crime Update: The View as We Exit 1984." *Western New England Law Review,* 7, no. 3 (1985), pp. 627-49.

744 BloomBecker, Jay Buck. "Cracking Down on Computer Crime." *Ethics: Easier Said Than Done,* 1991, no. 15 (1991), pp. 42-44.

745 Blouch, William E., Robert D. Smith, and Gary Saunders. "A Strategy for Disaster." *Information Strategy: The Executive's Journal,* 5, no. 4 (Summer 1989), pp. 4-10.

746 Blum, Andrew. "When a Virus Hit One Firm." *The National Law Journal,* 11, no. 35 (8 May 1989), p. 33.

747 Blume, Peter. "An EEC Policy for Data Protection." *Computer/Law Journal,* 11, no. 3 (Oct. 1992), pp. 399-440.

748 Bock, Gordon. "'The Chairman' and His Board: Embezzlers Nearly Get Away with $69 Million from First Chicago." *Time,* 131, no. 22 (30 May 1988), p. 45.

749 Boehmer, Robert G. "Artificial Monitoring and Surveillance of Employees: The Fine Line Dividing the Prudently Managed Enterprise from the Modern Sweatshop." *DePaul Law Review,* 41, no. 3 (Spring 1992), pp. 739-819.

750 Bohan, Thomas L. "The Performance Audit: Minimizing Software Liability (Part I)." *Idea,* 29, no. 2 (1988-89), pp. 127-35.

751 Bohan, Thomas L. "The Performance Audit: Minimizing Software Liability (Part II)." *Idea,* 29, no. 2 (1988-89), pp. 135-47.

752 Bologna, Jack. "Ethical Issues of the Information Era." *Computers and Security,* 9, no. 8 (Dec. 1990), pp. 689-92.

753 Bologna, Jack. "A Framework for the Ethical Analysis of Information Technologies." *Computers and Security,* 10, no. 4 (June 1991), pp. 303-7.

754 Bologna, Jack. "Soviet White-Collar Crime and Criminal Justice." *Computers and Security,* 7, no. 6 (Dec. 1988), pp. 553-56.

755 Bond, Andrea M. "Secured Lenders and Computerized Borrowers: An Introduction to Copyright and Trade Secret Law." *Hamline Law Review,* 13, no. 2 (Spring 1990), pp. 313-31.

756 Bond, Jonathan, and Laura F. H. McDonald. "The Proposed EC Database Directive: The 'Reversal' of *Feist v. Rural Telephone*." *The Computer Lawyer,* 9, no. 6 (June 1992), pp. 19-21.

757 Boockholdt, J. L. "Protecting Mainframe Data from PCs." *Journal of Accountancy,* 171, no. 4 (Apr. 1991), pp. 87-88, 90.

758 Boorstyn, Neil. "Infringement of Software Copyright." *California Lawyer,* 7, no. 10 (Oct. 1987), pp. 51-54.

759 Bora, Peter G. "*H/R Stone, Inc. v. Phoenix Business Systems, Inc.*: The Implied Covenant of Good Faith and Fair Dealing in Computer Contracts." *Software Law Journal,* 3, no. 1 (Winter 1989), pp. 117-29.

760 Borking, John J. "Results of a Socio-Legal Survey Regarding the Legal Protection of Software." *Software Protection,* 6, no. 6 (Nov. 1987), pp. 1-9.

761 Bornstein, Howard. "Beyond the Hype." *InfoWorld,* 11, no. 43 (23 Oct. 1989), p. 57.

762 Boshoff, W. H., and S. H. von Solms. "A Path Context Model for Addressing Security in Potentially Non-Secure Environments." *Computers and Security,* 8, no. 5 (Aug. 1989), pp. 417-25.

763 Boss, Amelia H. "Electronic Data Interchange Agreements: Private Contracting Toward a Global Environment." *Northwestern Journal of International Law and Business,* 13, no. 1 (Spring/Summer 1992), pp. 31-70.

764 Boss, Amelia H., Harold R. Weinberg, and William J. Woodward, Jr. "Scope of the Uniform Commercial Code: Advances in Technology and Survey of Computer Contracting Cases." *The Business Lawyer,* 44, no. 4 (Aug. 1989), pp. 1671-98.

765 Boss, Amelia H., and William J. Woodward. "Scope of the Uniform Commercial Code; Survey of Computer Contracting Cases." *The Business Lawyer,* 43, no. 4 (Aug. 1988), pp. 1513-44.

766 Bossert, Rex. "Circuit Panel OKs Reverse Engineering; Decision Allows Disassembly of Video Game Code; No Copyright Violation." *Los Angeles Daily Journal*, 105, no. 206 (21 Oct. 1992), pp. 1, 5.

767 "Boston ATC Center Software Error Causes East Coast Delays." *Aviation Week and Space Technology*, 129, no. 8 (22 Aug. 1988), p. 107.

768 "Boston Bookkeeper Accused of Tax Fraud by Computer." *The Wall Street Journal*, 214, no. 33 (17 Aug. 1989), p. A7.

769 Boudette, Neal E. "Computer Flu Is After You: Companies Shouldn't Feel Immune to Viruses." *Industry Week*, 238, no. 2 (16 Jan. 1989), pp. 39-40.

770 Bourgeois, Marie. "Protecting Business Confidences: A Comparative Study of Quebec and French Law." *Intellectual Property Journal*, 3, no. 3 (Jan. 1988), pp. 259-89.

771 Bown, Christopher M. "Liability for Defective Software in the United Kingdom." *Software Protection*, 5, no. 1 (June 1986), pp. 1-14.

772 Boyer, Helen A. "Using Software in Computer Networks: Avoiding Liability for Copyright Infringement." *Jurimetrics Journal*, 28, no. 3 (Spring 1988), pp. 275-83.

773 Bramson, Robert S. "Rights in Computer-Related Technology (with Forms)." *ALI-ABA Course Materials Journal*, 10, no. 1 (Aug. 1985), pp. 7-26.

774 Bramson, Robert S. "Two Computer Software Contracts." *ALI-ABA Course Materials Journal*, 9, no. 4 (Feb. 1985), pp. 61-73.

775 Brandt, Richard. "For Chipmakers, a Landmark Ruling Gets Wiped Off the Map." *Business Week*, no. 3033 (11 Jan. 1988), pp. 41-42.

776 Brandt, Richard. "Lotus the Copycat Killer Pounces Again: But Its Lawsuit Against Borland's Quattro Is No Sure Winner." *Business Week*, no. 3169 (16 July 1990), pp. 31-32.

777 Brandt, Richard. "Microsoft May Have Macro Worries: An Apple Lawsuit Just Got Stronger, and the FTC Has Questions, Too." *Business Week*, no. 3209 (25 Mar. 1991), p. 30.

778 Brannigan, Vincent. "The Regulation of Medical Expert Computer Software as a 'Device' Under the Food, Drug, and Cosmetic Act." *Jurimetrics Journal*, 27, no. 4 (Summer 1987), pp. 370-82.

779 Branscomb, Anne W. "Common Law for the Electronic Frontier: Networked Computing Challenges the Laws That Govern Information and Ownership." *Scientific American*, 265, no. 3 (Sept. 1991), pp. 154-58.

780 Branscomb, Anne W. "Rogue Computer Programs and Computer Rogues: Tailoring the Punishment to Fit the Crime." *Rutgers Computer and Technology Law Journal*, 16, no. 1 (1990), pp. 1- 61.

781 Branscomb, Anne W. "Who Owns Creativity? Property Rights in the Information Age." *Technology Review*, 91, no. 4 (May-June 1988), pp. 38-45.

782 Branwyn, Gareth. "Computers, Crime, and the Law." *The Futurist*, 24, no. 5 (Sept.-Oct. 1990), p. 48.

783 Bravo, Ellen. "Mistrust and Manipulation: Electronic Monitoring of the American Workforce." *USA Today*, 119, no. 2552 (May 1991), pp. 46-48.

784 Bray, Debra L. "Abuses of Attorneys' Computer Data Bases Threaten Professional Ethics." *Computer/Law Journal*, 7, no. 3 (Summer 1987), pp. 439-53.

785 "Brazil: Recent Developments and Their Application to Computer Software." *Software Protection*, 10, no. 4 (Sept. 1991), p. 14.

786 Brazil, Pat. "Infringement of Copyright and the Problem of 'Piracy.'" *The Australian Law Journal*, 61, no. 1 (Jan. 1987), pp. 12-24.

787 "Brazilian Software Copyright Protection Legislation Drafted." *The Computer Lawyer*, 4, no. 2 (Feb. 1987), p. 27.

788 "Brazil's Software Protection Law: Law nr. 7.646 of December 18, 1987." *Software Protection*, 6, no. 9 (Feb. 1988), pp. 4-8.

789 Brennan, Laura. "It Pays Back to Track Down Software Pirates." *PC Week*, 8, no. 2 (14 Jan. 1991), pp. 122, 131.

790 "Brief of ADAPSO (Amicus Curiae) in the Case of Whelan v. Jaslow Dental Laboratories, Inc." *Software Protection*, 4, no. 12 (May 1986), pp. 1-13.

791 "Briefs." *PC Magazine*, 11, no. 4 (25 Feb. 1992), p. 32.

792 "Briefs." *PC Magazine*, 11, no. 6 (31 Mar. 1992), pp. 60-66.

793 Brinson, J. Dianne. "Copyrighted Software: Separating the Protected Expression from Unprotected Ideas, a Starting Point." *Boston College Law Review*, 29, no. 4-5 (Sept. 1988), pp. 803-56.

794 Brinson, J. Dianne. "Software Distribution Agreements and Bankruptcy: The Licensor's Perspective." *Washington Law Review*, 64, no. 3 (July 1989), pp. 499-549.

795 Bromberg, Craig. "In Defense of Hackers." *New York Times Magazine* (21 Apr. 1991), pp. 44-49.

796 Bromley, Robert. "Virus Protection for Microcomputer Systems." *Journal of Accountancy*, 166, no. 6 (Dec. 1988), pp. 123-24, 126.

797 Brooks, David. "The New Look and Feel of Computer Software Protection." *Arizona Law Review*, 29, no. 2 (1987), pp. 281-94.

798 Brooks, Kenneth C. "Human Ingenuity: A Novel Standard for Patenting Algorithms." *Golden Gate University Law Review*, 22, no. 2 (Spring 1992), pp. 455-87.

799 Brotman, Stuart N. "Buying Computers Successfully: Knowledge of Contracts Is Essential to Sound Purchase." *Trial*, 23, no. 1 (Jan. 1987), pp. 33-34.

800 Brower, Steven. "Insurance Issues for the Computer Industry." *Boston Bar Journal*, 33, no. 5 (Sept.-Oct. 1989), pp. 21-24.

801 Brown, Harold R. "Fear and Loathing of the Paper Trail: Originality in Products of Reverse Engineering Under the Semiconductor Chip Protection Act as Analogized to the Fair Use of Nonfiction Literary Works." *Syracuse Law Review*, 41, no. 3 (1990), pp. 985-1020.

802 Brown, Jack E. "The Protection of High Technology Intellectual Property." *Computer/Law Journal*, 11, no. 1 (Feb. 1991), pp. 29-40.

803 Brown, Jack E. "Protection of Software Involves Several Options for Computer Industry." *The National Law Journal*, 13, no. 41 (17 June 1991), pp. 20-21.

804 Brown, Jack E. "Recent International Trends in the Legal Protection of Computer Software." *The Journal of Law and Technology*, 2, no. 1 (Winter 1987), pp. 167-81.

805 Brown, R. A. "Computer-Related Crime Under Commonwealth Law, and the Draft Federal Criminal Code." *Criminal Law Journal*, 10, no. 6 (Dec. 1986), pp. 376-93.

806 Brown, Ralph S. "Eligibility for Copyright Protection: A Search for Principled Standards." *Minnesota Law Review*, 70, no. 2 (Dec. 1985), pp. 579-609.

807 Brown, Richard L. "Copyright and Computer Databases: The Case of the Bibliographic Utility." *Rutgers Computer and Technology Law Journal*, 11, no. 1 (1985), pp. 17-49.

808 Brown, Turner Kenneth. "Compulsory Software Licenses Under EC Law." *Software Protection*, 9, no. 6-7 (Nov.-Dec. 1990), pp. 1-3.

809 Brown, Vance Franklin. "The Incompatibility of Copyright and Computer Software: An Economic Evaluation and a Proposal for a Marketplace Solution." *North Carolina Law Review*, 66, no. 5 (June 1988), pp. 977-1021.

810 Brownstein, Ronald. "Computer Communications Vulnerable as Privacy Laws Lag Behind Technology." *National Journal*, 16, no. 2 (14 Jan. 1984), pp. 52-57.

811 Bruzga, Charles E. "The *Benson* Court's Approach to Computer Software— or Other—Patent Claims Reciting a Mathematical Algorithm." *Journal of the Patent and Trademark Office Society*, 74, no. 2 (Feb. 1992), pp. 135-42.

812 Bruzzone, Lauren. "Copyright and License Protection for Computer Programs: A Market Oriented Assessment." *Pace Law Review*, 11, no. 2 (Winter 1991), pp. 303-56.

813 Bryan, E. Lewis. "Microcomputer Transmitted Disease." *The CPA Journal,* 62, no. 1 (Jan. 1992), pp. 75-79.

814 Buchsbaum, S. J. "Networked Computer Security." *Vital Speeches of the Day,* 58, no. 5 (15 Dec. 1991), pp. 150-55.

815 Budd, Steven W. "The Semiconductor Chip Protection Act of 1984: The Shape of Things to Come?" *Columbia-VLA Journal of Law and the Arts,* 10, no. 2 (1986), pp. 309-29.

816 Bulchis, Edward W., and Maurice J. Pirio. "Preserving Intellectual Property Rights During Software Beta Testing." *The Computer Lawyer,* 7, no. 6 (June 1990), pp. 1-6.

817 Bull, Jorgen. "Legal Protection of Computer Software in Norway." *Software Law Journal,* 1, no. 3 (Spring-Summer 1986), pp. 383-90.

818 Burchfiel, Kenneth J. "The Constitutional Intellectual Property Power: Progress of Useful Arts and the Legal Protection of Semiconductor Technology." *Santa Clara Law Review,* 28, no. 3 (1988), pp. 473-541.

819 Burgess, John. "Computer Virus Sparks a User Scare." *The Washington Post,* 112, no. 286 (17 Sept. 1989), p. H3.

820 Burgess, John. "Race to Secure Computers Threatens Free Exchange of Data." *The Washington Post,* 112, no. 89 (4 Mar. 1989), pp. D11-12.

821 Burgunder, Lee B. "Trademark and Copyright: How Intimate Should the Close Association Become?" *Santa Clara Law Review,* 29, no. 1 (Winter 1989), pp. 89-119.

822 Burk, Dan L., and Laurence H. Winer. "Failure to Prepare: Who's Liable in a Data Processing Disaster?" *Santa Clara Computer and High Technology Law Journal,* 5, no. 1 (Feb. 1989), pp. 19-50.

823 Burk, Daniel R. "Virginia's Response to Computer Abuses: An Act in Five Crimes." *University of Richmond Law Review,* 19, no. 1 (Fall 1984), pp. 85-106.

824 Burk, Holger, and Andreas Pfitzmann. "Digital Payment Systems Enabling Security and Unobservability." *Computers and Security,* 8, no. 5 (Aug. 1989), pp. 399-416.

825 Burkert, Herbert. "Public Sector Information: Towards a More Comprehensive Approach in Information Law?" *Journal of Law and Information Science,* 3, no. 1 (1992), pp. 47-62.

826 Burnett, Rachel. "Doing the Deal." *Solicitors Journal,* 135, no. 4 (1 Feb. 1991), pp. 124-25.

827 Burns, George S. "Litigating Computer Trade Secrets in California." *Computer/Law Journal,* 6, no. 3 (Winter 1986), pp. 485-511.

828 Burnside, Russell S. "The Electronic Communications Privacy Act of 1986: The Challenge of Applying Ambiguous Statutory Language to Intricate Telecommunication Technologies." *Rutgers Computer and Technology Law Journal,* 13, no. 2 (1987), pp. 451-517.

829 Burnson, Patrick. "IBM Offers Protection from Datacrime Virus." *Info-World,* 11, no. 41 (9 Oct. 1989), p. 13.

830 Burshtein, Sheldon. "Crown Copyright in Data Bases." *Software Protection,* 10, no. 1 (June 1991), pp. 5-15.

831 Busse, Torsten. "Latest Virus Scare Puts PC Buyers on Alert." *InfoWorld,* 14, no. 5 (3 Feb. 1992), pp. 1, 95.

832 Busse, Torsten. "Michelangelo: Hype or Threat?" *InfoWorld,* 14, no. 9 (2 Mar. 1992), pp. 1, 107.

833 Butler, Robert J. "In the Aftermath of *California v. FCC*: Computer III Remand Proceedings Pose Difficult Policy Choices for the Enhanced Services Industry." *The Computer Lawyer,* 8, no. 5 (May 1991), pp. 24-27.

834 "Byting Criminals: Computer Bills in Congress." *ABA Journal,* 71 (July 1985), p. 35.

835 "CBEMA Comments on Computer-Related Invention Patents." *The Computer Lawyer,* 8, no. 10 (Oct. 1991), pp. 32-40.

836 Calise, Angela K. "Diskless PCs Curb Theft, Virus." *National Underwriter-Property and Casualty/Risk and Benefits Management Edition,* 94, no. 35 (27 Aug. 1990), pp. 7, 31.

837 "Calling All Hackers: NTT Issues Security Challenge." *The Wall Street Journal,* 214, no. 43 (31 Aug. 1989), p. B6.

838 Calvo, Michel A. "Employees and Software Piracy in France." *Software Protection,* 10, no. 6 (Nov. 1991), pp. 1-5.

839 Cameron, Donald M., and Stephen J. Perry. "Computer Software–Related Patents in Canada." *The Computer Lawyer,* 7, no. 4 (Apr. 1990), pp. 8-12.

840 Campbell, Paul J. "The Impact of Computer Data Banks on the Law Enforcement Exemption of the Freedom of Information Act: *John Doe Agency v. John Doe Corporation*." *Software Law Journal,* 4, no. 4 (Dec. 1991), pp. 633-51.

841 "Can Software Makers Win the War Against Piracy?" *Business Week,* no. 2840 (30 Apr. 1984), pp. 108-9.

842 "Can We Stop a PC-Eater?" *Soviet Life,* 1989, no. 7 (July 1989), p. 39.

843 Candia, Tanya. "How VMS Keeps Out Intruders." *Computers and Security,* 9, no. 6 (Oct. 1990), pp. 499-502.

844 Canfield, James. "The Copyrightability of Object Code." *Notre Dame Law Review,* 59, no. 2 (1984), pp. 412-30.

845 Cangemi, Michael P. "Issues and Comments." *The EDP Auditor Journal,* 3 (1988), pp. 1-3.

846 Cangialosi, Charles. "The Electronic Underground: Computer Piracy and Electronic Bulletin Boards." *Rutgers Computer and Technology Law Journal,* 15, no. 2 (1989), pp. 265-301.

847 Capes, Nelson R. "Current Status of Patent Protection for Computer Software." *Journal of the Patent and Trademark Office Society,* 74, no. 1 (Jan. 1992), pp. 5-25.

848 Capes, Nelson R. "The Lotus Decision: Analysis and Recommendation for Non-Copyright Protection." *Software Protection,* 10, no. 2 (July 1991), pp. 5-15.

849 Capwell, Jeffrey R. "Secured Financing in Intellectual Property: Perfection of Security Interests in Copyrights to Computer Programs." *Syracuse Law Review,* 39, no. 3 (1988), pp. 1041-80.

850 Card, Duncan C. "Microchip Software Protection: Don't Get 'Burned.'" *Santa Clara Computer and High Technology Law Journal,* 7, no. 1 (July 1991), pp. 189-92.

851 Cardinali, Richard, and Ann Zakewicz. "Injuries Caused by Computer Systems: Who Is Liable?" *Journal of Products Liability,* 13, no. 4 (1991), pp. 347-59.

852 Carmichael, James T. "Protection of United States Semiconductor Designs in Foreign Countries Under the Semiconductor Chip Protection Act of 1984." *Rutgers Computer and Technology Law Journal,* 12, no. 2 (1987), pp. 433-45.

853 Carr, James G. "Privacy of Electronic Communications Under Title III." *Search and Seizure Law Report,* 14, no. 3 (Mar.-Apr. 1987), pp. 105-11.

854 Carrier, Joseph P. "Propriety Rights in Software: How Much Is Too Much?" *Journal of the Patent and Trademark Office Society,* 72, no. 1 (Jan. 1990), pp. 67-85.

855 Carroll, John M. "Conference Report: 2300 Brave Virus Threat to Attend National Security Conference." *Computers and Security,* 9, no. 1 (Feb. 1990), pp. 45-49.

856 Carroll, John M. "Security and Credibility in an Information-Intensive Society." *Computers and Security,* 9, no. 6 (Oct. 1990), pp. 489-98.

857 Carson, David O. "Copyright Protection for Factual Compilations After *Feist*: A Practitioner's View." *University of Dayton Law Review,* 17, no. 3 (Spring 1992), pp. 969-1018.

858 Carter, Craig C. "High-Tech Snooping." *Fortune,* 113, no. 8 (14 Apr. 1986), pp. 89-90.

859 "Cash-Machine Magician." *Time,* 129, no. 22 (1 June 1987), p. 61.

860 Cashell, James D., Jeri B. Waggoner. "Computer Viruses: The Risks Posed to CPAs and How to Deal with Them." *The CPA Journal,* 59, no. 7 (July 1989), pp. 66-71.

861 Castillo, Justin, Bill Doyle, and Susmita Dubey. "Computer Crime." *American Criminal Law Review,* 29, no. 2 (Winter 1992), pp. 221-41.

862 Castro, Janice. "Hey! Let's Send a Couple of Billion to Wolfgang." *Time,* 138, no. 12 (23 Sept. 1991), p. 13.

863 Caswell, Christopher K. "The Classification of Software: A Logical and Rational Approach." *Jurimetrics Journal,* 24, no. 4 (Summer 1984), pp. 377-95.

864 Catania, Phillip. "Expert Computer Witness: An Interview." *Law Institute Journal,* 62, no. 6 (June 1988), pp. 554-55.

865 "Caught in the Act." *Life,* 15, no. 12 (Nov. 1992), p. 21.

866 Cavaliere, Kevin F. "Protection of Proprietary Rights in Computer Programs: A 'Basic' Formula for Debugging the System." *Intellectual Property Law Review,* 16 (1984), pp. 57-91.

867 Cavasola, Pietro. "Legal Protection of Software Against Third Parties in Italy." *Software Law Journal,* 1, no. 3 (Spring-Summer 1986), pp. 367-71.

868 Cavazos, Edward A. "Computer Bulletin Board Systems and the Right of Reply: Redefining Defamation Liability for a New Technology." *The Review of Litigation,* 12, no. 1 (Fall 1992), pp. 231-48.

869 Celedonia, Baila H. "From Copyright to Copycat: Open Season on Data." *Publishers Weekly,* 238, no. 37 (16 Aug. 1991), pp. 34-35.

870 Celentino, Christopher, Robert Pressman, and Beth K. Eiseman. "*Vault Corp. v. Quaid Software Ltd.*: Invalidating Shrink-Wrap Licenses?" *The Journal of Law and Technology,* 2, no. 1 (Winter 1987), pp. 151-65.

871 Chalton, Simon. "Copyright Protection Extended: An English Comment on *Whelan v. Jaslow.*" *Software Protection,* 5, no. 9 (Feb. 1987), pp. 14-18.

872 Chalton, Simon. "Protecting Software Through Licensing — Part 1." *Software Protection,* 3, no. 10 (Mar. 1985), pp. 1-7.

873 Chalton, Simon. "Protecting Software Through Licensing — Part 2." *Software Protection,* 3, no. 11 (Apr. 1985), pp. 10-16.

874 Chandler, James P. "Protection of U. S. Competitiveness in the International Software Markets: Reexamining the Question of Copyrighting Government-Created Software." *George Washington Journal of International Law and Economics,* 25, no. 2 (1991), pp. 387-418.

875 Chang, Ching-Ning S. "Computer Software Protection in the Republic of China (Taiwan)." *Computer/Law Journal,* 7, no. 4 (Fall 1987), pp. 455-68.

876 Chang, Meredith. "The Patenting of MIS Computer Programs: One Step Beyond." *Pacific Law Journal,* 21, no. 3 (1990), pp. 761-99.

877 Chapman, James. "California Uniform Trade Secrets Act: A Comparative Analysis of the Act and the Common Law." *Santa Clara Computer and High-Technology Law Journal,* 2, no. 2 (1986), pp. 389-412.

878 Chapman, Michael T. "Copyright Law—Putting Too Much Teeth Into Software Copyright Infringement Claims: *Whelan Associates v. Jaslow Dental Laboratory.*" *The Journal of Corporation Law,* 12, no. 4 (Summer 1987), pp. 785-800.

879 Charles, Dan. "Can We Stop the Databank Robbers?" *New Scientist,* 129, no. 1753 (26 Jan. 1991), pp. 24-25.

880 Charles, Dan. "Computer Fraudsters Foiled by the Small Ads." *New Scientist,* 133, no. 1810 (29 Feb. 1992), p. 24.

881 Charles, Robert. "Computer Bulletin Boards and Defamation: Who Should Be Liable? Under What Standard?" *The Journal of Law and Technology,* 2, no. 1 (Winter 1987), pp. 121-50.

882 "A Charter of Rights for Creators: Report of the Sub-Committee on the Revision of Copyright (October 1985)." *Software Protection,* 5, no. 4 (Sept. 1986), pp. 4-9.

883 Chen, Christopher D. "Computer Crime and the Computer Fraud and Abuse Act of 1986." *Computer/Law Journal,* 10, no. 1 (Winter 1990), pp. 71-86.

884 Chesler, Lawrence. "Contractual Issues in the Remarketing of Systems." *The Computer Lawyer,* 7, no. 9 (Sept. 1990), pp. 1-9. (A slight variation of this article was published under the same title in *Computer/Law Journal,* 11, no. 2 [Apr. 1991], pp. 247-64.)

885 Chesser, James. "Semiconductor Chip Protection: Changing Roles for Copyright and Competition." *Virginia Law Review,* 71, no. 2 (Mar. 1985), pp. 249-95.

886 Chesser, James P. "Copyright Protection for Integrated Circuits: Reevaluating Old Ideas About New Competitive Processes." *The University of Western Ontario Law Review,* 22, no. 2 (1984), pp. 201-33.

887 Chester, Jeffrey A. "The Mob Breaks Into the Information Age." *Business and Society Review,* no. 59 (Fall 1986), pp. 4-8.

888 "Chips Get Copyright." *Science News,* 127, no. 2 (12 Jan. 1985), p. 23.

889 "Chips Successfully Enjoins OPTi's 'Page Interleaving' Designation." *The Computer Lawyer,* 9, no. 6 (June 1992), p. 35.

890 Chisum, Donald S. "The Patentability of Algorithms." *University of Pittsburgh Law Review,* 47, no. 4 (Summer 1986), pp. 959-1022.

891 Chlapowski, Francis S. "The Constitutional Protection of Informational Privacy." *Boston University Law Review,* 71, no. 1 (Jan. 1991), pp. 133-60.

892 Chock, Patricia N. "The Use of Computers in the Sexual Exploitation of Children and Child Pornography." *Computer/Law Journal,* 7, no. 3 (Summer 1987), pp. 383-407.

893 Chong, David K. K. "Should Developing Nations Grant Proprietary Rights to Foreign Works?" *Software Law Journal,* 1, no. 4 (Fall 1987), pp. 541-57.

894 Choy, Peter M. C. "Amicus Curiae Brief for the American Committee for Interoperable Systems." *Software Protection,* 10, no. 10 (Mar. 1992), pp. 2-10.

895 Christou, Richard. "The EEC Directive for Legal Protection of Computer Programs." *Solicitors' Journal,* 134, no. 46 (16 Nov. 1990), pp. 1342-43.

896 Churbuck, David. "Desktop Forgery." *Forbes,* 144, no. 12 (27 Nov. 1989), pp. 246-54.

897 Chwat, Anne. "Privacy Interests in Criminal Records: Accuracy and Dissemination." *1986 Annual Survey of American Law,* 2 (1986), pp. 545-67.

898 Ciarcia, Steve. "Build a Hardware Data Encryptor." *Byte,* 11, no. 9 (Sept. 1986), pp. 97-111.

899 Cipra, Barry. "Eternal Plague: Computer Viruses." *Science,* 249, no. 4975 (21 Sept. 1990), p. 1381.

900 Cirillo, Elisa. "The Legal Protection of Computer Software in the People's Republic of China." *Cardozo Arts and Entertainment Law Journal,* 7, no. 2 (1989), pp. 387-408.

901 Cirillo, Vincent A. "Liberty v. Tyranny: The Pennsylvania Supreme Court Encounters Old Combatants on a New Battlefield. III. Computer Files." *Temple Law Review,* 65, no. 2 (Summer 1992), pp. 619-20.

902 Cisler, Steve. "An Essay on the Openness of Networks, Electronic Free Speech, and the Security of Computers." *Online,* 14, no. 6 (Nov. 1990), pp. 101-3.

903 "Civil Defense: The Military Loses a Fight for Control of Data—Or Does It?" *Scientific American,* 258, no. 3 (Mar. 1988), pp. 18-20.

904 Clapes, Anthony L., and Jennifer M. Daniels. "Revenge of the Luddites: A Closer Look at *Computer Associates v. Altai.*" *The Computer Lawyer,* 9, no. 11 (Nov. 1992), pp. 11-19.

905 Clapes, Anthony L., Patrick Lynch, and Mark R. Steinberg. "Silicon Epics and Binary Bards: Determining the Proper Scope of Copyright Protection for Computer Programs." *UCLA Law Review,* 34, no. 5-6 (June-Aug. 1987), pp. 1493-594.

906 "Clarifying the Copyright Misuse Defense: The Role of Antitrust Standards and First Amendment Values." *Harvard Law Review,* 104, no. 6 (Apr. 1991), pp. 1289-1308.

907 Clarke, Roger. "The Resistible Rise of the National Personal Data System." *Software Law Journal,* 5, no. 1 (Feb. 1992), pp. 29-59.

908 Clarkson, John. "Don't Lose Your Data!" *Supervision,* 51, no. 2 (Feb. 1990), pp. 8-10.

909 "Clearpoint's Injunction Vacated." *The Computer Lawyer,* 9, no. 12 (Dec. 1992), p. 35.

910 Cleaver, Carole M. "Privacy Rights in Medical Records." *Fordham Urban Law Journal,* 13, no. 1 (1984-85), pp. 165-204.

911 Cleveland, Harlan. "How Can 'Intellectual Property' Be 'Protected'?" *Change,* 21, no. 3 (May-June 1989), pp. 10-11.

912 "Clever, Nasty and Definitely Antisocial." *Newsweek,* 112, no. 20 (14 Nov. 1988), pp. 24-25.

913 Cline, Dennis. "Copyright Protection of Software in the EEC: The Competing Policies Underlying Community and National Law and the Case for Harmonization." *California Law Review,* 75, no. 2 (Mar. 1987), pp. 633-80.

914 Clukey, Laura L. "The Electronic Communications Privacy Act of 1986: The Impact on Software Communication Technologies." *Software Law Journal,* 2, no. 2 (Spring 1988), pp. 243-63.

915 Coats, William S., and Heather D. Rafter. "*Accolade* and *Atari*: Reverse Engineering and the Right to Make Compatible Programs." *The Computer Lawyer,* 9, no. 10 (Oct. 1992), pp. 1-5.

916 "Code Green: The Cost of Perfect Security." *Canadian Business,* 62, no. 8 (Aug. 1989), p. 66.

917 Coffee, Peter. "A Holiday Cure for Causes of Computer Crime." *PC Week,* 8, no. 1 (7 Jan. 1991), p. 63.

918 Coffee, Peter. "Last Word on Viruses, the Ultimate Terrorist Act." *PC Week,* 7, no. 4 (29 Jan. 1990), p. 40.

919 Coffee, Peter. "Shareware Deserves a Chance to Prove Its Worth." *PC Week,* 7, no. 7 (19 Feb. 1990), p. 32.

920 Cogdell, Andrew. "Copyright Protection for Computer Programs in Object Code in ROM." *North Carolina Journal of International Law and Commercial Regulation,* 10 (1985), pp. 667-99.

921 Cohen, Bart D. "Computer Crime." *American Criminal Law Review*, 25, no. 3 (Winter 1988), pp. 367-70.

922 Cohen, F. B. "A Formal Definition of Computer Worms and Some Related Results." *Computers and Security*, 11, no. 7 (Nov. 1992), pp. 641-52.

923 Cohen, Fred. "Computational Aspects of Computer Viruses." *Computers and Security*, 8, no. 4 (June 1989), pp. 325-44.

924 Cohen, Fred. "Computer Viruses: Theory and Experiments." *Computers and Security*, 6, no. 1 (Feb. 1987), pp. 22-35.

925 Cohen, Fred. "A Cost Analysis of Typical Computer Viruses and Defenses." *Computers and Security*, 10, no. 3 (May 1991), pp. 239-50.

926 Cohen, Fred. "Models of Practical Defenses Against Computer Viruses." *Computers and Security*, 8, no. 2 (Apr. 1989), pp. 149-60.

927 Cohen, Fred. "On the Implications of Computer Viruses and Methods of Defense." *Computers and Security*, 7, no.2 (Apr. 1988), pp. 167-84.

928 Cole, George S. "Tort Liability for Artificial Intelligence and Expert Systems." *Computer/Law Journal*, 10, no. 2 (Apr. 1990), pp. 127-231.

929 Cole, Patrick, and Jonathan B. Levine. "Are ATMs Easy Targets for Crooks?" *Business Week*, no. 3094 (6 Mar. 1989), p. 30.

930 Cole, Patrick E. "New Challenges to the U.S. Multinational Corporation in the European Economic Community: Data Protection Laws." *New York University Journal of International Law and Politics*, 17, no. 4 (Summer 1985), pp. 893-947.

931 Coleman, Mitch, and Dave Jaffe. "DOS Hospital: When the Chips Are Down, the Physician Is In." *Omni*, 13, no. 12 (Sept. 1991), p. 104.

932 Collier, Paul Arnold, Robert Dixon, and Claire Lesley Marston. "Computer Fraud: Research Findings from the UK." *Internal Auditor*, 48, no. 4 (Aug. 1991), pp. 49-52.

933 Collingwood, Harris, ed. "The Virus Is Coming! The Virus Is Coming!" *Business Week*, no. 3256 (16 Mar. 1992), p. 48.

934 Collins, John, and Peter Knight. "Computer Contracts: Recent Developments in the Legal Liability of Vendors." *Software Law Journal*, 5, no. 1 (Feb. 1992), pp. 61-88.

935 "Colo. and Iowa Amend Dollar Limits." *The Computer Lawyer*, 9, no. 7 (July 1992), p. 42.

936 "Columbus Day Virus Proves a 'No Show' But Others Lurking." *Telecommunications*, 23, no. 12 (Dec. 1989), p. 15.

937 Comer, James P. "Computer Ethics." *Parents*, 60, no. 9 (Sept. 1985), p. 158.

938 Commins, Kevin. "Insurers Plan Computer Virus Coverage." *The Journal of Commerce and Commercial,* 380, no. 26994 (8 June 1989), pp. 1A, 9A.

939 The Committee on Computer Law. "The Applicability of the Magnuson–Moss Consumer Warranty Act to the Distribution of Personal Computer Products." *The Record of the Association of the Bar of the City of New York,* 43, no. 4 (May 1988), pp. 429-46.

940 The Committee on Computer Law. "Computer Law Reports." *The Record of the Association of the Bar of the City of New York,* 40, no. 7 (Dec. 1985), pp. 754-89.

941 The Committee on Computer Law. "Reverse Engineering and Intellectual Property Law." *The Record of the Association of the Bar of the City of New York,* 44, no. 2 (Mar. 1989), pp. 132-58.

942 "A Comprehensive Statute of Limitations for Litigation Arising from Defective Custom Computer Systems." *Stanford Law Review* (July 1985), pp. 1539-72.

943 "Computer Advisory Council Named to Aid SBA in Security, Education." *Journal of Accountancy,* 160, no. 3 (Sept. 1985), pp. 36-38.

944 "Computer Associates Found to Wrongfully Monopolize IBM Mainframe Software Business." *The Computer Lawyer,* 9, no. 6 (June 1992), pp. 37-38.

945 "Computer Associates Must Continue Maintenance Support on Bank's Computers." *The Computer Lawyer,* 9, no. 6 (June 1992), p. 36.

946 "Computer Crime." *American Criminal Law Review,* 24, no. 3 (Winter 1987), pp. 429-38.

947 "Computer Crime." *The Journal of the Law Society of Scotland,* 32, no. 8 (Aug. 1987), p. 314.

948 "Computer Crime Bill Passed." *The Computer Lawyer,* 4, no. 2 (Feb. 1987), p. 27.

949 "Computer Crime Deterrence." *American Journal of Criminal Law,* 13, no. 3 (Summer 1986), pp. 391-416.

950 "Computer Error Causes Secured Creditor to Lose Priority." *The Computer Lawyer,* 3, no. 9 (Sept. 1986), pp. 29-30.

951 "Computer Ethics." *The Futurist,* 18, no. 4 (Aug. 1984), pp. 68- 69.

952 "Computer Fraud." *The CPA Journal,* 57, no. 6 (June 1987), pp. 4- 15.

953 "Computer Intellectual Property and Conceptual Severance." *Intellectual Property Law Review,* 23 (1991), pp. 165-84. (First published in *Harvard Law Review,* 103, no. 5 [Mar. 1990], pp. 1046-65.)

954 "Computer Misuse Act 1990: No Peeking and Poking." *Journal of the Law Society of Scotland,* 36, no. 5 (May 1991), pp. 200-1.

955 "Computer Sabotage Charge." *The New York Times,* 137, no. 47515 (24 May 1988), p. D6.

956 "Computer Security: New Ways to Keep Hackers Out." *Fortune,* 124, no. 14 (16 Dec. 1991), p. 14.

957 "Computer Security Breaches." *Stores,* 72, no. 1 (Jan. 1990), p. 85.

958 "Computer Security Issues and Answers." *Datamation,* supplement, 31, no. 18 (15 Sept. 1985), [pp. 84/1-84/25].

959 "Computer Software and Copyright Protection: The 'Structure, Sequence and Organization' and 'Look and Feel' Questions." *Software Protection,* 8, no. 2 (July 1989), pp. 7-17.

960 "Computer Software Piracy." *World Press Review,* 31, no. 11 (Nov. 1984), pp. 56-58.

961 "Computer Software Protection: From Infancy to Adolescence." *Loyola Law Review,* 31, no. 2 (Spring 1985), pp. 301-26.

962 "The Computer Software Rental Act: Amending the 'First Sale Doctrine' to Protect Computer Software Copyright." *Loyola of Los Angeles Law Review,* 20, no. 4 (June 1987), pp. 1613-39.

963 "Computer Virus Doesn't Cause Much Lost Sleep." *The Wall Street Journal,* 214, no. 73 (13 Oct. 1989), pp. B1-B2.

964 "The Computer Virus Eradication Act of 1989: The War Against Computer Crime Continues." *Software Law Journal,* 3, no. 4 (Apr. 1990), pp. 717-53.

965 "Computer Virus Growth Could Chill PC Industry." *PC Week,* 7, no. 13 (2 Apr. 1990), p. 111.

966 "Computer Viruses: Information Age Vulnerability and the Technopath." *American Criminal Law Review,* 27, no. 3 (1990), pp. 525-43.

967 "Computer Viruses Act as Data System Time Bombs." *Software Protection,* 7, no. 6-7 (Nov.-Dec. 1988), pp. 20-22.

968 "Computer Whiz Guilty." *ABA Journal,* 76 (Apr. 1990), p. 20.

969 "Computers and Copyright—Copyright Protection for Computer Operating Systems Programs—*Apple Computer, Inc. v. Franklin Computer Corp.*" *University of Kansas Law Review,* 33, no. 1 (Fall 1984), pp. 167-87.

970 Condo, Joseph. "Computer Malpractice: Two Alternatives to the Traditional 'Professional Negligence' Standard." *Computer/Law Journal,* 11, no. 2 (Apr. 1991), pp. 323-40.

971 "Conference Report: ComPSEC International 90." *Computers and Security,* 10, no. 1 (Feb. 1991), pp. 75-77.

972 "Congress Passes Criminal Penalty Bill." *The Computer Lawyer,* 9, no. 11 (Nov. 1992), p. 29.

973 "Congress Puts Pressure on Japan and Other Nations Not Offering Software Copyright." *Software Protection,* 3, no. 12 (May 1985), pp. 3-5.

974 Conley, John M. "Tort Theories of Recovery Against Vendors of Defective Software." *Rutgers Computer and Technology Law Journal,* 13, no. 1 (1987), pp. 1-32.

975 Conley, John M., and David W. Peterson. "The Role of Experts in Software Infringement Cases." *Georgia Law Review,* 22, no. 2 (Winter 1988), pp. 425-68.

976 Conley, John M., and Robert M. Bryan. "Software Escrow in Bankruptcy: An International Perspective." *North Carolina Journal of International Law and Commercial Regulation,* 10 (1985), pp. 579-607.

977 Conley, John M., and Robert M. Bryan. "A Unifying Theory for the Litigation of Computer Software Copyright Cases." *Computer/Law Journal,* 6, no. 1 (Summer 1985), pp. 55-118. (First published in *North Carolina Law Review,* 63, no. 4 [Apr. 1985], pp. 563-616.)

978 Conly, Catherine H., and J. Thomas McEwen. "Computer Crime." *NIJ Reports,* no. 218 (Jan.-Feb. 1990), pp. 2-7.

979 Conner, Kathleen Reavis, and Richard P. Rumelt. "Software Piracy: An Analysis of Protection Strategies." *Management Science,* 37, no. 2 (Feb. 1991), pp. 125-39.

980 Connors, Daniel J., Jr., and Antje Westphal. "The European Community Directive on the Legal Protection of Computer Programs: A Comparison Between European and U.S. Copyright Law." *Communications and the Law,* 14, no. 1 (Mar. 1992), pp. 25-55.

981 Conour, William F. "Computer Services Theft: Follow Up." *Res Gestae,* 29, no. 3 (Sept. 1985), p. 141.

982 Conte, Christopher. "Computer Snooping Raises Privacy Concerns." *The Wall Street Journal,* 219, no. 102 (26 May 1992), p. A1.

983 "Contract: User Obtains Nearly $4 Million Jury Verdict for Vendor's Malicious Contract Breach Or Repudiation; Under UCC 2-207, Terms of Shrink-Wrap License Not Binding on Purchaser VAR." *The Computer Lawyer,* 8, no. 10 (Oct. 1991), pp. 42-44.

984 "Contract Damages Allowed Despite Copyright Misuse." *The Computer Lawyer,* 9, no. 9 (Sept. 1992), pp. 36-37.

985 Contreras, Jorge, Laura Handley, and Terrence Yang. "*NEC v. INTEL:* Breaking New Ground in the Law of Copyright." *Harvard Journal of Law and Technology,* 3 (Spring 1990), pp. 209-22.

986 Cook, Roger L. "Massive Damages and Other Tough Remedies for Patent Infringement: The Dawn of a New Era." *The Computer Lawyer*, 3, no. 11 (Nov. 1986), pp. 22-27.

987 Coolley, Ronald B. "RICO: Modern Weaponry Against Software Pirates." *Computer/Law Journal*, 5, no. 2 (Fall 1984), pp. 143-62.

988 Cooper, Frederick L., III, and Walter Sapronov. "Software Protection and Pricing in a LAN Environment." *Jurimetrics Journal*, 26, no. 2 (Winter 1986), pp. 162-79.

989 Cooper, Jeanne Dugan. "Banks Vulnerable to Computer Virus Infecting Europe." *American Banker*, 154, no. 245 (18 Dec. 1989), pp. 1, 11.

990 Cooper, Jeanne Dugan. "Computer Managers Unfazed by Virus Threat." *American Banker*, 154, no. 202 (16 Oct. 1989), p. 45.

991 Cope, Virginia. "Legislators Seek Cure for Computer Cold." *Trial*, 26, no. 1 (Jan. 1990), pp. 14-15.

992 "Copy or Inspiration? The 'Look and Feel' Debate." *Canadian Business*, 62, no. 4 (Apr. 1989), p. 108.

993 "Copy-Protected Software: Does It Need Legislative Protection as Well?" *Software Protection*, 4, no. 6 (Nov. 1985), pp. 9-12.

994 "Copyright Act Preempts Unfair Competition, Conversion, Unjust Enrichment and Accounting Claims." *The Computer Lawyer*, 8, no. 8 (Aug. 1991), pp. 37-38.

995 "Copyright, Computer Software, and Work Made for Hire." *Michigan Law Review*, 89, no. 3 (Dec. 1990), pp. 661-701.

996 "Copyright Law—The Idea/Expression Dichotomy: Where Has It Gone?" *Southern Illinois University Law Journal*, 11 (Winter 1987), pp. 411-25.

997 "Copyright Law—Scope of Protection of Non-Literal Elements of Computer Programs—Second Circuit Applies an 'Abstract-Filtration-Comparison' Test—*Computer Associates International, Inc. v. Altai, Inc.*, nos. 91-7893, 91-7935, 1992 U. S. App. LEXIS 14305 (2d Cir. June 22, 1992)." *Harvard Law Review*, 106, no. 2 (Dec. 1992), pp. 510-15.

998 "Copyright Law: Substantial Compliance; *Videotronics, Inc. v. Bend Electronics*, 586 F.Supp. 478 (D.C. Nev. 1984)." *Santa Clara Computer and High-Technology Law Journal*, 1, no. 1 (1985), pp. 175-78.

999 "Copyright Office Issues Final Regulations on Berne Implementation, Software Rental Legislation." *The Computer Lawyer*, 8, no. 5 (May 1991), p. 39.

1000 "Copyright Protection Extends to 'Structure, Sequence and Organization' of Computer Program." *The Computer Lawyer*, 3, no. 9 (Sept. 1986), pp. 23-24.

1001 "Copyright Protection for Citations to a Law Reporter: *West Publishing Co. v. Mead Data Central, Inc.*" *Minnesota Law Review,* 71, no. 4 (Apr. 1987), pp. 991-1034.

1002 "Copyright Protection for Computer Programs in Object Code in ROM." *North Carolina Journal of International Law and Commercial Regulation,* 10 (1985), pp. 667-99.

1003 "Copyright Protection for Computer Screen Displays." *Minnesota Law Review,* 72, no. 5 (May 1988), pp. 1123-58.

1004 "Copyrightability of Software: Piracy on the Waters of Protection." *South Carolina Law Review,* 37, no. 4 (Summer 1986), pp. 679-717.

1005 Cordova, Christina, and Nate Zelnick. "New and Improved: News of Announced Products and Upgrades." *PC Magazine,* 10, no. 4 (26 Feb. 1991), pp. 55-60.

1006 Corley, Eric. "Free the Hacker Two." *Harper's Magazine,* 279, no. 1672 (Sept. 1989), pp. 22-26.

1007 "The Corporate Director's Duty of Care and the Software Copying Policy." *The Journal of Law and Technology,* 2, no. 1 (Winter 1987), pp. 69-79.

1008 Correa, Carlos Maria. "Computer Software Protection in Developing Countries: A Normative Outlook." *Journal of World Trade,* 22, no. 1 (1988), pp. 23-31.

1009 Corsello, Kenneth R. "The Computer Software Rental Amendments Act of 1990: Another Bend in the First Sale Doctrine." *Catholic University Law Review,* 41, no. 1 (Fall 1991), pp. 177-209.

1010 Corson, Dale R. "What Is Federal Policy on Scientific Communication?" *Physics Today,* 40, no. 1 (Jan. 1987), p. 144.

1011 Cosentino, Caterina, and Rachel Falk. "Patentability of Computer Programs in Australia." *Software Protection,* 10, no. 11 (Apr. 1992), pp. 17-19.

1012 Costello, Thomas, Jr. "1990 Copyright Developments." *Michigan Bar Journal,* 70, no. 7 (July 1991), pp. 672-80.

1013 Costello, Thomas, Jr., Barbara Kovach, and Susan Mashour. "Computer Service Contracts and Software Licenses." *Michigan Bar Journal,* 56, no. 3 (Mar. 1986), pp. 298-302.

1014 Cottrell, Paul, and James Maron. "Professional Liability for Computer Design." *The Computer Lawyer,* 3, no. 8 (Aug. 1986), pp. 14-20.

1015 "Could a Virus Infect Military Computers?" *U.S. News and World Report,* 105, no. 19 (14 Nov. 1988), p. 13.

1016 "Council of European Economic Community Issues Amended Proposal for Software Protection Directive." *Software Protection,* 9, no. 5 (Oct. 1990), pp. 1-16.

1017 "Countering Computer Fraud: What Computer Frauds Have Been Committed in the UK?" *Accountancy*, 100, no. 1128 (Aug. 1987), p. 147.

1018 "Court Confirms Arbitration Award Because It Could Have Been Based on Adequate Theories." *The Computer Lawyer*, 8, no. 1 (Jan. 1991), pp. 35-36.

1019 "Court Declines to Order Withdrawal of Application for Copyright Registration That Allegedly Contains Another's Proprietary 'Security Code.'" *The Computer Lawyer*, 8, no. 1 (Jan. 1991), p. 29.

1020 "Court Enjoins Infringement of Reading Tutor Software's Structure, Sequence and Organization." *The Computer Lawyer*, 9, no. 8 (Aug. 1992), p. 34.

1021 "Court Finds in Favor of Galoob Toys on Appeal." *The Computer Lawyer*, 9, no. 6 (June 1992), p. 33.

1022 "Court Finds Lack of Price and Service Discrimination Allegations." *The Computer Lawyer*, 9, no. 12 (Dec. 1992), p. 35.

1023 "Court Finds Substantial Similarity in Two Computer Programs." *The Computer Lawyer*, 4, no. 5 (May 1987), pp. 32-33.

1024 "Court Grants Apple's Motion for Reconsideration." *The Computer Lawyer*, 9, no. 6 (June 1992), p. 34.

1025 "Court Has Inherent Power to Award Copyright Misuse Damages." *The Computer Lawyer*, 9, no. 6 (June 1992), pp. 35-36.

1026 "Court Outlines Lotus/Borland Trial." *The Computer Lawyer*, 9, no. 11 (Nov. 1992), p. 26.

1027 "Court Reconsiders, But Once Again Takes the Bite Out of Apple's Case." *The Computer Lawyer*, 9, no. 9 (Sept. 1992), p. 32.

1028 Cox, Gail Diane. "The Brave New World of Computer Law." *The National Law Journal*, 10, no. 41 (20 June 1988), p. 46.

1029 Cranston, Ross, ed. "The Law Commission's Report on Computer Misuse." *The Journal of Business Law*, 1989 (Nov. 1989), pp. 524-28.

1030 Cray, William C. "Software Licensing and Bankruptcy Law: *EI International*, a First and Confusing Interpretation of the 11 U.S.C. 365(n) Fix to *Lubrizol.*" *Software Protection*, 10, no. 7-8 (Dec. 1991-Jan. 1992), pp. 1-6.

1031 Crichton, Jean. "Counting on the Devil to Copyright Software." *Publishers Weekly*, 227, no. 7 (15 Feb. 1985), p. 80.

1032 Crichton, Michael. "Mousetrap." *Creative Computing*, 10, no. 6 (June 1984), p. 173.

1033 "Crimes; Comprehensive Computer Data Access and Fraud Act." *Pacific Law Journal*, 19 (1987-88), pp. 556-57.

1034 "Crimes; Computer Crimes." *Pacific Law Journal*, 16, no. 2 (Jan. 1985), pp. 610-11.

1035 "The Crimes of Hacking." *Solicitors' Journal*, 133, no. 42 (20 Oct. 1989), p. 1303.

1036 "Criminal Law A. Computer Crime Act Amended to Include Computer Tampering, False Claims for Payment, and Civil Actions." *Suffolk University Law Review*, 24, no. 1 (Spring 1990), pp. 427-32.

1037 "Criminal Penalties for Reproducing Or Distributing Multiple Copies of Copyrighted Software Proposed." *The Computer Lawyer*, 8, no. 6 (June 1991), pp. 37-38.

1038 Crino, Michael D., and Terry L. Leap. "What HR Managers Must Know About Employee Sabotage." *Personnel*, 66, no. 5 (May 1989), pp. 31-32, 34-36, 38.

1039 Crisp, Philip. "The Legal Protection of Computer Software: Recent Developments in Australia." *Software Law Journal*, 1, no. 3 (Spring-Summer 1986), pp. 289-302.

1040 Crisp, Phillip. "The Legal Protection of Computer Software—Recent Developments in Australia." *Journal of Law and Information Science*, 2, no. 1 (1986), pp. 53-67.

1041 Crockett, Barton. "San Diego Police Probe Card Fraud by Hackers." *American Banker*, 157, no. 76 (21 Aug. 1992), p. 2.

1042 Crowe, Daniel A. "The Scope of Copyright Protection for Non-Literal Design Elements of Computer Software: *Computer Associates International, Inc. v. Altai, Inc.*" *Saint Louis University Law Journal*, 37, no. 1 (Fall 1992), pp. 207-33.

1043 "The Crucial Case of the Copyrights." *Fortune*, 112, no. 1 (8 July 1985), p. 112.

1044 "Cruse, Rubin E., Jr. "Invasions of Privacy and Computer Matching Programs: A Different Perspective." *Computer/Law Journal*, 11, no. 3 (Oct. 1992), pp. 461-80.

1045 Cullen, Scott W. "The Computer Virus: Is There a Real Panacea?" *The Office*, 109, no. 3 (Mar. 1989), pp. 43-46.

1046 "Cuomo Signs Law Adding Six Offenses to Computer Crime." *New York Law Journal*, 196, no. 20 (29 July 1986), pp. 1, 15.

1047 "Current Topics: Data Protection." *Solicitors' Journal*, 130, no. 3 (17 Jan. 1986), p. 42.

1048 Currid, Cheryl. "Once More with Feeling: Spread Safe Computing Practices." *InfoWorld*, 14, no. 12 (23 Mar. 1992), p. 574.

1049 Currid, Cheryl. "Software Needs Easier Licensing Schemes." *PC Week*, 8, no. 22 (3 June 1991), p. 70.

1050 Curtin, Gerard V., Jr. "The Basics of ASICs: Protection for Semiconductor Mask Works in Japan and the United States." *Boston College International and Comparative Law Review*, 15, no. 1 (Winter 1992), pp. 113-39.

1051 Curtis, Bill. "Engineering Computer 'Look and Feel': User Interface Technology and Human Factors Engineering." *Jurimetrics Journal*, 30, no. 1 (Fall 1989), pp. 51-78.

1052 Cutrera, Terri A. "The Constitution in Cyberspace: The Fundamental Rights of Computer Users." *UMKC Law Review*, 60, no. 1 (Fall 1991), pp. 139-67.

1053 "DP Managers' Survey Cites Insiders as Prime Suspects in Computer Crime." *Journal of Accountancy*, 160, no. 2 (Aug. 1985), pp. 42-44.

1054 Dabich, Eli Jr. "More Disaster Planning Needed." *National Underwriter-Property and Casualty/Risk and Benefits Management Edition*, 93, no. 7 (13 Feb. 1989), pp. 19, 46.

1055 Dailey, Michael A., and Henry W. Jones, III. "Whelan Associates, Inc. v. Jaslow Dental Laboratories, Inc.: Towards a New Understanding of Copyrightable Expression." *Software Protection*, 5, no. 2 (July 1986), pp. 7-10.

1056 Dailey, Michael Alan. "Digital Communications Associates, Inc. v. Soft-Klone Distributing Corporation: The 'Look and Feel' of Copyrightable Expression." *Software Protection*, 6, no. 5 (Oct. 1987), pp. 11-17.

1057 Dallmeyer, Dorinda G. "The United States-Japan Semiconductor Accord of 1986: The Shortcomings of High-Tech Protectionism." *Maryland Journal of International Law and Trade*, 13, no. 2 (Spring 1989), pp. 179-222.

1058 Dam, Kenneth W. "The Growing Importance of International Protection of Intellectual Property." *The International Lawyer*, 21, no. 3 (Summer 1987), pp. 627-38.

1059 D'Amico, Thomas J. "Employer Liability for Unauthorized Copying of Software by Employees." *The Computer Lawyer*, 9, no. 2 (Feb. 1992), pp. 26-28.

1060 Damman, Gregory C. "Copyright of Computer Display Screens: Summary and Suggestions." *Computer/Law Journal*, 9, no. 4 (Fall 1989), pp. 417-45. (Also published in *Western State University Law Review*, 17, no. 1 [Fall 1989], pp. 31-58.)

1061 da Silva, Ricardo Barretto Ferreira, and Cristina Esperante Myrrha. "Update on the Brazilian Computer Industry." *Software Protection*, 10, no. 12 (May 1992), pp. 8-15.

1062 "Data Protection: A New Computer Game." *The Economist,* 296, no. 7409 (31 Aug. 1985), pp. 64, 67.

1063 "Data Protection Act." *Solicitors' Journal,* 128, no. 35 (31 Aug. 1984), p. 585.

1064 "Data Protection and the Right to Privacy in the United States and West Germany." *Arizona Journal of International and Comparative Law,* 1987 (1987), pp. 154-63.

1065 Dauer, Christopher. "Experts Eye Computer Virus Prevention." *National Underwriter-Property and Casualty/Risk and Benefits Management Edition,* 94, no. 18 (30 Apr. 1990), pp. 10, 75.

1066 Dauer, Christopher. "New Computer Policy Offers Virus Coverage." *National Underwriter-Property and Casualty/Risk and Benefits Management Edition,* 95, no. 38 (23 Sept. 1991), pp. 35, 42.

1067 Daughtrey, William H., Jr., and Peter L. Gibbes. "The Virginia Computer Crimes Act and Computer Security Systems: A Symbiotic Relationship." *The Virginia Bar Association Journal,* 15, no. 4 (Fall 1989), pp. 11-17.

1068 Daus, Donald G. "Patents and Commercial Success in the U.S. Federal Circuit." *Intellectual Property Journal,* 3, no. 3 (Jan. 1988), pp. 291-304.

1069 David, Jon. "LAN Security Standards." *Computers and Security,* 11, no. 7 (Nov. 1992), pp. 607-19.

1070 David, Jon. "The Novell Virus." *Computers and Security,* 9, no. 7 (Nov. 1990), pp. 593-99.

1071 David, Jon. "Treating Viral Fever." *Computers and Security,* 7, no. 3 (June 1988), pp. 255-58.

1072 Davidson, Duncan M. "Common Law, Uncommon Software." *University of Pittsburgh Law Review,* 47, no. 4 (Summer 1986), pp. 1037-117.

1073 Davidson, Stephen J. "'Box-Top' Software Licenses...." *The Bench and Bar of Minnesota,* 41, no. 3 (Mar. 1984), pp. 9-13.

1074 Davidson, Stephen J. "Reverse Engineering and the Development of Compatible and Competitive Products Under United States Law." *Santa Clara Computer and High Technology Law Journal,* 5, no. 2 (1989), pp. 401-34.

1075 Davis, Barton Bolling. "Acquisition of Rights in Computer Software by the Department of Defense." *Public Contract Law Journal,* 17, no. 1 (Sept. 1987), pp. 77-151.

1076 Davis, Bob. "Abusive Computers." *The Wall Street Journal,* 210, no. 37 (20 Aug. 1987), pp. 1, 12.

1077 Davis, Bob. "GAO, in Its Study of Computer Virus, Cites Lax Security." *The Wall Street Journal,* 214, no. 13 (20 July 1989), p. B4.

1078 Davis, Daniel A. *"Feist Publications, Inc. v. Rural Telephone Service Co.*: Opening the Door to Information Pirates?" *Saint Louis University Law Journal*, 36, no. 2 (Winter 1991), pp. 739-73.

1079 Davis, Fred. "Technology Follows Biology as Computer Viruses Proliferate." *PC Week*, 8, no. 3 (21 Jan. 1991), p. 142.

1080 Davis, Phillip M. "Invasion of the Data Snatchers." *Design News*, 45, no. 14 (17 July 1989), p. 174.

1081 Davis, Phillip M. "More Ways to Prevent Computer Tampering." *Design News*, 45, no. 15 (7 Aud. 1989), p. 148.

1082 Davis, Randall. "The Nature of Software and Its Consequences for Establishing and Evaluating Similarity." *Software Law Journal*, 5, no. 2 (Apr. 1992), pp. 299-330.

1083 Davis, Theodore H., Jr. "Combatting Piracy of Intellectual Property in International Markets: A Proposed Modification of the Special 301 Action." *Vanderbilt Journal of Transnational Law*, 24, no. 3 (1991), pp. 505-33.

1084 Dayan, Leon. "The Scope of Copyright in Information: An Alternative to Classic Theory." *Federal Communications Law Journal*, 42, no. 2 (Apr. 1990), pp. 239-75.

1085 DeBenedictis, Don J. "dBase Copyright Invalidated: Critics Say Judge Misapplied Patent Law in Dismissing Software Maker's Suit." *ABA Journal*, 77 (Mar. 1991), pp. 30-31.

1086 DeBenedictis, Don J. "E-Mail Snoops: Reading Others' Computer Messages May Be Against the Law." *ABA Journal*, 76 (Sept. 1990), pp. 26-27.

1087 DeBenedictis, Don J. "Never Mind: Judge Reverses Himself on Copyright Ruling." *ABA Journal*, 77 (July 1991), pp. 30-31.

1088 DeBenedictis, Don J. "One Opinion, Two Controversies: 2nd Circuit Limits Copyright Protection for Software, Approves Court Expert." *ABA Journal*, 78 (Sept. 1992), p. 26.

1089 Debes, Cheryl, Dorinda Elliot, and Anne R. Field. "Busting Software Pirates." *Business Week*, no. 2899 (17 June 1985), p. 56.

1090 Deeks, D. Brian, and Carol Paradine. "EDI Security: The Feeling's Mutual." *CA Magazine*, 124, no. 10 (Oct. 1991), pp. 49-51.

1091 "Default Entered for Code Destruction." *The Computer Lawyer*, 8, no. 2 (Feb. 1991), p. 37.

1092 "Defendant Cypress Wins Jury Verdict in Patent Suit." *The Computer Lawyer*, 9, no. 8 (Aug. 1992), pp. 35-36.

1093 "Defendant Liable for Patent Infringement Despite Additional Features Present in Infringing Device." *The Computer Lawyer*, 4, no. 5 (May 1987), pp. 34-35.

1094 "Defending Secrets, Sharing Data: New Locks and Keys for Electronic Information." *Software Protection,* 6, no. 11 (Apr. 1988), pp. 1-24.

1095 "Defining the Scope of Copyright Protection for Computer Software." *Stanford Law Review,* 38 (Jan. 1986), pp. 497-534.

1096 De Gorgey, Andrea. "The Advent of DNA Databanks: Implications for Information Privacy." *American Journal of Law and Medicine,* 16, no. 3 (1990), pp. 381-98.

1097 De Groot, Katja C. "An Overview of Recent Changes in California Computer Crime Laws: The Criminalization of Computer Contamination and Strengthend Penalty Provisions." *Santa Clara Computer and High Technology Law Journal,* 6, no. 1 (Mar. 1990), pp. 135-42.

1098 Dehnad, Khosrow. "A Simple Way of Improving the Login Security." *Computers and Security,* 8, no. 7 (Nov. 1989), pp. 607-11.

1099 de Jersey, Paul. "Protection of Computer Programs: The Current Position." *Australian Law Journal,* 62 (Apr. 1988), pp. 255-67.

1100 De Lacy, Justine. "The Sexy Computer." *The Atlantic,* 260, no. 1 (July 1987), pp. 18-26.

1101 Delaney, Richard C. "Warding Off a Computer Virus." *Datamation,* 35, no. 14 (15 July 1989), pp. 64-66.

1102 De Lorenzo, Edward. "How Secure Are Your Files? It Takes Careful Planning to Keep Electronic Data Safe from Prying Eyes or Inadvertent Destruction." *The American Lawyer: Technology 1992,* (May 1992), pp. 13-14, 18.

1103 DeLoughry, Thomas J. "Court Will Not Hear Case Accusing UCLA of Copying Software: Ruling a Blow to Copyright Holders; Victory Seen for Public Universities." *The Chronicle of Higher Education,* 35, no. 29 (29 Mar. 1989), pp. A1, A18.

1104 DeMaio, Harry. "Guarding Against Viruses." *American City and County,* 107, no. 4 (Apr. 1992), p. 8.

1105 DeMaio, Harry B. "Viruses—A Management Issue." *Computers and Security,* 8, no. 5 (Aug. 1989), pp. 381-88.

1106 Dembart, Lee. "Attack of the Computer Virus." *Discover,* 3, no. 11 (Nov. 1984), pp. 90-92.

1107 Denning, Dorothy E., Selim G. Akl, Mark Heckman, Teresa F. Lunt, Matthew Morgenstern, Peter G. Neumann, and Roger R. Schell. "Views for Multilevel Database Security." *IEEE Transactions on Software Engineering,* SE-13, no. 2 (Feb. 1987), pp. 129-40.

1108 Denning, Peter J. "The Internet Worm." *American Scientist,* 77, no. 2 (Mar.-Apr. 1989), pp. 126-28.

1109 Denning, Peter J. "Stopping Computer Crimes." *American Scientist,* 78, no. 1 (Jan.-Feb. 1990), pp. 10-12.

1110 Dennis, Terry L., and Daniel A. Joseph. "Protecting Your PC Data." *Business,* 39, no. 2 (Apr.-June 1989), pp. 9-13.

1111 de Oliveria Novaes, Noemia. "Software Protection in Brazil." *Software Law Journal,* 1, no. 3 (Spring-Summer 1986), pp. 309-18.

1112 Depke, Deidre A., ed. "How to Hack Your Way to the Tropics." *Business Week,* no. 3127 (9 Oct. 1989), p. 148A.

1113 Derra, Skip. "PC Users Should Be Prepared for Outbreak of Computer Viruses." *Research and Development,* 31, no. 10 (Oct. 1989), pp. 20-21.

1114 Derwin, Douglas K., and Daniel R. Siegel. "Microcode Copyright Infringement." *The Computer Lawyer,* 4, no. 4 (Apr. 1987), pp. 1-8.

1115 Desilets, Roland B., Jr. "Software Vendors' Exposure to Products Liability for Computer Viruses." *Computer/Law Journal,* 9, no. 4 (Fall 1989), pp. 509-26.

1116 Desjeux, Xavier. "From Design to Software: Software, Video Games and Copyright — The Analytical Method in the Test of Technology." *Journal of Law and Information Science,* 2, no. 1 (1986), pp. 18-52.

1117 Deutsch, Dennis. "Preparing the Breach of Contract Computer Law Case." *Trial Diplomacy Journal,* 8, no. 2 (Summer 1985), pp. 20-22.

1118 Deutsch, Dennis S. "The 'Demo' as the Basis of the Fraud and Breach of Contract Claim." *The Computer Lawyer,* 8, no. 5 (May 1991), pp. 22-23.

1119 Deutsch, Dennis S. "Litigate and Arbitrate: A Hybrid Method of Alternative Dispute Resolution." *Computer/Law Journal,* 10, no. 4 (Dec. 1990), pp. 517-50.

1120 "Develop Hard-Nosed Security Standards and Educate Users Why They're Important." *Communications News,* 26, no. 7 (July 1989), p. 49.

1121 "Developer of Software Program Retains Ownership in Source Code." *The Computer Lawyer,* 4, no. 6 (June 1987), pp. 40-41.

1122 "Developers Fight to Strengthen Virus Protection." *PC Week,* 7, no. 36 (10 Sept. 1990), p. 49.

1123 Deveza, Robert R. "Legal Protection of Computer Software in Major Industrial Countries: A Survey of Copyright and Patent Protection for Computer Software." *UCLA Pacific Basin Law Journal,* 9, no. 1-2 (Spring 1991), pp. 166-209.

1124 Dewdney, A. K. "A Core War Bestiary of Viruses, Worms and Other Threats to Computer Memories." *Scientific American,* 252, no. 3 (Mar. 1985), pp. 14-23.

1125 Dewdney, A. K. "Of Worms, Viruses, and Core War." *Scientific American,* 260, no. 3 (Mar. 1989), pp. 110-13.

1126 Dewdney, A. K. "A Program Called MICE Nibbles Its Way to Victory at the First Core War Tournament." *Scientific American,* 256, no. 1 (Jan. 1987), pp. 14-20.

1127 DiBattista, Ron A. "Designing a Program to Manage the Risk of Sabotage." *Supervision,* 50, no. 10 (Oct. 1989), pp. 6-8.

1128 Di Cato, Edward M. "Operator Liability Associated with Maintaining a Computer Bulletin Board." *Software Law Journal,* 4, no. 1 (Oct. 1990), pp. 147-59.

1129 Dickinson, M. Lee. "'Total Concept and Feel' Test for Substantial Similarity in Copyright Infringement Extended to Nongame Audiovisual Displays. *Broderbund Software, Inc. v. Unison World, Inc.,* 648 F.Supp. 1127 (N.D. Cal. 1986)." *Santa Clara Computer and High-Technology Law Journal,* 3, no. 2 (1987), pp. 415-19.

1130 Dickman, Steven. "Hackers Revealed as Spies." *Nature,* 338, no. 6211 (9 Mar. 1989), p. 108.

1131 "Dictionary of Hacking Terms." *U.S. News and World Report,* 108, no. 3 (22 Jan. 1990), p. 25.

1132 "Dictum Suggests Software Which Fails to Yield Result for Which It Was Designed May Be Proper Subject of Products Liability Suit." *The Computer Lawyer,* 8, no. 8 (Aug. 1991), p. 35.

1133 Diebel, Linda. "Privacy and the Computer State." *Maclean's,* 97, no. 2 (9 Jan. 1984), pp. 34-37.

1134 Diehl, Stanford, Stan Wszola, Bradley Kliewer, and Larry Stevens. "Rx for Safer Data." *Byte,* 16, no. 8 (Aug. 1991), pp. 218-30, 234-35.

1135 Dietz, James R. "Federal Government Computer Data Sharing and the Threat to Privacy." *University of Detroit Journal of Urban Law,* 61, no. 4 (Summer 1984), pp. 605-23.

1136 Dik, Daniel K. "Copyrighted Software and Tying Arrangements: A Fresh Appreciation for *Per Se* Illegality." *Computer/Law Journal,* 10, no. 3 (Oct. 1990), pp. 413-52.

1137 "Disablement of Software Pursuant to Contract Clause Permissible." *The Computer Lawyer,* 8, no. 9 (Sept. 1991), pp. 32-33.

1138 "Disassembly Permitted to Gain Understanding." *The Computer Lawyer,* 9, no. 11 (Nov. 1992), p. 24.

1139 "Discussion Following the Remarks of Mr. James Keon and Mr. Michael Keplinger." *Canada–United States Law Journal,* 11 (1986), pp. 65-68.

1140 Dixon, R., C. Marston, and P. Collier. "A Report on the Joint CIMA and IIA Computer Fraud Survey." *Computers and Security,* 11, no. 4 (July 1992), pp. 307-13.

1141 Doheny, Donald A., Sr. "Modern Banking: Easy Access vs. Privacy." *Journal of the Missouri Bar,* 48, no. 4 (June 1992), pp. 287-99.

1142 Doheny, Donald A., Sr., and Graydon John Forrer. "Electronic Access to Account Information and Financial Privacy." *The Banking Law Journal,* 109, no. 5 (Sept.-Oct. 1992), pp. 436-55.

1143 Donahue, Gary. "What Is Protected by a Program Copyright?" *New England Law Review,* 27, no. 1 (Fall 1992), pp. 61-83.

1144 Donner, Irah H. "Two Decades of *Gottschalk v. Benson*: Putting the 'Rithm' Back into the Patenting of Mathematical Algorithms." *Software Law Journal,* 5, no. 2 (Apr. 1992), pp. 419-59.

1145 "Don't Use Copyright to Shackle Software." *Business Week,* no. 3107 (29 May 1989), p. 122.

1146 Doost, Roger K. "Accounting Irregularities and Computer Fraud." *The National Public Accountant,* 35, no. 5 (May 1990), pp. 36-39.

1147 Doost, Roger K. "How to Improve Client's Access Control Over Programs and Files." *The CPA Journal,* 59, no. 3 (Mar. 1989), pp. 44-46.

1148 Dorman, Christopher G., and Robert G. Miller. "Computer Software Piracy: The Need for Integration of Statutory and Technological Protections of Intellectual Property." *St. John's Journal of Legal Commentary,* 4, no. 1 (1988), pp. 37-63.

1149 Dorny, Brett N., and Michael K. Friedland. "Copyrighting 'Look and Feel': *Manufacturers Technologies v. CAMS.*" *Harvard Journal of Law and Technology,* 3 (Spring 1990), pp. 195-208.

1150 Dorr, Robert C., and William P. Eigles. "Ownership of Software and Computer-Stored Data." *Colorado Lawyer,* 13, no. 4 (Apr. 1984), pp. 577-88.

1151 Dorr, Robert C., and William P. Eigles. "Resolving Claims to Ownership of Software and Computer-Stored Data—The Importance or Temporary Restraining Orders and Preliminary Injunctions." *Computer/Law Journal,* 5, no. 1 (Summer 1984), pp. 1-24.

1152 Dratler, Jay, Jr. "Trade Secret Law: An Impediment to Trade in Computer Software." *Santa Clara Computer and High-Technology Law Journal,* 1, no. 1 (Jan. 1985), pp. 27-58.

1153 Dreier, Thomas, and Gunnar W. G. Karnell. "Originality of the Copyrighted Work: A European Perspective." *Journal of the Copyright Society of the U.S.A.,* 39, no. 4 (Summer 1992), pp. 289-302.

1154 Dreier, Thomas, and Silke von Lewinski. "The European Commission's Activities in the Field of Copyright." *Journal of the Copyright Society of the U.S.A.*, 39, no. 2 (Winter 1991), pp. 96-120.

1155 Dreyfuss, Rochelle Cooper. "Information Products: A Challenge to Intellectual Property Theory." *New York University Journal of International Law and Politics*, 20, no. 4 (Summer 1988), pp. 897-927.

1156 Driscoll, Faith F. "Why Not Patent 'Software?'" *Women Lawyers Journal*, 72, no. 4 (Summer 1986), pp. 17-18.

1157 Droke, Michael W. "Private, Legislative and Judicial Options for Clarification of Employee Rights to the Contents of Their Electronic Mail Systems." *Santa Clara Law Review*, 32, no. 1 (1992), pp. 167-98.

1158 "Drop the Phone: Busting a Computer Whiz." *Time*, 133, no. 2 (9 Jan. 1989), p. 49.

1159 Dror, Asael. "Secret Codes." *Byte*, 14, no. 6 (June 1989), pp. 267-70.

1160 DuBoff, Leonard D. "High-Tech Law." *INTER-ALIA*, 51, no. 5 (Nov.-Dec. 1986), pp. F5-F11.

1161 DuBoff, Leonard D. "High-Tech Law—Protecting Computer Software." *Journal of the Missouri Bar*, 42, no. 2 (Mar. 1986), pp. 112-19.

1162 DuBoff, Leonard D. "Introduction to Computer Law." *Comm/Ent*, 14, no. 2 (Winter 1992), pp. 215-34.

1163 DuBoff, Leonard D., and Sally Holt Caplan. "The Berne Convention: New Dimensions in Copyright." *Los Angeles Lawyer*, 12, no. 2 (Apr. 1989), pp. 41-45, 58.

1164 DuCharme, Nancy Kemp, and Robert F. Kemp. "Copyright Protection for Computer Software in Great Britain and the United States: A Comparative Analysis." *Santa Clara Computer and High-Technology Law Journal*, 3, no. 2 (1987), pp. 257-82.

1165 Duckworth, Matthew. "Computer Snoopers and the Computer Misuse Act 1990." *Solicitors Journal*, 136, no. 38 (2 Oct. 1992), pp. 964-65.

1166 Duflock, Walter G. "'Look and Feel': A Proposed Solution to the Diverging Views Between the Software Industry and the Courts." *Santa Clara Computer and High Technology Law Journal*, 8, no. 2 (Aug. 1992), pp. 447-68.

1167 Dukarich, Gary. "Patentability of Dedicated Information Processors and Infringement Protection of Inventions That Use Them." *Jurimetrics Journal*, 29, no. 2 (Winter 1989), pp. 135-220.

1168 Du Mesnil de Rochemont, Rudolf. "Copyright and Fair Trade Laws Against Software Piracy in European Civil Law Countries." *Software Protection*, 6, no. 4 (Sept. 1987), pp. 1-7.

1169 Dunaway, Robert W., and Michael A. Dillon. "*B. V. Engineering v. University of California, Los Angeles*: A License to Steal?" *Santa Clara Computer and High Technology Law Journal*, 5 (1989), pp. 349-61.

1170 Dunlap, F. Thomas, Jr. "The Copyrightability of Microcode." *Software Protection*, 4, no. 4 (Sept. 1985), pp. 2-4.

1171 Dunlap, F. Thomas, Jr. "*NEC v. INTEL*: A Challenge to the Developing Law of Copyright in the Protection of Computer Programs." *Santa Clara Computer and High-Technology Law Journal*, 3, no. 1 (Jan. 1987), pp. 3-22.

1172 Dunlap, Tom. "NEC CORP. v. INTEL CORP.: Microcode Held Protected by Copyright Law - The Intel Perspective." *Software Protection*, 5, no. 6 (Nov. 1986), p. 7.

1173 Durney, Edward G. "Japan: Software Protection After *Microsoft*." *Software Protection*, 6, no. 12 (May 1988), pp. 6-11.

1174 Durney, Edward G. "Protection of Computer Programs Under Japanese Copyright Law." *UCLA Pacific Basin Law Journal*, 9, no. 1-2 (Spring 1991), pp. 17-77.

1175 Durney, Edward G. "The Warranty of Merchantability and Computer Software Contracts: A Square Peg Won't Fit in a Round Hole." *Washington Law Review*, 59, no. 3 (July 1984), pp. 511-31.

1176 Duvall, Donald K. "Fair Trade and the Protection of Intellectual Property Rights in U.S.-Korean Economic Relations." *Law/ Technology*, 21, no. 1 (1988), pp. 18-35.

1177 Dvorak, John C. "The Software Piracy Bluff." *PC Magazine*, 11, no. 9 (12 May 1992), p. 93.

1178 Dysart, Joe. "Is Your Software About to Drop Dead?" *Restaurant Hospitality*, 76, no. 2 (Feb. 1992), p. 65.

1179 Dyson, Esther. "Hackers' Rights." *Forbes*, 147, no. 1 (7 Jan. 1991), p. 288.

1180 Dyson, Esther. "Intellectual Property." *Forbes*, 144 (18 Sept. 1989), p. 202.

1181 Dyson, Esther. "New Product or Knockoff?" *Forbes*, 139, no. 13 (15 June 1987), p. 272.

1182 "EC Adopts Software Directive." *The Computer Lawyer*, 8, no. 6 (June 1991), p. 39.

1183 "EC Council of Ministers Approves Amended Software Directive." *The Computer Lawyer*, 8, no. 2 (Feb. 1991), pp. 36-37.

1184 "EC Directive on the Legal Protection of Computer Programs." *Software Protection*, 9, no. 6-7 (Nov.-Dec. 1990), pp. 18-22.

1185 "The EC Software Directive: Meeting the Challenges of the Information Age: Legislative History and Bibliography." *Cardozo Arts and Entertainment Law Journal*, 10, no. 1 (1991), pp. 191-276.

1186 "EDP-Related Fraud Is Subject of Report by AICPA Task Force." *Journal of Accountancy*, 157, no. 6 (June 1984), pp. 26-28.

1187 "EFT Losses Aren't Due to High-Tech Raids, Study Reveals." *Commercial Law Bulletin*, 1, no. 4 (July-Aug. 1986), pp. 9-10.

1188 Earley, William. "The Protection of Computer Software Against Third Parties in Ireland." *Software Law Journal*, 1, no. 3 (Spring-Summer 1986), pp. 361-66.

1189 Edwards, Lynda. "Samaurai Hackers." *Rolling Stone*, no. 613 (19 Sept. 1991), pp. 67-69.

1190 Effros, Robert C. "A Banker's Primer on the Law of Electronic Funds Transfers." *The Banking Law Journal*, 105, no. 6 (Nov.-Dec. 1988), pp. 510-43.

1191 Eidelman, James A., and Carol R. Shepherd. "Living Among Pirates: Practical Strategies to Protect Computer Software." *Michigan Bar Journal*, 56, no. 3 (Mar. 1986), pp. 284-90.

1192 Einhorn, Bruce, and Dori Jones. "Fake Windows, Ersatz DOS, Angry Uncle Sam." *Business Week*, no. 3266 (18 May 1992), p. 130.

1193 Einhorn, David A. "Box-Top Licenses and the Battle-of-the-Forms." *Software Law Journal*, 5, no. 2 (Apr. 1992), pp. 401-18.

1194 Einhorn, David A. "Copyright and Patent Protection for Computer Software: Are They Mutually Exclusive?" *Software Protection*, 8, no. 12 (May 1990), pp. 1-9. (First published in *Idea*, 30, no. 3 [1989-90], pp. 265-78.)

1195 Einhorn, David. "The Enforceability of 'Tear-Me-Open' Software License Agreements." *Journal of the Patent and Trademark Office Society*, 67, no. 10 (Oct. 1985), pp. 509-29.

1196 Eitel, Mitchell S. "Microcode Copyright and the Protection of Microprocessors Under Current Intellectual Property Law." *Columbia Journal of Law and Social Problems*, 21, no. 1 (1987), pp. 53-85.

1197 "Electronic Contracts: Are They Enforceable Under Article 2 on the U.C.C.?" *Software Law Journal*, 4, no. 2 (Apr. 1991), pp. 247-69.

1198 Electronic Messaging Services Task Force. "Model Electronic Data Interchange Trading Partner Agreement and Commentary." *Software Law Journal*, 4, no. 2 (Apr. 1991), pp. 179-208.

1199 "Electronic Tax Returns and the Preparer Penalties." *Computer/ Law Journal*, 10, no. 4 (Dec. 1990), pp. 551-79.

1200 "Eleventh Amendment Protects State Against Damages Suit for Copyright Infringement." *The Computer Lawyer*, 4, no. 5 (May 1987), pp. 31-32.

1201 Elkin, Bradley J. "Breach of Contract and Fraud: Computer Sales Distributorship Agreement—*Computer Systems Engineering, Inc. v. Qantel Corp.* 740 F.2d 59 (1st Cir. 1984)." *Santa Clara Computer and High-Technology Law Journal,* 1, no. 1 (Jan. 1985), pp. 169-73.

1202 Elkins, David S. "*NEC v. Intel*: A Guide to Using 'Clean Room' Procedures as Evidence." *Computer/Law Journal,* 10, no. 4 (Dec. 1990), pp. 453-81.

1203 Elliott, Lawrence. "Hunt for the Hacker Spy." *Reader's Digest,* 136, no. 816 (Apr. 1990), pp. 185-91, 194-232.

1204 Elliott, Raymond W. "Protection Against Computer Viruses." *Journal of Accountancy,* 171, no. 5 (May 1991), pp. 121, 123-24.

1205 Ellis, Anne Welles. "Computer Viruses: Working Out the Bugs." *Best's Review-Property/Casualty Insurance Edition,* 90, no. 1 (May 1989), pp. 84, 86, 88.

1206 Ellis, David. "After You've Beat 'em—Join 'em." *Time,* 137, no. 25 (24 June 1991), p. 13.

1207 Ellis, David R. "Computer Law—A Primer on the Law of Software Protection." *Florida Bar Journal,* 60, no. 4 (Apr. 1986), pp. 81-84.

1208 Ellis, David R. "Ownership of Computer Programs and Other Copyrighted Works." *Florida Bar Journal,* 64, no. 9 (Oct. 1990), pp. 82-85.

1209 Ellis, David R. "Technology Transfer and Licensing." *Florida Bar Journal,* 63, no. 4 (Apr. 1989), pp. 58-60.

1210 Ellis, Leslie P. "Only Audit Around the Computer?—No!" *The National Public Accountant,* 34, no. 5 (May 1989), pp. 14-16.

1211 Ellison, Carol. "On Guard: 20 Utilities That Battle the Virus Threat." *PC Magazine,* 10, no. 18 (29 Oct. 1991), pp. 199-208.

1212 Elmer-DeWitt, Philip. "A Bold Raid on Computer Security: The Hannover Hacker Is Tracked Down by a Berkeley Whiz." *Time,* 131, no. 18 (2 May 1988), p. 58.

1213 Elmer-DeWitt, Philip. "Can a System Keep a Secret? The Iranscam Revelations Raise Thorny Issues About Privacy." *Time,* 129, no. 14 (6 Apr. 1987), pp. 68-69.

1214 Elmer-DeWitt, Philip. "Cyberpunk!: With Virtual Sex, Smart Drugs and Synthetic Rock 'n' Roll, a New Counterculture Is Surfing the Dark Edges of the Computer Age." *Time,* 141, no. 6 (8 Feb. 1993), pp. 58-65.

1215 Elmer-DeWitt, Philip. "Cyberpunks and the Constitution." *Time,* 137, no. 14 (8 Apr. 1991), p. 81.

1216 Elmer-DeWitt, Philip. "Ding! Whrrrrrrrrrrrr. Crash!" *Time,* 139, no. 11 (16 Mar. 1992), p. 56.

1217 Elmer-DeWitt, Philip. "Don't Tread on My Data: Protecting Individual Privacy in the Information Age." *Time*, 130, no. 1 (6 July 1987), p. 84.

1218 Elmer-DeWitt, Philip. "An Electronic Assault on Privacy? Computer Blacklists Have Become a New Growth Industry." *Time*, 127, no. 20 (19 May 1986), p. 104.

1219 Elmer-DeWitt, Philip. "The Great Satellite Caper: Hackers' Arrests Point Up the Growing Problem of System Security." *Time*, 126, no. 4 (29 July 1985), p. 65.

1220 Elmer-DeWitt, Philip. "Imitation or Infringement? An Apple Copyright Suit Casts a Pall Over the Computer Industry." *Time*, 131, no. 14 (4 Apr. 1988), p. 60.

1221 Elmer-DeWitt, Philip. "In Search of Hackers." *Time*, 133, no. 15 (10 Apr. 1989), p. 95.

1222 Elmer-DeWitt, Philip. "Invasion of the Data Snatchers! A 'Virus' Epidemic Strikes Terror in the Computer World." *Time*, 132, no. 13 (26 Sept. 1988), pp. 62-67.

1223 Elmer-DeWitt, Philip. "'The Kid Put Us Out of Action': A Grad- school Whiz Injects a Virus Into a Huge Computer Network." *Time*, 132, no. 20 (14 Nov. 1988), p. 76.

1224 Elmer-DeWitt, Philip. "Let Us Now Praise Famous Hackers." *Time*, 124, no. 23 (3 Dec. 1984), p. 76.

1225 Elmer-DeWitt, Philip. "Surveying the Data Diddlers: A New Study Takes the Measure of Computer Crime." *Time*, 127, no. 7 (17 Feb. 1986), p. 95.

1226 Elmer-DeWitt, Philip. "Triumph of a Hacker Sleuth." *Time*, 125, no. 4 (28 Jan. 1985), p. 91.

1227 Eloff, Jan H. P. "Computer Security Policy: Important Issues." *Computers and Security*, 7, no. 6 (Dec. 1988), pp. 559-62.

1228 Elsom, S. M. "Protection of Computer Software by Technical Measures." *Software Protection*, 4, no. 6 (Nov. 1985), pp. 1-6.

1229 Emanuel, Harold M. "Reviewing Your Computer Contract." *California Lawyer*, 4, no. 4 (Apr. 1984), pp. 42-44.

1230 Emmerson, J. McL. "Computer Software: Detailed Enquiry Needed Before Litigation." *Law Institute Journal*, 58, no. 5 (May 1984), pp. 514-15, 517-18.

1231 Emmett, Arielle. "Thwarting the Data Thief." *Personal Computing*, 8, no. 1 (Jan. 1984), pp. 98-105, 204-5.

1232 "Employer Not Liable for Employee's Misappropriation of Plaintiff's Trade Secrets." *The Computer Lawyer*, 4, no. 5 (May 1987), p. 34.

1233 Eng, Paul M. "A Better Vaccine for Computer Viruses." *Business Week*, no. 3228 (26 Aug. 1991), p. 64A.

1234 Eng, Paul M. "This Security System Dares You to Hack Away." *Business Week*, no. 3210 (22 Apr. 1991), p. 100A.

1235 Eng, Paul M. "Will Michelangelo Chisel Away at Your Hard Disk?" *Business Week*, no. 3254 (2 Mar. 1992), p. 94E.

1236 Engel, G. Larry, and Mark F. Radcliffe. "Intellectual Property Financing for High Technology Companies." *The Computer Lawyer*, 3, no. 10 (Oct. 1986), pp. 20-31.

1237 Englander, Bradford Frost. "Copyrightability of Computer Operating Systems." *Washington and Lee Law Review*, 41, no. 4 (Fall 1984), pp. 1361-85.

1238 Englund, Steven R. "Idea, Process, or Protected Expression?: Determining the Scope of Copyright Protection of the Structure of Computer Programs." *Michigan Law Review*, 88, no. 4 (Feb. 1990), pp. 866-909.

1239 Epner, Steven A. "Computer Security: Plenty of Questions But No Easy Answers." *The Office*, 101, no. 3 (Mar. 1985), pp. 74-76.

1240 Erickson, William J. "Computer Abuse Insurance: An Analysis of the Risk and a Comparison of Current Policies." *Federation of Insurance and Corporate Counsel Quarterly*, 36, no. 1 (Fall 1985), pp. 65-85.

1241 Erlewine, Christopher, and Helene Cavior. "Inmates and Computers: Managing Access, Preventing Abuse." *Federal Prisons Journal*, 1, no. 2 (Fall 1989), pp. 28-31.

1242 Erstling, Jay A. "The Semiconductor Chip Protection Act and Its Impact on the International Protection of Chip Designs." *Rutgers Computer and Technology Law Journal*, 15, no. 2 (1989), pp. 303-49.

1243 Eskew, Joy L. "The Copyright Dilemma Facing Texas Educators as They Implement Computer Literacy Into the Curriculum." *Houston Law Review*, 22, no. 4 (July 1985), pp. 1011-44.

1244 Eskow, Dennis, and Lee Green. "Catching Computer Crooks." *Popular Mechanics*, 161, no. 6 (June 1984), pp. 63-65, 98-99.

1245 Essinger, James. "Prevention Is the Priority." *Accountancy*, 108, no. 1177 (Sept. 1991), pp. 64-66.

1246 Estadella-Yuste, Olga. "The Draft Directive of the European Community Regarding the Protection of Personal Data." *International and Comparative Law Quarterly*, 41, no. 1 (Jan. 1992), pp. 170-79.

1247 Estadella-Yuste, Olga. "Transborder Data Flows and the Sources of Public International Law." *North Carolina Journal of International Law and Commercial Regulation*, 16, no. 2 (Fall 1991), pp. 379-433.

1248 Esters, Stephanie D. "Avoid It Like the Plague: Protecting Yourself from Computer Virus Attacks." *Black Enterprise,* 19, no. 7 (Feb. 1989), pp. 55-56.

1249 "European Commission Plans to Harmonise Database Protection (Based Upon an EC Press Release)." *Software Protection,* 10, no. 9 (Feb. 1992), pp. 14-15.

1250 Evans, Christopher. "Protection of Software Against Third Parties in the United Kingdom." *Software Law Journal,* 1, no. 3 (Spring-Summer 1986), pp. 407-15.

1251 Evans, John. "Computer Blackmail Reported at Five Leading British Banks." *American Banker,* 155, no. 201 (16 Oct. 1990), p. 27.

1252 Evans, Paul. "Computer Fraud – The Situation, Detection and Training." *Computers and Security,* 10, no. 4 (June 1991), pp. 325-27.

1253 "Expert Software Systems: The Legal Implications." *Computer/Law Journal,* 8, no. 4 (Fall 1988), pp. 455-77.

1254 "Extending Copyright Protection to a Computer Program's Structure: *Whelan Associates, Inc. v. Jaslow Dental Laboratory, Inc.,* 797 F.2d 1222 (3d Cir. 1986)." *Washington University Law Quarterly,* 65, no. 2 (1987), pp. 471-80.

1255 Fahle, Becki. "The Effect of the Directive on the Legal Protection of Computer Programs on Copyright Law in the EC." *Houston Journal of International Law,* 14, no. 3 (Spring 1992), pp. 659-86.

1256 Fainberg, Tony. "The Night the Network Failed." *New Scientist,* 121, no. 1654 (4 Mar. 1989), pp. 38-42.

1257 Fakes, Arthur. "The Abduction of Licensed Software Technology by the People's Republic of China." *Software Law Journal,* 3, no. 2 (Spring 1989), pp. 223-93.

1258 Fakes, Arthur. "The Application of the United Nations Convention on Contracts for the International Sale of Goods to Computer, Software, and Database Transactions." *Software Law Journal,* 3, no. 4 (Apr. 1990), pp. 559-614.

1259 Fakes, Arthur. "The EEC's Directive on Software Protection and Its Moral Rights Loophole." *Software Law Journal,* 5, no. 3 (Oct. 1992), pp. 531-633.

1260 Farhoomand, Ali F., and Michael Murphy. "Managing Computer Security." *Datamation,* 34, no. 26 (1 Jan. 1989), pp. 67-68.

1261 Farr, Evan H. "Copyrightability of Computer-Created Works." *Rutgers Computer and Technology Law Journal,* 15, no. 1 (1989), pp. 63-80.

1262 "Fear and Loathing of the Paper Trail: Originality in Products of Reverse Engineering Under the Semiconductor Chip Protection Act as Analogized to the Fair Use of Nonfiction Literary Works." *Syracuse Law Review,* 41, no. 3 (1990), pp. 985-1020.

1263 Feder, Daniel G. "Computer Software: Hybrid Technology Demanding a Unique Combination of Copyright and Patent Protection." *UMKC Law Review,* 59, no. 4 (Summer 1991), pp. 1037-74.

1264 "Federal Clearinghouse to Track Computer Viruses Planned." *The Computer Lawyer,* 8, no. 1 (Jan. 1991), p. 42.

1265 "Federal Copyright Law in the Computer Era: Protection for the Authors of Video Games." *University of Puget Sound Law Review,* 7, no. 2 (Winter 1984), pp. 425-40.

1266 "Federal Court Has Jurisdiction Over Unfair Competition Counterclaim Against Copyright Holder's Attorney for Obtaining Software Copyright." *The Computer Lawyer,* 8, no. 9 (Sept. 1991), pp. 37-38.

1267 Feldman, Robert A. "Bankruptcy and Software Licenses: Some Proposed Drafting Solutions." *The Computer Lawyer,* 4, no. 5 (May 1987), pp. 13-26.

1268 Feldman, Robert A. "Warranties and Disclaimers in Computer Contracts." *The Computer Lawyer,* 8, no. 2 (Feb. 1991), pp. 1-12.

1269 Feldman, Robert A., and Michael S. Khoury. "Software Licensing and Bankruptcy." *Michigan Bar Journal,* 67, no. 10 (Oct. 1988), pp. 991-95.

1270 Fenster, Stephen B., and Dennis S. Deutsch. "Computer and EDP Claims: Risk Management, Coverage and Potential Liabilities." *Software Law Journal,* 4, no. 2 (Apr. 1991), pp. 209-29.

1271 Fent, Tomme Jeanne. "Commercial Law: Electronic Funds Transfer: How New U. C. C. Article 4A May Affect Consumers." *Oklahoma Law Review,* 43, no. 2 (Summer 1990), pp. 339-56.

1272 Fenwick and West. "International Legal Protection for Software— 1991Update." *Software Protection,* 9, no. 8 (Jan. 1991), pp. 1-12.

1273 Ferranti, Marc. "SPA Cases Show Software Pirates Can Be Developers Themselves." *PC Week,* 9, no. 18 (4 May 1992), p. 38.

1274 Ferron, William O., Jr. "The Patent/Copyright Interface: Protecting Software Methods, Ideas, Systems, and Sequences." *Software Law Journal,* 4, no. 3 (Oct. 1991), pp. 377-98.

1275 Fersko-Weiss, Henry. "Firmloc: Simple, Effective Security for $249.95." *PC Magazine,* 11, no. 20 (24 Nov. 1992), p. 56.

1276 Fetterman, Daniel J. "The Scope of Copyright Protection for Computer Programs: Exploring the Idea/Expression Dichotomy." *Intellectual Property Law Review,* 20 (1988), pp. 399-435. (First published in *Washington and Lee Law Review,* 43, no. 4 [Fall 1986], pp. 1373-409.)

1277 Fiatal, Robert A. "The Electronic Communications Privacy Act: Addressing Today's Technology." *The Prosecutor,* 22, no. 1 (Summer 1988), pp. 15-28.

1278 Fifield, Ken J. "Smartcards Outsmart Computer Crime." *Computers and Security,* 8, no. 3 (May 1989), pp. 247-55.

1279 "15 Tips to Forestall Viruses." *Personal Computing,* 14, no. 3 (20 Mar. 1990), p. 24.

1280 "Fighting Parasites." *The Futurist,* 22, no. 4 (July-Aug. 1988), p. 54.

1281 Fikeys, Nelka. "Some Opinions on the Legal Protection of Computer Programs in Yugoslavia." *Software Protection,* 6, no. 1 (June 1987), pp. 6-8.

1282 Filipski, Alan, and James Hanko. "Making UNIX Secure." *Byte,* 11, no. 4 (Apr. 1986), pp. 113-28.

1283 Finkel, Evan. "Copyright Protection for Computer Software in the Nineties." *Santa Clara Computer and High Technology Law Journal,* 7, no. 2 (Dec. 1991), pp. 201-89.

1284 Finkel, Evan. "Update to: Copyright Protection for Computer Software in the Nineties." *Santa Clara Computer and High Technology Law Journal,* 8, no. 1 (May 1992), pp. 99-119.

1285 Finlay, Doug. "Management Has Key to Data Security." *The Office,* 114, no. 5 (Nov. 1991), pp. 76, 85.

1286 "First European Conference on Computer Audit, Control and Security." *Computers and Security,* 6 (1987), pp. 173-76.

1287 Fischer, Mark A. "Entertainment/Computer Law: Converging Industries, Converging Law." *Trial,* 20, no. 9 (Sept. 1984), pp. 42-44.

1288 Fisher, Francis Dummer. "Are Plato and the Parthenon Copyrighted?" *Change,* 21, no. 3 (May-June 1989), p. 15.

1289 Fisher, Francis Dummer. "The Electronic Lumberyard and Builders' Rights: Technology, Copyrights, Patents, and Academe." *Change,* 21, no. 3 (May-June 1989), pp. 12-21.

1290 Fisher, Janet E. "Copyright: Copyright Act of 1976—Operating System Computer Programs Expressed in Object Code and Stored on ROM Are Copyrightable: *Apple Computer, Inc. v. Franklin Computer Corp.* (1983)." *Villanova Law Review,* 29, no. 3-4 (June 1984), pp. 894-931.

1291 Fisher, Lawrence M. "Dreaded Virus Said to Cause Little Damage to Computers." *The New York Times,* 139, no. 48023 (14 Oct. 1989), p. 37.

1292 Fisher, Lawrence M. "On the Front Lines in Battling Electronic Invaders." *The New York Times,* 138, no. 47680 (5 Nov. 1988), p. 7.

1293 Fisher, Susan E. "California Police Confiscate MS-DOS Copies, Nab 2 Execs." *PC Week,* 9, no. 8 (24 Feb. 1992), p. 168.

1294 Fisher, Susan E. "Group to Address Computer Users' Rights." *PC Week,* 7, no. 32 (13 Aug. 1990), p. 117.

1295 Fisher, Susan E. "Softmart Offers On-Line Software Licensing Plan." *PC Week,* 9, no. 8 (24 Feb. 1992), p. 165.

1296 Fisk, George E., and Jane E. Clark. "Hardware and Software Protection in Canada." *Computer/Law Journal,* 10, no. 4 (Dec. 1990), pp. 483-516.

1297 Fitch, Thomas P. "A Rogue in the Spreadsheet: Are Computer Viruses Really Someone Else's Problem Now That PCs Are Part of Nearly Every Bank's Environment?" *American Banker,* 154, no. 23 (2 Feb. 1989), p. 6.

1298 Fitzgerald, Karen. "The Quest for Intruder-Proof Computer Systems." *IEEE Spectrum,* 26, no. 8 (Aug. 1989), pp. 22-26.

1299 Fitzpatrick, Edmund W. "Protecting Against PC Viruses and Other Risks." *Journal of the American Society of CLU and ChFC,* 46, no. 4 (July 1992), pp. 28, 30.

1300 "Five Convicted in Scheme to Steal Using Computer." *The Wall Street Journal,* 213, no. 123 (26 June 1989), p. B5.

1301 Flaherty, David H. "The Need for an American Privacy Protection Commission." *Government Information Quarterly,* 1, no. 3 (1984), pp. 235-58.

1302 Flaherty, David H. "On the Utility of Constitutional Rights to Privacy and Data Protection." *Case Western Reserve Law Review,* 41, no. 3 (1991), pp. 831-55.

1303 Flaherty, David H. "Protecting Privacy in Police Information Systems: Data Protection in the Canadian Police Information Centre." *University of Toronto Law Journal,* 36 (1986), pp. 116-48.

1304 Flanagan, William G., and Brigid McMenamin. "'The Playground Bullies Are Learning How to Type.'" *Forbes,* 150, no. 14 (21 Dec. 1992), pp. 184-89.

1305 "The 'Flexibility Factor' in Copyright, Trade Secret and Patent Law for Computer Software: The Aftermath of *Sony.*" *Ohio Northern University Law Review,* 11, no. 2 (1984), pp. 333-63.

1306 Flumenbaum, Martin, and Brad S. Karp. "Infringement of Computer Software Copyright." *New York Law Journal,* 208, no. 15 (22 July 1992), pp. 3, 27.

1307 Flynn, Mary Kathleen. "Avoiding Viruses from Vendors." *PC Magazine,* 11, no. 6 (31 Mar. 1992), pp. 30-31.

1308 Fonda, David B. "The Interdependent Nature of Computer Software; Another Reason Why User-Interfaces Should Not Be Protected by Copyright Law." *The John Marshall Law Review,* 25, no. 4 (Summer 1992), pp. 737-67.

1309 "For Sale: Data About You." *Harper's,* 284, no. 1702 (Mar. 1992), pp. 26-27.

1310 Forcht, Karen A., Daphyne Thomas, and Karen Wigginton. "Computer Crime: Assessing the Lawyer's Perspective." *Journal of Business Ethics,* 8, no. 4 (Apr. 1989), pp. 243-51.

1311 Forester, Tom. "Computers and Behavior." *National Forum: Phi Kappa Phi Journal,* 71, no. 3 (Summer 1991), pp. 18-20.

1312 Forgione, Dana, and Alan Blankley. "Microcomputer Security and Control: Six Inexpensive and Simple Techniques." *Journal of Accountancy,* 169, no. 6 (June 1990), pp. 83-90.

1313 Fortnow, Matthew J. "Why the 'Look and Feel' of Computer Software Should Not Receive Copyright Protection." *Cardozo Law Review,* 14, no. 2 (Nov. 1992), pp. 421-48.

1314 Fossett, John J. "The Development of Negligence in Computer Law." *Northern Kentucky Law Review,* 14, no. 2 (1987), pp. 289-310.

1315 "Fourth Amendment Rights Not Violated By Confiscation of Computer Items." *The Computer Lawyer,* 9, no. 9 (Sept. 1992), pp. 37-38.

1316 Fox, Barry. "Computers Get Stoned on Patent Discs." *New Scientist,* 131, no. 1781 (10 Aug. 1991), p. 24.

1317 Fox, Barry. "The Key to Locking Out Computer Saboteurs." *New Scientist,* 133, no. 1809 (22 Feb. 1992), p. 22.

1318 Fox, Bob. "Meet and Beat the Ego-Driven Systems Hacker." *Communications News,* 29, no. 1 (Jan. 1992), p. 23.

1319 Francis, Bob. "PC Security Grows Up." *Datamation,* 38, no. 22 (1 Nov. 1992), pp. 61-64.

1320 Francis, Bob. "A Secure Future for Diskless Workstations." *Datamation,* 36, no. 22 (15 Nov. 1990), pp. 53-54, 56.

1321 Francis, Ted. "Do Computer Viruses Pose a Threat?" *Bank Administration,* 65, no. 1 (Jan. 1989), pp. 6-10.

1322 Frank, Nancy K. "Export Controls on High Technology." *Santa Clara Computer and High-Technology Law Journal,* 3, no. 1 (Jan. 1987), pp. 105-40.

1323 Frank, Steven J. "Tort Adjudication and the Emergence of Artificial Intelligence Software." *Suffolk University Law Review,* 21, no. 3 (Fall 1987), pp. 623-77.

1324 Franklin, Carl J. "Computer Software Copyright Protection: Infringement and Eleventh Amendment Immunity." *Computer/Law Journal,* 9, no. 2 (Spring 1989), pp. 163-75.

1325 "Franklin Claims Infringement of Booting Program." *The Computer Lawyer,* 4, no. 2 (Feb. 1987), p. 26.

1326 Franklin, J. Thomas. "Misappropriation Law, Copyright Law, and Product Compatibility." *The Computer Lawyer,* 4, no. 2 (Feb. 1987), pp. 8-13.

1327 Franklin, Jeffrey A. "Copyright Protection of Computer Software After *Vault Corp. v. Quaid Software Ltd.,* Reinterpreting Section 117." *The Journal of Law and Commerce,* 9, no. 1 (1989), pp. 133-65.

1328 Franks, Renae Angeroth. "The National Security Agency and Its Interference with Private Sector Computer Security." *Iowa Law Review,* 72, no. 4 (May 1987), pp. 1015-39.

1329 "Free the Hacker Two." *Harper's,* 279, no. 1672 (Sept. 1989), pp. 22-26.

1330 Freed, Roy N. "Copyright in the Computer Age and Beyond: Some Thoughts on the British Intellectual Property White Paper with Particular Reference to Software Programs." *Software Protection,* 6, no. 2-3 (July-Aug. 1987), pp. 2-11.

1331 Freed, Roy N. "Legal Interests Related to Software Programs." *Jurimetrics Journal,* 25, no. 4 (Summer 1985), pp. 347-76.

1332 Freed, Roy N. "Legal Protection of Software – A Global View from Japan." *Software Law Journal,* 2, no. 1 (Winter 1987), pp. 17-27.

1333 Freed, Roy N. "Security Interests in the Computer Age: Practical Advice for the Secured Lender." *The Banking Law Journal,* 101, no. 5 (July-Aug. 1984), pp. 404-29.

1334 Freedman, Beth. "Look-and-Feel Lawsuit Expected to Go to Trial." *PC Week,* 9, no. 8 (24 Feb. 1992), p. 168.

1335 Freedman, Beth. "Software Publishers Association Seeks Damages for Alleged Piracy." *PC Week,* 9, no. 24 (15 June 1992), p. 162.

1336 Freedman, Beth. "Survey Reveals Alarming Percentage of Ailing PCs." *PC Week,* 8, no. 48 (2 Dec. 1991), p. 141.

1337 Freeman, Layton, and Peter P. Mykytyn. "Computer Crime and Data Copyright: Issues for Management." *Journal of Systems Management,* 42, no. 11 (Nov. 1991), p. 18.

1338 Freidheim, Elizabeth A. "Singapore's New Copyright Law: Turning Pirates Into Discounters?" *Software Law Journal,* 2, no. 2 (Spring 1988), pp. 203-20.

1339 "French Law on Software Copyright." *Bulletin of Legal Developments,* 1985, no. 24 (13 Dec. 1985), p. 255.

1340 "French Law Provides Protection for Computer Software." *Software Protection,* 2, no. 7 (Mar.-Apr. 1984), pp. 15-17.

1341 "French Legislation on Computer Misuse." *Bulletin of Legal Developments,* 1988, no. 2 (29 Jan. 1988), p. 13.

1342 Frenchman, Beth. "An Action for Contributory Copyright Infringement: Are Copy Program Manufacturers Liable?" *Software Law Journal,* 2, no. 2 (Spring 1988), pp. 265-81.

1343 Freund, Jim. "PC MagNet: Virus Defense." *PC Magazine,* 11, no. 6 (31 Mar. 1992), p. 359.

1344 Friedland, David K. "Computer Software Patentability: The Dilemma of Defining an Algorithm." *Software Law Journal,* 2, no. 4 (Fall 1988), pp. 537-58.

1345 Friedman, Herb. "Computer Security." *Radio-Electronics,* 56, no. 6 (June 1985), pp. 78-79.

1346 Friedman, Lawrence M. "*Broderbund Software, Inc. v. Unison World, Inc.*: Confusing the 'Look' and the 'Feel' of Computer Software in Copyright Infringement Cases." *Software Law Journal,* 2, no. 1 (Winter 1987), pp. 113-24.

1347 Friedman, Lawrence M., and Mark E. Wojcik. "Computer Software as Articles of Commerce in International Trade: The Surprising Study of Singapore's Software Subsidies." *Software Law Journal,* 4, no. 3 (Oct. 1991), pp. 399-419.

1348 Friedman, Marc S., and Andrew J. Siegel. "From Flour Barrel to Computer Systems: The Applicability of Theories of Alternative Liability to Shift the Burdens of Proof in Cases of Intermingled Causation and Damages Within a Modern Computer Scenario." *Rutgers Computer and Technology Law Journal,* 14, no. 2 (1988), pp. 289-310.

1349 Friedman, Marc S., and Helene Hirsch Wingens. "Averting Disaster When a Software Supplier Goes Bankrupt." *The Computer Lawyer,* 8, no. 2 (Feb. 1991), pp.13-15.

1350 Friedman, Marc S., and Helene Hirsch Wingens. "Averting Disaster When a Software Supplier Goes Bankrupt." *New Jersey Lawyer,* no. 143 (Nov.-Dec. 1991), pp. 33-37.

1351 Friedman, Mark M. "Copyrighting Machine Language Computer Software—The Case Against." *Computer/Law Journal,* 9, no. 1 (Winter 1989), pp. 1-36. (Also published in *Houston Law Review,* 26, no. 2 [Mar. 1989], pp. 275-320.)

1352 Friedman, Michael Todd. "The Misuse of Electronically Transferred Confidential Information in Interstate Commerce: How Well Do Our Present Laws Address the Issue?" *Software Law Journal,* 4, no. 3 (Oct. 1991), pp. 529-66.

1353 Friis, M. William. "Is Your PC Infected?" *ABA Banking Journal,* 81, no. 5 (May 1989), pp. 49, 51-52.

1354 Fugere, Kathryn A. "Reverse Engineering Under the Semiconductor Chip Protection Act: An Argument in Favor of a 'Value-Added' Approach." *Golden Gate University Law Review*, 22, no. 2 (Spring 1992), pp. 515-27.

1355 Fuller, Grover F., Jr. "Commentary—New Legislation: Copyright Protection for Semiconductor Chip Masks." *Idea*, 25, no. 4 (1984), pp. 199-204.

1356 Fuller, William P., V. "The Protection of Computer Software in the People's Republic of China." *Boston College Third World Law Journal*, 9, no. 1 (Winter 1989), pp. 57-79.

1357 "GATT Update; PTO Extends Interim Chip Protection Orders; USTR Seeks Comment on Priority List Factors." *The Computer Lawyer*, 8, no. 3 (Mar. 1991), pp. 35-36.

1358 Gable, R. Lewis, and J. Bradford Leaheey. "The Strength of Patent Protection for Computer Products: The Federal Circuit and the Patent Office Refine the Test for Determining Which Computer-Related Inventions Constitute Patentable Subject Matter." *Rutgers Computer and Technology Law Journal*, 17, no. 1 (1991), pp. 87-137.

1359 Gadbaw, R. Michael. "Intellectual Property and International Trade: Merger or Marriage of Convenience?" *Vanderbilt Journal of Transnational Law*, 22, no. 2 (1989), pp. 223-42.

1360 Gage, Thomas M. "*Whelan Associates v. Jaslow Dental Laboratories*: Copyright Protection for Computer Software Structure—What's the Purpose?" *Wisconsin Law Review*, 1987, no. 5 (1987), pp. 859-94.

1361 Galen, Michele. "Software: In for a Patent Pounding?" *Business Week*, no. 3121 (28 Aug. 1989), pp. 30-31.

1362 Galloway, Joseph L. "How Your Privacy Is Being Stripped Away." *U.S. News and World Report*, 96, no. 17 (30 Apr. 1984), pp. 46-48.

1363 Gang, Liu. "Copyright Protection of Computer Software in the People's Republic of China." *Software Protection*, 10, no. 3 (Aug. 1991), pp. 4-9.

1364 Gantz, John. "Metamorphosis of the Leaves Heralds Return of the Worm." *Infoworld*, 11, no. 39 (25 Sept. 1989), p. 46.

1365 Garby, Thierry. "Software Protection Against Third Parties in France." *Software Law Journal*, 1, no. 3 (Spring-Summer 1986), pp. 333-39.

1366 Garcia, Robert. "'Garbage In, Gospel Out': Criminal Discovery, Computer Reliability, and the Constitution." *UCLA Law Review*, 38, no. 5 (June 1991), pp. 1043-145.

1367 Gardner, Jeff. "Preventing a Computer Virus Attack." *Parks and Recreation*, 24, no. 4 (Apr. 1989), pp. 14-15, 64.

1368 Gardner, Phillip E. "The Internet Worm: What Was Said and When." *Computers and Security*, 8, no. 4 (June 1989), pp. 291-96.

1369 Garfinkel, Simson L. "How to Protect Computer Programs." *The Christian Science Monitor,* 81, no. 223 (13 Oct. 1989), p. 12.

1370 Garfinkel, Simson L. "Lax Security Lets Hackers Attack." *The Christian Science Monitor,* 81, no. 223 (13 Oct. 1989), pp. 12-13.

1371 Garfinkel, Simson L., Richard M. Stallmar, and Mitchell Kapor. "Why Patents Are Bad for Software." *Issues in Science and Technology,* 8, no. 1 (Fall 1991), pp. 50-55.

1372 Gastineau, John. "Bent Fish: Issues of Ownership and Infringement in Digitally Processed Images." *Indiana Law Journal,* 67, no. 1 (Winter 1991), pp. 95-128.

1373 Gates, George H., III. "Trade Secret Software: Is It Prior Art?" *The Computer Lawyer,* 6, no. 8 (Aug. 1989), pp. 11-17.

1374 Gaudio, Ginamarie A. "*Manufacturers Technologies, Inc. v. Cams, Inc.* — The Legal Fiction Created by a Single Copyright Registration of a Computer Program and Its Display Screens." *Notre Dame Law Review,* 65, no. 3 (1990), pp. 536-63.

1375 Gelfond, Susan M. "The 'Core-Walker' That Stalled American Airlines." *Business Week,* no. 3109 (12 June 1989), p. 98C.

1376 Gelfond, Susan M. "Just When You Thought Your PC Was Safe from Hackers...." *Business Week,* no. 3107 (29 May 1989), p.102O.

1377 Gelfond, Susan M. "A New Report Says Hackers Are Still Taking Their Bite." *Business Week,* no. 3113 (3 July 1989), p. 64A.

1378 Gemignani, Michael. "A College's Liability for Unauthorized Copying of Microcomputer Software by Students." *Journal of Law and Education,* 15, no. 4 (Fall 1986), pp. 421-37.

1379 Gemignani, Michael. "Copyright Protection: Computer-Related Dependent Works." *Rutgers Computer and Technology Law Journal,* 15, no. 2 (1989), pp. 383-410.

1380 Gemignani, Michael C. "More on the Use of Computers by Professionals." *Rutgers Computer and Technology Law Journal,* 13, no. 2 (1987), pp. 317-39.

1381 Gemignani, Michael C. "Potential Liability for Use of Expert Systems." *Idea,* 29, no. 2 (1988-89), pp. 120-27.

1382 Gemignani, Michael C. "What Is Computer Crime, and Why Should We Care?" *University of Arkansas at Little Rock Law Journal,* 10, no. 1 (1987-88), pp. 55-67.

1383 George, B. J., Jr. "Contemporary Legislation Governing Computer Crimes." *Criminal Law Bulletin,* 21, no. 5 (Sept.-Oct. 1985), pp. 389-412.

1384 Geraldi, Alan R. "Misuse: An Equitable Defense to Intellectual Property Infringement Actions." *Comm/Ent*, 14, no. 2 (Winter 1992), pp. 235-58.

1385 Gerber, Barry. "Sometimes 'Abort, Retry' Means 'Network Virus.'" *PC Week*, 7, no. 13 (2 Apr. 1990), p. 57.

1386 Gerritzen, Theresa M. "Copyrighting the Book of Numbers—Protecting the Compiler: *West Publishing Co. v. Mead Data Central, Inc.*" *Creighton Law Review*, 20 (1986-87), pp. 1133-66.

1387 Gerth, Jeff. "Intruders Into Computer Systems Still Hard to Prosecute." *The New York Times*, 138, no. 47,680 (5 Nov. 1988), p. 7.

1388 Gesmer, Lee T. "Developments in the Law of Computer Software Copyright Infringement." *Jurimetrics Journal*, 26, no. 3 (Spring 1986), pp. 224-34.

1389 Gesmer, Lee T. "Protection of Trade Secrets in the Computer Industry." *Boston Bar Journal*, 33, no. 5 (Sept.-Oct. 1989), pp. 18-20.

1390 Giannetti, Thomas. "Software Protection Expanded by Controversial 'Lotus' Decision." *The National Law Journal*, 12, no. 48 (6 Aug. 1990), pp. 39-40.

1391 Gibson, Steve. "At Last, How to Protect Yourself from Polymorphic Viruses." *InfoWorld*, 14, no. 17 (27 Apr. 1992), p. 36.

1392 Gibson, Steve. "Polymorphic Software Viruses Present a Daunting Challenge." *InfoWorld*, 14, no. 15 (13 Apr. 1992), p. 40.

1393 Gibson, Steve. "Polymorphic Viruses Escape Detection But Get Our Attention." *InfoWorld*, 14, no. 16 (20 Apr. 1992), p. 33.

1394 Gilbert, Francoise. "Breach of System Security and Theft of Data: Legal Aspects and Preventive Measures." *Computers and Security*, 11, no. 6 (Oct. 1992), pp. 508-17.

1395 Gilbert, Francoise. "Louisiana Software License Enforcement Act Under Judicial Scrutiny: What Impact on Shrink-Wrap License Agreements?" *Software Protection*, 5, no. 12 (May 1987), pp. 1-11.

1396 Gilbert, Jerome. "Computer Crime: Detection and Prevention." *Journal of Property Management*, 54, no. 2 (Mar.-Apr. 1989), pp. 64-66.

1397 Gilbert, Jonathan. "Computer Bulletin Board Operator Liability for User Misuse." *Fordham Law Review*, 54, no. 3 (Dec. 1985), pp. 439-54.

1398 Gilbert, Steven W., and Peter Lyman. "Intellectual Property in the Information Age: Issues Beyond the Copyright Law." *Change*, 21, no. 3 (May-June 1989), pp. 22-28.

1399 Gilder, George. "How the Computer Companies Lost Their Memories." *Forbes*, 141, no. 13 (13 June 1988), pp. 79-82, 84.

1400 Gill, Sylvia R. "Computer Technology Exports Under the Export Administration Amendments Act of 1985: Taking Competitive Advantage of China's Open Door." *Hastings International and Comparative Law Review,* 10, no. 3 (Spring 1987), pp. 669-703.

1401 Giller, Richard C. "Roms, Rams, and Copyright: The Copyrightability of Computer Chips." *Southwestern University Law Review,* 14, no. 4 (1984), pp. 685-744.

1402 Gilroy, James V. "Computer Crimes." *Barrister,* 14, no. 3 (Summer 1987), pp. 49-52.

1403 Ginsburg, Jane C. "Creation and Commercial Value: Copyright Protection of Works of Information." *Columbia Law Review,* 90, no. 7 (Nov. 1990), pp. 1865-938.

1404 Ginsburg, Jane C. "French Copyright Law: A Comparative Overview." *Journal of the Copyright Society of the U.S.A.,* 36 (1988-89), pp. 269-85.

1405 Ginsburg, Jane C. "No 'Sweat'? Copyright and Other Protection of Works of Information After *Feist v. Rural Telephone.*" *Columbia Law Review,* 92, no. 2 (Mar. 1992), pp. 338-88.

1406 Given, Kim Marie. "Unravelling Copyrighted Software from a Tying Arrangement Presumption: *3 P. M., Inc. v. Basic Four Corp.,* an Alternative to *Digidyne Corp. v. Data General.*" *Rutgers Computer and Technology Law Journal,* 12, no. 2 (1987), pp. 447-69.

1407 Glick, Martin R., and M. Patricia Thayer. "*Galoob v. Nintendo*: When Is a Modified Computer Program an Infringing Derivative Work?" *The Computer Lawyer,* 8, no. 9 (Sept. 1991), pp. 1-10.

1408 Gligor, Virgil D., C. S. Chandersekaren, Wen-Der Jiang, Abhai Johri, Gary L. Luckenbaugh, and L. Edward Reich. "A New Security Testing Method and Its Application to the Secure Xenix Kernel." *IEEE Transactions on Software Engineering,* SE-13, no. 2 (Feb. 1987), pp. 169-83.

1409 Gliss, Hans. "East Germany—Haven for Software Piracy." *Computers and Security,* 9, no. 5 (Aug. 1990), pp. 391-93.

1410 Glynn, Elizabeth A. "Computer Abuse: The Emerging Crime and the Need for Legislation." *Fordham Urban Law Journal,* 12 (1983-84), pp. 73-101.

1411 Gobey, Nancilynn B. "Trade Secret—The Most Widely Used Method of Protecting Proprietary Interests in Computer Software. Is It the Most Effective?" *Capital University Law Review,* 17, no. 2 (1988), pp. 291-316.

1412 Godbey, David C. "Comment: Legal Documents as a Metaphor for Computer Programs in Copyright Analysis - A Critique of *Whelan* and *Plains Cotton.*" *The Computer Lawyer,* 6, no. 8 (Aug. 1989), pp. 1-10.

1413 Godes, James N. "Developing a New Set of Liability Rules for a New Generation of Technology: Assessing Liability for Computer-Related Injuries in the Health Care Field." *Computer/Law Journal,* 7, no. 4 (Fall 1987), pp. 517-34.

1414 Goldberg, David, and Robert J. Bernstein. "District Court Invalidates Software Copyright." *New York Law Journal,* 205, no. 50 (15 Mar. 1991), pp. 3, 30-31.

1415 Goldberg, Jeff. "Computerized Breaking and Entering: When a Kid Worms Into a Computer Network, the System Must Fish Or Cut Bait." *Omni,* 12, no. 12 (Sept. 1990), p. 18.

1416 Goldberg, Morton David, and David O. Carson. "Copyright Protection for Artificial Intelligence Systems." *Journal of the Copyright Society of the U.S.A.,* 39, no. 1 (Fall 1991), pp. 57-75.

1417 Goldberg, Morton David, and John F. Burleigh. "Copyright Protection for Computer Programs: Is the Sky Falling?" *AIPLA Quarterly Journal,* 17, no. 3 (1989), pp. 294-322.

1418 Golden, Jeffrey S. "Information on the Federal Government's Electronic Databases: Is There a First Amendment Right of Access?" *Software Law Journal,* 3, no. 1 (Winter 1989), pp. 65-90.

1419 Golden, Kevin. "Transborder Data Flows and the Possibility of Guidance in Personal Data Protection by the ITU." *Houston Journal of International Law,* 6, no. 2 (Spring 1984), pp. 215-41.

1420 Goldhammer, Joel S. "Computer Programs and Technological Innovation: Testing the Copyright Law." *The Journal of Law and Technology,* 2, no. 1 (Winter 1987), pp. 17-23.

1421 Goldman, Neil A. "Microcomputer Viruses: Strategies for Reducing Exposure." *The Ohio CPA Journal,* 48, no. 2 (Summer 1989), pp. 37-38.

1422 Goldstein, Mark L. "Time to Lock the Door." *Industry Week,* 233, no. 7 (29 June 1987), pp. 58, 61.

1423 Goldstein, Paul. "Copyright in the Information Age." *Stanford Lawyer,* 26, no. 1 (Fall 1991), pp. 4-9.

1424 Goldstein, Paul. "Copyright in the New Information Age." *Catholic University Law Review,* 40, no. 4 (Summer 1991), pp. 829-37.

1425 Goldstein, Paul. "Infringement of Copyright in Computer Programs." *University of Pittsburgh Law Review,* 47, no. 4 (Summer 1986), pp. 1119-30.

1426 Gollhofer, Richard A. "Copyright Protection of Computer Software: What Is It and How Did We Get It?" *Software Law Journal,* 5, no. 4 (Dec. 1992), pp. 695-713.

1427 Goodman, Jeffrey S. "The Policy Implications of Granting Patent Protection to Computer Software: An Economic Analysis." *Vanderbilt Law Review,* 37, no. 1 (Jan. 1984), pp. 147-81.

1428 Goodman, Mark. "Hacker for Hire." *People Weekly,* 38, no. 16 (19 Oct. 1992), pp. 151-53.

1429 Goodwin, Irwin. "In Rough Waters, White House Cancels Controls on Databases." *Physics Today,* 40, no. 5 (May 1987), p. 66.

1430 Goodwin, Irwin. "Making Waves: Poindexter Sails Into Scientific Databases." *Physics Today,* 40, no. 1 (Jan. 1987), pp. 51-52.

1431 Gordon, Marcy J. "Derivative Work Protection for Computer Software Conversions." *Communications and the Law,* 7, no. 5 (Oct. 1985), pp. 3-24.

1432 Gordon, Mark L. "Key Issues in Contracting for the Development of Joint and Derived Products." *Computer/Law Journal,* 11, no. 1 (Feb. 1991), pp. 1-27.

1433 Gordon, Mark L., and Eric G. Grossman. "Computer System Failures: Practical Resolution Considerations." *Software Law Journal,* 4, no. 3 (Oct. 1991), pp. 421-41.

1434 Gordon, Noah J. "Copyrightability of Object Code and ROM in Japan, Australia, and Germany: Surpassing Traditional Copyright Limits." *Computer/Law Journal,* 6, no. 3 (Winter 1986), pp. 513-41.

1435 Gorman, John. "18-Year-Old Chicagoan Charged in Computer Break- ins, Thefts." *The Washington Post,* 111, no. 248 (9 Aug. 1988), p. C5.

1436 Gorman, Robert A. "The *Feist* Case: Reflections on a Pathbreaking Copyright Decision." *Rutgers Computer and Technology Law Journal,* 18, no. 2 (1992), pp. 731-72.

1437 Gouras, Eckhart K. "The Reform of West German Data Protection Law as a Necessary Correlate to Improving Domestic Security." *Columbia Journal of Transnational Law,* 24, no. 3 (1986), pp. 597-621.

1438 "Government Data Bases and Privacy." *The Futurist,* 20, no. 5 (Sept.-Oct. 1986), pp. 52-53.

1439 Gozzi, Raymond, Jr. "The Computer 'Virus' as Metaphor." *ETC.: A Review of General Semantics,* 47, no. 2 (Summer 1990), pp. 177-80.

1440 Graft, William Christopher. "Combating Software Piracy: A Statutory Proposal to Strengthen Software Copyright." *Depaul Law Review,* 34, no. 4 (Summer 1985), pp. 993-1031.

1441 Graham, Carol, and Melanie Freely. "Keep Your Data Secure." *Datamation,* 36, no. 23 (1 Dec. 1990), pp. 97-100.

1442 Graham, Gord. "Slipped Disks." *Canadian Business,* 62, no. 4 (Apr. 1989), pp. 107-10.

1443 Graham, John M. "Fair Administration of the Freedom of Information Act After the Computer Revolution." *Computer/Law Journal,* 5, no. 1 (Summer 1984), pp. 51-76.

1444 Graham, Jonathan P. "Privacy, Computers, and the Commercial Dissemination of Personal Information." *Texas Law Review,* 65, no. 7 (June 1987), pp. 1395-1439.

1445 Graham, Kent, and William S. Wyler. "Report of the Joint Study Subcommittee of the Criminal Justice and Computer Law Committees." *Ohio State Bar Association Report,* 60, no. 43 (26 Oct. 1987), pp. 1658-62.

1446 Grammas, George N. "The Test for Proving Copyright Infringement of Computer Software: 'Structure, Sequence, and Organization' and 'Look and Feel' Cases." *William Mitchell Law Review,* 14, no. 1 (Winter 1988), pp. 105-40.

1447 Graziano, Sue Ganske. "Computer Malpractice - A New Tort on the Horizon." *Rutgers Computer and Technology Law Journal,* 17, no. 1 (1991), pp. 177-87.

1448 Graziano, Sue Ganske. "Current Legal Issues in Computer Software Protection." *Whittier Law Review,* 12, no. 3 (1991), pp. 357-66.

1449 Green, Lee D., and Glenn P. Rickards. "Taking a Multi-Front War to Software Pirates in Taiwan." *The Computer Lawyer,* 6, no. 6 (June 1989), pp. 12-17.

1450 Green, Lisa A. "Copyright Protection and Computer Programs: Identifying Creative Expression in a Computer Program's Nonliteral Elements." *Fordham Entertainment, Media and Intellectual Property Law Forum,* 3, no. 1 (Autumn 1992), pp. 89-137.

1451 Greenberg, Ross M. "Know Thy Viral Enemy." *Byte,* 14, no. 6 (June 1989), pp. 275-80.

1452 Greenleaf, Graham. "Computers and Crime — The Hacker's New Rules." *The Australian Law Journal,* 64 (May 1990), pp. 284-86.

1453 Greenleaf, Graham. "Information Technology and the Law: Can the Data Matching Epidemic Be Controlled?" *The Australian Law Journal,* 65, no. 4 (Apr. 1991), pp. 220-23.

1454 Greenleaf, Graham. "Information Technology and the Law: The Literature of Information Technology Law." *The Australian Law Journal,* 65 (Aug. 1991), pp. 472-73.

1455 Greenleaf, Graham. "Information Technology and the Law: Software Copyright - Form Follows Function, OK?" *The Australian Law Journal,* 63 (Nov. 1989), pp. 764-66.

1456 Greenleaf, Graham. "Intellectual Property and Data Protection: No Confidence in the Commonwealth Privacy Bill." *The Australian Law Journal,* 62, no. 1 (Jan. 1988), pp. 78-81.

1457 Greenleaf, Graham. "Intellectual Property and Data Protection: Screens, Structures and Ideas on the Boundary of Copyright." *The Australian Law Journal,* 62, no. 8 (Aug. 1988), pp. 630-35.

1458 Greenleaf, Graham. "Intellectual Property and Data Protection: Software Copyright: FAST and Loose Amendments." *The Australian Law Journal,* 62, no. 6 (June 1988), p. 457.

1459 Greenleaf, Graham. "Intellectual Property and Data Protection: Technology-Driven Copyright." *The Australian Law Journal,* 62, no. 2 (Feb. 1988), pp. 164-67.

1460 Greenleaf, Graham. "Intellectual Property and Data Protection: The Privacy Act 1988: Half a Loaf and Other Matters." *The Australian Law Journal,* 63, no. 2 (Feb. 1989), pp. 116-18.

1461 Greenleaf, Graham, and Roger Clarke. "A Critique of the Australian Law Reform Commission's Information Privacy Proposals." *Journal of Law and Information Science,* 2, no. 1 (1986), pp. 83-110.

1462 Greenstein, Seth. "Is Software 'Goods'? Intangibility Revisited Under the UCC and the National Stolen Property Act." *The Computer Lawyer,* 8, no. 4 (Apr. 1991), pp. 30-34.

1463 Greguras, Fred. "The European Community's Proposed Directive on the Legal Protection of Computer Programs: Comments from the Silicon Valley." *Software Protection,* 8, no. 8 (Jan. 1990), pp. 11-12.

1464 Greguras, Fred, Gary Reback, and Joel Riff. "Software's Legal Protection Around the World." *Information Strategy: The Executive's Journal,* 7, no. 1 (Fall 1990), pp. 23-29.

1465 Greguras, Fred M. "Checklist for U.S. Software Licensors for End-User Licenses in Japan." *Software Protection,* 6, no. 9 (Feb. 1988), pp. 9-11.

1466 Greguras, Fred M. "Final Regulations on Federal Government Rights in Computer Software." *Software Protection,* 6, no. 2-3 (July-Aug. 1987), pp. 12-14.

1467 Greguras, Fred M. "Implications of Lotus 1-2-3 Copyright Infringement Decision." *Software Protection,* 9, no. 2-3 (July-Aug. 1990), pp. 1-5.

1468 Greguras, Fred M. "Misuse of Copyright Defense to Software Infringement Claim." *Software Protection,* 9, no. 11 (Apr. 1991), pp. 1-3.

1469 Greguras, Fred M. "Software Licensing in Japan: 1991 Checklist for United States Licensors." *Software Law Journal,* 4, no. 4 (Dec. 1991), pp. 567-75. (First published in *Software Protection,* 9, no. 10 [Mar. 1991], pp. 7-12.)

1470 Greguras, Fred M., and Frances Foster-Simons. "Software Protection in the People's Republic of China. Part 1." *Software Protection,* 4, no. 1 (June 1985), pp. 1-7.

1471 Greguras, Fred M., and Frances Foster-Simons. "Software Protection in the People's Republic of China. Part 2." *Software Protection,* 4, no. 2 (July 1985), pp. 6-9.

1472 Greguras, Fred M., and Ivan H. Humphreys. "International Taxation of Software." *Software Protection*, 4, no. 4 (Sept. 1985), pp. 17-19.

1473 Greguras, Fred M., and Moon Sung Lee. "Checklist for U.S. Software Licensors for End-Use Licenses in the Republic of Korea." *Software Protection*, 10, no. 12 (May 1992), pp. 1-7.

1474 Grehan, Rick. "Cloak and Data." *Byte*, 15, no. 6 (June 1990), pp. 311-24.

1475 Gres, Viktoria L. "Rejection of Computer Software Licensing Agreements in Bankruptcy." *Cardozo Law Review*, 8, no. 2 (Dec. 1986), pp. 361-96.

1476 Grevstad, Eric. "Be Smart: Use Norton Antivirus to Protect PCs Against Viruses." *PC Computing*, 4, no. 1 (Jan. 1991), pp. 37-38.

1477 Griffin, Jennifer J. "The Monitoring of Electronic Mail in the Private Sector Workplace: An Electronic Assault on Employee Privacy Rights." *Software Law Journal*, 4, no. 3 (Oct. 1991), pp. 493-527.

1478 Griffin, Patricia A. "Copyright Law and Computer Software: The Third and Ninth Circuits Take Another Bite of the Apple." *Albany Law Review*, 49, no. 1 (Fall 1984), pp. 170-200.

1479 Griffith, Dodd S. "The Computer Fraud and Abuse Act of 1986: A Measured Response to a Growing Problem." *Vanderbilt Law Review*, 43, no. 2 (Mar. 1990), pp. 453-90.

1480 Grilk, Thomas S., and Lindsey Kiang. "Marketing Computer Products in Japan: Is It Safe?" *Boston Bar Journal*, 33, no. 5 (Sept.-Oct. 1989), pp. 25-28.

1481 Grimes, Thomas A. "Computer Security Programs for Law Firms: How to Protect Sensitive and Confidential Client Data." *Los Angeles Lawyer*, 14, no. 4 (June 1991), pp. 61-62.

1482 Grimley, Vikki. "Copyright: Penalty for Possession of Infringing Copies of Computer Programs." *Software Protection*, 10, no. 12 (May 1992), pp. 15-17.

1483 Gritzalis, D., A. Tomaras, S. Katsikas, and J. Keklikoglou. "Data Security in Medical Information Systems: The Greek Case." *Computers and Security*, 10, no. 2 (Apr. 1991), pp. 141-59.

1484 Gritzalis, D., S. Katsikas, J. Keklikoglou, and A. Tomaras. "Determining Access Rights for Medical Information Systems." *Computers and Security*, 11, no. 2 (Apr. 1992), pp. 149-61.

1485 Gritzalis, Dimitris, Sokratis Katsikas, and Stefanos Gritzalis. "A Zero Knowledge Probabilistic Login Protocol." *Computers and Security*, 11, no. 8 (Dec. 1992), pp. 733-45.

1486 Grodsky, Allen B. "Recent Developments in Intellectual Property Law." *Tort and Insurance Law Journal*, 27, no. 2 (Winter 1992), pp. 310-21.

1487 Grogan, Allen R. "Acquiring Content for New Media Works." *The Computer Lawyer*, 8, no. 1 (Jan. 1991), pp. 2-9.

1488 Grogan, Allen R. "Copyright Considerations in the Use of Computer Software on Local Area Networks and Multi-User Configurations." *The Computer Lawyer*, 3, no. 8 (Aug. 1986), pp. 1-8.

1489 Grogan, Allen R., and Ron Ben-Yehuda. "Outsourcing of Data Processing Operations." *The Computer Lawyer*, 8, no. 12 (Dec. 1991), pp. 1-12.

1490 Grogan, Allen R., and Ronald L. Johnston. "Differentiating System from Expression: The Potential Significance of *Lotus v. Borland*." *The Computer Lawyer*, 9, no. 5 (May 1992), pp. 18-20.

1491 Grogan, Allen R., and Ronald L. Johnston. "Reconciling Copyright Protection for Computer Programs with the Exclusion of Protection for Systems." *The Computer Lawyer*, 9, no. 2 (Feb. 1992), pp. 1-12.

1492 Groner, Jonathan. "Swatting Back at Software Pirates." *Legal Times*, supplement, 14, no. 52 (18 May 1992), pp. 7-8, 10, 13.

1493 Gross, Neil, and John W. Verity. "Can Fujitsu Break Big Blue's Grip?" *Business Week*, no. 3084 (19 Dec. 1988), pp. 100-2.

1494 Gross, Steve. "Computer Virus." *Omni*, 8, no. 9 (June 1986), p. 35.

1495 Grossberg, Michael. "Some Queries About Privacy and Constitutional Rights." *Case Western Reserve Law Review*, 41, no. 3 (1991), pp. 857-66.

1496 Grossblatt, Robert. "Copy Protection and a Z-80 Reset." *Radio- Electronics*, 59, no. 9 (Sept. 1988), pp. 82-83, 86, 104.

1497 "The Gulf War Flu." *U.S. News and World Report*, 112, no. 2 (20 Jan. 1992), p. 50.

1498 Gupta, Rajat K. "*Koontz v. Jaffarian*: The Unit Publication Doctrine." *Rutgers Computer and Technology Law Journal*, 14, no. 1 (1988), pp. 261-83.

1499 Guren, Marc D. "International Trade in Software and Data Bases: Restrictions on Imports Under Section 337 of the Tariff Act of 1933." *Software Law Journal*, 1, no. 4 (Fall 1987), pp. 471-522.

1500 Gutterman, Alan S. "International Intellectual Property: A Summary of Recent Developments and Issues for the Coming Decade." *Santa Clara Computer and High Technology Law Journal*, 8, no. 2 (Aug. 1992), pp. 335-405.

1501 Gutwirth, Serge, and Tony Joris. "Electronic Funds Transfer and the Consumer: The 'Soft Law' Approach in the European Community and Australia." *International and Comparative Law Quarterly*, 40, no. 2 (Apr. 1991), pp. 265-301.

1502 Guyon, Janet. "AT&T Tests a Solution to Computer Break-Ins." *The Wall Street Journal*, 213, no. 10 (16 Jan. 1989), p. B1.

1503 Gyngell, Julian. "Compilations of Computer Programmes: *Total Information Processing Systems Limited v. Daman Limited*—A Case Commentary." *Software Protection,* 10, no. 10 (Mar. 1992), pp. 10-16.

1504 Haaf, Joseph. "The EC Directive on the Legal Protection of Computer Programs: Decompilation and Security for Confidential Programming Techniques." *Columbia Journal of Transnational Law,* 30, no. 2 (1992), pp. 401-30.

1505 "The Hacker Report." *Science News,* 129, no. 16 (19 Apr. 1986), p. 248.

1506 "The Hacker Tracker." *Nation's Business,* 73, no. 2 (Feb. 1985), p. 58.

1507 "Hackers Beware: Computer Law Strengthened." *ABA Journal,* 72 (Sept. 1986), p. 32.

1508 "The Hacker's Return." *The Economist,* 312, no. 7611 (15 July 1989), pp. 81-82.

1509 "'Hackers' Score a New Pentagon Hit." *U.S. News and World Report,* 99, no. 5 (29 July 1985), p. 7.

1510 Hackett, George, and Hilliard Harper. "The Hacker Who Vanished." *Newsweek,* 109, no. 3 (19 Jan. 1987), p. 22.

1511 "Hacking Overkill." *New Statesman and Society,* 2, no. 71 (13 Oct. 1989), p. 5.

1512 Haeck, Louis. "The Protection of Personal Data Used for the Purposes of Direct Marketing and the IATA Recommended Practice on Transborder Data Flows." *Air Law,* 13, no. 4-5 (1988), pp. 178-86.

1513 Hafner, Katherine M., Geoff Lewis, Kevin Kelly, Mario Shao, Chuck Hawkins, and Paul Angiolillo. "Is Your Computer Secure?: Hackers, High-Tech Bandits, and Disasters Cost Billions—and as PCs Proliferate, the Problem Can Only Grow Worse." *Business Week,* no. 3063 (1 Aug. 1988), pp. 64-72.

1514 Hafner, Katherine M., and Richard Brandt. "Does This Lawsuit Compute for Apple?" *Business Week,* no. 3045 (4 Apr. 1988), pp. 32-33.

1515 Hafner, Katie. "Morris Code." *The New Republic,* 202, no. 8 (19 Feb. 1990), pp. 15-16.

1516 Haggerty, Alfred G. "Insurers Prepare to Foil 'Virus.'" *National Underwriter-Property and Casualty/Risk and Benefits Management Edition,* 93, no. 7 (13 Feb. 1989), pp. 9, 40-41.

1517 Haggerty, Alfred G. "Insurers View Virus Cure with Skepticism." *National Underwriter-Property and Casualty/Risk and Benefits Management Edition,* 93, no. 35 (28 Aug. 1989), pp. 9, 24.

1518 Hahm, Heon. "Computer Protection Against Foreign Competition in the United States." *Computer/Law Journal,* 10, no. 3 (Oct. 1990), pp. 393-412.

1519 Halal, William E. "Computer Viruses: The 'AIDS' of the Information Age?" *The Futurist,* 22, no. 5 (Sept.-Oct. 1988), p. 60.

1520 Hale, D. J. *"Vault Corp. v. Quaid Software Ltd.*: Limits to Copyright Protection for Computer Programs." *Tulane Law Review,* 64, no. 1 (Nov. 1989), pp. 270-79.

1521 Hale, Tim, and Jack Russo. "The Computer Software Copyright Rental Act." *Software Protection,* 9, no. 10 (Mar. 1991), pp. 6-7.

1522 Haley, Jeffrey T. "Enforcing Intellectual Property Rights in Computer Software." *Washington State Bar News,* 39, no. 7 (July 1985), pp. 10-13.

1523 "Halting Hackers." *The Economist,* 313, no. 7626 (28 Oct. 1989), p. 18.

1524 Halvey, John K. "A Rose by Any Other Name: Computer Programs and the Idea-Expression Distinction." *Copyright Law Symposium,* 35 (1988), pp. 1-40. (First published in *Emory Law Journal,* 34, no. 3-4 [Summer-Fall 1985], pp. 741-76.)

1525 Hamilton, David P. "Can Electronic Property Be Protected?" *Science,* 253, no. 5015 (5 July 1991), p. 23.

1526 Hamilton, Pamela L. "Protections for Software Under U.S. and Japanese Law: A Comparative Analysis." *Boston College International and Comparative Law Review,* 7, no. 2 (Summer 1984), pp. 353-401.

1527 Hammalian, John. "To What Extent Are Computer Programs in Machine-Readable Form Appropriate for Copyright Protection: A Critical Analysis and a Proposed Standard of Protection." *The Journal of Law and Commerce,* 7 (1987), pp. 183-223.

1528 Hammond, Herbert J. "Intellectual Property." *Texas Tech Law Review,* 19, no. 2 (1988), pp. 707-29.

1529 Hammond, Herbert J. "Intellectual Property." *Texas Tech Law Review,* 20, no. 2 (1989), pp. 495-516.

1530 Hammond, Herbert J. "Limiting and Dealing with Liability in Software Contracts." *The Computer Lawyer,* 9, no. 6 (June 1992), pp. 22-30.

1531 Hammond, R. Grant. "Electronic Crime in Canadian Courts." *Oxford Journal of Legal Studies,* 6, no. 1 (Spring 1986), pp. 145-50.

1532 Hammond, R. Grant. "Theft of Information." *The Law Quarterly Review,* 100 (Apr. 1984), pp. 252-64.

1533 Hammonds, Keith. "Don't Bury Software's Promise in a Legal Bog." *Business Week,* no. 3106 (22 May 1989), p. 86.

1534 Hanan, Rubin, and Allan R. Palliotta. "Perimeter Security for Telecommunication with External Entities." *Internal Auditor,* 46, no. 2 (Apr. 1989), pp. 40-45.

1535 Handley, Curtis E. "Menu Structures and User Interfaces: What Aspects of Computer Software Are Copyrightable in the Aftermath of *Lotus Development Corporation v. Paperback Software International*: and *Stephenson Software Limited.*" *Thomas M. Cooley Law Review*, 9, no. 1 (1992), pp. 233-51.

1536 Hanneman, Henri W. "International Aspects of Software Protection - Patents." *Software Protection*, 7, no. 6-7 (Nov.-Dec. 1988), pp. 14-20.

1537 Hanotiau, Bernard, and Philippe Peters. "Software Protection Against Third Parties in Belgium." *Software Law Journal*, 1, no. 3 (Spring-Summer 1986), pp. 303-8.

1538 Hansen, Ann C. "Criminal Law—Theft of Use of Computer Services—*State v. McGraw*, 459 N.E.2d 61 (Ind. App. Ct. 1984)." *Western New England Law Review*, 7, no. 3 (1985), pp. 823-28.

1539 Harborth, Nelson L., Bartholomew Rice, and Richard Snow. "Malicious Computer Logic." *Government Accountants Journal*, 40, no. 4 (Winter 1992), pp. 49-52.

1540 Harburg, Dale R. "Recent Amendments to the U.S. Copyright Act." *The Washington Lawyer*, 6, no. 4 (Mar.-Apr. 1992), pp. 42-43.

1541 Hardy, Gary. "Case Study: Closing 'Windows' Against Intruders." *Computers and Security*, 11, no. 8 (Dec. 1992), pp. 711-14.

1542 Hardy, I. T. "The Policy, Law, and Facts of Copyrighting Computer Screen Displays: An Essay." *Computer/Law Journal*, 11, no. 3 (Oct. 1992), pp. 371-97.

1543 Hardy, I. Trotter. "A Response to Gregg Williams' 'A Threat to Future Software.'" *Software Protection*, 4, no. 12 (May 1986), pp. 13-14.

1544 Hardy, I. Trotter, Jr. "Six Copyright Theories for the Protection of Computer Object Programs." *Arizona Law Review*, 26, no. 4 (1984), pp. 845-70.

1545 Hardy, Kelly Ann. "Contracts—Box-Top License Agreements—Uniform Commercial Code Section 2-207 Precludes Enforcement of Box-Top License Agreements When Terms Do Not Correspond with Previously-Reached Agreements—*Step-Saver Data Systems, Inc. v. Wyse Technology*, 939 F.2d 91 (3d Cir. 1991)." *Seton Hall Law Review*, 22, no. 2 (1992), pp. 615-19.

1546 Harn, Lein, Hung-Yu Lin, and Shoubao Yang. "A Software Authentication System for Information Integrity." *Computers and Security*, 11, no. 8 (Dec. 1992), pp. 747-52.

1547 Harper, Blaney. "Domestic Manufacturer Infringement Liability Under the Process Patent Act." *The Computer Lawyer*, 8, no. 10 (Oct. 1991), pp. 24-31.

1548 Harper, Blaney. "Intellectual Property and State Sovereign Immunity: The Eleventh Amendment Under Scrutiny." *The Computer Lawyer,* 9, no. 7 (July 1992), pp. 21-27.

1549 Harper, Doug. "Is Something Bugging Your Computer?" *Industrial Distribution,* 80, no. 4 (Mar. 1991), p. 49.

1550 Harper, Doug. "An Ounce of Prevention on Viruses Can Save a Megabyte of Data." *The Journal of Commerce and Commercial,* 390, no. 27583 (15 Oct. 1991), p. 4B.

1551 Harper, Doug. "Who Watches Your Computer Watching the Store? Make It Tough for Electronic Muggers to Tamper with Your Business." *Industrial Distribution,* 79, no. 8 (Aug. 1990), pp. 41.

1552 Harris, John R. "Legal Protection for Microcode and Beyond: A Discussion of the Applicability of the Semiconductor Chip Protection Act and the Copyright Laws to Microcode." *Computer/Law Journal,* 6, no. 2 (Fall 1985), pp. 187-222.

1553 Harris, John R. "A Market-Oriented Approach to the Use of Trade Secret or Copyright Protection (or Both?) for Software." *Jurimetrics Journal,* 25, no. 2 (Winter 1985), pp. 147-67.

1554 Harris, Julian. "Copyright Protection for Electronic Databases." *Solicitors Journal,* 136, no. 21 (29 May 1992), p. 532.

1555 Harris, Michael D. "Anti-Viral Policies Are a Necessity." *Los Angeles Daily Journal, California Law Business,* supplement, 105, no. 76 (20 Apr. 1992), pp. S14-15.

1556 Harris, Tommy, Cindy C. Barnes, and Beheruz Sethna. "A Survey of Microcomputer Security Procedures Used by Law Firms." *Law Office Economics and Management,* 32 (1992), pp. 466-72.

1557 Harrold, C. L. "An Introduction to the SMITE Approach to Secure Computing." *Computers and Security,* 8, no. 6 (Oct. 1989), pp. 495-505.

1558 Hart, Joseph P. "From Facts to Form: Extension and Application of the *Feist* 'Practical Inevitability' Test and Creativity Standard." *Golden Gate University Law Review,* 22, no. 2 (Spring 1992), pp. 549-66.

1559 Hart, R. J. "Semiconductor Chip: Reverse Engineering Revisited." *Software Protection,* 8, no. 2 (July 1989), pp. 4-6.

1560 Hart, Robert. "Maintenance Under the EEC Directive on the Legal Protection of Computer Programs." *Software Protection,* 10, no. 9 (Feb. 1992), pp. 11-13.

1561 Hart, Robert J. "The Legal Protection of Semiconductor Chips in the United Kingdom." *Software Law Journal,* 1, no. 3 (Spring-Summer 1986), pp. 273-88.

1562 Hart, Robert J. "Semiconductor Topography: Protection in the U.K. Contrasted with the U.S. Semiconductor Chip Protection Act and the EEC Directive on Topographies." *Software Protection*, 7, no. 3 (Aug. 1988), pp. 6-20.

1563 Hartnick, Alan J. "A Primer on the Interface of Trade Secrets and Copyright on Software Protection." *Communications and the Law*, 6, no. 5 (Oct. 1984), pp. 3-9.

1564 Hatch, Orrin G. "Better Late Than Never: Implementation of the 1986 Berne Convention." *Cornell International Law Journal*, 22, no. 2 (Spring 1989), pp. 171-95.

1565 Hauptman, Gunter A. "Computer Software Protection Chart." *Idea*, 28, no. 1 (1987-88), p. 1.

1566 Hauptman, Gunter A. "How Computer Software Has Come to Be Protected Under the U.S. Patent Law." *The Computer Lawyer*, 6, no. 12 (Dec. 1989), pp. 11-20.

1567 Hawkins, Corinne C. "What Users Should Know About Computer Viruses." *Telecommunications*, 23, no. 7 (July 1989), pp. 42-44.

1568 Hayden, John F. "Copyright Protection of Computer Databases After *Feist.*" *Harvard Journal of Law and Technology*, 5 (Fall 1991), pp. 215-43.

1569 Hayes, David L. "Acquiring and Protecting Technology: The Intellectual Property Audit." *The Computer Lawyer*, 8, no. 4 (Apr. 1991), pp. 1-20.

1570 Hayes, David L. "Shrinkwrap License Agreements: New Light on a Vexing Problem." *The Computer Lawyer*, 9, no. 9 (Sept. 1992), pp. 1-9.

1571 Haynes, C. Leigh. "The Envelope, Please: Problems and Proposals for Electronic Mail Surveillance." *Hastings Constitutional Law Quarterly*, 14, no. 2 (Winter 1987), pp. 421-49.

1572 Haynes, Mark A. "A Programmer's Right of Renewal and Right of Termination of Transfers and Licenses Under Copyright." *Software Protection*, 8, no. 1 (June 1989), pp. 1-10.

1573 Haynes, Mark A., and Stephen C. Durant. "Patents and Copyrights in Computer Software Based Technology: Why Bother with Patents?" *The Computer Lawyer*, 4, no. 2 (Feb. 1987), pp. 1-7.

1574 Hazan, Yves. "No Design Protection for Computer Screens in Australia." *Software Protection*, 10, no. 3 (Aug. 1991), pp. 3-4.

1575 Hazen, Thomas Lee. "Contract Principles as a Guide for Protecting Intellectual Property Rights in Computer Software: The Limits of Copyright Protection, the Evolving Concept of Derivative Works, and the Proper Limits of Licensing Arrangements." *U.C. Davis Law Review*, 20, no. 1 (Fall 1986), pp. 105-58.

1576 Hearn, Patrick. "Patent Licensing in the EEC - I." *Solicitors' Journal*, 128, no. 31 (3 Aug. 1984), pp. 523-25.

1577 Hearn, Patrick. "Patent Licensing in the EEC - II." *Solicitors' Journal*, 128, no. 32 (10 Aug. 1984), pp. 542-44.

1578 Hearn, Patrick. "Patent Licensing in the EEC - III." *Solicitors' Journal*, 128, no. 33 (17 Aug. 1984), pp. 559-62.

1579 Hearnden, Keith. "How to Combat Computer Crime." *Management Today*, (Dec. 1984), pp. 37-40.

1580 Heckel, Paul. "The Software-Patent Controversy." *The Computer Lawyer*, 9, no. 12 (Dec. 1992), pp. 13-23.

1581 Heimbecher, Reed R. "Proposed Prior Art Legislation for Computer Program Patent Applications: Creating a Potential for Coexisting Patents " *Comm/Ent*, 13, no. 1 (1990), pp. 57-88.

1582 Heitke, Sheila. "Work for Hire After *CCNV v. Reid*: Adequacy of Protection for Artists and Extent of the Doctrine's Applicability to Software Developers." *Northern Illinois University Law Review*, 10, no. 2 (1990), pp. 331-63.

1583 Helein, Charles H. "Software Lock-In and Antitrust Tying Arrangements: The Lessons of *Data General*." *Computer/Law Journal*, 5, no. 3 (Winter 1985), pp. 329-45.

1584 Hemnes, Thomas M. S. "Three Common Fallacies in the User Interface Copyright Debate." *The Computer Lawyer*, 7, no. 2 (Feb. 1990), pp. 14-20.

1585 Hemnes, Thomas M. S., and Susan Barbieri Montgomery. "The Bankruptcy Code, the Copyright Act, and Transactions in Computer Software." *Computer/Law Journal*, 7, no. 3 (Summer 1987), pp. 327-81.

1586 Hennessey, Gilbert H. "Software Patents in the Nineties." *Boston Bar Journal*, 33, no. 5 (Sept.-Oct. 1989), pp. 12-17.

1587 Hennington, Boyett Judson, III. "Computer Arbitration: Taking the Byte Out of Data Processing Disputes." *Cumberland Law Review*, 19, no. 2 (1989), pp. 279-308.

1588 Heredero, Manuel. "The Rights of the Users of Computer Programs in the New Spanish Act on the Law of Copyright." *Software Protection*, 7, no. 4 (Sept. 1988), pp. 1-4.

1589 Hernandez, Ruel Torres. "ECPA and Online Computer Privacy." *Federal Communications Law Journal*, 41, no. 1 (Nov. 1988), pp. 17-41.

1590 Herrera, Rosario. "Computerized Check Processing: *De minimis* Errors in Check Description on Stop Payment Orders." *Computer/Law Journal*, 9, no. 2 (Spring 1989), pp. 205-21.

1591 Herschberg, I. S. "Make the Tigers Hunt for You." *Computers and Security*, 7, no. 2 (Apr. 1988), pp. 197-203.

1592 Herschberg, I. S., and R. Paans. "Friday the 13th, Facts and Fancies." *Computers and Security*, 9, no. 2 (Apr. 1990), pp. 125-30.

1593 Herschberg, Israel Samuel. "The Hackers' Comfort." *Computers and Security*, 6 (1987), pp. 133-38.

1594 Hicks, Jack B. "Copyright and Computer Databases: Is Traditional Compilation Law Adequate?" *Texas Law Review*, 65, no. 5 (Apr. 1987), pp. 993-1028.

1595 Higashima, Takaharu, and Kenji Ushiku. "A New Means of International Protection of Computer Programs Through the Paris Convention – A New Concept of Utility Model." *Computer/Law Journal*, 7, no. 1 (Summer 1986), pp. 1-22.

1596 Higgins, Steve. "Tough New Law Deters Software Piracy." *PC Week*, 9, no. 49 (7 Dec. 1992), p. 17.

1597 Higgins, Willis E. "The Case for Software Patent Protection." *Comm/Ent*, 14, no. 2 (Winter 1992), pp. 315-22.

1598 Higgins, Willis E. "Technological Poetry: The Interface Between Copyrights and Patents for Software." *Comm/Ent*, 12, no. 1 (Fall 1989), pp. 67-80.

1599 Highland, Harold Joseph. "The BRAIN Virus: Fact and Fantasy." *Computers and Security*, 7, no. 4 (Aug. 1988), pp. 367-70.

1600 Highland, Harold Joseph. "Computer Viruses Can Be Deadly!" *EDPACS*, 15, no. 12 (June 1988), pp. 1-6.

1601 Highland, Harold Joseph. "Data Physician – A Virus Protection Program." *Computers and Security*, 6, no. 1 (Feb. 1987), pp. 73-79.

1602 Highland, Harold Joseph. "Datacrime Virus and New Anti-Virus Products." *Computers and Security*, 8, no. 8 (Dec. 1989), pp. 659-61.

1603 Highland, Harold Joseph. "How Secure Are Fiber Optics Communications?" *Computers and Security*, 7, no. 1 (Feb. 1988), pp. 25-26.

1604 Highland, Harold Joseph. "How to Combat a Computer Virus." *Computers and Security*, 7, no. 2 (Apr. 1988), pp. 157-63.

1605 Highland, Harold Joseph. "IFIP TC11 News." *Computers and Security*, 11, no. 7 (Nov. 1992), pp. 625-28.

1606 Highland, Harold Joseph. "IFIP TC11 News." *Computers and Security*, 11, no. 8 (Dec. 1992), pp. 715-19.

1607 Highland, Harold Joseph. "Random Bits & Bytes: Access Control/Menu Security Program." *Computers and Security*, 11, no. 8 (Dec. 1992), pp. 683-88.

1608 Highland, Harold Joseph. "Random Bits & Bytes: Access Control Weakness." *Computers and Security,* 11, no. 5 (Sept. 1992), pp. 390-91.

1609 Highland, Harold Joseph. "Random Bits & Bytes: Anatomy of Three Computer Virus Attacks." *Computers and Security,* 8, no. 6 (Oct. 1989), pp. 461-66.

1610 Highland, Harold Joseph. "Random Bits & Bytes: Another Case History of a Virus Attack." *Computers and Security,* 8, no. 7 (Nov. 1989), pp. 559-60.

1611 Highland, Harold Joseph. "Random Bits & Bytes: Australian Computer Virus Infector Charged." *Computers and Security,* 8, no. 7 (Nov. 1989), p. 554.

1612 Highland, Harold Joseph. "Random Bits & Bytes: 'Back Door' Trespassing." *Computers and Security,* 5 (1986), p. 94.

1613 Highland, Harold Joseph. "Random Bits & Bytes: Briefs and Comments." *Computers and Security,* 9, no. 5 (Aug. 1990), pp. 373-75.

1614 Highland, Harold Joseph. "Random Bits & Bytes: Case History of a Virus Attack." *Computers and Security,* 7, no. 1 (Feb. 1988), pp. 3-5.

1615 Highland, Harold Joseph. "Random Bits & Bytes: Computer Abuse and Managerial Response." *Computers and Security,* 6 (1987), p. 448.

1616 Highland, Harold Joseph. "Random Bits & Bytes: Computer Security-U.S.A." *Computers and Security,* 9, no. 8 (Dec. 1990), pp. 660-64.

1617 Highland, Harold Joseph. "Random Bits & Bytes: Computer Security and a Litigious Society." *Computers and Security,* 10, no. 6 (Oct. 1991), pp. 489-91.

1618 Highland, Harold Joseph. "Random Bits & Bytes: Computer Security and Law." *Computers and Security,* 6 (1987), pp. 203-5.

1619 Highland, Harold Joseph. "Random Bits & Bytes: Computer Viruses—The Lighter (?) Side." *Computers and Security,* 10, no. 1 (Feb. 1991), pp. 8-12.

1620 Highland, Harold Joseph. "Random Bits & Bytes: Computer Viruses: Media Hyperbole, Errors and Ignorance." *Computers & Security,* 7, no. 5 (Oct. 1988), pp. 442-49.

1621 Highland, Harold Joseph. "Random Bits & Bytes: Computer Viruses—A Post Mortem." *Computers and Security,* 7, no. 2 (Apr. 1988), pp. 117-25.

1622 Highland, Harold Joseph. "Random Bits & Bytes: Computer Viruses—A Status Report." *Computers and Security,* 10, no. 1 (Feb. 1991), pp. 4-8.

1623 Highland, Harold Joseph. "Random Bits & Bytes: Computer Viruses and Free Speech." *Computers and Security,* 9, no. 1 (Feb. 1990), pp. 8-9.

1624 Highland, Harold Joseph. "Random Bits & Bytes: Computer Viruses and Sudden Death!" *Computers and Security,* 6, no. 1 (Feb. 1987), pp. 8-10.

1625 Highland, Harold Joseph. "Random Bits & Bytes: Computer Viruses Strike 50% of the Microcomputers in China." *Computer and Security,* 9, no. 5 (Aug. 1990), pp. 369-70.

1626 Highland, Harold Joseph. "Random Bits & Bytes: The Cornell Report— The Internet Virus." *Computers and Security,* 8, no. 5 (Aug. 1989), pp. 371-73.

1627 Highland, Harold Joseph. "Random Bits & Bytes: Definition of a Computer Virus." *Computers and Security,* 8, no. 5 (Aug. 1989), pp. 376-77.

1628 Highland, Harold Joseph. "Random Bits & Bytes: Emerging Viruses, Emerging Threat." *Computers and Security,* 9, no. 2 (Apr. 1990), pp. 104-7.

1629 Highland, Harold Joseph. "Random Bits & Bytes: Faulty Software—Not a Virus." *Computers and Security,* 10, no. 7 (Nov. 1991), pp. 594-95.

1630 Highland, Harold Joseph. "Random Bits & Bytes: The Federal Government's Role in Non-Defense Information Security." *Computers and Security,* 9, no. 1 (Feb. 1990), pp. 6-7.

1631 Highland, Harold Joseph. "Random Bits & Bytes: Forged E-Mail." *Computers and Security,* 10, no. 1 (Feb. 1991), pp. 12-13.

1632 Highland, Harold Joseph. "Random Bits & Bytes: The Good Side of a Computer Virus." *Computers and Security,* 8, no. 8 (Dec. 1989), pp. 648-49.

1633 Highland, Harold Joseph. "Random Bits & Bytes: Hackers Revisited." *Computers and Security,* 7, no. 4 (Aug. 1988), pp. 339-40.

1634 Highland, Harold Joseph. "Random Bits & Bytes: Harmless Viruses Do *Not* Exist." *Computers and Security,* 8, no. 4 (June 1989), pp. 276-78.

1635 Highland, Harold Joseph. "Random Bits & Bytes: How Secure Is Your Network?" *Computers and Security,* 9, no. 6 (Oct. 1990), pp. 470-72.

1636 Highland, Harold Joseph. "Random Bits & Bytes: In Brief...." *Computers and Security,* 5 (1986), pp. 187-88.

1637 Highland, Harold Joseph. "Random Bits & Bytes: In the Defense of Hackers." *Computers and Security,* 9, no. 6 (Oct. 1990), pp. 473-76.

1638 Highland, Harold Joseph. "Random Bits & Bytes: In the News...." *Computers and Security,* 10, no. 2 (Apr. 1991), pp. 99-100.

1639 Highland, Harold Joseph. "Random Bits & Bytes: In the News...." *Computers and Security,* 10, no. 5 (Aug. 1991), pp. 393-94.

1640 Highland, Harold Joseph. "Random Bits & Bytes: Internet 'Hacked' Again!" *Computers and Security,* 9, no. 4 (June 1990), pp. 282-86.

1641 Highland, Harold Joseph. "Random Bits & Bytes: Internet Hacked Again." *Computers and Security*, 10, no. 5 (Aug. 1991), pp. 384-85.

1642 Highland, Harold Joseph. "Random Bits & Bytes: Internet Redux." *Computers and Security*, 9, no. 3 (May 1990), pp. 200-3.

1643 Highland, Harold Joseph. "Random Bits & Bytes: The Internet Worm...Continued." *Computers and Security*, 8, no. 6 (Oct. 1989), pp. 460-61.

1644 Highland, Harold Joseph. "Random Bits & Bytes: It Had to Happen!" *Computers and Security*, 9, no. 3 (May 1990), pp. 204-5.

1645 Highland, Harold Joseph. "Random Bits & Bytes: The Italian or Ping-Pong Virus." *Computers and Security*, 8, no. 2 (Apr. 1989), pp. 91-94.

1646 Highland, Harold Joseph. "Random Bits & Bytes: Items in the News." *Computers and Security*, 10, no. 7 (Nov. 1991), pp. 595-96.

1647 Highland, Harold Joseph. "Random Bits & Bytes: A Macro Virus." *Computers and Security*, 8, no. 3 (May 1989), pp. 178-82.

1648 Highland, Harold Joseph. "Random Bits & Bytes: The Marijuana Virus Revisited." *Computers and Security*, 8, no. 2 (Apr. 1989), p. 97.

1649 Highland, Harold Joseph. "Random Bits & Bytes: The Marijuana Virus Revisited." *Computers and Security*, 8, no. 5 (Aug. 1989), pp. 369-71.

1650 Highland, Harold Joseph. "Random Bits & Bytes: The Maturing of the Anti-Virus Product Market." *Computers and Security*, 10, no. 5 (Aug. 1991), pp. 388-90.

1651 Highland, Harold Joseph. "Random Bits & Bytes: Michelangelo—Part I." *Computers and Security*, 11, no. 3 (May 1992), pp. 200-2.

1652 Highland, Harold Joseph. "Random Bits & Bytes: Michelangelo—Part II." *Computers and Security*, 11, no. 4 (July 1992), pp. 294-99.

1653 Highland, Harold Joseph. "Random Bits & Bytes: Microcomputer Security." *Computers & Security*, 10, no. 2 (Apr. 1991), pp. 95-97.

1654 Highland, Harold Joseph. "Random Bits & Bytes: The Milnet/Arpanet Attack." *Computers and Security*, 8, no. 1 (Feb. 1989), pp. 3-10.

1655 Highland, Harold Joseph. "Random Bits & Bytes: The MOD Squad—Hacker vs Hacker." *Computers and Security*, 11, no. 7 (Nov. 1992), pp. 593-94.

1656 Highland, Harold Joseph. "Random Bits & Bytes: NSDD 145 Revised." *Computers and Security*, 9, no. 7 (Nov. 1990), pp. 576-80.

1657 Highland, Harold Joseph. "Random Bits & Bytes: nVIR Strikes Again—This Time Around the World." *Computers and Security*, 8, no. 1 (Feb. 1989), pp. 10-11.

1658 Highland, Harold Joseph. "Random Bits & Bytes: Near-Miss Census Bureau Virus." *Computers and Security,* 9, no. 2 (Apr. 1992), p. 108.

1659 Highland, Harold Joseph. "Random Bits & Bytes: Network Communications Security." *Computers and Security,* 8, no. 7 (Nov. 1989), pp. 553-54.

1660 Highland, Harold Joseph. "Random Bits & Bytes: A Network Virus?" *Computers and Security,* 9, no. 6 (Oct. 1990), pp. 476-77.

1661 Highland, Harold Joseph. "Random Bits & Bytes: A New Attempt to Control Sensitive but Unclassified Data?" *Computers and Security,* 9, no. 1 (Feb. 1990), pp. 4-6.

1662 Highland, Harold Joseph. "Random Bits & Bytes: The New Brain Goes to School." *Computers and Security,* 8, no. 1 (Feb. 1989), pp. 12-13.

1663 Highland, Harold Joseph. "Random Bits & Bytes: New Deadly Computer Virus Surfaces." *Computers and Security,* 8, no. 7 (Nov. 1989), pp. 560-61.

1664 Highland, Harold Joseph. "Random Bits & Bytes: New Directions for Anti-Virus Measures." *Computers and Security,* 9, no. 1 (Feb. 1990), pp. 7-8.

1665 Highland, Harold Joseph. "Random Bits & Bytes: New Zealand's Marijuana Virus." *Computers and Security,* 8, no. 1 (Feb. 1989), pp. 11-12.

1666 Highland, Harold Joseph. "Random Bits & Bytes: News and Comments." *Computers and Security,* 10, no. 8 (Dec. 1991), pp. 694-97.

1667 Highland, Harold Joseph. "Random Bits & Bytes: News from the Peoples Republic of China." *Computers and Security,* 5, no. 1 (Mar. 1986), p. 3.

1668 Highland, Harold Joseph. "Random Bits & Bytes: 1984 in 1990." *Computers and Security,* 10, no. 8 (Dec. 1991), pp. 690-94.

1669 Highland, Harold Joseph. "Random Bits & Bytes: Novell Network Virus Alert." *Computers and Security,* 9, no. 7 (Nov. 1990), pp. 570-71.

1670 Highland, Harold Joseph. "Random Bits & Bytes: Open Sesame—Hackers Welcome." *Computers and Security,* 7, no. 3 (June 1988), pp. 232-33.

1671 Highland, Harold Joseph. "Random Bits & Bytes: 'Other' Sources of Computer Virus Infection." *Computers and Security,* 8, no. 8 (Dec. 1989), pp. 649-53.

1672 Highland, Harold Joseph. "Random Bits & Bytes: Password Integrity and Secrecy." *Computers and Security,* 8, no. 4 (June 1989), p. 276.

1673 Highland, Harold Joseph. "Random Bits & Bytes: Postgiro Hit—Some Questions Raised." *Computers and Security,* 8, no. 8 (Dec. 1989), pp. 655-57.

1674 Highland, Harold Joseph. "Random Bits & Bytes: Protecting Hardware and Software." *Computers and Security,* 8, no. 8 (Dec. 1989), pp. 647-48.

1675 Highland, Harold Joseph. "Random Bits & Bytes: Security Conundrum." *Computers and Security,* 10, no. 2 (Apr. 1991), pp. 94-95.

1676 Highland, Harold Joseph. "Random Bits & Bytes: Security Press Briefs." *Computers and Security,* 9, no. 1 (Feb. 1990), pp. 9-11.

1677 Highland, Harold Joseph. "Random Bits & Bytes: Security Snippets." *Computers and Security,* 11, no. 8 (Dec. 1992), pp. 682-83.

1678 Highland, Harold Joseph. "Random Bits & Bytes: A Spate of New Viruses." *Computers and Security,* 9, no. 3 (May 1990), pp. 205-6.

1679 Highland, Harold Joseph. "Random Bits & Bytes: Testing a Password System." *Computers and Security,* 11, no. 2 (Apr. 1992), pp. 110-13.

1680 Highland, Harold Joseph. "Random Bits & Bytes: U.S. Congress Computer Virus Report." *Computers and Security,* 7, no. 5 (Oct. 1988), pp. 439-40.

1681 Highland, Harold Joseph. "Random Bits & Bytes: U.S. Government's Security Program in the Black?" *Computers and Security,* 9, no. 7 (Nov. 1990), pp. 574-76.

1682 Highland, Harold Joseph. "Random Bits & Bytes: Using and Breaking Encryption." *Computers and Security,* 9, no. 8 (Dec. 1990), pp. 668-71.

1683 Highland, Harold Joseph. "Random Bits & Bytes: The Vienna Virus." *Computers and Security,* 8, no. 5 (Aug. 1989), pp. 375-76.

1684 Highland, Harold Joseph. "Random Bits & Bytes: Would You Report a Suspected Data Crime to the Authorities?" *Computers and Security,* 6 (1987), pp. 288-95.

1685 Highland, Harold Joseph. "Report on the Fourth National Computer Security Conference: COMPSEC IV." *Computers and Security,* 7, no. 3 (June 1988), pp. 309-11.

1686 Highland, Harold Joseph. "Secret Disk II — Administrator." *Computers and Security,* 8, no. 7 (Nov. 1989), pp. 563-68.

1687 Highland, Harold Joseph. "Secret Disk II — Transparent Automatic Encryption." *Computers and Security,* 7, no. 1 (Feb. 1988), pp. 27-34.

1688 Highland, Harold Joseph. "What If a Computer Virus Strikes?" *EDPACS,* 17, no. 1 (July 1989), pp. 11-17.

1689 Highley, Robert. "Copyright Law and Computer Screen Displays." *University of Toronto Faculty of Law Review,* 48, no. 1 (Winter 1990), pp. 48-91.

1690 Hild, John. "Piracy and Protection." *Editor and Publisher,* 122, no. 35 (2 Sept. 1989), pp. 22PC, 39PC.

1691 Hiles, Andrew. "Protecting PC Accounting Systems." *The Accountant's Magazine,* 93, no. 998 (Sept. 1989), p. 24.

1692 Hilton, William E. "Quantifying Originality: A Logical Analysis for Determining Substantial Similarity in Computer Software Copyright Infringement Actions." *Idea,* 31, no. 4 (1991), pp. 269-96.

1693 Hilton, William E. "Survey of Computers, Software, and Information Processing." *Idea,* 31, no. 2 (1990), pp. 67-84.

1694 Hilts, Philip J. "'Virus' Hits Vast Computer Network." *The Washington Post,* 111, no. 335 (4 Nov. 1988), pp. A1, A4.

1695 Himelson, David. "Frankly, Incredible: Unconscionability in Computer Contracts." *Computer/Law Journal,* 4, no. 4 (Spring 1984), pp. 695-736.

1696 Hinckley, Robert C. "*NEC v. INTEL:* Will Hardware Be Drawn Into the Black Hole of Copyright?" *Santa Clara Computer and High-Technology Law Journal,* 3, no. 1 (Jan. 1987), pp. 23-72.

1697 Hirakawa, Osamu, and Kenichi Nakano. "Copyright Protection of Computer 'Interfaces' in Japan." *The Computer Lawyer,* 7, no. 12 (Dec. 1990), pp. 1-16.

1698 Hirasawa, Takami. "Program Registration in Japan." *Software Protection,* 9, no. 2-3 (July-Aug. 1990), pp. 5-8.

1699 Hitt, Jack, and Paul Tough. "Terminal Delinquents." *Esquire,* 114, no. 6 (Dec. 1990), pp. 174-83, 211-19.

1700 Hobbs, Pamela. "Methods of Determining Substantial Similarity in Copyright Cases Involving Computer Programs." *University of Detroit Law Review,* 67, no. 3 (Spring 1990), pp. 393-411.

1701 Hochman, Marilyn. "The Flagler Dog Track Case." *Computer/Law Journal,* 7, no. 1 (Summer 1986), pp. 117-27.

1702 Hoffer, Jeffrey A., and Detmar W. Straub, Jr. "The 9 to 5 Underground: Are You Policing Computer Crimes?" *Sloan Management Review,* 30, no. 4 (Summer 1989), pp. 35-43.

1703 Hoffman, Gary M., and Jon D. Grossman. "Substantial Similarity at Issue in Software Infringement Cases." *The National Law Journal,* 12, no. 26 (5 Mar. 1990), pp. 34, 37-38.

1704 Hoffman, Gary, and Jon Grossman. "Software Ideas, Expression Need a Uniform System of Protection." *The National Law Journal,* 10, no. 47 (1 Aug. 1988), pp. 27-29.

1705 Hoffman, Gary M., George T. Marcou, and Charles Murray. "Commercial Piracy of Intellectual Property." *Journal of the Patent and Trademark Office Society,* 71, no. 7 (July 1989), pp. 556-67.

1706 Hoffman, Lance J. "Risk Analysis and Computer Security: Towards a Theory at Last." *Computers and Security,* 8, no. 1 (Feb. 1989), pp. 23-24.

1707 Hoffman, Paul S. "A Primer on Disclosure Agreements." *Software Law Journal*, 3, no. 3 (Summer 1989), pp. 531-41.

1708 Hoffman, Paul S. "Who Has the Right to License Software?" *New York State Bar Journal*, 64, no. 3 (Mar.-Apr. 1992), pp. 10-15.

1709 Hogan, Thomas M., and Ruth C. Schoenbeck. "Trade Secret Preliminary Hearings: Does the Press Have a Right to Know?" *Santa Clara Computer and High Technology Law Journal*, 3, no. 2 (1987), pp. 329-50.

1710 Holgate, Geoff. "Hacking—A Ground for Dismissal?" *Solicitors Journal*, 135, no. 35 (13 Sept. 1991), pp. 1008-10.

1711 Hollander, Patricia A. "An Introduction to Legal and Ethical Issues Relating to Computers in Higher Education." *The Journal of College and University Law*, 11, no. 2 (Fall 1984), pp. 215-32.

1712 Hollinger, Richard C., and Lonn Lanza-Kaduce. "The Process of Criminalization: The Case of Computer Crime Laws." *Criminology*, 26, no. 1 (Feb. 1988), pp. 101-26.

1713 Hollingsworth, Mark A. "Is the Medium the Message? Extending Copyright Protection to Logic Devices." *Whittier Law Review*, 12, no. 3 (1991), pp. 383-401.

1714 Holman, Richard L. "Bogus Software in Europe." *The Wall Street Journal*, 214, no. 26 (29 June 1992), p. A10.

1715 Holt, Mary Kathryn. "In Search of Equilibrium: Intellectual Property, Antitrust, and the Personal Computer Industry." *Software Law Journal*, 2, no. 4 (Fall 1988), pp. 577-95.

1716 Holtzman, Jeff. "Guard Against Disk Errors and Viruses with Disk Watcher." *Radio-Electronics*, 60, no. 5 (May 1989), pp. 77-80.

1717 Honan, Patrick. "Avoiding Virus Hysteria." *Personal Computing*, 13, no. 5 (May 1989), pp. 84-92.

1718 Honan, Patrick. "Beware: It's Virus Season." *Personal Computing*, 12, no. 7 (July 1988), p. 36.

1719 Honan, Patrick. "Data Security." *Personal Computing*, 11, no. 1 (Jan. 1987), pp. 101-7.

1720 Honan, Patrick. "Never Lose Data Again." *Personal Computing*, 10, no. 11 (Nov. 1986), pp. 71-75.

1721 Honan, Patrick. "Security On-Line." *Personal Computing*, 11, no. 1 (Jan. 1987), p. 107.

1722 Hootman, Joseph T. "A Gentle Knock." *Information Strategy: The Executive's Journal*, 5, no. 3 (Spring 1989), pp. 41-44.

1723 Hopkins, Catherine E. "The Status of Patent Law Concerning Computer Programs: The Proper Form for Legal Protection." *Drake Law Review,* 33, no. 1 (1983-84), pp. 155-75.

1724 Horgan, Sherry M. "Foreign Data: Is It Safe in United States Data Banks?" *California Western International Law Journal,* 16, no. 2 (Summer 1986), pp. 346-72.

1725 Hornick, John F. "Computer Program Copyrights: Look and Feel No Evil." *Software Law Journal,* 5, no. 2 (Apr. 1992), pp. 355-84.

1726 Horovitz, Bonna Lynn. "Computer Software as a Good Under the Uniform Commercial Code: Taking a Byte Out of the Intangibility Myth." *Boston University Law Review,* 65, no. 1 (Jan. 1985), pp. 129-64.

1727 Horton, Thomas R. "Computer Security: Gaining the CEO's Support." *Vital Speeches of the Day,* 56, no. 10 (1 Mar. 1990), pp. 307-10.

1728 Horton, William. "Copyright Protection for Software." *Michigan Bar Journal,* 67, no. 10 (Oct. 1988), pp. 964-67.

1729 Horwitz, Stuart. "Proposed Changes in the Regulations Governing Deposits of Computer Programs with the Copyright Office." *Jurimetrics Journal,* 26, no. 3 (Spring 1986), pp. 305-27.

1730 "House Bill Makes Computer Crimes a Federal Case." *The Office,* 104, no. 1 (July 1986), p. 16.

1731 "How To Find and Whip Michelangelo." *U.S. News and World Report,* 112, no. 8 (2 Mar. 1992), p. 19.

1732 "How to Hold the Electronic Vandal at Bay." *New Scientist,* 121, no. 1654 (4 Mar. 1989), p. 42.

1733 Howard, Bill. "Virus Protection: Scan, Cleanup." *PC Magazine,* 9, no. 12 (26 June 1990), p. 181.

1734 Hoyt, Michael. "The Tampa Media-Espionage Case: Was the Computer Used as a Weapon in a TV Ratings War?" *Columbia Journalism Review,* 28, no. 1 (May-June 1989), pp. 27-31.

1735 Hruska, Andrew C. "A Broad Market Approach to Antitrust Product Market Definition in Innovative Industries." *The Yale Law Journal,* 102, no. 1 (Oct. 1992), pp. 305-31.

1736 Huang, C. Y., and Jeffrey H. Chen. "Copyright Protection of Computer Software in Taiwan." *Software Protection,* 9, no. 10 (Mar. 1991), pp. 1-5.

1737 Huber, Peter. "Madonna Ain't Software." *Forbes,* 146 (3 Sept. 1990), p. 104.

1738 Huet, Jerome, and Jane C. Ginsburg. "Computer Programs in Europe: A Comparative Analysis of the 1991 EC Software Directive." *Columbia Journal of Transnational Law,* 30, no. 2 (1992), pp. 327-73.

1739 Hughes, Gordon. "Computer Contracts: The Rise of the GITC." *Law Institute Journal,* 66, no. 5 (May 1992), pp. 404-6.

1740 Hughes, Gordon. "Computer Copyright - Wombat Eats Apple and Leaves." *Law Institute Journal,* 60, no. 8 (Aug. 1986), pp. 802-7.

1741 Hughes, Gordon. "The Criminalisation of Computer Abuse in Victoria." *Law Institute Journal,* 61, no. 9 (Sept. 1987), pp. 930-1.

1742 Hughes, Gordon. "Current Issues in Australian Computer Law." *Law Institute Journal,* 61, no. 10 (Oct. 1987), pp. 1034-37.

1743 Hughes, Gordon. "Data Protection at Common Law." *Law Institute Journal,* 62, no. 10 (Oct. 1988), pp. 971-73.

1744 Hughes, Gordon. "The Implications of Australian Consumer Protection Legislation on Software Licences." *Software Law Journal,* 5, no. 1 (Feb. 1992), pp. 89-96.

1745 Hughes, Gordon. "Landmark Ruling on Computer Copyright." *Law Institute Journal,* 64, no. 12 (Dec. 1990), pp. 1184-85.

1746 Hughes, Gordon. "Legislative Responses to Computer Crime." *Law Institute Journal,* 63, no. 6 (June 1989), pp. 507-9.

1747 Hughet, William N. "The Computer Software Rental Amendments Act of 1990: A Solution to the Problem of Pirating Computer Programs or an Exercise in Futility?" *Journal of Corporation Law,* 16, no. 1 (Fall 1990), pp. 931-62.

1748 Hulbert, Bradley J. "Special Considerations for Obtaining and Litigating Software Patents." *Software Law Journal,* 4, no. 1 (Oct. 1990), pp. 1-14.

1749 Hunter, Daniel. "Secure in the Knowledge." *Law Institute Journal,* 65, no. 6 (June 1991), pp. 494-95.

1750 Hunter, Daniel. "Virally-Induced Stress: A Guide to How Computer Viruses Operate and Practical Ways to Protect Yourself Against Them." *Law Institute Journal,* 65, no. 4 (Apr. 1991), pp. 252-53.

1751 Hunter, Daniel A. D. "Protecting the 'Look and Feel' of Computer Software in the United States and Australia." *Santa Clara Computer and High Technology Law Journal,* 7, no. 1 (July 1991), pp. 95-155.

1752 Hurford, Chris. "Help Yourself." *The Accountant's Magazine,* 96, no. 1026 (Jan. 1992), pp. 48, 50.

1753 Hurt, Tracy L. "*NEC v. INTEL*: Copyright and the Mysteries of Embedded Microcode." *Jurimetrics Journal,* 29, no. 3 (Spring 1989), pp. 311-31.

1754 Hyde, Edward R. "Legal Protection of Computer Software." *Connecticut Bar Journal,* 59 (1985), pp. 298-319.

1755 "IBM Brings Copycats in from the Cold." *New Scientist,* 131, no. 1779 (27 July 1991), p. 11.

1756 "ITC to Review ALJ Initial 337 Ruling on Infringement of TI Patents by Encapsulated Devices." *The Computer Lawyer,* 9, no. 2 (Feb. 1992), pp. 29-30.

1757 Iannotta, Mark W. "Protecting Individual Privacy in the Shadow of a National Data Base: The Need for Data Protection Legislation." *Capital University Law Review,* 17, no. 1 (1987), pp. 117-41.

1758 "If Your Computer Catches a Virus on Friday the 13th, Who You Gonna Call? John McAfee." *People Weekly,* 32, no. 16 (16 Oct. 1989), p. 77.

1759 Ignatin, Gary R. "Let the Hackers Hack: Allowing the Reverse Engineering of Copyrighted Computer Programs to Achieve Compatibility." *University of Pennsylvania Law Review,* 140, no. 5 (May 1992), pp. 1999-2050.

1760 Iida, Jeanne. "Growing Number of Viruses Seen as Danger to Bank Data." *American Banker,* 157, no. 41 (2 Mar. 1992), p. 3.

1761 "Illegal Copying of Software Is Termed Felony in Bill." *The Wall Street Journal,* 220, no. 73 (12 Oct. 1992), p. B8.

1762 "I'm OK; You Could Have a Virus." *Modern Office Technology,* 34, no. 1 (Jan. 1989), pp. 44-45.

1763 "Improving the International Framework for the Protection of Computer Software." *University of Pittsburgh Law Review,* 48, no. 4 (Summer 1987), pp. 1151-84.

1764 "Information on Perot Supporters Is Erased." *The New York Times,* 141, no. 48993 (10 June 1992), p. A20.

1765 Ingram, Jeffrey L. "Intellectual Property - Copyright Law - 'Look and Feel' in Copyright Infringement Actions for Nonliteral Elements of Computer Software. *Lotus Development Corp. v. Paperback Software International,* 740 F. Supp. 37." *Cumberland Law Review,* 22, no. 1 (1991-92), pp. 135-48.

1766 "Intel Sues AMD for Infringement of Microcode and 'Control' Program; Some AMD Antitrust Allegations Against Intel Dismissed as Time-Barred." *The Computer Lawyer,* 9, no. 2 (Feb. 1992), p. 36.

1767 "Intel v. NEC: Does Copyright Protect Microcode?" *Software Protection,* 4, no. 4 (Sept. 1985), p. 1.

1768 "Intel v. NEC Decision Clarifies Several Important Issues." *Software Protection,* 7, no. 10 (Mar. 1989), p. 1.

1769 "Intellectual Property and Innovation." *Software Protection,* 5, no. 2 (July 1986), pp. 13-14.

1770 "The Intellectual Property Protection of Computer Programs." *Software Protection,* 4, no. 1 (June 1985), pp. 8-12.

1771 "Intentionality for Purposes of Insurance Coverage Not Amenable to Summary Disposition and Coverage for Personal Injury Includes Copyright Infringement." *The Computer Lawyer*, 8, no. 1 (Jan. 1991), pp. 33-34.

1772 "Interim Chip Protection Authority Extended." *The Computer Lawyer*, 8, no. 8 (Aug. 1991), p. 38.

1773 "International Business Machines Corporation vs. Fujitsu Limited. Case No. 13T-117-0636-85." *Software Protection*, 6, no. 6 (Nov. 1987), pp. 11-19.

1774 "International Legal Protection for Software." *Software Protection*, 8, no. 9 (Feb. 1990), pp. 1-11.

1775 "International Legal Protection for Software - 1991 Update." *Software Protection*, 9, no. 8 (Jan. 1991), pp. 1-12.

1776 Intindola, Brendan. "Software and Back-Ups Ease Threat of Virus." *National Underwriter-Property and Casualty/Risk and Benefits Management Edition*, 95, no. 34 (26 Aug. 1991), pp. 9, 40.

1777 Irwin, Stephen T. "What Corporate Users Should Know About Data Network Security." *Telecommunications*, 25, no. 5 (May 1991), pp. 49-51.

1778 "Is Computer Hacking a Crime?" *Harper's*, 280, no. 1678 (Mar. 1990), pp. 45-57.

1779 Ishizumi, Kanji. "Copyright Protection of Computer Programs and Semi-Conductors in Japan." *International Business Lawyer*, 15, no. 4-5 (Apr.-May 1987), pp. 207-11.

1780 Ishizumi, Kanji. "Copyright Protection of Computer Programs and Semiconductors in Japan." *Software Law Journal*, 2, no. 3 (Summer 1988), pp. 305-18.

1781 Jacobs, Michael A. "Copyright and Compatibility." *Jurimetrics Journal*, 30, no. 1 (Fall 1989), pp. 91-106.

1782 Jamieson, Rodger, and Graham Low. "Security and Control Issues in Local Area Network Design." *Computers and Security*, 8, no. 4 (June 1989), pp. 305-16.

1783 Jander, Mary. "The Naked Network." *Computer Decisions*, 21, no. 4 (Apr. 1989), pp. 39-42.

1784 "Japan Stops Fighting and Switches to Copyright Protection." *Software Protection*, 3, no. 12 (May 1985), pp. 5-6.

1785 "Japanese Patent Statutes Do Not Provide for Agent-Client Privilege." *The Computer Lawyer*, 9, no. 6 (June 1992), pp. 36-37.

1786 Jarett, Stacy L. "Joint Ownership of Computer Software Copyright: A Solution to the Work for Hire Dilemma." *University of Pennsylvania Law Review*, 137, no. 4 (Apr. 1989), pp. 1251-79.

1787 Jaspin, Elliot, and Mark Sableman. "News Media Access to Computer Records: Updating Information Laws in the Electronic Age." *Saint Louis University Law Journal,* 36, no. 2 (Winter 1991), pp. 349-407.

1788 Jehoram, Herman Cohen. "From Copyright Law to Information Law." *Journal of the Copyright Society of the U.S.A.,* 34 (Oct. 1986-July 1987), pp. 380-88.

1789 Jehoram, Herman Cohen. "Some Curious Problems Caused by Semiconductor Chip Protection: A European View." *Journal of the Copyright Society of the U.S.A.,* 36 (1989), pp. 295-99.

1790 Jenero, Kenneth A., and Lynne D. Mapes-Riordan. "Electronic Monitoring of Employees and the Elusive 'Right to Privacy.'" *Employee Relations Law Journal,* 18, no. 1 (Summer 1992), pp. 71-102.

1791 Jenish, D'Arcy. "A 'Terrorist' Virus: Michelangelo Stirs Fears of Future Shocks." *Maclean's,* 105, no. 11 (16 Mar. 1992), pp. 48, 50-51.

1792 Jenkins, Jolyon. "Hacked to Pieces." *New Statesman and Society,* 3, no. 87 (9 Feb. 1990), p. 27.

1793 Jensen, Eric C. "An Electronic Soapbox: Computer Bulletin Boards and the First Amendment." *Federal Communications Law Journal,* 39, no. 3 (Oct. 1987), pp. 217-58.

1794 Jensen, Mary Brandt. "The Preemption of Shrink Wrap Licenses in the Wake of *Vault Corp. v. Quaid Software Ltd.*" *Computer/Law Journal,* 8, no. 2 (Spring 1988), pp. 157-69.

1795 Jeong, Young-Cheol, and Yoong Neung Kee. "Protection and Licensing of Software in Korea." *The Computer Lawyer,* 8, no. 7 (July 1991), pp. 25-35.

1796 Jerrard, Donald G. "Latest Developments in the Computer and Software Industry in Europe." *Software Protection,* 9, no. 6-7 (Nov.-Dec. 1990), pp. 3-9.

1797 Jobusch, David L., and Arthur E. Oldehoeft. "A Survey of Password Mechanisms: Weaknesses and Potential Improvements. Part 1." *Computers and Security,* 8, no. 7 (Nov. 1989), pp. 587-604.

1798 Jobusch, David L., and Arthur E. Oldehoeft. "A Survey of Password Mechanisms: Weaknesses and Potential Improvements. Part 2." *Computers and Security,* 8, no. 8 (Dec. 1989), pp. 675-89.

1799 Johansen, Dag. "*Lotus Development v. Paperback Software*: The Overextension of Copyright Protection to Functional Aspects of Computer Software." *Hastings Communications and Entertainment Law Journal,* 14, no. 2 (Winter 1992), pp. 271-94.

1800 Johnson, Bradley. "Michelangelo's Revenge." *Advertising Age,* 63, no. 10 (9 Mar. 1992), p. 50.

1801 Johnson, Brian. "An Analysis of the Copyrightability of the 'Look and Feel' of a Computer Program: *Lotus v. Paperback Software.*" *Ohio State Law Journal*, 52, no. 3 (1991), pp. 947-90.

1802 Johnson, David R. "Electronic Communications Privacy: Good Sysops Should Build Good Fences." *The Computer Lawyer*, 6, no. 1 (Jan. 1989), pp. 26-31.

1803 Johnson, Dawn E. "Computer Software: Enforceable Protection Versus the Free Use of Ideas." *Western State University Law Review*, 17, no. 2 (Spring 1990), pp. 373-414.

1804 Johnson, Deborah G. "Should Computer Programs Be Owned?" *Metaphilosophy*, 16, no. 4 (Oct. 1985), pp. 276-88.

1805 Johnson, Gregory L. "Electronic Contracts: Are They Enforceable Under Article 2 of the U. C. C.?" *Software Law Journal*, 4, no. 2 (Apr. 1991), pp. 247-69.

1806 Johnson, Tom. "Protecting Privacy in the Face of Technology." *Risk Management*, 39, no. 5 (May 1992), p. 88.

1807 Johnson, Virginia. "Copyright Protection for Computer Flow Logic and Algorithms." *Computer/Law Journal*, 5, no. 2 (Fall 1984), pp. 257-85.

1808 Johnson-Laird, Andrew. "Reverse Engineering of Software: Separating Legal Mythology from Actual Technology." *Software Law Journal*, 5, no. 2 (Apr. 1992), pp. 331-54.

1809 Johnson-Laird, Andy. "Neural Networks: The Next Intellectual Property Nightmare?" *The Computer Lawyer*, 7, no. 3 (Mar. 1990), pp. 7-16.

1810 Johnston, Ronald L. "The *IBM-Fujitsu* Arbitration Revisited - A Case Study in Effective ADR." *The Computer Lawyer*, 7, no. 5 (May 1990), pp. 13-17.

1811 Johnston, Ronald L., and Allen R. Grogan. "Copyright Protection for Command Driven Interfaces." *The Computer Lawyer*, 8, no. 6 (June 1991), pp. 1-12.

1812 "Joint Ventures in the Semiconductor Industry." *Computer/Law Journal*, 10, no. 4 (Dec. 1990), pp. 581-602.

1813 Jones, David C. "Harsh Computer Virus Penalties Proposed." *National Underwriter-Property and Casualty/Risk and Benefits Management Edition*, 93, no. 24 (12 June 1989), pp. 6, 41.

1814 Jones, David C. "Insurers Brace for Computer Virus." *National Underwriter-Property and Casualty/Risk and Benefits Management Edition*, 96, no. 9 (2 Mar. 1992), pp. 3, 20.

1815 Jones, David C. "Michelangelo Computer Virus Time Bomb a Dud." *National Underwriter-Property and Casualty/Risk and Benefits Management Edition*, 96, no. 11 (16 Mar. 1992), p. 5.

1816 Jones, Laurie Ganong. "Computer Viruses: Threat or Media Hype?" *The EDP Auditor Journal*, 3 (1988), pp. 25-32.

1817 Jordahl, Gregory. "The Computer Virus Menace: PC Users Are Learning the Hard Way That Computer Vandalism Is More Than Just Media Hype." *Insurance Review*, 51, no. 1 (Jan. 1990), pp. 41-44.

1818 Jordan, Dawn. "Software Piracy: The United States Needs to Utilize the Protection Provided by the Berne Convention in the Pacific Rim." *Emory Journal of International Dispute Resolution*, 3, no. 1 (Fall 1988), pp. 133-55.

1819 Jordan, Richard A. "On the Scope of Protection for Computer Programs Under Copyright." *AIPLA Quarterly Journal*, 17, no. 3 (1989), pp. 199-214.

1820 Joseph, Jonathan. "Computer Contract Challenges." *Computer/Law Journal*, 5, no. 3 (Winter 1985), pp. 379-91.

1821 Joyce, Edward J. "Software Viruses: Pc Health Enemy Number One." *Datamation*, 34, no. 20 (15 Oct. 1988), pp. 27-28, 30.

1822 Joyce, Jennifer M. "The Battle Against Piracy: Hard Times for Software." *St. Louis University Law Journal*, 34, no. 2 (Winter 1990), pp. 325-43.

1823 Juceam, Michael S. "Protection of Computer Software — Legal, Commercial and Technical Methods — Part 1." *Software Protection*, 3, no. 6 (Nov. 1984), pp. 1-11.

1824 Juceam, Michael S. "Protection of Computer Software — Legal, Commercial and Technical Methods — Part 2." *Software Protection*, 3, no. 7 (Dec. 1984), pp. 1-8.

1825 "Judge Rules in Favor of Lotus in Suit Against Borland." *The Computer Lawyer*, 9, no. 9 (Sept. 1992), pp. 31-32.

1826 "Judgment to Be Entered Against Mosaic." *The Computer Lawyer*, 8, no. 3 (Mar. 1991), p. 27.

1827 Jung, William F. "Detecting and Preventing Computer Crime in the Office Setting." *Florida Bar Journal*, 65, no. 11 (Dec. 1991), pp. 50-51.

1828 Jurkat, M. Alexander. "Computer Crime Legislation: Survey and Analysis." *1986 Annual Survey of American Law*, 2 (1986), pp. 511-44.

1829 "Jury Award Affirmed for Employee Who Was Forced to Destroy Software." *The Computer Lawyer*, 9, no. 2 (Feb. 1992), pp. 35-36.

1830 "Jury Awards $3.5 Million for Hayes Modem Infringement." *The Computer Lawyer*, 8, no. 3 (Mar. 1991), p. 27.

1831 "Jury Decides Intel/AMD 287 Suit." *The Computer Lawyer*, 9, no. 7 (July 1992), p. 37.

1832 "Jury Finds Infringement Based on Literal Code Copying and Structural Similarity of Databases." *The Computer Lawyer*, 8, no. 1 (Jan. 1991), p. 22.

1833 "Justice Department Letter." *Software Protection*, 4, no. 8 (Jan. 1986), pp. 2-4.

1834 "KLH Agrees Not to Distribute GeoWorks' Ensemble." *The Computer Lawyer*, 9, no. 11 (Nov. 1992), p. 25.

1835 Kagan, Daniel. "Locking Up Data." *Omni*, 6, no. 6 (Mar. 1984), pp. 28, 30.

1836 Kahin, Brian. "The Software Patent Crisis." *Technology Review*, 93, no. 3 (Apr. 1990), pp. 52-58.

1837 Kahin, Brian. "Software Patents: Franchising the Information Infrastructure." *Change*, 21, no. 3 (May-June 1989), pp. 24-25.

1838 Kalinka, Edward M., Jeffery M. Brinka, and Gregory J. Parry. "Protecting Software in the Scale of Equipment from Reverse Engineering." *Michigan Bar Journal*, 69, no. 6 (June 1990), pp. 564-67.

1839 Kane, Dan. "'Sorcerer's Apprentice' Meets Less Benign Fate." *The National Law Journal*, 12, no. 22 (5 Feb. 1990), p. 8.

1840 Kang, Peter Heeseok. "Canada, Copyright, Computers: Impact and Analysis in an International Perspective or from Gutenberg to Uruguay: Protecting the Soul of a New Machine." *Computer/Law Journal*, 10, no. 3 (Oct. 1990), pp. 265-334.

1841 "Kansas Amends Computer Crime Statute." *The Computer Lawyer*, 9, no. 8 (Aug. 1992), p. 37.

1842 Kaplan, James M., and Bob Evart. "Protecting Information Assets: Antivirus Software." *Internal Auditor*, 48, no. 4 (Aug. 1991), pp. 15-19.

1843 Kapor, Mitch. "Litigation vs. Innovation." *Byte*, 15, no. 9 (Sept. 1990), p. 520.

1844 Kapor, Mitchell. "Civil Liberties in Cyberspace: When Does Hacking Turn from an Exercise of Civil Liberties Into a Crime?" *Scientific American*, 265, no. 3 (Sept. 1991), pp. 158-60, 162-64.

1845 Kapor, Mitchell. "Computer Spies." *Forbes*, 150, no. 11 (9 Nov. 1992), p. 288.

1846 Kapor, Mitchell. "Piracy and Software Protection." *Creative Computing*, 10, no. 11 (Nov. 1984), pp. 236, 239.

1847 Kappel, Cary S. "Copyright Protection of SSO: Replete with Internal Deficiencies and Practical Dangers." *Fordham Law Review*, 59, no. 4 (Mar. 1991), pp. 699-717.

1848 Karam, Ronald E. "Countervailing Considerations." *The Journal of Law and Technology,* 2, no. 1 (Winter 1987), pp. 25-34.

1849 Karger, Paul A. "Authentication and Discretionary Access Control in Computer Networks." *Computers and Security,* 5 (1986), pp. 314-24.

1850 Karjala, Dennis S. "Copyright and Misappropriation." *University of Dayton Law Review,* 17, no. 3 (Spring 1992), pp. 885-942.

1851 Karjala, Dennis S. "Copyright, Computer Software, and the New Protectionism." *Jurimetrics Journal,* 28, no. 1 (Fall 1987), pp. 33-96.

1852 Karjala, Dennis S. "Japanese Courts Interpret the 'Algorithm' Limitation on the Copyright Protection of Computer Programs." *Jurimetrics Journal,* 31, no. 2 (Winter 1991), pp. 233-45.

1853 Karjala, Dennis S. "Lessons from the Computer Software Protection Debate in Japan." *Arizona State Law Journal,* 1984, no. 1 (1984), pp. 53-82.

1854 Karjala, Dennis S. "The Protection of Operating Software Under Japanese Copyright Law." *Jurimetrics Journal,* 29, no. 1 (Fall 1988), pp. 43-66.

1855 Karjala, Dennis S. "United States Adherence to the Berne Convention and Copyright Protection of Information-Based Technologies." *Jurimetrics Journal,* 28, no. 2 (Winter 1988), pp. 147-52.

1856 Karol, Michael. "ATypI Aims to End Font Piracy." *Graphic Arts Monthly,* 64, no. 10 (Oct. 1992), p. 115.

1857 Kastenmeier, Robert W. "The 1989 Horace S. Manges Lecture — 'Copyright in an Era of Technological Change: A Political Perspective.'" *Columbia-VLA Journal of Law and the Arts,* 14, no. 1 (Fall 1989), pp. 1-24.

1858 Kastenmeier, Robert W., and David Beier. "International Trade and Intellectual Property: Promise, Risks, and Reality." *Vanderbilt Journal of Transnational Law,* 22, no. 2 (1989), pp. 285-307.

1859 Kastenmeier, Robert W., and Michael J. Remington. "The Semiconductor Chip Protection Act of 1984: A Swamp or Firm Ground?" *Minnesota Law Review,* 70, no. 2 (Dec. 1985), pp. 417-70. (A "slight variation" of this article was published under the same title in *Journal of the Copyright Society of the U.S.A.,* 33, (Oct. 1985-July 1986), pp. 110-61.)

1860 Katsh, Ethan, and Janet Rifkin. "The New Media and a New Model of Conflict Resolution: Copying, Copyright, and Creating." *Notre Dame Journal of Law, Ethics and Public Policy,* 6, no. 1 (1992), pp. 49-74.

1861 Katz, James E. "Telecommunications and Computers: Whither Privacy Policy?" *Society,* 25, no. 1 (Nov.-Dec. 1987), pp. 81-86.

1862 Katz, Ronald S. "Independent Computer Maintainers Win Antitrust Verdicts Against Two Computer Manufacturers." *The Computer Lawyer,* 8, no. 6 (June 1991), pp. 13-16.

1863 Kauffman, Susan. "Outwitting the Hackers." *Nation's Business,* 77, no. 9 (Sept. 1989), p. 17.

1864 Kaufman, Marjorie Hope. *"Pearl Systems,* Functionality, Protection for Structure, and the Boundaries of Copyright Protection: An Ad Hoc Forum." *The Computer Lawyer,* 6, no. 1 (Jan. 1989), pp. 1-4.

1865 Kaufman, Page M. "The Enforceability of State 'Shrink-Wrap' License Statutes in Light of *Vault Corp. v. Quaid Software, Ltd."* *Cornell Law Review,* 74, no. 1 (Nov. 1988), pp. 222-44.

1866 Kearney, Kerry A. "Computer Dissatisfaction: Should Tort Remedies Be Permitted Or Does the U.C.C. Still Govern?" *The Journal of Law and Commerce,* 7 (1987), pp. 243-62.

1867 Keating, William J. "Copyright Protection and the Information Explosion." *Dickinson Law Review,* 88, no. 2 (Winter 1984), pp. 268-78.

1868 Keays, Anne C. "Software Trade Secret Protection." *Software Law Journal,* 4, no. 4 (Dec. 1991), pp. 577-95.

1869 Keefe, T. F., W. T. Tsai, and M. B. Thuraisingham. "SODA: A Secure Object-Oriented Database System." *Computers and Security,* 8, no. 6 (Oct. 1989), pp. 517-33.

1870 Keenan, Thomas P. "Emerging Vulnerabilities in Office Automation Security." *Computers and Security,* 8, no. 3 (May 1989), pp. 223-27.

1871 Kehoe, Louise. "Physical Traits." *The Banker,* 139, no. 766 (Dec. 1989), p. 78.

1872 Kehoe, Louise. "Terminal Virus." *The Banker,* 139, no. 764 (Oct. 1989), p. 118.

1873 Kelman, Alistair. "Latent Exemption Clause Problems in UK Computer Contracts." *International Business Lawyer,* 15, no. 5 (May 1987), pp. 211-12.

1874 Kelsey, David. "Computer Ethics: An Overview of the Issues." *Ethics: Easier Said Than Done,* 1991, no. 15 (1991), pp. 330-33.

1875 Kemp, Deborah. "Limitations Upon the Software Producer's Rights: *Vault Corp. v. Quaid Software Ltd."* *Rutgers Computer and Technology Law Journal,* 16, no. 1 (1990), pp. 85-127.

1876 Kemp, Deborah. "Mass Marketed Software: The Legality of the *Form* License Agreement." *Intellectual Property Law Review 1989,* 1989, no. 3 (1989), pp. 515-56. (First published in *Louisiana Law Review,* 48, no. 1 [Sept. 1987], pp. 87-128.)

1877 Kemp, Deborah. "Trade Secret and Copyright Protection for Mass Marketed Computer Programs." *Commercial Law Journal,* 90, no. 10 (Dec. 1985), pp. 625-31.

1878 Kemp, Norman. "Software Rights Affirmed." *Datamation,* 30, no. 12 (1 Aug. 1984), p. 54.

1879 Kendall, Megan A. *"AFSCME v. County of Cook*: Access to Information Beyond Reach as Computer Tape Lengthens Bureaucratic Red Tape." *Software Law Journal,* 3, no. 4 (Apr. 1990), pp. 775-91.

1880 Kenfield, Dexter L. "Remedies in Software Copyright Cases." *Computer/Law Journal,* 6, no. 1 (Summer 1985), pp. 1-33.

1881 Kenfield, Dexter L., and Eric G. Woodbury. "Import/Customs Regulation of Computer Technology." *North Carolina Journal of International Law and Commercial Regulation,* 10 (1985), pp. 609-15.

1882 Kennedy, David. "Chipping Away at Electronic Piracy." *Technology Review,* 88, no. 4 (May-June 1985), pp. 60-62.

1883 Kenner, Hugh. "Stomping the Nasties." *Byte,* 15, no. 12 (Nov. 1990), pp. 466-67.

1884 Kent, Marianne L. "Computers and the Law." *Solicitors' Journal,* 129, no. 16 (19 Apr. 1985), pp. 279-80.

1885 Kenyon, David M. "The Computer Contagion." *ABA Journal,* 75 (June 1989), pp. 116-17.

1886 Keon, Jim. "Intellectual Property Protection in Canada: The Technology Challenge." *Canada-United States Law Journal,* 11 (1986), pp. 27-50.

1887 Keplinger, Michael S. "Authorship in the Information Age: Protection for Computer Programs Under the Berne and Universal Copyright Conventions." *Software Law Journal,* 1, no. 2 (Winter 1986), pp. 167-86.

1888 Keplinger, Michael S. "International Protection for Computer Programs." *Software Law Journal,* 4, no. 1 (Oct. 1990), pp. 15-50.

1889 Keplinger, Michael S. "Overview of the United States Intellectual Property System: Current Issues." *Canada-United States Law Journal,* 11 (1986), pp. 51-64.

1890 Kernochan, John M. "Some Observations on the Protection of Semiconductor Chip Design." *Rutgers Computer and Technology Law Journal,* 13, no. 2 (1987), pp. 287-95.

1891 Kerr, Susan. "A Secret No More." *Datamation,* 35, no. 13 (1 July 1989), pp. 53-55.

1892 Kerr, Susan. "Using AI to Improve Security." *Datamation,* 36, no. 3 (1 Feb. 1990), pp. 57-58, 60.

1893 Kesler, Christopher A. *"Galoob v. Nintendo*: Derivative Works, Fair Use and Section 117 in the Realm of Computer Program Enhancements." *Golden Gate University Law Review,* 22, no. 2 (Spring 1992), pp. 489-513.

1894 Keustermans, Jozef A. "Semiconductor Chip Protection in the European Community: The Council Directive on the Legal Protection of Topographies of Semiconductor Products." *The Computer Lawyer*, 4, no. 2 (Feb. 1987), pp. 17-22.

1895 Kevlin, Mary L. "Computer Cases—Bound for the Supreme Court?" *New York Law Journal*, 208, no. 22 (31 July 1992), pp. 3, 29.

1896 Kidwell, John A. "Software and Semiconductors: Why Are We Confused?" *Minnesota Law Review*, 70, no. 2 (Dec. 1985), pp. 533-77.

1897 Kienast, Peter J. "Protection of Computer Software Against Third Parties in Switzerland." *Software Law Journal*, 1, no. 3 (Spring-Summer 1986), pp. 397-406.

1898 Kim, Yong Hak. "New Information Technology and Copyright Law Principles in the Information Age." *ILSA Journal of International Law*, 11 (1987), pp. 113-47.

1899 King, Harriet. "Microsoft Nails Some Pirates: An International Far Eastern Chase Catches Counterfeiters." *The New York Times*, 141, no. 48962 (10 May 1992), p. F7.

1900 King, Judith. "X.400 Security." *Computers and Security*, 11, no. 8 (Dec. 1992), pp. 707-10.

1901 Kingery, John C. "The U.S.-Japan Semiconductor Arrangement and the GATT: Operating in a Legal Vacuum." *Stanford Journal of International Law*, 25 (Spring 1989), pp. 467-97.

1902 Kinnon, Andrew, and Robert Davis. "Audit and Security Implications of Electronic Funds Transfer." *Computers and Security*, 5, no. 1 (Mar. 1986), pp. 17-23.

1903 Kirby, Michael. "Information Security—OECD Initiatives." *Journal of Law and Information Science*, 3, no. 1 (1992), pp. 25-46.

1904 Kirby, Michael. "Legal and Ethical Issues in Artificial Intelligence." *Law Institute Journal*, 63, no. 6 (June 1989), pp. 513-15.

1905 Kirby, Michael. "Legal Aspects of Transborder Data Flows." *Computer/Law Journal*, 11, no. 2 (Apr. 1991), pp. 233-45.

1906 Kirby, Michael. "Toronto Statement on the International Legal Vulnerability of Financial Information." *Computer/Law Journal*, 11, no. 1 (Feb. 1991), pp. 75-96.

1907 Kirk, Robert. "Data Protection Update." *International Business Lawyer*, 14, no. 2-4 (Feb.-Apr. 1986), pp. 89-92.

1908 Kirvan, Paul. "Is a Hacker Hovering in Your Horoscope?" *Communications News*, 29, no. 11 (Nov. 1992), p. 48.

1909 Kleiman, Matthew N. "The Right to Financial Privacy Versus Computerized Law Enforcement: A New Fight in an Old Battle." *Northwestern University Law Review,* 86, no. 4 (Summer 1992), pp. 1169-228.

1910 Kline, Michael J. "Requiring an Election of Protection for Patentable/Copyrightable Computer Programs." *Computer/Law Journal,* 6, no. 4 (Spring 1986), pp. 607-75. (First published in *Journal of the Patent and Trademark Office Society,* 67, no. 6 [June 1985], pp. 280-314.)

1911 Klopp, Charlotte. "Software Vendors Capitalize on Security Needs." *Computers and Security,* 9, no. 1 (Feb. 1990), pp. 33-35.

1912 Kluth, Daniel J. "The Computer Virus Threat: A Survey of Current Criminal Statutes." *Hamline Law Review,* 13, no. 2 (Spring 1990), pp. 297-312.

1913 Kochanski, Martin. "How Safe Is It?" *Byte,* 14, no. 6 (June 1989), pp. 257-64.

1914 Kolata, Gina. "NSA to Provide Secret Codes." *Science,* 230, no. 4721 (4 Oct. 1985), pp. 45-46.

1915 Kopf, Lisa. "Debugging the Computer Contract: A Preventive Strategy Based on a Review of Vendor Liability." *Uniform Commercial Code Law Journal,* 20, no. 2 (Fall 1987), pp. 130-58.

1916 Kostal, Susan. "Apple Alters Strategy in Its Copyright Case." *Los Angeles Daily Journal* (28 May 1991), p. 4.

1917 Kostal, Susan. "Apple Decision Cuts the Core of 'Look and Feel.'" *Los Angeles Daily Journal,* 105, no. 74 (16 Apr. 1992), pp. 1, 18.

1918 Kostal, Susan. "Business Booms for Software Police." *Los Angeles Daily Journal* (9 Oct. 1991), p. 7.

1919 Kostal, Susan. "Copyright Ruling Provokes Dissent." *Los Angeles Daily Journal,* 105, no. 97 (19 May 1992), p. II-1.

1920 Kostal, Susan. "Decision Explains 'Look and Feel.'" *Los Angeles Daily Journal,* 105, no. 68 (8 Apr. 1992), p. 18.

1921 Kostal, Susan. "'Electronic Joyriding' Raises Legal Issues." *Los Angeles Daily Law Journal* (19 June 1991), p. 7.

1922 Kostal, Susan. "'Feist' Fallout Has Lawyers Searching." *Los Angeles Daily Journal* (6 Nov. 1991), p. 7.

1923 Kostal, Susan. "Firms in the Chips; Judge Guts Patent." *Los Angeles Daily Journal* (18 Oct. 1991), p. 9.

1924 Kostal, Susan. "Firms Ready to Crash Michelangelo's Birthday." *Los Angeles Daily Journal,* 105, no. 45 (5 Mar. 1992), pp. 1, 10.

1925 Kostal, Susan. "Firms Wage Battle by Press Release." *Los Angeles Daily Journal,* 105, no. 107 (3 June 1992), p. 7.

1926 Kostal, Susan. "'Look and Feel' Decision Stands." *Los Angeles Daily Journal*, 105, no. 197 (9 Oct. 1992), p. 3.

1927 Kostal, Susan. "Professors Target Copyright Ruling on Software: Amicus Brief Asks Federal Judge in Boston to Abandon Earlier Opinion and Follow Traditional Standard." *Los Angeles Daily Journal* (7 Oct. 1991), p. B1.

1928 Kostal, Susan. "2nd Circuit Speaks Up on Compatibility." *Los Angeles Daily Journal*, 105, no. 127 (1 July 1992), p. 7.

1929 Kostal, Susan. "Software Protection Discussed: Report Looks Ahead." *Los Angeles Daily Journal*, 105, no. 92 (12 May 1992), p. 8.

1930 Kostal, Susan. "State Seems Left Out of Software Report." *Los Angeles Daily Journal*, 105, no. 98 (20 May 1992), p. 7.

1931 Knight, Peter. "Computer Products, Parallel Imports and Copyright in Australia and New Zealand." *Software Law Journal*, 5, no. 1 (Feb. 1992), pp. 97-126.

1932 Kovach, Karen S. "Computer Software Design: User Interface - Idea or Expression?" *University of Cincinnati Law Review*, 60, no. 1 (Summer 1991), pp. 161-90.

1933 Kramer, Matt. "Fighting Back Against Feds' BBS Crackdown." *PC Week*, 7, no. 29 (23 July 1990), p. 53.

1934 Kramsky, Elliott N. "The Semiconductor Chip Protection Act." *Software Protection*, 3, no. 11 (Apr. 1985), pp. 1-10.

1935 Kratofil, Bruce. "The PC Corner: Computer Viruses." *Business Economics*, 25, no. 1 (Jan. 1990), pp. 52-54.

1936 Kravetz, Paul I. "Copyright Protection of Screen Displays After *Lotus Development Corporation v. Paperback Software International.*" *DePaul Business Law Journal*, 4, no. 2 (Spring-Summer 1992), pp. 485-518.

1937 Kreimer, Seth F. "Sunlight, Secrets, and Scarlet Letters: The Tension Between Privacy and Disclosure in Constitutional Law." *University of Pennsylvania Law Review*, 140, no. 1 (Nov. 1991), pp. 1-147.

1938 Kreiss, Robert A. "Copyright Symposium Part I: Copyright Protection for Computer Databases, CD-ROMs and Factual Compilations: Introduction." *University of Dayton Law Review*, 17, no. 2 (Winter 1992), pp. 323-30.

1939 Kreiss, Robert A. "Copyright Symposium Part II: Copyright Protection for Computer Databases, CD-ROMs and Factual Compilations: Introduction." *University of Dayton Law Review*, 17, no. 3 (Spring 1992), pp. 731-35.

1940 Kreiss, Robert A. "Section 117 of the Copyright Act." *Brigham Young University Law Review*, 1991, no. 4 (1991), pp. 1497-546.

1941 Kreiss, Robert A. "Ten Theories for Hiring Parties Who Want to Own Works Created or Invented by Independent Contractors." *The Computer Lawyer*, 8, no. 5 (May 1991), pp. 10-21.

1942 Krema, James F. "Computer Crime: What It Is and How to Counter It." *The Office*, 103, no. 3 (Mar. 1986), pp. 95-96.

1943 Kretschmer, Marc T. "Copyright Protection for Software Architecture: Just Say No!" *Columbia Business Law Review*, 1988, no. 3 (1988), pp. 823-53.

1944 Krieger, Sibylle I. "*Apple v. Wombat*: Australian Developments in the Copyright Protection of Computer Software." *Art and the Law*, 9, no. 4 (1985), pp. 455-76.

1945 Krivulka, Thomas. "Constitutional Law—Limits of Privacy Expectations Within Seized Electronic Data—*Commonwealth v. Copenhefer*, 587 A.2d 1353 (Pa. 1991)." *Temple Law Review*, 65, no. 2 (Summer 1992), pp. 645-61.

1946 Krohn, Nico. "Novell Ships Its Second Patch for NetWare Hole." *PC Week*, 9, no. 47 (23 Nov. 1992), p. 6.

1947 Krohn, Nico. "Novell Signs Pact with Intel for In-House Virus Protection." *PC Week*, 9, no. 18 (4 May 1992), pp. 47, 56.

1948 Kruys, Jan P. "Security of Open Systems." *Computers and Security*, 8, no. 2 (Apr. 1989), pp. 139-47.

1949 Ku, Linlin. "Does Software Need More Copyright Protection?" *Communications and the Law*, 11, no. 4 (Dec. 1989), pp. 3-23.

1950 Kullby, Laurie Zeeb. "The Copyrightability of Computer Program Screen Displays." *Comm/Ent*, 10, no. 3 (1987-88), pp. 859-84.

1951 Kunen, James S., and S. Avery Brown. "Astronomer Cliff Stoll Stars in the Espionage Game, But for Him Spying Doesn't Really Compute." *People Weekly*, 32, no. 24 (11 Dec. 1989), pp. 118-20.

1952 Kuntz, Mary Ann, and Michael Maingot. "Viruses Are Alive and Well." *CA Magazine*, 122, no. 12 (Dec. 1989), pp. 60-61.

1953 Kutten, L. J. "Enough Already." *Software Protection*, 4, no. 8 (Jan. 1986), pp. 12-14.

1954 Kutten, L. J. "Is It Copyright or Money?" *Software Protection*, 3, no. 12 (May 1985), pp. 6-8.

1955 Kutten, L. J. "Legal Problems of Software Publishing Contracts." *Software Law Journal*, 1, no. 1 (Fall 1985), pp. 1-31.

1956 Kutten, L. J. "Trade Secret Preemption and Use of a Copyright Notice." *Software Protection*, 5, no. 5 (Oct. 1986), pp. 8-9.

1957 Kutten, L. J. "Where to Place the Copyright Notice on Software." *Software Protection*, 5, no. 5 (Oct. 1986), pp. 7-8.

1958 Kutz, Robin K. "Computer Crime in Virginia: A Critical Examination of the Criminal Offenses in the Virginia Computer Crimes Act." *William and Mary Law Review,* 27, no. 4 (Summer 1986), pp. 783-831.

1959 Kwok, Edward C. "An Erroneous Decision or a Ground-Breaking Case? *Pearl Systems v. Competition Electronics, Inc.,* No. 87-6728." *Santa Clara Computer and High Technology Law Journal,* 5, no. 2 (1989), pp. 573-78.

1960 Lacayo, Richard. "Nowhere to Hide: Using Computers, High-tech Gadgets and Mountains of Data, an Army of Snoops Is Assaulting Our Privacy." *Time,* 138, no. 19 (11 Nov. 1991), pp. 34-40.

1961 "Lack of Controversy Ends in Dismissal." *The Computer Lawyer,* 9, no. 10 (Oct. 1992), p. 35.

1962 Ladd, David, and Bruce G. Joseph. "Expanding Computer Software Protection by Limiting the Idea." *The Journal of Law and Technology,* 2, no. 1 (Winter 1987), pp. 5-15.

1963 Lake, William T., John H. Harwood, II, and Thomas P. Olson. "Tampering with Fundamentals: A Critique of Proposed Changes in EC Software Protection." *The Computer Lawyer,* 6, no. 12 (Dec. 1989), pp. 1-10.

1964 Lamberson, John C. "Curbing Computer Virus Infections." *National Underwriter-Property and Casualty/Risk and Benefits Management Edition,* 93, no. 32 (7 Aug. 1989), pp. 9, 20-21.

1965 Lamoree, Paul R. "Expanding Copyrights in Software: The Struggle to Define 'Expression' Begins." *Santa Clara Computer and High-Technology Law Journal,* 4, no. 1 (Jan. 1988), pp. 49-86.

1966 Land, John. "Pitfalls in Registering Software Program Copyrights." *Software Protection,* 10, no. 5 (Oct. 1991), pp. 1-3.

1967 Landever, Arthur R. "Electronic Surveillance, Computers, and the Fourth Amendment—The New Telecommunications Environment Calls for Reexamination of Doctrine." *The University of Toledo Law Review,* 15, no. 2 (Winter 1984), pp. 597-640.

1968 Lang, Charles Victor. "Stolen Bytes: Business Can Bite Back." *Columbia Business Law Review,* 1986, no. 1 (1986), pp. 251-62.

1969 Lang, Marsha. "Trade Secret Protection of Mass-Distributed Software in the Personal Computer Marketplace." *Utah Bar Journal,* 13, no. 7-12 (Fall-Winter 1985), pp. 49-54.

1970 Lang, Wesley M. "The Semiconductor Chip Protection Act: A New Weapon in the War Against Computer Software Piracy." *Utah Law Review,* 1986, no. 2 (1986), pp. 417-38.

1971 Lange, David. "Sensing the Constitution in *Feist.*" *University of Dayton Law Review,* 17, no. 2 (Winter 1992), pp. 367-84.

1972 Laperriere, R., R. Cote, and G. A. LeBel. "The Transborder Flow of Personal Data from Canada: International and Comparative Law Issues." *Jurimetrics*, 32, no. 4 (Summer 1992), pp. 547-69.

1973 LaPolla, Stephanie. "High Tech's Dark Side: Fraud, Forgery, Check Swindles; Scanners, Printers Are Accomplices in Crime." *PC Week*, 9, no. 29 (20 July 1992), p. 23.

1974 Lappa, Karen. "Computer Virus Prescription: 'Safe Computing.'" *Hospitals*, 63, no. 11 (5 June 1989), p. 64.

1975 Larson, Erik. "Crook's Tool: Computers Turn Out to Be Valuable Aid in Employee Crime; Machines Facilitate Stealing, Extortion and Sabotage." *The Wall Street Journal*, 205, no. 9 (14 Jan. 1985), pp. 1, 10.

1976 LaRue, James. "Micro Biology." *Wilson Library Bulletin*, 65, no. 1 (Sept. 1990), pp. 88-89, 133.

1977 "The Last Adventure of Dark Dante?" *Newsweek*, 115, no. 5 (29 Jan. 1990), p. 73.

1978 Lastova, John R., and Gary M. Hoffman. "Patent Protection for Software Gives Businesses Extra Leverage." *The National Law Journal*, 11, no. 42 (26 June 1989), pp. 38-39.

1979 Lathrop, David L. "Perestroika and Its Implications for Computer Security in the U.S.S.R." *Computers and Security*, 9, no. 8 (Dec. 1990), pp. 693-96.

1980 Laurie, Ronald S. "Comment: Use of a 'Levels of Abstraction' Analysis for Computer Programs." *AIPLA Quarterly Journal*, 17, no. 3 (1989), pp. 232-36.

1981 Laurie, Ronald S. "*NEC v. Intel*: Compatibility, Constraints, and Choices." *The Computer Lawyer*, 3, no. 10 (Oct. 1986), pp. 9-17.

1982 Laurie, Ronald S., and Stephen M. Everett. "The Copyrightability of Microcode: Is It Software or Hardware...or Both?" *The Computer Lawyer*, 2, no. 3 (Mar. 1985), pp. 1-11.

1983 Laurie, Samantha. "Embarrassment of Losses." *The Banker*, 141, no. 779 (Jan. 1991), pp. 34-36.

1984 Lautsch, John C. "Justification for Software Protection: Why Be Concerned About Proprietary Protection of Software?" *Software Protection*, 4, no. 3 (Aug. 1985), pp. 1-4.

1985 Lavenue, Lionel M. "*Lotus Development Corp. v. Paperback Software Int'l*: Copyrightability for the User Interface of Computer Software in the United States and the International Realm." *The American University Journal of International Law and Policy*, 7, no. 2 (Winter 1992), pp. 289-343.

1986 "The Law in Computerland." *Canadian Business,* 58, no. 9 (Sept. 1985), pp. 123, 150-51.

1987 "The Law Plods After Computer Crime." *Economist,* 300, no. 7464 (20 Sept. 1986), p. 75.

1988 Law Reform Committee. "The Data Protection Act 1984: Subject Access Provisions." *Journal of the Law Society of Scotland,* 32, no. 10 (Oct. 1987), pp. 378-80.

1989 "Lawmakers Tackle Computer Crime." *Trial,* 20, no. 2 (Feb. 1984), p. 8.

1990 Lawren, Bill. "Breaking and Entering: Did the Government Confiscate Hackers' Rights in Its Raids on Computer Crime?" *Omni,* 13, no. 3 (Dec. 1990), p. 17.

1991 Lawrence, Diane B. "Strict Liability, Computer Software and Medicine: Public Policy at the Crossroads." *Tort and Insurance Law Journal,* 23, no. 1 (Fall 1987), pp. 1-18.

1992 Layne, Richard. "Multiplying Viruses Spawn Growth Market." *American Banker,* 155, no. 149 (1 Aug. 1990), p. 10.

1993 Lazzareschi, Carla. "IBM Virus Not Widespread, Experts Say." *Los Angeles Times* (14 Sept. 1989), pp. IV-3, 5.

1994 Leach, Nicholas N. "Protection of Computers and Computer Software Before the United States International Trade Commission: In Re Certain Personal Computers and Components Thereof." *Georgia Journal of International and Comparative Law,* 15, no. 3 (1985), pp. 627-55.

1995 Leahy, Patrick. "Privacy and Progress." *Computers and Security,* 5 (1986), pp. 347-49.

1996 Leccese, Mark. "Of *Phrack* and Freedom." *Columbia Journalism Review,* 30, no. 4 (Nov.-Dec. 1991), p. 30.

1997 Lederman, Eli. "Criminal Liability for Breach of Confidential Commercial Information." *Emory Law Journal,* 38, no. 4 (Fall 1989), pp. 921-1004.

1998 Ledsinger, Deborah. "Copyright Protection of Object Code Computer Programs: Can Courts Determine Copying?" *Comm/Ent,* 9, no. 2 (1986-87), pp. 255-77.

1999 Lee, J. A. N., and Gerald Segal. "Positive Alternatives to Computer Misuse: A Report of the Proceedings of an ACM Panel on Hacking." *Computers and Security,* 6 (1987), pp. 177-79.

2000 Lee, Mark S. "Prejudgment Asset Freezes Against Software Pirates." *The Computer Lawyer,* 9, no. 10 (Oct. 1992), pp. 22-27.

2001 Lee, Tae Hee. "The Korean Computer Program Protection Act." *Software Protection,* 9, no. 11 (Apr. 1991), pp. 5-6.

2002 Lee, Tae Hee. "Legal Protection for Computer Software: Korea's Careful Progress Toward International Standards." *Law/Technology*, 19, no. 1 (1986), pp. 27-50.

2003 Lee, Tae Hee. "Protection of Software in Korea: Current Remedies, Future Laws and the International Perspective of Korean Policy." *Software Protection*, 4, no. 7 (Dec. 1985), pp. 6-12.

2004 Lefever, Andrew. "Exploitation of Intellectual Property Overseas." *Solicitors Journal*, 132, no. 27 (8 July 1988), pp. 980-81.

2005 Leggett, Ellen L., and Dan R. Gallipeau. "Computer Litigation: Jurors' Perceptions and Reactions." *The Computer Lawyer*, 9, no. 8 (Aug. 1992), pp. 18-21.

2006 Lehman, Bruce A. "Brief Amicus Curiae of the Software Publishers Association." *Software Protection*, 10, no. 9 (Feb. 1992), pp. 3-11.

2007 Leinicke, Linda Marie, W. Max Rexroad, and Jon D. Ward. "Computer Fraud Auditing: It Works." *Internal Auditor*, 47, no. 4 (Aug. 1990), pp. 26-33.

2008 Leland, Clyde. "One for the Law Books: Lexis and Westlaw Battle Over Copyrights." *California Lawyer*, 8, no. 1 (Jan.-Feb. 1988), pp. 22-23.

2009 Lemberg, Jonathan H. "Semiconductor Protection: Foreign Responses to a U.S. Initiative." *Columbia Journal of Transnational Law*, 25, no. 2 (1987), pp. 345-76.

2010 Lemley, Mark A. "The Economic Irrationality of the Patent Misuse Doctrine." *California Law Review*, 78, no. 6 (Dec. 1990), pp. 1599-632.

2011 "Lender/Security Interest Holder Not Liable for Lessor's Allegedly Unreasonable Interference with Proposed Settlement." *The Computer Lawyer*, 9, no. 2 (Feb. 1992), pp. 33-34.

2012 Levary, Reuven R., and Karen K. Duke. "Some Aspects of Potential Disclosure of Confidential Computerized Legal Materials." *Defense Law Journal*, 33, no. 5 (1984), pp. 569-78.

2013 Levenfeld, Barry. "Copyright Protection for Computer Software in Israel." *Computer/Law Journal*, 8, no. 1 (Winter 1987), pp. 23-41.

2014 Levenfeld, Barry. "Israel Amends Copyright Laws to Apply to Computer Software." *Software Protection*, 7, no. 5 (Oct. 1988), pp. 1-7.

2015 Levenfeld, Barry. "'Look and Feel' Comes to Israel: A Critique of *Ahitov* v. *Harpaz*." *Software Protection*, 8, no. 4 (Sept. 1989), pp. 1-7.

2016 Levenfeld, Barry. "A New Proposed Computer Law in Israel." *Software Protection*, 9, no. 2-3 (July-Aug. 1990), pp. 9-22.

2017 Leverett, E. J., Jr., and Brenda F. Powell. "Computer Systems on the Brink of Destruction." *Risk Management*, 36, no. 11 (Nov. 1989), pp. 22-26.

2018 Levy, Lawrence B., and Suzanne Y. Bell. "Software Product Liability: Understanding and Minimizing the Risks." *High Technology Law Journal*, 5, no. 1 (Spring 1990), pp. 1-27.

2019 Levy, Steven M. "Single Copyright Registration for Computer Programs: Outdated Perceptions Byte the Dust." *Brooklyn Law Review*, 54, no. 3 (Fall 1988), pp. 965-90.

2020 Lewis, Denise W. "Apple 'Bytes' Back: Copyrightability of Computer Programs: *Apple Computer, Inc. v. Franklin Computer Corp.*" *University of Bridgeport Law Review*, 5, no. 2 (1984), pp. 363-92.

2021 Lewis, Geoff. "Tougher Medicine May Prevent Computer Viruses." *Business Week*, no. 3118 (7 Aug. 1989), p. 66A.

2022 Lewis, Gerard J., Jr. "Copyright Protection for Purely Factual Compilations Under *Feist Publications, Inc. v. Rural Telephone Service Co.*: How Does *Feist* Protect Electronic Data Bases of Facts?" *Santa Clara Computer and High Technology Law Journal*, 8, no. 1 (May 1992), pp. 169-207.

2023 Lewis, Gerard J., Jr. "*Lotus Development Corp. v. Paperback Software International*: Broad Copyright Protection for User Interfaces Ignores the Software Industry's Trend Toward Standardization." *University of Pittsburgh Law Review*, 52, no. 3 (Spring 1991), pp. 689-722.

2024 Lewis, Mike. "Computer Crime: Theft in Bits and Bytes." *Nation's Business*, 73, no. 2 (Feb. 1985), pp. 57-58.

2025 Lewis, Mike. "Scuttling Software Pirates." *Nation's Business*, 73, no. 3 (Mar. 1985), p. 28.

2026 Lewis, Peter. "Computer Fraud at VW." *Maclean's*, 100, no. 13 (30 Mar. 1987), p. 32.

2027 Lewis, Peter H. "Building a Moat with Software." *The New York Times*, 138 (3 Sept. 1989), p. 7.

2028 Lewis, Peter H. "Friday the 13th: A Virus Is Lurking." *The New York Times*, 139, no. 48017 (8 Oct. 1989), p. F12.

2029 Lewis, Peter H. "Medicine, and Common Sense, for Virus Problems: A Company with No Policy Should Write One; Others Should Enforce Their Rules." *The New York Times*, 141, no. 49004 (21 June 1992), p. 9.

2030 Lewis, Robert M. "Allocation of Loss Due to Fraudulent Wholesale Wire Transfers: Is There a Negligence Action Against a Beneficiary's Bank After Article 4A of the Uniform Commercial Code?" *Michigan Law Review*, 90, no. 8 (Aug. 1992), pp. 2565-611.

2031 Lewyn, Mark. "Hackers: Is a Cure Worse Than the Disease?" *Business Week*, no. 3136 (4 Dec. 1989), pp. 37-38.

2032 Lewyn, Mark. "'Killer' Computer Viruses: An Idea Whose Time Shouldn't Come." *Business Week*, no. 3170 (23 July 1990), p. 30.

2033 Lewyn, Mark, and Evan I. Schwartz. "Why 'The Legion of Doom' Has Little Fear of the Feds: Nailing Computer Hackers Is Proving Harder Than Prosecutors Imagined." *Business Week,* no. 3209 (15 Apr. 1991), p. 31.

2034 Liberman, Adam. "*Apple Computer, Inc. v. Computer Edge Pty. Limited*: Repercussions for the Protection of Computer Software in Australia." *Software Protection,* 2, no. 6 (Feb. 1984), pp. 12-16.

2035 "The Licensing and Protection of Software in Europe: An International Roundtable." *Software Protection,* 4, no. 2 (July 1985), pp. 1-5.

2036 Liebman, Ken, Gary Frischling, and Andre Brunel. "The Shape of Things to Come: Design-Patent Protection for Computers." *The Computer Lawyer,* 9, no. 11 (Nov. 1992), pp. 1-10.

2037 Liebman, Ken, Gary Frischling, and Andre Brunel. "The Shape of Things to Come: Trademark Protection for Computers." *The Computer Lawyer,* 9, no. 12 (Dec. 1992), pp. 1-8.

2038 Lim, Byungkwon. "Protection of Computer Programs Under the Computer Program Protection Law of the Republic of Korea." *Harvard International Law Journal,* 30, no. 1 (Winter 1989), pp. 171-93.

2039 Lin, M. S., and Ross Katchman. "Intellectual Property Protection of Integrated Circuit Design in the Republic of China." *The Computer Lawyer,* 4, no. 4 (Apr. 1987), pp. 19-22.

2040 Lindley, David. "Problems of Security." *Nature,* 340, no. 6231 (27 July 1989), p. 252.

2041 Lingenfelter, David Blair. "Differentiating Idea and Expression in Copyrighted Computer Software: The Tests for Infringement." *The Journal of Law and Commerce,* 6 (1986), pp. 419-41.

2042 Linowes, David F., and Colin Bennett. "Privacy: Its Role in Federal Government Information Policy." *Library Trends,* 35, no. 1 (Summer 1986), pp. 19-42.

2043 Linsalata, Phil. "The Octopus File." *Columbia Journalism Review,* 30, no. 4 (Nov.-Dec. 1991), pp. 76-82.

2044 Liskin, Miriam. "Can You Trust Your Database?" *Personal Computing,* 14, no. 6 (29 June 1990), pp. 129-34.

2045 Liskin, Miriam. "Protecting the Corporate Database." *Personal Computing,* 13, no. 8 (Aug. 1989), pp. 51-54.

2046 "Litigating a Standard." *Personal Computing,* 13, no. 3 (Mar. 1989), p. 73.

2047 "Litigation: Default Judgment Entered for Source Code Destruction; Another Default Judgment Vacated." *The Computer Lawyer,* 9, no. 3 (Mar. 1992), p. 38.

2048 "Litigation: Trade Secrets Case Ends with Consent Injunction." *The Computer Lawyer,* 9, no. 3 (Mar. 1992), pp. 38-39.

2049 Litman, Jessica. "After *Feist.*" *University of Dayton Law Review,* 17, no. 2 (Winter 1992), pp. 607-29.

2050 Litvinov, A. V. "Legal Issues in the Protection of Computer Information." *Soviet Law and Government,* 27, no. 1 (Summer 1988), pp. 86-96.

2051 Liu, Hong, and Jun Wei. "Technology Transfer to China: The Patent System." *Santa Clara Computer and High Technology Law Journal,* 5 (1989), pp. 363-98.

2052 Livingston, Ann, and Leif M. Clark. "Technology Transfers: What If the Other Party Files Bankruptcy?" *St. Mary's Law Journal,* 21, no. 1 (1989), pp. 173-208.

2053 Llewelyn, David. "Computers, Software and International Protection." *Columbia-VLA Journal of Law and the Arts,* 11, no. 1 (Fall 1986), pp. 183-93.

2054 Llewelyn, David, and Harry Small. "Copyright in Computer Software: A Reply." *Solicitors' Journal,* 128, no. 21 (25 May 1984), pp. 358-60.

2055 Lloyd, Ian. "Computer Abuse and the Law." *Law Quarterly Review,* 104 (Apr. 1988), pp. 202-7.

2056 Lloyd, Ian J. "The Data Protection Act - Little Brother Fights Back?" *Modern Law Review,* 48, no. 2 (Mar. 1985), pp. 190-200.

2057 "Lock Up Your Software." *The Economist,* 310, no. 7585 (14 Jan. 1989), pp. 77-78.

2058 Lockhart, Thomas L., and Richard J. McKenna. "Software License Agreements in Light of the UCC and the Convention on the International Sale of Goods." *Michigan Bar Journal,* 70, no. 7 (July 1991), pp. 646-55.

2059 Loewenheim, Ulrich. "Legal Protection for Computer Programs in West Germany." *High Technology Law Journal,* 4, no. 2 (Fall 1989), pp. 187-215.

2060 Long, William J. "The U.S.-Japan Semiconductor Dispute: Implications for U.S. Trade Policy." *Maryland Journal of International Law and Trade,* 13, no. 1 (Fall 1988), pp. 1-37.

2061 "'Look and Feel' as a Copyrightable Element: The Legacy of *Whelan v. Jaslow?* Or, Can Equity in Computer Program Infringement Cases Be Found Instead by the Proper Allocation of Burden of Persuasion?" *Louisiana Law Review,* 51, no. 1 (Sept. 1990), pp. 177-216.

2062 "Look But Don't Touch: Software Companies Battle Over Intellectual Property Rights." *Scientific American,* 261, no. 3 (Sept. 1989), pp. 101-2.

2063 Lopez, Rodrigo, Tom Kristensen, and Hans Prydz. "Database Contamination." *Nature*, 355, no. 6357 (16 Jan. 1992), p. 211.

2064 Losey, Ralph C. "Legal Protection of Computer Databases." *Florida Bar Journal*, 65, no. 9 (Oct. 1991), pp. 80-85.

2065 "Lotus Denied 'Visual Arts' Copyright." *The Computer Lawyer*, 4, no. 4 (Apr. 1987), p. 24.

2066 *"Lotus* Leaves Software Copyright in a Dream State: Defining Protection of the User Interface Following *Lotus Development Corp. v. Paperback Software International." Loyola of Los Angeles Law Review*, 24, no. 4 (June 1991), pp. 1301-32.

2067 "Lotus Sues Software 'Clone' Vendors." *Software Protection*, 6, no. 1 (June 1987), pp. 8-15.

2068 "Lotus Sues to Protect 'Look and Feel' of Software." *The Computer Lawyer*, 4, no. 2 (Feb. 1987), p. 26.

2069 "Lotus Takes the Offensive." *Personal Computing*, 11, no. 3 (Mar. 1987), pp. 29-30.

2070 Louderback, Jim. "Stamp Out Michelangelo Virus with an Ounce of Prevention." *PC Week*, 9, no. 8 (24 Feb. 1992), p. 16.

2071 "Louisiana Proposes New Law to Protect 'Box-Top' Licenses." *Software Protection*, 2, no. 7 (Mar.-Apr. 1984), pp. 12-15.

2072 Lowenstein, Frank. "Software Liability." *Technology Review*, 90, no. 1 (Jan. 1987), pp. 9-10.

2073 Lowry, Elizabeth G. "Copyright Protection for Computer Languages: Creative Incentive or Technological Threat?" *Emory Law Journal*, 39, no. 4 (Fall 1990), pp. 1293-1349.

2074 Lowry, Houston Putnam. "Transborder Data Flow: Public and Private International Law Aspects." *Houston Journal of International Law*, 6, no. 2 (Spring 1984), pp. 159-74.

2075 Lubasch, Arnold H. "Arrest in a Theft from New York City." *The New York Times*, 108, no. 47897 (10 June 1989), p. A31.

2076 Lucas, Andre. "Copyright in the European Community: The Green Paper and the Proposal for a Directive Concerning Legal Protection of Computer Programs." *Columbia Journal of Transnational Law*, 29, no. 1 (1991), pp. 145-67.

2077 Lundberg, Steven W., George H. Gates, III, and John P. Sumner. "Baker v. Selden, Computer Programs, 17 U.S.C. Section 102(b) and Whelan Revisited." *Hamline Law Review*, 13, no. 2 (Spring 1990), pp. 221-52.

2078 Lundberg, Steven W., and John P. Sumner. "Patent Preemption of Shrink-Wrap Prohibitions on Reverse Engineering." *The Computer Lawyer*, 4, no. 4 (Apr. 1987), pp. 9-12.

2079 Lundberg, Steven W., and John P. Sumner. "Software Is Patentable: The Emerging Importance of Software Patents." *Bench & Bar of Minnesota,* 43, no. 11 (Dec. 1986), pp. 12-18.

2080 Lundberg, Steven W., Michelle M. Michel, and John P. Sumner. "The Copyright/Patent Interface: Why Utilitarian 'Look and Feel' Is Uncopyrightable Subject Matter." *The Computer Lawyer,* 6, no. 1 (Jan. 1989), pp. 5-11.

2081 Lunney, Glynn S., Jr. "Atari Games v. Nintendo: Does a Closed System Violate the Antitrust Laws?" *High Technology Law Journal,* 5, no. 1 (Spring 1990), pp. 29-73.

2082 Lunney, Glynn S., Jr. "Copyright Protection for ASIC Gate Configurations: PLDs, Custom and Semicustom Chips." *Stanford Law Review,* 42 (Nov. 1989), pp. 163-206.

2083 Lunt, Teresa F. "Access Control Policies: Some Unanswered Questions." *Computers and Security,* 8, no. 1 (Feb. 1989), pp. 43-54.

2084 Lurie, Paul M., and Barry D. Weiss. "Computer Assisted Mistakes: Changing Standards of Professional Liability." *Software Law Journal,* 2, no. 3 (Summer 1988), pp. 283-303.

2085 Lurie, Paul M., and Barry D. Weiss. "Computers: Changing the Legal Rules." *Architectural Record,* 175 (Apr. 1987), pp. 35, 37, 39.

2086 Lyman, Susan C. "Civil Remedies for the Victims of Computer Viruses." *Southwestern University Law Review,* 21, no. 3 (1992), pp. 1169-97.

2087 Lyons, Virginia R. "Carrying Copyright Too Far: The Inadequacy of the Current System of Protection for Computer Programs." *Comm/Ent,* 12, no. 1 (Fall 1989), pp. 81-98.

2088 Lytle, Susan S., and Hal W. Hall. "Software, Libraries, & the Copyright Law." *Library Journal,* 110, no. 12 (July 1985), pp. 33-39.

2089 McAdam, Steve. "Locking Up Computers with Encryption." *Accountant's Magazine,* 93, no. 995 (June 1989), pp. 29-30.

2090 McAfee, John. "The Virus Cure." *Datamation,* 35, no. 4 (15 Feb. 1989), pp. 29-40.

2091 McAllister, Celia F. "Throwing the Book at Computer Hackers." *Business Week,* no. 3160 (21 May 1990), p. 148E.

2092 McBroom, Viki. "Computer Viruses: What They Are, How to Protect Against Them." *Software Protection,* 8, no. 3 (Aug. 1989), pp. 1-16.

2093 McCall, Carol C. "Computer Crime Statutes: Are They Bridging the Gap Between Law and Technology?" *Criminal Justice Journal,* 11, no. 1 (Fall-Winter 1988), pp. 203-33.

2094 McCandless, Holloway. "Are These Software Pirates Lurking Among Your Staff?" *Working Woman*, 14, no. 1 (Jan. 1989), p. 27.

2095 McCandless, Holloway. "Computer Monitoring: Is It 'Big Brother' Watching?" *Working Woman*, 13, no. 11 (Nov. 1988), pp. 38-40.

2096 McCandless, Holloway. "An Rx for Healthy Software." *Working Woman*, 13, no. 9 (Sept. 1988), p. 33.

2097 McCarroll, Thomas. "Whose Bright Idea? Companies Are Cracking Down on Pirates Who Steal Designs, Movies and Computer Programs. The Battle Is Getting Hotter—and More Important." *Time*, 137, no. 23 (10 June 1991), pp. 44-46.

2098 McCartney, Robert J. "Computer Hackers Face Spy Charges." *The Washington Post*, 112, no. 255 (17 Aug. 1989), p.A32.

2099 McCartney, Sheila J. "Moral Rights Under the United Kingdom's Copyright, Designs and Patents Act of 1988." *Columbia-VLA Journal of Law and the Arts*, 15, no. 2 (Winter 1991), pp. 205-45.

2100 McCarty, Joseph G. "U.C.C. Article 4A—Wire or Wire Not? Consequential Damages Under Article 4A and a Critical Analysis of *Evra v. Swiss Bank*." *Computer/Law Journal*, 11, no. 2 (Apr. 1991), pp. 341-69.

2101 McClanahan, John Baker. "Copyright Misuse as a Defense in an Infringement Action: *Lasercomb America, Inc. v. Reynolds*." *Washington and Lee Law Review*, 49, no. 1 (Winter 1992), pp. 213-35.

2102 McClinchie, Malcolm U., III. "Criminal Law—Computer Crimes— New Texas Penal Code Provision Establishing Criminal Penalties for Unauthorized Use and Tampering with Computers and Computer Data Bases." *St. Mary's Law Journal*, 17, no. 2 (1986), pp. 591-95.

2103 McClure, Carma, and Michael D. Sher. "Evaluating Claims of Software Copying Through Data Analysis—Part 1." *Software Protection*, 3, no. 2 (July 1984), pp. 8-15.

2104 McClure, Carma, and Michael D. Sher. "Evaluating Claims of Software Copying Through Data Analysis—Part 2." *Software Protection*, 3, no. 3 (Aug. 1984), pp. 6-20.

2105 McDermott, P. M. "Computers—False Representation—Crimes Act 1914." *Criminal Law Journal*, 11, no. 6 (Dec. 1987), pp. 382-84.

2106 McDonough, Patrick. "Are Your Electronic Files Secure? A Guide to Computer Security." *Trial*, 25, no. 1 (Jan. 1989), pp. 56-59.

2107 McDougall, Rosamund. "Attack of the Killer Viruses!!" *The Banker*, 141, no. 789 (Nov. 1991), pp. 12, 15-16, 18.

2108 McGrath, Richard J. "The Unauthorized Use of Patents by the United States Government or Its Contractors." *AIPLA Quarterly Journal*, 18, no. 4 (1991), pp. 349-70.

2109 McGrath, William T. "Copyright Protection for User Interfaces in the Nineties: Of Perilous Journeys on the Drooping Shoulders of Giants." *Software Law Journal*, 4, no. 4 (Dec. 1991), pp. 597-610.

2110 McGrath, William T. "Who Owns the Copyrights?" *Byte*, 15, no. 4 (Apr. 1990), pp. 269-71.

2111 McGue, Joan A. "Software Protection Under U.S. Membership in the Berne Convention: Transplanting a New Moral Right Into U.S. Soil." *Software Law Journal*, 2, no. 3 (Summer 1988), pp. 339-71.

2112 Machrone, Bill. "Viruses: Sense and Nonsense." *PC Magazine*, 8, no. 4 (28 Feb. 1989), pp. 65-66.

2113 MacKay, J. Scott. "*Broderbund Software, Inc. v. Unison World, Inc.*: 'Look and Feel' Copyright Protection for the Display Screens of an Application Microcomputer Program." *Rutgers Computer and Technology Law Journal*, 13, no. 1 (1987), pp. 105-36.

2114 Mackay, John. "Parallel Importation of Computer Software and Restrictive Trade Practices—Exclusive Distributorship Agreement." *Software Protection*, 10, no. 12 (May 1992), pp. 17-20.

2115 Mackay, John, and James McLachelan. "Are Computer Screen Displays and Their 'Look and Feel' Capable of Copyright Protection in Australia?" *Software Protection*, 10, no. 7-8 (Dec. 1991-Jan. 1992), pp. 15-22.

2116 McKelvey, Tina Eubanks. "Article 4A of the Uniform Commercial Code: Finally, Banks and Their Customers Know Where They Stand and Who Pays When a Wire Transfer Goes Awry." *Memphis State University Law Review*, 21, no. 2 (Winter 1991), pp. 351-85.

2117 McKenna, Marshall. "*Dyason v. Autodesk Inc.*: Copyright Protection for Computer Software in the 1990s." *University of Western Australia Law Review*, 21, no. 1 (June 1991), pp. 183-95.

2118 McKeown, M. Margaret. "Trade Secrets Litigation: Noncompetition Covenants, Nondisclosure Agreements." *Software Protection*, 10, no. 6 (Nov. 1991), pp. 5-13.

2119 McLellan, Vin. "Computer Systems Under Seige." *The EDP Auditor Journal*, 3 (1988), pp. 33-38.

2120 McManis, Charles R. "International Protection for Semiconductor Chip Designs and the Standard of Judicial Review of Presidential Proclamations Issued Pursuant to the Semiconductor Chip Protection Act of 1984." *The George Washington Journal of International Law and Economics*, 22, no. 2 (1988), pp. 331-78.

2121 McMillan-McCartney, Elizabeth A. "The Future of Copyright Protection and Computer Programs—Beyond *Apple v. Franklin*." *Northern Kentucky Law Review*, 13, no. 1 (1986), pp. 97-127.

2122 McNeil, Michael B. "Copyright Ownership of Commissioned Computer Software in Light of Current Developments in the Work Made for Hire Doctrine." *Indiana Law Review,* 24, no. 1 (1990), pp. 135-59.

2123 McNeil, Michael J. "Trade Secret Protection for Mass Market Computer Software: Old Solutions for New Problems." *Albany Law Review,* 51, no. 2 (Winter 1987), pp. 293-331.

2124 MacPherson, Alan. "Impact of Partial Findings of Fact and Conclusions of Law in NEC v. INTEL: View of Plaintiffs." *Software Protection,* 5, no. 6 (Nov. 1986), pp. 8-10.

2125 MacPherson, Alan H. "Response to Mr. Dunlap's Article." *Software Protection,* 4, no. 4 (Sept. 1985), pp. 5-6.

2126 MacPherson, Alan H., Robert Morrill, and Richard Franklin. "Microcode: Patentable Or Copyrightable?" *Software Protection,* 4, no. 4 (Sept. 1985), pp. 7-10.

2127 MacQueen, Hector L. "Design Right and Semiconductor Topographies." *Journal of the Law Society of Scotland,* 35, no. 10 (Oct. 1990), pp. 422-24.

2128 Madsen, Wayne. "Government Sponsored Computer Warfare and Sabotage." *Computers and Security,* 11, no. 3 (May 1992), pp. 233-36.

2129 Magnier, Mark. "Copyright Suit Against Singapore Firm Dropped." *Journal of Commerce and Commercial,* 391, no. 27657 (4 Feb. 1992), p. 5A.

2130 Magnier, Mark. "Two US Software Firms in Legal Mess After Suit Flops in Singapore." *Journal of Commerce and Commercial,* 390, no. 27627 (19 Dec. 1991), pp. 1A-2A.

2131 Magrab, E. Brendan. "Computer Software Protection in Europe and the EC Parliamentary Directive on Copyright for Computer Software." *Law and Policy in International Business,* 23, no. 3 (Spring 1992), pp. 709-23.

2132 Mahan, Jeffrey B. "Federal Copyright Law in the Computer Era: Protection for the Authors of Video Games." *University of Puget Sound Law Review,* 7, no. 2 (Winter 1984), pp. 425-40.

2133 Maher, David W. "The Shrink-Wrap License: Old Problems in a New Wrapper." *Journal of the Copyright Society of the U.S.A.,* 34 (Apr. 1987), pp. 292-312.

2134 Maher, John J., and James O. Hicks. "Computer Viruses: Controller's Nightmare." *Management Accounting,* 71, no. 4 (Oct. 1989), pp. 44-49.

2135 Maier, Gregory J. "Software Protection—Integrating Patent, Copyright and Trade Secret Law." *Idea,* 28, no. 1 (1987), pp. 13-28. (Also published in *Journal of the Patent and Trademark Office Society,* 69, no. 3 [Mar. 1987], pp. 151-65.)

2136 "Making 'Big Brother' Obsolete." *Science News,* 128, no. 18 (2 Nov. 1985), p. 281.

2137 Malloy, Rich. "Technology Is Not the Problem; Legal Squabbles Focus on Competition and Threaten Innovation." *Byte,* 16, no. 11 (1991), p. 40.

2138 Mamis, Robert A. "Curing Computer Viruses." *Inc.,* 14, no. 4 (Apr. 1992), p. 131.

2139 Mamlet, Alfred M. "Liability for Defective Information." *Barrister,* 17, no. 1 (Spring 1990), pp. 43-44.

2140 Mandel, Lawrence D. *"Digital Communications Associates, Inc. v. Soft-Klone Distributing Corporation*: Copyright Protection for the Status Screen of a Computer Program." *Rutgers Computer and Technology Law Journal,* 15, no. 1 (1989), pp. 169-89.

2141 Manes, Stephen. "No, Virginia, There's No Such Thing as Total Electronic Privacy." *PC Computing,* 4, no. 4 (Apr. 1991), p. 72.

2142 Manes, Stephen. "Think Your Computer Is Safe from Outsiders' Attempts to Access It? A True Tale of Computer Espionage May Convince You Otherwise." *PC Magazine,* 9, no. 8 (24 Apr. 1990), pp. 91-92.

2143 Mann, J. Fraser. "Comment on *Apple Computer v. Mackintosh Computers.*" *McGill Law Journal,* 32, no. 2 (Mar. 1987), pp. 437-47.

2144 Mann, Paul. "GE Charged with $21-Million Fraud Scheme Against Army." *Aviation Week and Space Technology,* 129, no. 23 (5 Dec. 1988), p. 33.

2145 Mantle, Ray A. "Trade Secret and Copyright Protection of Computer Software." *Computer/Law Journal,* 4, no. 4 (Spring 1984), pp. 669-94.

2146 Manuel, Tom. "The Assault on Data Security Is Getting a Lot of Attention." *Electronics,* 61, no. 17 (Nov. 1988), pp. 136-38, 142.

2147 "Manufacturer Liable for Malfunction of Computer Operated Machine." *The Computer Lawyer,* 3, no. 10 (Oct. 1986), pp. 43-44.

2148 *"Manufacturers Technologies, Inc. v. CAMS, Inc.*: A False Hope for Software Developers Seeking Copyright Protection for Their Generated Screen Displays." *Rutgers Computer and Technology Law Journal,* 17, no. 1 (1991), pp. 211-50.

2149 Marbach, William D. "Booting Out Viruses While Booting Up the PC." *Business Week,* no. 3291 (2 Nov. 1992), p. 123.

2150 Marbach, William D., Andrew Nagorski, and Richard Sandza. "Hacking Through NASA." *Newsweek,* 110, no. 13 (28 Sept. 1987), p. 38.

2151 Marbach, William D., Martin Kasindorf, and Richard Sandza. "Was It Really WarGames?" *Newsweek,* 106, no. 5 (29 July 1985), p. 23.

2152 Marbach, William D., Richard Sandza, and Michael Rogers. "Is Your Computer Infected?" *Newsweek,* 111, no. 5 (1 Feb. 1988), p. 48.

2153 Marcellino, James J. "Expert Witnesses in Software Copyright Infringement Actions." *Computer/Law Journal,* 6, no. 1 (Summer 1985), pp. 35-54.

2154 Marcellino, James J., and Dexter L. Kenfield. "Legislative Developments in High-Tech." *Boston Bar Journal,* 28, no. 1-3 (Jan.-June 1984), pp. 19-23.

2155 Marconda, Scott M. "*NEC Corp. v. INTEL Corp.*: A Brief Synopsis." *Santa Clara Computer and High Technology Law Journal,* 5, no. 2 (1989), pp. 559-72.

2156 Marcuss, Stanley J., and Arthur R. Watson. "Technology Transfer in the People's Republic of China: An Assessment." *Syracuse Journal of International Law and Commerce,* 15, no. 2 (Winter 1989), pp. 141-85.

2157 Margolis, Stephen E. "Comments on 'Copyright and Computer Software.'" *Research in Law and Economics,* 8 (1986), pp. 227-31.

2158 Marinos, Michail. "Developments in Greek Copyright Law." *Software Protection,* 10, no. 11 (Apr. 1992), pp. 16-17.

2159 Marion, Camille Cardoni. "Computer Viruses and the Law." *Dickinson Law Review,* 93, no. 3 (Spring 1989), pp. 625-42.

2160 Mark, Julie A. "Software Copying Policies: The Next Step in Piracy Prevention?" *The Journal of Law and Technology,* 2, no. 1 (Winter 1987), pp. 43-68.

2161 Marke, Julius J. "'Jump Cites' and Computer-Assisted Legal Research." *New York Law Journal,* 194, no. 74 (15 Oct. 1985), p. 4.

2162 Marke, Julius J. "Public Access to Computerized Government Information." *New York Law Journal,* 207, no. 18 (28 Jan. 1992), pp. 4, 8.

2163 Markoff, John. "Author of Computer 'Virus' Is Son of N.S.A. Expert on Data Security." *The New York Times,* 138, no. 47680 (5 Nov. 1988), pp. 1, 7.

2164 Markoff, John. "Computer Network at NASA Attacked by Rogue Program." *The New York Times,* 139, no. 48027 (18 Oct. 1989), p. B10.

2165 Markoff, John. "Computer Virus Cure May Be Worse Than Disease." *The New York Times,* 139, no. 48016 (7 Oct. 1989), pp. 1, 35.

2166 Markoff, John. "Cornell Suspends Computer Student: School Says He Was Author of Program That Jammed a Nationwide Network." *The New York Times,* 108, no. 47881 (25 May 1989), p. A16.

2167 Markoff, John. "How a Need for Challenge Seduced Computer Expert." *The New York Times,* 138, no. 47681 (6 Nov. 1988), pp. 1, 30.

2168 Markoff, John. "Paper on Codes Is Sent Despite U.S. Objections." *The New York Times,* 108, no. 47957 (9 Aug. 1989), p. A16.

2169 Markoff, John. "Student, After Delay, Is Charged in Crippling of Computer Network." *The New York Times,* 108, no. 47944 (27 July 1989), p. A17.

2170 Markoff, John. "Top-Secret, and Vulnerable." *The New York Times*, 137, no. 47486 (25 Apr. 1988), pp. D1, D4.

2171 Markoff, John. "Virus Outbreaks Thwart Computer Experts." *The New York Times*, 108, no. 47886 (30 May 1989), pp. C1, C9.

2172 Markoff, John, Phillip Robinson, and Ezra Shapiro. "Up to Date." *Byte*, 10, no. 3 (Mar. 1985), pp. 355-58.

2173 Marsa, Linda, and Ray Don. "Crime Bytes Back." *Omni*, 12, no. 11 (Aug. 1990), pp. 34-38, 96-102.

2174 Marshall, Eliot. "Computer Security: NAS Sounds the Alarm." *Science*, 250, no. 4986 (7 Dec. 1990), p. 1330.

2175 Marshall, Eliot. "German Computer Spy Ring Broken." *Science*, 243, no. 4898 (24 Mar. 1989), p. 1545.

2176 Marshall, Eliot. "Statisticians at Odds Over Software Ownership." *Science*, 255, no. 5041 (10 Jan. 1992), pp. 152-53.

2177 Marsland, Vanessa. "International Software Licensing and Database Issues in Europe." *Software Protection*, 7, no. 11-12 (Apr.-May 1989), pp. 4-12.

2178 Marsteller, Thomas F., Jr., and Robert L. Tucker. "Copyrighting Trade Secrets Under the 1976 Copyright Act." *Idea*, 25, no. 4 (1984), pp. 211-23.

2179 Martin, Anne Crawford, and Kevin Deasy. "Licensing of Intellectual Property Rights Needed for Software Support: A Life Cycle Approach." *Jurimetrics Journal*, 28, no. 2 (Winter 1988), pp. 223-41.

2180 Martin, Nicholas. "Revenge of the Nerds: The Real Problem with Computer Viruses Isn't Genius Programmers, It's Careless Ones." *The Washington Monthly*, 20, no. 12 (Jan. 1989), pp. 21-24.

2181 Martin, Shannon E. "Analysis of the Computer Security Act of 1987 and Its Consequences for the Freedom of Information Act." *Communications and the Law*, 14, no. 3 (Sept. 1992), pp. 73-90.

2182 Marx, Gary T., and Nancy Reichman. "Routinizing the Discovery of Secrets: Computers as Informants." *Software Law Journal*, 1, no. 1 (Fall 1985), pp. 95-121.

2183 Marx, Gary T., and Sanford Sherizen. "Monitoring on the Job: How to Protect Privacy as Well as Property." *Technology Review*, 89, no. 8 (Nov.-Dec. 1986), pp. 62-72.

2184 Marx, Peter. "The Legal Risks of Using Information as a Competitive Weapon." *Software Law Journal*, 2, no. 2 (Spring 1988), pp. 185-201.

2185 Mashour, Susan L. "Proposed Judicial Guidelines for Deciding Software Infringement Actions." *Wayne Law Review*, 32, no. 3 (Spring 1986), pp. 1191-216.

2186 Mason, Paul E., and Denise Foley. "International Protection of Computer Software: The Japanese Experiment." *Boston Bar Journal,* 29, no. 5 (Nov.-Dec. 1985), pp. 28-34.

2187 Massingale, Cheryl S., and A. Faye Borthick. "Risk Allocation for Computer System Security Breaches: Potential Liability for Providers of Computer Services." *Western New England Law Review,* 12, no. 2 (1990), pp. 167-94.

2188 Massingale, Cheryl S., and A. Faye Borthick. "Risk Allocation for Injury Due to Defective Medical Software." *Journal of Products Liability,* 11, no. 3 (1988), pp. 181-98.

2189 Mathew, Paul A. "Computers: Where You and They Stand with the Law." *Architectural Record,* 173 (Sept. 1985), pp. 35-39.

2190 Mathewson, William. "Computer Fraud in China." *The Wall Street Journal,* 214, no. 80 (24 Oct. 1989), p. A21.

2191 Mattera, Philip. "Caught in the Crossfile: In Its Fight Against Fraud, the Government Strikes a Dangerous Match." *The Progressive,* 49, no. 3 (Mar. 1985), pp. 30-32.

2192 Mattfeld, Antje. "Protection of Software Against Third Parties in the Federal Republic of Germany." *Software Law Journal,* 1, no. 3 (Spring-Summer 1986), pp. 341-59.

2193 Matthes, Karen. "Is There a Doctor in the House?" *Management Review,* 80, no. 7 (July 1991), pp. 5-6.

2194 Matthews, Byron. "Editorial: Privacy and Technology." *Current Municipal Problems,* 11 (1984-85), p. 249.

2195 Matthews, Rosalyn Clive. "Protection of Rights of Individuals in the EEC in Relation to Automatic Processing of Personal Data." *International Business Lawyer* (Oct. 1984), pp. 410-14.

2196 Maule, Michael R. "Applying Strict Products Liability to Computer Software." *Tulsa Law Journal,* 27, no. 4 (Summer 1992), pp. 735-56.

2197 Maune, James J. "Computer Software as Property." *Journal of the Suffolk Academy of Law,* 5 (1988), pp. 21-34.

2198 Maxey, Brigitte. "Experts Expect Limited Claims from March 6 Computer Virus." *Journal of Commerce and Commercial,* 391, no. 27670 (24 Feb. 1992), p. 9A.

2199 Maybury, Neil M. "Computer Contracts and the Protection of Computer Software." *Solicitors Journal,* 132, no. 27 (8 July 1988), pp. 978-79.

2200 Meadows, James E. "*Lubrizol*: What Will It Mean for the Software Industry?" *Santa Clara Computer and High-Technology Law Journal,* 3, no. 1 (Jan. 1987), pp. 311-28.

2201 Meadows, James E. "Software Protection in Transactions with the Soviet Union." *Rutgers Computer and Technology Law Journal,* 12, no. 1 (1986), pp. 133-67.

2202 "The Medium Is the Message: *Apple Computer, Inc. v. Franklin Computer Corporation." University of San Francisco Law Review,* 18, no. 2 (Winter 1984), pp. 351-69.

2203 Meijboom, Alfred P. "New Developments Regarding the Patentability of Software-Related Inventions in Europe." *Journal of the Patent and Trademark Office Society,* 72 (June 1990), pp. 583-85.

2204 Meijboom, Alfred P. "Software Protection in 'Europe 1992.'" *Rutgers Computer and Technology Law Journal,* 16, no. 2 (1990), pp. 407-43.

2205 Meiklejohn, Ian. "How to Avoid a Hack Attack." *Management Today* (Jan. 1990), pp. 89-90.

2206 Meisner, Mary M. "Archival Backup Copying of Software: How Broad a Right?" *Rutgers Computer and Technology Law Journal,* 14, no. 2 (1988), pp. 391-412.

2207 Melka, Paul. "Wishful Thinking Will Not Make Publicity-Seeking Viruses Go Away." *InfoWorld,* 14, no. 17 (27 Apr. 1992), p. 47.

2208 Mell, Patricia. "The Criminal Law Aspects of Unauthorized Access, Information Theft and Other Pests Associated with Computer Use." *Delaware Lawyer,* 7, no. 5 (Fall 1989), pp. 28-31.

2209 Mellema, Cynthia L. "Copyright Protection for Computer Software: An International View." *Syracuse Journal of International Law and Commerce,* 11, no. 1 (Summer 1984), pp. 87-120.

2210 Menell, Peter S. "An Analysis of the Scope of Copyright Protection for Application Programs." *Stanford Law Review,* 41 (May 1989), pp. 1045-104.

2211 Menell, Peter S. "Tailoring Legal Protection for Computer Software." *Stanford Law Review,* 39 (July 1987), pp. 1329-72.

2212 Menelly, Lisa. "Prosecuting Computer-Related Crime in the United States, Canada, and England: New Laws for Old Offenses?" *Boston College International and Comparative Law Review,* 8, no. 2 (Summer 1985), pp. 551-74.

2213 Menkus, Belden. "Breakpoints." *Computers and Security,* 7, no. 3 (June 1988), pp. 261-68.

2214 Menkus, Belden. "The 'Computer Virus' Danger Grows." *Modern Office Technology,* 34, no. 2 (Feb. 1989), pp. 38, 40.

2215 Menkus, Belden. "The Computer Virus Situation Is Not Encouraging." *Computers and Security,* 8, no. 2 (Apr. 1989), pp. 115-19.

2216 Menkus, Belden. "Computer Virus Update." *Modern Office Technology,* 35, no. 1 (Jan. 1990), p. 150.

2217 Menkus, Belden. "Concerns in Computer Security." *Computers and Security,* 11, no. 3 (May 1992), pp. 211-15.

2218 Menkus, Belden. "'Crime Prevention' in System Design." *Journal of Systems Management,* 42, no. 5 (May 1991), p. 19.

2219 Menkus, Belden. "Eight Factors Contributing to Computer Fraud." *Internal Auditor,* 47, no. 5 (Oct. 1990), pp. 71-73.

2220 Menkus, Belden. "Eight Unfortunate Facts About Computer Fraud." *Internal Auditor,* 47, no. 3 (June 1990), pp. 70-71.

2221 Menkus, Belden. "'Hackers': Know the Adversary." *Computers and Security,* 10, no. 5 (Aug. 1991), pp. 405-9.

2222 Menkus, Belden. "How to Begin Dealing with Computer Security." *Computers and Security,* 10, no. 3 (May 1991), pp. 199-203.

2223 Menkus, Belden. "Introduction to Computer Security." *Computers and Security,* 11, no. 2 (Apr. 1992), pp. 121-27.

2224 Menkus, Belden. "Physical Security: Selecting an Access Control System." *Computers and Security,* 8, no. 3 (May 1989), pp. 201-5.

2225 Menkus, Belden. "U.S. Government Agencies Belatedly Address Information System Security Issues." *Computers and Security,* 7, no. 4 (Aug. 1988), pp. 361-66.

2226 Menosky, Joseph. "Technopranks." *Science 84,* 5, no. 6 (July- Aug. 1984), pp. 89-92.

2227 Mensik, Michael S. "Latin America: Protecting and Marketing Software Programs." *Software Protection,* 4, no. 8 (Jan. 1986), pp. 6-12.

2228 Mensik, Michael S. "Software Localization: Hidden Issues That Arise When Software Is Translated Abroad." *The Computer Lawyer,* 8, no. 5 (May 1991), pp. 1-9.

2229 Mensik, Michael S., and A. John Radsan. "Copyright Protection and the Marketing of Software in Brazil: The New Legal Framework." *The International Lawyer,* 24, no. 1 (Spring 1990), pp. 153-78.

2230 "Menu Screens of Computer Program Held to Be Copyrightable Audiovisual Displays." *The Computer Lawyer,* 3, no. 11 (Nov. 1986), pp. 27-29.

2231 Mercer, Lindsay C. J. "Tailor-Made Auditing of Information Systems for the Detection of Fraud." *Computers and Security,* 9, no. 1 (Feb. 1990), pp. 59-66.

2232 Merges, Robert P. "Editor, Jurimetrics." *Jurimetrics Journal,* 24, no. 2 (Winter 1984), pp. 195-96.

2233 Merritt, Deborah Jones. "The Constitution in a Brave New World: A Century of Technological Change and Constitutional Law." *Oregon Law Review*, 69, no. 1 (1990), pp. 1-45.

2234 Messick, Robert. "IRS Computer Data Bank Searches: An Infringement of the Fourth Amendment Search and Seizure Clause." *Santa Clara Law Review*, 25, no. 1 (Winter 1985), pp. 153-89.

2235 Metalitz, Steven J. "Copyright Registration After *Feist*: New Rules and New Roles?" *University of Dayton Law Review*, 17, no. 3 (Spring 1992), pp. 763-95.

2236 Meyer, David J. "*Paine, Webber, Jackson and Curtis, Inc. v. Merrill Lynch, Pierce, Fenner and Smith*: Methods of Doing Business Held Patentable Because Implemented on a Computer." *Computer/Law Journal*, 5, no. 1 (Summer 1984), pp. 101-24.

2237 Meyer, Howard. "Lawyer Software Copyright Infringers Flee, All Is Discovered!'" *New York State Bar Journal*, 64, no. 6 (Sept.-Oct. 1992), pp. 18-19.

2238 Meyer, Jim. "The Perils of Piracy: What Every Lawyer Should Know About Copying Disks." *ABA Journal*, 78 (Oct. 1992), p. 104.

2239 Meyer, Stuart P. "Obtaining and Enforcing Patents for Software-Related Inventions: Avoiding the Pitfalls." *Software Law Journal*, 5, no. 4 (Dec. 1992), pp. 715-38.

2240 Meyers, Tedson J. "Liability Limitations in International Data Traffic: The Consequences of Deregulation." *Case Western Reserve Journal of International Law*, 16, no. 2 (1984), pp. 203-22.

2241 Meza, Ricardo. "*Analysts International Corporation v. Recycled Paper Products, Inc.*: Is Custom-Designed Software a 'Good' Under Article 2 of the Uniform Commercial Code?" *Software Law Journal*, 3, no. 3 (Summer 1989), pp. 543-55.

2242 Mezzacappa, John, and Karen M. Cooke. "Computer Viruses and the All Risk Policy." *Best's Review-Property/Casualty Insurance Edition*, 91, no. 3 (July 1990), p. 80.

2243 Miastkowski, Stan. "Put a Positive Lock on Your Data." *Byte*, 14, no. 2 (Feb. 1989), p. 100.

2244 Michael, James. "Protecting Privacy." *Solicitors Journal*, 135, no. 10 (15 Mar. 1991), pp. 304-5.

2245 Michael, Robin. "17 U. S. C. 117: Is the Amendment to the Copyright Act Adequate to Regulate the Computer Software Market?" *Computer/Law Journal*, 7, no. 2 (Fall 1986), pp. 227-44.

2246 Michaelson, Peter L. "The 1984 Semiconductor Chip Protection Act: A Comprehensive View." *Communications and the Law*, 8, no. 5 (Oct. 1986), pp. 23-55.

2247 "'Michelangelo' Computer Virus Triggered." *Facts on File,* 52, no. 2677 (12 Mar. 1992), p. 163.

2248 "Micro Computer Software Warranties." *Software Protection,* 5, no. 5 (Oct. 1986), pp. 1-7.

2249 "Microchips Prevent Copies of Software When Desired." *Wall Street Journal,* 219, no. 113 (10 June 1992), p. B6.

2250 "Microcom Utility Combats Three New Mac Viruses." *PC Week,* 7, no. 50 (17 Dec. 1990), p. 40.

2251 "Microsoft's Mouse Held Noninfringing." *The Computer Lawyer,* 9, no. 10 (Oct. 1992), p. 34.

2252 Middleton, Alan S. "A Thousand Clones: The Scope of Copyright Protection in the 'Look and Feel' of Computer Programs— *Digital Communications Associates, Inc. v. SoftKlone Distributing Corp.,* 659 F.Supp. 449 (N.D. Ga. 1987)." *Washington Law Review,* 63, no. 1 (Jan. 1988), pp. 195-220.

2253 Mihm, Michael W. "The 'Soft' Existing Legal Protection of Software and the Preemption of State Shrink-Wrap License Enforcement Acts." *Northern Illinois University Law Review,* 8, no. 2 (1988), pp. 531-63.

2254 Milenbach, Julian. "Windows Virus Program Has Sluggish Symptoms." *PC Week,* 8, no. 23 (10 June 1991), pp. 33, 41.

2255 Millard, Christopher J. "Software Protection in the United Kingdom: The Copyright, Designs and Patents Act 1988." *Software Protection,* 7, no. 6-7 (Nov.-Dec. 1988), pp. 1-10.

2256 Mille, Antonio. "Idea and Expression in Software Works." Translated by Leslie Williams. *Software Protection,* 7, no. 4 (Sept. 1988), pp. 6-13.

2257 Mille, Antonio. "Shrink Wrap Package Licenses in Argentina." *Software Protection,* 4, no. 10-11 (Mar.-Apr. 1986), pp. 30-31.

2258 Mille, Antonio. "Software Protection in the Latin American Countries." *Software Protection,* 4, no. 7 (Dec. 1985), pp. 1-5.

2259 Miller, Clifford. "The Enforceability of Shrinkwraps as Bare Intellectual Property Licenses." *The Computer Lawyer,* 9, no. 8 (Aug. 1992), pp. 15-17.

2260 Miller, Fred H., Robert G. Ballen, William B. Davenport, and James V. Vergari. "Commercial Paper, Bank Deposits and Collections, and Commercial Electronic Fund Tranfers." *The Business Lawyer,* 42, no. 4 (Aug. 1987), pp. 1269-1305.

2261 Miller, Philip H. "Life After *Feist*: Facts, the First Amendment, and the Copyright Status of Automated Databases." *Fordham Law Review,* 60, no. 3 (Dec. 1991), pp. 507-39.

2262 Millett, P. J. "Tracing the Proceeds of Fraud." *The Law Quarterly Review,* 107 (Jan. 1991), pp. 71-85.

2263 Millstein, Ira M. "The Role of Antitrust in an Age of Technology." *Cardozo Law Review,* 9, no. 4 (Mar. 1988), pp. 1175-202.

2264 Milor, G. Will. "The Computer Security Act of 1987." *Computers and Security,* 7, no. 3 (June 1988), pp. 251-53.

2265 Min, Byoung Kook. "The Law of Technology Transfer and Economic Development: The Next Phase of Korea's Course Towards Economic Parity." *Law/Technology,* 21, no. 1 (1988), pp. 1-17.

2266 Minard, Lawrence. "New Hoods on the Block." *Forbes,* 150, no. 14 (21 Dec. 1992), p. 10.

2267 "Minimum Quantum of Evidence Defeats Laches." *The Computer Lawyer,* 9, no. 8 (Aug. 1992), pp. 34-35.

2268 Minsk, Alan D. "The Patentability of Algorithms: A Review and Critical Analysis of the Current Doctrine." *Santa Clara Computer and High Technology Law Journal,* 8, no. 2 (Aug. 1992), pp. 251-300.

2269 Mirabito, Jason. "Technology Transfers of Patent/Data Rights in the Commercial Sector: A Primer." *Boston College International and Comparative Law Review,* 7, no. 2 (Summer 1984), pp. 251-68.

2270 Miskiewicz, Jim "States Put 'Byte' Into Their Laws." *The National Law Journal,* 8, no. 50 (25 Aug. 1986), pp. 1, 22-23.

2271 Mislow, Christopher M. "Necessity May Be the Mother of Invention, But Who Gets Custody?: The Ownership of Intellectual Property Created by an Employed Inventor." *Santa Clara Computer and High-Technology Law Journal,* 1, no. 1 (1985), pp. 59-106.

2272 Mislow, Christopher M. "Protecting Source Code from Disclosure During Pretrial Discovery." *The Utah Bar Journal,* 12, no. 7-12 (Fall-Winter 1984), pp. 39-47.

2273 Mislow, Christopher M. "Reducing the High Risk of High Tech: Legal Planning for the Marketing of Computer Systems." *American Business Law Journal,* 23, no. 1 (Spring 1985), pp. 123-39.

2274 Misutka, Frances. "Stand on Guard." *Canadian Business,* 62, no. 8 (Aug. 1989), pp. 65-70.

2275 Mital, Vijay, and Les Johnson. "Professional Negligence and Financial-Legal Expert Systems: Architectures to Enable the Reasonableness Defence." *Law, Computers and Artificial Intelligence,* 1, no. 1 (1992), pp. 53-77.

2276 Mitchell, Christine. "Copyright: The Great Debate." *Law Institute Journal,* 65, no. 6 (June 1991), pp. 462-63.

2277 Miyaki, Patrick T. "Computer Software Defects: Should Computer Software Manufacturers Be Held Strictly Liable for Computer Software Defects?" *Santa Clara Computer and High Technology Law Journal*, 8, no. 1 (May 1992), pp. 121-44.

2278 Miyashita, Yoshiyuki. "International Protection of Computer Software." *Computer/Law Journal*, 11, no. 1 (Feb. 1991), pp. 41-73.

2279 Moad, Jeff. "Avoid Distributed Disasters." *Datamation*, 38, no. 22 (1 Nov. 1992), pp. 97-99.

2280 "Model Electronic Payments Agreement and Commentary." *Jurimetrics Journal*, 32, no. 4 (Summer 1992), pp. 601-70.

2281 Moody, Michael C. "The Intellectual Property Bankruptcy Protection Act: Legislative Relief for Software Licensees from Licensor Bankruptcy." *Software Law Journal*, 3, no. 1 (Winter 1989), pp. 91-115.

2282 Moor, James. "Computing and the Ring of Invisibility: A Philosopher Explains Why We Shouldn't Trust Computers." *Ethics: Easier Said Than Done*, 1991, no. 15 (1991), pp. 40-41.

2283 Moore, Gregory E., and Akiyo Fujii. "Managing Computer Software Liability." *Boston Bar Journal*, 33, no. 5 (Sept.-Oct. 1989), pp. 8-11.

2284 Moore, Harold C. "*Atari v. Nintendo*: Super Mario Uses 'Expressive' Security Feature to 'Lock' Out the Competition." *Rutgers Computer and Technology Law Journal*, 18, no. 2 (1992), pp. 919-40.

2285 Moore, Thomas H. "Colleges Seen Vulnerable to Legal Actions Arising from Computer Viruses." *The Chronicle of Higher Education*, 35, no. 42 (28 June 1989), pp. A1, A20.

2286 Morddel, Anne. "Data Protection in the United Kingdom." *Records Management Quarterly*, 20, no. 3 (July 1986), pp. 58, 60, 62.

2287 Morgan, Derek. "Cable, Computers, Copyright and Canadian Culture." *Intellectual Property Journal*, 2, no. 1 (Nov. 1985), pp. 69-91.

2288 Morgan, Derek. "Copyright—Computer Programs—Is Copyright Protection Desirable?" *Canadian Bar Review*, 63, no. 2 (June 1985), pp. 412-23.

2289 Morris, Lewis C. "It's Far Too Easy for Outsiders to Grab Your Information and Run." *Communications News*, 26, no. 7 (July 1989), p. 49.

2290 Morrison, Linda G. "The EC Directive on the Legal Protection of Computer Programs: Does It Leave Room for Reverse Engineering Beyond the Need for Interoperability?" *Vanderbilt Journal of Transnational Law*, 25, no. 2 (1992), pp. 293-332.

2291 Morrison, Perry R. "Computer Parasites: Software Diseases May Cripple Our Computers." *The Futurist*, 20, no. 2 (Mar.-Apr. 1986), pp. 36-38.

2292 Morrissey, Jane. "Bankruptcy Ruling Puts Software Pirates on the Spot." *PC Week*, 9, no. 28 (13 July 1992), p. 118.

2293 Morrissey, Jane. "Piracy Wars Obscure Licensing Dilemmas." *PC Week*, 8, no. 21 (27 May 1991), pp. 1, 6.

2294 Morrow, A. David. "The Protection of Software Against Third Parties in Canada." *Software Law Journal*, 1, no. 3 (Spring-Summer 1986), pp. 319-32.

2295 Mortimer, Hope. "Computer-Aided Medicine: Present and Future Issues of Liability." *Computer/Law Journal*, 9, no. 2 (Spring 1989), pp. 177-203.

2296 Moses, Jonathan M. "Wiretap Inquiry Spurs Computer Hacker Charges." *The Wall Street Journal*, 220, no. 7 (9 July 1992), p. B8.

2297 Moulton, Rolf, and Robert P. Bigelow. "Protecting Ownership of Proprietary Information." *Computers and Security*, 8, no. 1 (Feb. 1989), pp. 15-21.

2298 Mueller, Janice M. "Determining the Scope of Copyright Protection for Computer/User Interfaces." *Computer/Law Journal*, 9, no. 1 (Winter 1989), pp. 37-59.

2299 Muenchinger, Nancy E. "American Case Law on Copyright Protection of Electronic Games." *International Business Lawyer*, 15, no. 2-4 (Feb.-Apr. 1987), pp. 107-13.

2300 Muftic, Sead, and Edina Hatunic. "CISS: Generalized Security Libraries." *Computers and Security*, 11, no. 7 (Nov. 1992), pp. 653-59.

2301 Muggridge, Les. "FAST and Loose." *The Accountant's Magazine*, 96, no. 1028 (Mar. 1992), pp. 50-51.

2302 Mulhall, Lisa. "Computer Crime — New Legislation." *Law Institute Journal*, 61, no. 8 (Aug. 1987), p. 820.

2303 Murphy, Brian J. "Telecommunications Talk." *Creative Computing*, 10, no. 1 (Jan. 1984), pp. 266-70.

2304 Murphy, Brian J. "Telecommunications Talk." *Creative Computing*, 10, no. 5 (May 1984), pp. 184-88.

2305 Murphy, Jamie. "A Threat from Malicious Software: Hackers Are Slipping Dangerous Miniprograms Into Big Systems." *Time*, 126, no. 18 (4 Nov. 1985), p. 94.

2306 Murray, W. H. "The Application of Epidemiology to Computer Viruses." *Computers and Security*, 7, no. 2 (Apr. 1988), pp. 139-45.

2307 Murray, William Hugh. "Computer Viruses — Is There a Vaccine?" *Financial Executive*, 5, no. 2 (Mar.-Apr. 1989), pp. 39-41.

2308 "Musings on a Software Piracy Survey: An Editorial." *Software Protection*, 3, no. 9 (Feb. 1985), pp. 1-4.

2309 Myara, Alicia S. "An Attorney's Duty to Advise a Corporate Client Concerning Computer Software Copying: The Ethical Considerations." *The Journal of Law and Technology,* 2, no. 1 (Winter 1987), pp. 81-99.

2310 Myles-Sanders, Leslie. "Who Owns the Software? Intellectual Property in the Computer Industry After *CCN v. Reid.*" *Michigan Bar Journal,* 70, no. 7 (July 1991), pp. 664-71.

2311 Mylott, Thomas R., III. "Computer Professional Malpractice." *Santa Clara Computer and High-Technology Law Journal,* 2, no. 1 (1986), pp. 239-70.

2312 Mylott, Thomas R., III. "Computer Security and the Threats from Within." *The Office,* 101, no. 3 (Mar. 1985), pp. 45-46, 190.

2313 "NEC CORP. v. INTEL CORP.: Microcode Held Protected by Copyright Law." *Software Protection,* 5, no. 6 (Nov. 1986), pp. 2-6.

2314 "NEC Corporation v. INTEL Corporation, Memorandum of Decision." *Software Protection,* 7, no. 10 (Mar. 1989), pp. 2-15.

2315 Nabhan, Victor. "A Glance Over the Amendments to Canada's Copyright Law." *Columbia-VLA Journal of Law and the Arts,* 14, no. 3 (1990), pp. 397-413.

2316 Nakajima, Tohru. "Legal Protection of Computer Programs in Japan: The Conflict Between Economic and Artistic Goals." *Columbia Journal of Transnational Law,* 27, no. 1 (1988), pp. 143-68.

2317 Napier, B. W. "An End to Hacking?" *Solicitors' Journal,* 133, no. 49 (8 Dec. 1989), pp. 1554-56.

2318 Napier, B. W. "The Future of Information Technology Law." *The Cambridge Law Journal,* 51, no. 1 (Mar. 1992), pp. 46-65.

2319 Naumann, Steven T. "Compliance with 35 U.S.C. 112 for Inventions Containing Computer Software: Is Disclosure of the Computer Code Required?" *Software Law Journal,* 4, no. 3 (Oct. 1991), pp. 443-55.

2320 Neely, R. E. "Australian Federal Court Hands Down Its Decision in *Autodesk.*" *Software Protection,* 9, no. 11 (Apr. 1991), pp. 3-4.

2321 Neill, Torrey M. "Copyright Law — Copyright Protection for the User Interface of a Computer Program: *Digital Communications Associates v. Soft-Klone Distributing.*" *The Journal of Corporation Law,* 13, no. 3 (Spring 1988), pp. 919-39.

2322 Nelson, Brenda. "Straining the Capacity of the Law: The Idea of Computer Crime in the Age of the Computer Worm." *Computer/Law Journal,* 11, no. 2 (Apr. 1991), pp. 299-321.

2323 Nesset, D. M. "Factors Affecting Distributed System Security." *IEEE Transactions on Software Engineering,* SE-13, no. 2 (Feb. 1987), pp. 233-48.

2324 Neuner, Robert. "Trade Secret Protection for Computer Software." *New York Law Journal,* 207, no. 22 (3 Feb. 1992), pp. 3, 5-6.

2325 "New Locks and Keys for Electronic Information." *Computers and Security,* 7, no. 1 (Feb. 1988), pp. 89-93.

2326 "A New Strain of Electronic Vandalism." *Newsweek,* 114, no. 26 (25 Dec. 1989), p. 82.

2327 Newell, Allen. "*Response:* The Models Are Broken, the Models Are Broken." *University of Pittsburgh Law Review,* 47, no. 4 (Summer 1986), pp. 1023-35.

2328 Newman, Jon O. "Copyright Law and the Protection of Privacy." *Columbia-VLA Journal of Law and the Arts,* 12, no. 4 (1988), pp. 459-79.

2329 Newport, John Paul, Jr. "A Maker of Chips That Won't Forget." *Fortune,* 111, no. 12 (10 June 1985), p. 106.

2330 "News Briefs: Symantec Bolsters Anti-Virus Software." *PC Week,* 8, no. 24 (17 June 1991), p. 39.

2331 "Newspaper's Computer Is Infected with a 'Virus.'" *The New York Times,* 137, no. 47516 (25 May 1988), p. D18.

2332 Ney, Bruce A. "Copyright Law: Copyright Protection for Facts and Factual Compilations? [*Feist Publications v. Rural Telephone Service Co.,* 111 S.Ct. 1282 (1991)]." *Washburn Law Journal,* 31, no. 1 (Fall 1991), pp. 141-54.

2333 Niblett, Bryan. "Software Protection: Proposals in the United Kingdom White Paper." *Software Protection,* 5, no. 6 (Nov. 1986), pp. 10-13.

2334 Nicholson, Cynthia K., and Robert Cunningham. "Computer Crime." *American Criminal Law Review,* 28, no. 3 (1991), pp. 393-405.

2335 Nielsen, Paul. "Norton AntiVirus Battles 142 Threats with Three Methods." *PC Week,* 8, no. 1 (7 Jan. 1991), pp. 30, 35.

2336 Nielsen, Paul. "Software Copyright in the Nordic Countries." *The Computer Lawyer,* 9, no. 3 (Mar. 1992), pp. 1-12.

2337 Niemic, Robert J. "The Electronic Tax Return: Is Paperless Filing Here?" *Jurimetrics Journal,* 26, no. 2 (Winter 1986), pp. 138-61.

2338 Nilles, Andrew J. "Copyright Protection for Programs Stored in Computer Chips: Competing with IBM and Apple." *Hamline Law Review,* 7, no. 1 (Jan. 1984), pp. 103-30.

2339 Nimmer, David, Richard L. Bernacchi, and Gary N. Frischling. "Analyzing Substantial Similarity in Computer Software Infringement Cases." *The Computer Lawyer,* 6, no. 1 (Jan. 1989), pp. 17-25.

2340 Nimmer, David, Richard L. Bernacchi, and Gary N. Frischling. "A Structured Approach to Analyzing the Substantial Similarity of Computer Software in Copyright Infringement Cases." *Arizona State Law Journal*, 20, no. 3 (Fall 1988), pp. 625-56.

2341 Nimmer, Raymond, and Patricia A. Krauthaus. "Computer Error and User Liability Risk." *Defense Law Journal*, 35, no. 4 (1986), pp. 579-99. (First published in *Jurimetrics Journal*, 26, no. 2 [Winter 1986], pp. 121-37.)

2342 Nimmer, Raymond, and Patricia A. Krauthaus. "Copyright and Software Technology Infringement: Defining Third Party Development Rights." *Indiana Law Journal*, 62, no. 1 (1986-87), pp. 13-62.

2343 Nimmer, Raymond T. "Uniform Codification of Commercial Contract Law." *Rutgers Computer and Technology Law Journal*, 18, no. 2 (1992), pp. 465-97.

2344 Nimmer, Raymond T., and Angel L. Franqui. "United States Protection of Computer Software Technology." *Software Law Journal*, 1, no. 3 (Spring-Summer 1986), pp. 417-55.

2345 Nimmer, Raymond T., and Patricia Krauthaus. "Classification of Computer Software for Legal Protection: International Perspectives." *The International Lawyer*, 21, no. 3 (Summer 1987), pp. 733-54.

2346 "The 1989 John Marshall National Moot Court Competition in Information Law and Privacy." *Software Law Journal*, 4, no. 2 (Apr. 1991), pp. 271-375.

2347 "9th Circuit Follows *Apple v. Franklin* Decision and Upholds Software Copyrights." *Software Protection*, 2, no. 7 (Mar.-Apr. 1984), pp. 17-20.

2348 Nixon, Larry S. "Protection of Intellectual Property Rights in the United States for Computer-Aided Processes, Machines and Audio-Visual Displays: Part 1." *Software Protection*, 3, no. 8 (Jan. 1985), pp. 1-11.

2349 Nixon, Larry S. "Protection of Intellectual Property Rights in the United States for Computer-Aided Processes, Machines and Audio-Visual Displays: Part 2." *Software Protection*, 3, no. 9 (Feb. 1985), pp. 5-16.

2350 "No Copyright Protection for 'Indispensable Elements' of Videogame." *The Computer Lawyer*, 4, no. 5 (May 1987), p. 32.

2351 Nolan, Anthony R. G. "Brave New World? Copyright Protection of Computer Programs in Germany and France in Light of the European Community Software Directive." *Journal of the Copyright Society of the U.S.A.*, 39, no. 2 (Winter 1991), pp. 121-62.

2352 "Nonliteral Elements Not Dictated by Market Forces." *The Computer Lawyer*, 9, no. 12 (Dec. 1992), p. 34.

2353 "Nonregistration Defeats Arbitration Award." *The Computer Lawyer*, 9, no. 11 (Nov. 1992), pp. 26-27.

2354 Nordwall, Bruce D., and Breck W. Henderson. "Rapid Spread of Virus Confirms Fears About Danger to Computers." *Aviation Week and Space Technology,* 129, no. 20 (14 Nov. 1988), p. 44.

2355 Norman, Geoff. "PC Security Issues." *Computers and Security,* 11, no. 5 (Sept. 1992), pp. 412-16.

2356 Norman, Leslie Susan. "Unauthorized Access To EFT Information: Who Should Be Responsible?" *Computer/Law Journal,* 6, no. 1 (Summer 1985), pp. 171-85.

2357 "A Normative Analysis of Disclosure, Privacy, and Computers: The State Cases." *Computer/Law Journal,* 10, no. 4 (Dec. 1990), pp. 603-34.

2358 "Norton AntiVirus Utility Wipes Out PC, Network Bugs." *PC Week,* 7, no. 50 (17 Dec. 1990), p. 4.

2359 Nota, Peter. "Data Manipulation in a Secure Environment." *Accountancy,* 103, no. 1150 (June 1989), pp. 142-43.

2360 "Nothing to Sneeze At." *Time,* 131, no. 15 (11 Apr. 1988), p. 52.

2361 Nussbaum, Jan L. "*Apple Computer, Inc. v. Franklin Computer Corporation* Puts the Byte Back Into Copyright Protection for Computer Programs." *Golden Gate University Law Review,* 14, no. 2 (Summer 1984), pp. 281-308.

2362 Nycum, Susan H., Dexter L. Kenfield, and Margaret A. Keenan. "Debugging Software Escrow: Will It Work When You Need It?" *Computer/ Law Journal,* 4, no. 3 (Winter 1984), pp. 441-63.

2363 Nydegger, Rick D. "Practical and Legal Considerations in Drafting a U.S. Patent Application for Computer-Related Inventions." *Rutgers Computer and Technology Law Journal,* 18, no. 1 (1992), pp. 109-363.

2364 "OCR Action Reinstated, *Aukerman* Cited for Support." *The Computer Lawyer,* 9, no. 10 (Oct. 1992), p. 33.

2365 "OPTi Did Not Infringe Chip's Patent." *The Computer Lawyer,* 9, no. 8 (Aug. 1992), p. 34.

2366 Oberdorfer, Dan. "West-Mead Data Copyright Suit Hearing Slated." *National Law Journal,* 7, no. 52 (9 Sept. 1985), p. 20.

2367 Oberst, Gary. "A Vacuum Tube Decision in the Microchip Age: *Plains Cotton Coop. Ass'n. v. Goodpasture Computer Serv.*" *Southern University Law Review,* 16 (1989), pp. 365-78.

2368 Oddi, A. Samuel. "Functional and Free Market Theory." *AIPLA Quarterly Journal,* 17, no. 3 (1989), pp. 173-98.

2369 "Offers Users Can't Refuse: Shrink-Wrap License Agreements as Enforceable Adhesion Contracts." *Cardozo Law Review,* 10, no. 7 (June 1989), pp. 2105-35.

2370 Ogilvie, John W. L. "Defining Computer Program Parts Under Learned Hand's Abstractions Test in Software Copyright Infringement Cases." *Michigan Law Review,* 91, no. 3 (Dec. 1992), pp. 526-70.

2371 Ognibene, Peter J. "Computer Saboteurs." *Science Digest,* 92, no. 7 (July 1984), pp. 58-61.

2372 Ognibene, Peter J. "Secret Ciphers Solved: Artificial Intelligence." *Omni,* 7, no. 2 (Nov. 1984), pp. 38, 144.

2373 Ojanen, Karla. "Intellectual Property Considerations for Computer Software." *Barrister,* 17, no. 1 (Spring 1990), pp. 49-51.

2374 Oliver, Peter, and Reimer von Borries. "Data Protection and Censuses Under the West German Constitution." *Public Law,* 1984 (Summer 1984), pp. 199-206.

2375 Olson, Eric W. "*Galoob v. Nintendo*: Subject Matter Fixation and Consumer Fair Use Define the Scope of Copyright Protection for Interoperable Works." *Rutgers Computer and Technology Law Journal,* 18, no. 2 (1992), pp. 879-918.

2376 Oman, Ralph. "The Copyright Clause: 'A Charter for a Living People.'" *University of Baltimore Law Review,* 17, no. 1 (Fall 1987), pp. 99-113.

2377 Oman, Ralph. "The 1976 Copyright Revision Revisited: '*Lector, si monumentum requiris, circumspice.*'" *Journal of the Copyright Society of the U.S.A.,* 34 (Oct. 1986-July 1987), pp. 29-37.

2378 Oman, Ralph. "Software as Seen by the U.S. Copyright Office." *Idea,* 28, no. 1 (1987), pp. 29-38.

2379 "On-Line Information Service Not Liable for Defamatory Statements Posted on Electronic Bulletin Board." *The Computer Lawyer,* 9, no. 2 (Feb. 1992), pp. 34-35.

2380 "On-Line Software Licensee's Production of Offline Add-On Product Violates Best Efforts Clause." *The Computer Lawyer,* 8, no. 8 (Aug. 1991), pp. 31-32.

2381 Onyshko, Tom. "Access to Personal Information: British and Canadian Legislative Approaches." *Manitoba Law Journal,* 18, no. 2 (1989), pp. 213-48.

2382 "Order Invalidating dBASE Line Rescinded." *The Computer Lawyer,* 8, no. 5 (May 1991), p. 28.

2383 O'Regan, Ron. "D & T Offers Software-Auditing Service." *PC Week,* 9, no. 29 (20 July 1992), p. 17.

2384 O'Reilly, Brian. "Making Computers Snoop-Proof." *Fortune,* 113, no. 6 (17 Mar. 1986), p. 65.

2385 Ortner, Charles B. "Current Trends in Software Protection—A Litigation Perspective." *Jurimetrics Journal*, 25, no. 3 (Spring 1985), pp. 319-32.

2386 Oshins, Alice H. "Computer Protection Should Not Be Left to Chance." *Risk Management*, 36, no. 10 (Oct. 1989), p. 60.

2387 Oshins, Alice H. "Making Sure Your Equipment and Information Are Safe." *Working Woman*, 12, no. 5 (May 1987), pp. 28-30.

2388 Ottaviano, Carla. "Computer Crime." *Idea*, 26, no. 4 (1985-86), pp. 163-72.

2389 Overstreet, Keith A. "Copyrightable Expression in the User Interface of a Computer Program: *Lotus Development Corporation v. Paperback Software International.*" *Rutgers Computer and Technology Law Journal*, 18, no. 2 (1992), pp. 941-69.

2390 Owen, David A. "The Application of Article 2 of the Uniform Commercial Code to Computer Contracts." *Northern Kentucky Law Review*, 14, no. 2 (1987), pp. 277-88.

2391 Owen, Kenneth. "Computer Security: IFIP Addresses the Practical Issues." *Computers and Security*, 5, no. 1 (Mar. 1986), pp. 68-72.

2392 Paans, Ronald. "The Second European Conference on Computer Audit, Control and Security." *Computers and Security*, 7, no. 3 (June 1988), pp. 312-15.

2393 Paans, Ronald, and I. S. Herschberg. "How to Control MVS User Supervisor Calls." *Computers and Security*, 5, no. 1 (Mar. 1986), pp. 46-54.

2394 Paans, Ronald, and Israel Samuel Herschberg. "Computer Security: The Long Road Ahead." *Computers and Security*, 6 (1987), pp. 403-16.

2395 Paciaroni, Richard F. "Copyright Law—Computer Programs—The Ninth Circuit Court of Appeals Has Held That All Computer Programs Are Copyrightable Regardless of Their Function. *Apple Computer, Inc. v. Formula Int'l, Inc.*, 725 F.2d 521." *Duquesne Law Review*, 23, no. 2 (Winter 1985), pp. 457-75.

2396 Padgett, Donald F. "Copyright Protection of Computer Software." *Texas Bar Journal*, 48, no. 3 (Mar. 1985), pp. 258-67.

2397 Palca, Joseph. "Culprit Found at Cornell." *Nature*, 338, no. 6216 (13 Apr. 1989), p. 530.

2398 Palenski, Ronald J. "The EC Software Directive: Meeting the Challenges of the Information Age." *Cardozo Arts and Entertainment Law Journal*, 10, no. 1 (1991), pp. 191-276.

2399 Paley, Mark Aaron. "Lotus Lookalike Litigation: Landmark or Limbo?" *Buffalo Law Review*, 40, no. 1 (Winter 1992), pp. 283-319.

2400 Palmer, Alan K., and Thomas C. Vinje. "The EC Directive on the Legal Protection of Computer Software: New Law Governing Software Development." *Duke Journal of Comparative and International Law*, 2, no. 1 (Winter 1992), pp. 65-87.

2401 Palmer, John P. "Copyright and Computer Software." *Research in Law and Economics*, 8 (1986), pp. 205-25.

2402 Panchak, Patricia. "Products and Services That Help Your Company Stay Competitive." *Modern Office Technology*, 36, no. 1 (Jan. 1991), p. 90.

2403 "Panel Discussion." *Idea*, 29, no. 2 (1988-89), pp. 153-65.

2404 "Panel Discussion: Are Computer Viruses Here to Stay." *Computers and Security*, 9, no. 4 (June 1990), pp. 305-7.

2405 Paquette, Paul N. "State Public Records Act Gives Inadequate Protection to Police Files." *Los Angeles Daily Journal*, 105, no. 146 (28 July 1992), p. 6.

2406 Paray, Paul E. "Freedom of Contract Under the UCC: The Ability of Software Vendors to Exclude Recovery of Consequential Damages." *Uniform Commercial Code Law Journal*, 25, no. 2 (Fall 1992), pp. 133-68.

2407 Paray, Paul E. "Judicial Treatment of Damages Exclusions Negotiated in Custom Software Licenses." *Uniform Commercial Code Law Journal*, 25, no. 3 (Winter 1993), pp. 240-56.

2408 Park, Edwards. "Around the Mall and Beyond." *Smithsonian*, 20, no. 11 (Feb. 1990), pp. 20-26.

2409 Parker, Donn. "Computer Crime: As Computer Literacy Increases, Can the Corporate Database Ever Be Safe?" *FE*, 2, no. 12 (Dec. 1986), pp. 31-33.

2410 Parker, Rachel. "Docucomp Has Code to Detect Virus Presence." *InfoWorld*, 11, no. 35 (28 Aug. 1989), p. 38.

2411 Parkhurst, Beverly Susler. "Airline Computer Reservation Systems—A National and International View of Current Legal Issues." *Software Law Journal*, 4, no. 2 (Apr. 1991), pp. 231-46.

2412 "Parol Evidence May Be Considered in Determining Whether 'Property' Conveyed by Writing Included Copyright in Programs." *The Computer Lawyer*, 8, no. 1 (Jan. 1991), pp. 21-22.

2413 Parry, John. "Pirates in the Dock." *International Management*, 46, no. 4 (May 1991), pp. 56-57, 59.

2414 "Passwords Protect ABA/Net Mail." *ABA Journal*, 76 (Sept. 1990), p. 27.

2415 "The Patent Law Equivalency Doctrine and Reduced Instruction Set Computing Technology: If It Computes Like a Duck, Is It Still a Duck?" *Rutgers Computer and Technology Law Journal*, 16, no. 2 (1990), pp. 571-602.

2416 "Patentability of Computer-Related Inventions: A Criticism of the PTO's View on Algorithms." *The George Washington Law Review,* 54, no. 5 (Aug. 1986), pp. 871-914.

2417 Patterson, L. Ray. "Copyright Overextended: A Preliminary Inquiry Into the Need for a Federal Statute of Unfair Competition." *University of Dayton Law Review,* 17, no. 2 (Winter 1992), pp. 385-422.

2418 Paul, Bill. "Electronic Theft Is Routine and Costs Firms Billions, Security Experts Say." *The Wall Street Journal,* 214, no. 78 (20 Oct. 1988), p. B2A.

2419 Pearson, Hilary. "The Last Days of the Clones? Protecting the 'Look and Feel' of Software." *Software Protection,* 6, no. 1 (June 1987), pp. 2-6.

2420 Pearson, Hilary E. "Computer Databases: Copyright and Other Protection." *The Computer Lawyer,* 4, no. 6 (June 1987), pp. 28-36.

2421 Pearson, Hilary E. "Data Protection in Europe." *The Computer Lawyer,* 8, no. 8 (Aug. 1991), pp. 24-29.

2422 Pearson, Hilary E. "Shrink-Wrap Licensing in England." *Software Protection,* 5, no. 3 (Aug. 1986), pp. 1-4.

2423 Pearson, Hilary, Clifford Miller, and Nigel Turtle. "Commercial Implications of the European Software Copyright Directive." *International Quarterly,* 5, no. 1 (Jan. 1993), pp. 108-26. (First published in *The Computer Lawyer,* 8, no. 11 [Nov. 1991], pp. 13-21.)

2424 Peck, Robert S. "Extending the Constitutional Right to Privacy in the New Technological Age." *Hofstra Law Review,* 12, no. 4 (Summer 1984), pp. 893-912.

2425 Peck, Robert S. "The Right to Be Left Alone." *Human Rights,* 15, no. 1 (Fall 1987), pp. 27-31, 50-51.

2426 Pedersen, Robin Lee. "*West Publishing Co. v. Mead Data Central, Inc. (Lexis)*." *Rutgers Computer and Technology Law Journal,* 14, no. 2 (1988), pp. 359-89.

2427 Penney, Brian. "Computer Viruses." *Journal of Housing,* 47, no. 5 (Sept.-Oct. 1990), pp. 235-36.

2428 Perritt, Henry H., Jr. "Electronic Records Management and Archives." *University of Pittsburgh Law Review,* 53, no. 4 (Summer 1992), pp. 963-1024.

2429 Perritt, Henry H., Jr. "Federal Electronic Information Policy." *Temple Law Review,* 63, no. 2 (Summer 1990), pp. 201-50.

2430 Perschke, Gerard A., and Stephen J. Karabin. "Four Steps to Information Security." *Journal of Accountancy,* 161, no. 4 (Apr. 1986), pp. 104-11.

2431 Peters, Marybeth. "The Copyright Office and the Formal Requirements of Registration of Claims to Copyright." *University of Dayton Law Review,* 17, no. 3 (Spring 1992), pp. 737-62.

2432 Peterson, I. "The Complexity of Computer Security." *Science News,* 134, no. 13 (24 Sept. 1988), p. 199.

2433 Peterson, I. "Computing a Bit of Security." *Science News,* 133, no. 3 (16 Jan. 1988), p. 38.

2434 Peterson, I. "Federal Computer Security Concerns." *Science News,* 128, no. 15 (12 Oct. 1985), p. 230.

2435 Peterson, I. "Phone Glitches and Other Computer Faults." *Science News,* 140, no. 1 (6 July 1991), p. 7.

2436 Peterson, I. "Risky Business: Tackling Computer Security." *Science News,* 138, no. 24 (15 Dec. 1990), p. 373.

2437 Peterson, I. "Software Failure: Counting Up the Risks." *Science News,* 140, no. 24 (14 Dec. 1991), pp. 388-89.

2438 Peterson, Ivars. "Bits of Ownership: Growing Computer Software Sales Are Forcing Universities to Rethink Their Copyright and Patent Policies." *Science News,* 128, no. 12 (21 Sept. 1985), pp. 188-90.

2439 Peterson, Ivars. "A Digital Matter of Life and Death: Concerns About Potentially Life-Threatening Software Errors Bring Government Regulation of Computer-Controlled Medical Devices." *Science News,* 133, no. 11 (12 Mar. 1988), pp. 170-71.

2440 Peterson, Ivars. "Warning: This Software May Be Unsafe." *Science News,* 130, no. 11 (13 Sept. 1986), pp. 171-73.

2441 Peterson, Scott K. "Introduction. (Patenting Software Conference Papers)." *Idea,* 31, no. 3 (1991), pp. 181-83.

2442 Peterzell, Jay. "Spying and Sabotage by Computer: The U.S. and Its Adversaries Are Tapping Data Bases — and Spreading Viruses." *Time,* 133, no. 12 (20 Mar. 1989), pp. 25-26.

2443 Petraske, Eric W. "An Infringement Test for Comprehensive Similarity in Software Cases." *The Computer Lawyer,* 7, no. 8 (Aug. 1990), pp. 12-24.

2444 Petraske, Eric W. "Non-Protectible Elements of Software: The Idea/Expression Distinction Is Not Enough." *Idea,* 29, no. 1 (1988-89), pp. 35-67.

2445 Pevzner, Pavel. "No Immunity for Moscow." *Nature,* 338, no. 6210 (2 Mar. 1989), p. 9.

2446 Peys, James T. "Commercial Law — The Enforceability of Computer 'Box-Top' License Agreements Under the U.C.C." *Whittier Law Review,* 7, no. 3 (1985), pp. 881-914.

2447 Phillips, Jeremy. "Literary Works Produced by a Computer." *The Journal of Business Law,* 1985 (1985), pp. 491-92.

2448 Phillips, John C. "Sui Generis Intellectual Property Protection for Computer Software." *The George Washington Law Review,* 60, no. 4 (Apr. 1992), pp. 997-1041.

2449 Picanol, Enric. "The Protection of Software Against Third Parties in Spain." *Software Law Journal,* 1, no. 3 (Spring-Summer 1986), pp. 391-95.

2450 Picarille, Lisa. "Firms Exploit Loophole in Rental Act." *InfoWorld,* 14, no. 2 (13 Jan. 1992), pp. 1, 121.

2451 Pichirallo, Joe, and Philip J. Hilts. "FBI to Question Student About Computer 'Virus.'" *The Washington Post,* 111, no. 337 (6 Nov. 1988), pp. A1, A8-9.

2452 Pickett, John L. "CBEMA Comments on Computer-Related Invention Patents." *The Computer Lawyer,* 8, no. 10 (Oct. 1991), pp. 32-40.

2453 Pierson, Lyndon E., and Edward L. Witzke. "A Security Methodology for Computer Networks." *AT&T Technical Journal,* 67, no. 3 (May/June 1988), pp. 28-36.

2454 Pietrantoni, Michael. "Viruses That Infect Computers." *USA Today,* 117, no. 2524 (Jan. 1989), pp. 64-66.

2455 Pilarski, John H. "User Interfaces and the Idea-Expression Dichotomy, Or, Are the Copyright Laws User Friendly?" *AIPLA Quarterly Journal,* 15, no. 4 (1987), pp. 325-53.

2456 Pincus, Laura B. "Legal Liability for the Health Hazards Resulting from the Use of Video Display Terminals: Who Must Pay?" *Computer/Law Journal,* 11, no. 1 (Feb. 1991), pp. 131-71.

2457 Pines, Deborah. "Criteria for Software Infringement Adopted: Circuit Court Limits Copyright Protections." *New York Law Journal,* 207, no. 121 (24 June 1992), pp. 1-2.

2458 Pines, Deborah. "Federal, State Courts Attack Computer Virus and Prevail—So Far." *New York Law Journal,* 207, no. 42 (4 Mar. 1992), pp. 1-2.

2459 Pinheiro, John, and Gerard Lacroix. "Protecting the 'Look and Feel' of Computer Software." *High Technology Law Journal,* 1, no. 2 (Fall 1986), pp. 411-45.

2460 Piragoff, Donald K. "Computers." *Ottawa Law Review,* 16, no. 2 (1984), pp. 306-15.

2461 Pittman, Margaret L. "What the Judge Sees Is What You Get: The Implications of *Lotus v. Paperback* for Software Copyright." *Wayne Law Review,* 37, no. 3 (Spring 1991), pp. 1527-1613.

2462 Platton, Guy. "The Council Directive on the Legal Protection of Computer Programs: An Unsatisfactory Balance of Competing Interests." *The American University Journal of International Law and Policy*, 7, no. 2 (Winter 1992), pp. 235-88.

2463 "Playing the Data Game: A Congressman and a Computer Magazine Editor Choose Sides Over Privacy." *Omni*, 12, no. 11 (Aug. 1990), p. 16.

2464 Polek, Anastasia. "Back to the Basics: Copyright Protection for Computer Display Screens." *Software Law Journal*, 2, no. 3 (Summer 1988), pp. 373-90.

2465 "Police Computers Used for Improper Tasks." *The New York Times*, 142, no. 49137 (1 Nov. 1992), p. 38.

2466 Pollack, Howard G. "The Gordian Algorithm: An Attempt to Untangle the International Dilemma Over the Protection of Computer Software." *Law and Policy in International Business*, 22, no. 4 (1991), pp. 815-56.

2467 Poore, Ralph Spencer, and David R. Brockman. "Barring Unauthorized Access: The Threats to Computer Security." *The National Law Journal*, 8, no. 5 (14 Oct. 1985), pp. 14, 17.

2468 Port, Otis. "How Uncle Sam's Cloak-and-Data Boys Are Fighting Back." *Business Week*, no. 3063 (1 Aug. 1988), p. 72.

2469 Porter, Janet. "Computer Crime Rise Predicted for Shipping." *Journal of Commerce and Commercial*, 388, no. 27470 (3 May 1991), p. 12B.

2470 Posner, Ronald S., and George T. DeBakey. "Software Piracy Limits U.S. Export Growth." *Software Protection*, 5, no. 2 (July 1986), pp. 11-12.

2471 Posner, Steve. "Can a Computer Language Be Copyrighted? The State of Confusion in Computer Copyright Law." *Computer/Law Journal*, 11, no. 1 (Feb. 1991), pp. 97-130.

2472 "Possible Computer Fraud by Bank Found in London." *Wall Street Journal*, 212, no. 2 (5 July 1988), p. 17.

2473 Post, Gerald V., and Karen-Ann Kievit. "Accessibility vs. Security: A Look at the Demand for Computer Security." *Computers and Security*, 10, no. 4 (June 1991), pp. 331-44.

2474 "Post-Copyright Injunction Damages Pursuable." *The Computer Lawyer*, 9, no. 11 (Nov. 1992), pp. 24-25.

2475 Postell, Claudia J. "Does Strict Liability Apply to Computer Software?" *Trial*, 25, no. 3 (Mar. 1989), pp. 93-95.

2476 Postell, Claudia J. "States Enact Legislation to Target Computer Crime." *Trial*, 25, no. 1 (Jan. 1989), pp. 119-20.

2477 Pournelle, Jerry. "A Confederation of Hackers." *Byte*, 12, no. 2 (Feb. 1987), pp. 267-84.

2478 Pournelle, Jerry. "Dr. Pournelle vs. the Virus." *Byte*, 13, no. 7 (July 1988), pp. 197-207.

2479 Pournelle, Jerry. "On the Road: Hackercon and COMDEX." *Byte*, 10, no. 3 (Mar. 1985), pp. 313-46.

2480 Powell, Mark. "Software Licenses and the Application of the EC Competition Rules." *The Computer Lawyer*, 8, no. 7 (July 1991), pp. 13-24.

2481 Powell, Norma C., and Sherre G. Strickland. "Security in the Microcomputer Environment." *The Ohio CPA Journal*, 48, no. 3 (Autumn 1989), pp. 20-23.

2482 Pozzo, Maria M., and Terence E. Gray. "An Approach to Containing Computer Viruses." *Computers and Security*, 6 (1987), pp. 321-31.

2483 Prasinos, Nicholas. "International Legal Protection of Computer Programs." *Idea*, 26, no. 4 (1985-86), pp. 173-240.

2484 Pratt, Thomas K. "A Legal Test for the Copyrightability of a Computer Program's User Interface." *The University of Kansas Law Review*, 39, no.4 (Summer 1991), pp. 1045-69.

2485 "Preliminary Injunction Inappropriate Because Defendant Did Not Change Its Use of Source Code." *The Computer Lawyer*, 8, no. 9 (Sept. 1991), pp. 30-31.

2486 Price, R. Leon, John S. Cotner, and Warren L. Dickson. "Computer Fraud in Commercial Banks: Management's Perception of Risk." *Journal of Systems Management*, 40, no. 10 (Oct. 1989), pp. 28-32.

2487 Primak, L. Scott. "Computer Software: Should the U.N. Convention on Contracts for the International Sale of Goods Apply? A Contextual Approach to the Question." *Computer/Law Journal*, 11, no. 2 (Apr. 1991), pp. 197-231.

2488 Prins, Corien. "Software Protection in Eastern Europe." *Software Protection*, 6, no. 2-3 (July-Aug. 1987), pp. 14-23.

2489 Pritt, Jeffry A. "Computer Crime in West Virginia: A Statutory Proposal." *West Virginia Law Review*, 91, no. 2 (Winter 1988-89), pp. 569-96.

2490 "Privacy Versus Database Statistics." *Science News*, 140, no. 20 (16 Nov. 1991), p. 315.

2491 Probst, Franz, and Georg Rauber. "Swiss Copyright Law Revisions and Protection of Computer Programs and Integrated Circuits." *The Computer Lawyer*, 7, no. 4 (Apr. 1990), pp. 1-7.

2492 "Product Liability Suit Against Lotus Dropped." *The Computer Lawyer*, 4, no. 2 (Feb. 1987), p. 26.

2493 "Programmer Convicted After Planting a 'Virus.'" *The New York Times*, 138, no. 47635 (21 Sept. 1988), p. D15.

2494 "Programmer Convicted for Computer Virus." *The National Law Journal,* 11, no. 4 (3 Oct. 1988), p. 6.

2495 "A Promise of Conformity in the Area of 'Look and Feel'?; *Data East U.S.A., Inc. v. Epyx, Inc.* 862 F.2d 204 (9th Cir. 1988)." *Santa Clara Computer and High Technology Law Journal,* 5 (1989), pp. 547-57.

2496 "Proposed Copyright Reform in Sweden: The Swedish Copyright Committee Report." *Software Protection,* 5, no. 7 (Dec. 1986), pp. 13-17.

2497 "Proprietary Rights: Consultant's Software Was Not Work Made for Hire." *The Computer Lawyer,* 9, no. 3 (Mar. 1992), pp. 32-33.

2498 "Proprietary Rights: *Feist* Originality Standard Does Not Apply to One of Several Tapes Constituting 3090 Microcode; No Preliminary Injunction on SSO Infringement and Trade Secrets Claims Against Former Principal; Fifth Circuit Law Precludes Copyright Protection for User Interfaces; Component Program Need Not Be Separately Registered, and Trade Secrets Claim Preempted." *The Computer Lawyer,* 8, no. 11 (Nov. 1991), pp. 30-35.

2499 "Proprietary Rights: Plaintiff Misused Copyright by Asserting Similarities Between Defendant's Work and Derivative Matter in Own Work." *The Computer Lawyer,* 8, no. 10 (Oct. 1991), pp. 41-42.

2500 "Protecting Computer Software: Lessons from the Chip Act." *Arizona State Law Journal,* 1986, no. 2 (1986), pp. 337-59.

2501 "Protecting Intellectual Property: An Introductory Guide for U.S. Businesses on Protecting Intellectual Property Abroad." *Business America* (1 July 1991), pp. 2-7.

2502 "Proving Copyright Infringement of Computer Software: An Analytical Framework." *Loyola of Los Angeles Law Review,* 18, no. 3 (1985), pp. 919-48.

2503 Puhala, Karen. "The Protection of Computer Software Through Shrink-Wrap License Agreements." *Washington and Lee Law Review,* 42, no. 4 (Fall 1985), pp. 1347-82.

2504 "Punitives Awarded for Intentional Bug." *The Computer Lawyer,* 9, no. 10 (Oct. 1992), pp. 33-34.

2505 Puri, K. "Copyright Protection in Australia." *Law, Computers and Artificial Intelligence,* 1, no. 1 (1992), pp. 79-114.

2506 Quade, Vicki. "The Law of a New Machine: Making Sense, and New Opportunities, Out of Today's Fast-Growing Computer Law." *Barrister,* 15, no. 3 (Fall 1988), pp. 14-17, 38-42.

2507 Quraishi, Jim, and Julian Milenbach. "Antiviral Utilities Lack Network Punch: Scanners, Monitoring Programs Still Comprise Only One Part of Network Security." *PC Week,* 8, no. 1 (7 Jan. 1991), pp. 93, 96-97.

2508 "ROMs, RAMs, and Copyright: The Copyrightability of Computer Chips." *Southwestern University Law Review*, 14, no. 4 (1984), pp. 685-744.

2509 Rabinowitz, David, and Mark G. Lake. "Security Interests in Computer Programs—Perfection and Enforcement." *Practical Lawyer*, 32, no. 1 (Jan. 1986), pp. 53-64.

2510 Racicot, Michel. "Copyright Reform in Canada as It Relates to Computer Programs." *Software Protection*, 4, no. 9 (Feb. 1986), pp. 1-6.

2511 Racicot, Michel. "Copyright Reform in Canada as It Relates to Computer Programs: Part II." *Software Protection*, 5, no. 4 (Sept. 1986), pp. 1-3.

2512 Racicot, Michel. "Copyright Reform in Canada—Phase I Legislation." *Software Protection*, 6, no. 5 (Oct. 1987), pp. 1-11.

2513 Racicot, Michel. "Protection of Software in Canadian Law· Part 1." *Software Protection*, 8, no. 10 (Mar. 1990), pp. 1-12.

2514 Racicot, Michel. "Protection of Software in Canadian Law: Part 2." *Software Protection*, 8, no. 11 (Apr. 1990), pp. 1-10.

2515 Radai, Yisrael. "The Israeli PC Virus." *Computers and Security*, 8, no. 2 (Apr. 1989), pp. 111-13.

2516 Radcliffe, Mark, and Dianne Brinson. "Security Interests in Copyright: The New Learning." *Software Protection*, 10, no. 7-8 (Dec. 1991-Jan. 1992), pp. 6-14.

2517 Radcliffe, Mark F. "The Future of Computer Law: Ten Challenges for the Next Decade." *The Computer Lawyer*, 8, no. 8 (Aug. 1991), pp. 1-11.

2518 Radcliffe, Mark F. "Recent Developments in Copyright Law Related to Computer Software." *Software Protection*, 4, no. 5 (Oct. 1985), pp. 1-8.

2519 Radcliffe, Mark F. "Trademarks: The Computer Industry's Forgotten Asset." *The Computer Lawyer*, 9, no. 8 (Aug. 1992), pp. 10-14.

2520 Radding, Alan. "Plans for a Safer System." *Computer Decisions*, 19, no. 7 (6 Apr. 1987), pp. 36-38.

2521 Raffel, Dawn. "They Just Can't 'Hack' It Anymore." *Seventeen*, 43, no. 2 (Feb. 1984), p. 54.

2522 Raloff, Janet. "Coming: The Big Chill." *Science News*, 131, no. 20 (16 May 1987), pp. 314-17.

2523 Ramaswamy, Raju. "Placement of Data Integrity Security Services in Open Systems Interconnection Architecture." *Computers and Security*, 8, no. 6 (Oct. 1989), pp. 507-16.

2524 Ramirez, Anthony. "The Password Is...." *The New York Times*, 141, no. 49036 (23 July 1992), p. B7(L).

2525 Ramirez, Anthony. "A Wiretap of Computers Leads to Arrest of Hackers." *The New York Times*, 141, no. 49025 (12 July 1992), p. E2.

2526 Ramos, Gregory J. "*Lotus v. Paperback*: Confusing the Idea-Expression Distinction and Its Application to Computer Software." *University of Colorado Law Review*, 63, no. 1 (1992), pp. 267-90.

2527 Rankin, Murray. "Privacy and Technology: A Canadian Perspective." *Alberta Law Review*, 22, no. 3 (1984), pp. 323-47.

2528 Ranii, David. "Computer Laws Add Up: Do They Go Far Enough?" *The National Law Journal*, 6, no. 34 (30 Apr. 1984), pp. 1, 34, 36-37.

2529 Raphael, Lance A. "Teaching an Old Law a New Trick: Repossessing Software Through Disablement." *Commercial Law Journal*, 97, no. 2 (Summer 1992), pp. 276-94.

2530 Raphelson, Jeffrey G. "Limits on Warranties, Remedies and Damages in Computer Contracts." *Michigan Bar Journal*, 67, no. 10 (Oct. 1988), pp. 976-81.

2531 Rash, Wayne, Jr. "Be Secure, Not Sorry." *Byte*, 13, no. 10 (Oct. 1988), pp. 129-30.

2532 Rash, Wayne, Jr. "Security." *Byte*, 14, no. 6 (June 1989), p. 254.

2533 Raskind, Leo J. "Assessing the Impact of *Feist*." *University of Dayton Law Review*, 17, no. 2 (Winter 1992), pp. 331-65.

2534 Raskind, Leo J. "Reverse Engineering, Unfair Competition, and Fair Use." *Minnesota Law Review*, 70, no. 2 (Dec. 1985), pp. 385-415.

2535 Raskind, Leo J. "The Uncertain Case for Special Legislation Protecting Computer Software." *University of Pittsburgh Law Review*, 47, no. 4 (Summer 1986), pp. 1131-84.

2536 Ratner, Allan, and Kenneth N. Nigon. "The Patentability of Computer Programs: The PTO Guidelines, *In re Grams* and *In re Iwahashi*." *The Computer Lawyer*, 6, no. 12 (Dec. 1989), pp. 21-29.

2537 Raubitschek, John H. "Legislative Update on DOD Patent and Data Rights." *The Army Lawyer*, 1987 (Jan. 1987), pp. 32-34.

2538 Rauenhorst, Amy M. "Software Production and Development Policy Alternatives: Brazil and Singapore." *The Fletcher Forum of World Affairs*, 13, no. 1 (Winter 1989), pp. 127-42.

2539 Rauf, Naeem M. "Recent Developments in Wire-Tap Law." *The Criminal Law Quarterly*, 31 (1988-89), pp. 208-39.

2540 Ray, Paul Chastain. "Computer Viruses and the Criminal Law: A Diagnosis and a Prescription." *Georgia State University Law Review*, 7, no. 2 (Spring 1991), pp. 455-94.

2541 Rayl, A. J. S. "Secrets of the Cyberculture." *Omni,* 15, no. 2 (Nov. 1992), pp. 58-67.

2542 Raysman, Richard, and Peter Brown. "'Best Efforts' Obligations in Licensing Accords." *New York Law Journal,* 206, no. 6 (9 July 1991), pp. 3, 6.

2543 Raysman, Richard, and Peter Brown. "Confidentiality Agreements." *New York Law Journal,* 194, no. 50 (10 Sept. 1985), pp. 1-2.

2544 Raysman, Richard, and Peter Brown. "Consumer Fraud Act—Litigation Tool Useful." *New York Law Journal,* 199, no. 54 (22 Mar. 1988), pp. 1, 32.

2545 Raysman, Richard, and Peter Brown. "Copyright and Programs." *New York Law Journal,* 205, no. 10 (15 Jan. 1991), pp. 3, 6.

2546 Raysman, Richard, and Peter Brown. "Copyright Protection for Software Redefined." *New York Law Journal,* 208, no. 9 (14 July 1992), pp. 3-4, 7.

2547 Raysman, Richard, and Peter Brown. "Effective Establishment of a Software Patent Claim." *New York Law Journal,* 206, no. 43 (29 Aug. 1991), pp. 3, 30.

2548 Raysman, Richard, and Peter Brown. "Jail Term for Theft of Software." *New York Law Journal,* 207, no. 28 (11 Feb. 1992), pp. 3, 5.

2549 Raysman, Richard, and Peter Brown. "Liability for Unauthorized Changes in Software." *New York Law Journal,* 202, no. 94 (15 Nov. 1989), pp. 3-4.

2550 Raysman, Richard, and Peter Brown. "Limited Availability of Headstart Defense." *New York Law Journal,* 199, no. 89 (10 May 1988), pp. 1-2.

2551 Raysman, Richard, and Peter Brown. "New Legislation on Computer Crime." *New York Law Journal,* 196, no. 113 (12 Dec. 1986), pp. 1, 3.

2552 Raysman, Richard, and Peter Brown. "Pending Legislation on Computer Crime." *New York Law Journal,* 191, no. 89 (8 May 1984), pp. 1-2.

2553 Raysman, Richard, and Peter Brown. "Privacy and Computer Data Issues." *New York Law Journal,* 202, no. 84 (31 Oct. 1989), pp. 3, 5.

2554 Raysman, Richard, and Peter Brown. "Privity in Systems Agreements." *New York Law Journal,* 205, no. 111 (11 June 1991), pp. 3, 7.

2555 Raysman, Richard, and Peter Brown. "Recent Copyright Decisions." *New York Law Journal,* 207, no. 91 (12 May 1992), pp. 3, 6.

2556 Raysman, Richard, and Peter Brown. "Recent Developments in Legislation." *New York Law Journal,* 196, no. 5 (8 July 1986), pp. 1, 26.

2557 Raysman, Richard, and Peter Brown. "Recent Federal, State Computer-Crime Statutes." *New York Law Journal,* 193, no. 5 (8 Jan. 1985), pp. 1-2.

2558 Raysman, Richard, and Peter Brown. "Recent Software Copyright Decisions." *New York Law Journal,* 208, no. 72 (13 Oct. 1992), pp. 3, 5.

2559 Raysman, Richard, and Peter Brown. "'Shrink-Wrap' Licenses and Implied Warranties." *New York Law Journal,* 205, no. 55 (22 Mar. 1991), pp. 3, 31.

2560 Raysman, Richard, and Peter Brown. "Software Ownership and Work for Hire." *New York Law Journal,* 207, no. 46 (10 Mar. 1992), p. 3-4.

2561 Raysman, Richard, and Peter Brown. "Tampering with New York's Computer Crime Statute." *New York Law Journal,* 199, no. 113 (14 June 1988), pp. 3, 6.

2562 Raysman, Richard, and Peter Brown. "Trade Secret Protection and Generic Programs." *New York Law Journal,* 203, no. 20 (30 Jan. 1990), pp. 3, 5.

2563 Raysman, Richard, and Peter Brown. "Trademark Protection for Computer Products." *New York Law Journal,* 207, no. 71 (14 Apr. 1992), pp. 3, 5.

2564 Raysman, Richard, and Peter Brown. "The U.K.'s Data Protection Act." *New York Law Journal,* 200, no. 7 (12 July 1988), pp. 3, 6.

2565 Raysman, Richard, and Peter Brown. "Unauthorized Employee Use of Computers." *New York Law Journal,* 195, no. 10 (15 Jan. 1986), pp. 1, 28.

2566 Raysman, Richard, and Peter Brown. "Viruses and How to Prevent Them." *New York Law Journal,* 202, no. 50 (12 Sept. 1989), pp. 3, 6.

2567 Raysman, Richard, and Peter Brown. "Whelan Standards Attacked." *New York Law Journal,* 207, no. 9 (14 Jan. 1992), pp. 3, 7.

2568 Rebello, Kathy, Michele Galen, and Evan I. Schwartz. "It Looks and Feels as If Apple Lost." *Business Week,* no. 3263 (27 Apr. 1992), p. 36.

2569 "Red Ink Is a Symptom of Virus Epidemic." *PC Week,* 7, no. 12 (26 Mar. 1990), p. 117.

2570 Reece, Laurence H., III. "Computer Monitoring and Privacy: Is the Orwellian Nightmare Here?" *The National Law Journal,* 10, no. 23 (15 Feb. 1988), pp. 20-21.

2571 Reece, Laurence H., III. "Legal Theories in Actions Against Software Developers for Defective Software." *Idea,* 29, no. 2 (1988-89), pp. 113-20.

2572 Reed, C. M. "Negligence and Computer Software." *Journal of Business Law,* 1987 (Nov. 1987), pp. 444-53.

2573 Reed, Chris. "Authenticating Electronic Mail Messages—Some Evidential Problems." *Software Law Journal,* 4, no. 2 (Apr. 1991), pp. 161-72.

2574 Reed, Chris. "EC Antitrust Law and the Exploitation of Intellectual Property Rights in Software." *Jurimetrics,* 32, no. 3 (Spring 1992), pp. 431-46.

2575 Reed, Sandra R. "See You in Court." *Personal Computing,* 13, no. 8 (Aug. 1989), pp. 179-80.

2576 Reetz, C. Ryan. "Warrant Requirement for Searches of Computerized Information." *Boston University Law Review,* 67, no. 1 (Jan. 1987), pp. 179-212.

2577 Regan, Priscilla M. "Privacy, Government Information, and Technology." *Public Administration Review,* 46, no. 6 (Nov.-Dec. 1986), pp. 629-34.

2578 Regis, Ed. "A Science Court: Case 6. Computer Privacy." *Omni,* 10. no. 4 (Jan. 1988), pp. 99-100.

2579 "Registration of Claims to Copyright; Mandatory Deposit of Machine-Readable Copies." *Software Protection,* 8, no. 8 (Jan. 1990), pp. 2-8.

2580 "Registration Under the Data Protection Act 1984 " *The Journal of the Law Society of Scotland,* 30, no. 12 (Dec. 1985), pp. 470-72.

2581 Reich, John C. "Guidelines for Evaluating Whether a Claim That Embodies an Algorithm Constitutes Patentable Subject Matter." *Software Law Journal,* 5, no. 2 (Apr. 1992), pp. 461-91.

2582 Reichman, J. H. "Computer Programs as Applied Scientific Know-How: Implications of Copyright Protection for Commercialized University Research." *Vanderbilt Law Review,* 42, no. 3 (Apr. 1989), pp. 639-723.

2583 Reichman, J. H. "Electronic Information Tools—The Outer Edge of World Intellectual Property Law." *University of Dayton Law Review,* 17, no. 3 (Spring 1992), pp. 797-851.

2584 Reichman, Nancy. "Computer Matching Toward Computerized Systems of Regulation." *Law and Policy,* 9, no. 4 (Oct. 1987), pp. 387-415.

2585 Reid, Calvin. "Facts on File Settles Claims in Software Copyright Suit." *Publishers Weekly,* 235, no. 25 (23 June 1989), pp. 9-10.

2586 Reidenberg, Joel R. "Privacy in the Information Economy: A Fortress or Frontier for Individual Rights?" *Federal Communications Law Journal,* 44, no. 2 (Mar. 1992), pp. 195-243.

2587 Reidenberg, Joel R. "The Privacy Obstacle Course: Hurdling Barriers to Transnational Financial Services." *Fordham Law Review,* 60, no. 6 (May 1992), pp. S137-77.

2588 Reidenberg, Joel R. "U.S. Software Protection: Problems of Trade Secret Estoppel Under International and Brazilian Technology Transfer Regimes." *Columbia Journal of Transnational Law,* 23, no. 3 (1985), pp. 679-704.

2589 Reidinger, Paul. "Cite Wars: Lexis Can't Use West's Pages." *ABA Journal,* 72, no. 14 (Dec. 1986), p. 78.

2590 Reidinger, Paul. "Soft Selling: U.C.C. Covers Computer Software." *ABA Journal,* 77 (May 1991), pp. 87-88.

2591 Reilly, Ann. "Computer Crackdown: Washington Is Finally Getting Around to Doing Something About Computer Crime." *Fortune,* 110, no. 6 (17 Sept. 1984), pp. 141-42.

2592 Reimer, Douglas M. "Judicial and Legislative Responses to Computer Crimes." *Insurance Counsel Journal,* 53, no. 3 (July 1986), pp. 406-30.

2593 Reimer, Douglas M. "The Low Side of High Tech." *The Brief,* 14, no. 4 (Summer 1985), pp. 9-12, 16.

2594 Reimer, Douglas M. "12 Ways to Con a Computer." *The Brief,* 14, no. 4 (Summer 1985), pp.13-15.

2595 Reinhardt, Andy. "The Lotus Case: Judge Rules User Interface Is Protected by Copyright." *Byte,* 15, no. 9 (Sept. 1990), pp. 19-20.

2596 Render, Barry, Richard Coffinberger, Ella P. Gardner, Stephen R. Ruth, and Linda Samuels. "Perspectives on Computer Ethics and Crime." *Business,* 36, no. 1 (Jan.-Mar. 1986), pp. 30-36.

2597 Rensberger, Boyce, and R. Jeffrey Smith. "'Virus' Illustrates Security Problems." *The Washington Post,* 111, no. 336 (5 Nov. 1988), p. A4.

2598 Renton, Paul. "Secure Your Hard Disk with PC Access." *Radio-Electronics,* 61, no. 4 (Apr. 1990), pp. 69, 73-76.

2599 Reske, Henry J. "Inslaw Investigator Appointed: Allegations of Stolen Software, International Conspiracy Dog Justice." *ABA Journal,* 78 (Feb. 1992), pp. 22, 24.

2600 Resnick, Rosalind. "The Outer Limits: As Personal Computers Proliferate, the Technology Raises New Civil Liberties Issues That Test the Bounds of Existing Laws." *The National Law Journal,* 14, no. 2 (16 Sept. 1991), pp. 1, 32-33.

2601 "Retroviral Michelangelo." *Nature,* 356, no. 6365 (12 Mar. 1992), p. 92.

2602 "Reverse Engineering Defense Unsubstantiated; $26M Verdict Left Intact." *The Computer Lawyer,* 9, no. 12 (Dec. 1992), pp. 33-34.

2603 Reynolds, Larry. "Constitutional Law in the Electronic Age." *Management Review,* 81, no. 9 (Sept. 1992), pp. 24-25.

2604 Rice, Charles M. "Computer Law for the Non-Specialist." *Journal of the Missouri Bar,* 41, no. 8 (Dec. 1985), pp. 489-95.

2605 Rice, David A. "Lessons About the Realities of Contract for U.C.C. Article 2 Revision and a Future Software Contract Statute." *Rutgers Computer and Technology Law Journal,* 18, no. 2 (1992), pp. 499-520.

2606 Rice, David A. "Licensing the Use of Computer Program Copies and the Copyright Act First Sale Doctrine." *Jurimetrics Journal,* 30, no. 2 (Winter 1990), pp. 157-87.

2607 Rice, David A. "Public Goods, Private Contract and Public Policy: Federal Preemption of Software License Prohibitions Against Reverse Engineering." *University of Pittsburgh Law Review,* 53, no. 3 (Spring 1992), pp. 543-630.

2608 Rice, David A. "Whither (No Longer Whether) Software Copyright." *Rutgers Computer and Technology Law Journal,* 16, no. 2 (1990), pp. 341-55.

2609 Rice, Susan Dianne. "AMD's 'Smoking Guns' Used Bullets from Intel." *Los Angeles Daily Journal,* 105, no. 39 (26 Feb. 1992), pp. 1, 10.

2610 Rice, Susan Dianne "$85,000 Awarded in Software Suit." *Los Angeles Daily Journal,* 105, no. 68 (8 Apr. 1992), p. 3.

2611 Rice, Susan Dianne. "Jurors Deliberate Copyright Claim at San Jose Trial on Computer Chip." *Los Angeles Daily Journal,* 105, no. 113 (11 June 1992), p. 3.

2612 Rice, Susan Dianne. "Largest Software Seizure Made: California Attorneys for Microsoft Obtain Order for Severe Remedy." *Los Angeles Daily Journal,* 105, no. 197 (9 Oct. 1992), p. 3.

2613 Rich, Patricia L. "When Technology and the Law Collide—Look and Feel Copyright Evolves." *Western State University Law Review,* 16, no. 1 (Fall 1988), pp. 183-99.

2614 Richards, Evelyn. "Behind Computer 'Virus': Network's Lax Oversight." *The Washington Post,* 112, no. 227 (20 July 1989), p. A21.

2615 Richards, Evelyn. "Viruses Pull Computer Underground Into Spotlight." *The Washington Post,* 112, no. 62 (5 Feb. 1989), pp. H1, H6.

2616 Richards, Evelyn, and John Burgess. "New U.S.-Soviet Computer Links Raising Questions About Security." *The Washington Post,* 112, no. 67 (10 Feb. 1989), pp. F1, F3.

2617 Richards, John. "10 Years of Substantive Law Development in the European Patent Office." *Journal of the Patent and Trademark Office Society,* 71, no. 4 (Apr. 1989), pp. 320-42.

2618 Richards, Roy Martin, and Jan Yestingsmeier. "Risk Management—A Key to Security in the Electronic Funds Transfer System." *Computers and Security,* 5 (1986), pp. 135-40.

2619 Ricketson, Sam. "The Use of Copyright Works in Electronic Databases." *Law Institute Journal,* 63, no. 6 (June 1989), pp. 480-82.

2620 Riddle, Bruce L., Murray S. Miron, and Judith A. Semo. "Passwords in Use in a University Time Sharing Environment." *Computers and Security*, 8, no. 7 (Nov. 1989), pp. 569-79.

2621 Riley, Tom. "Data Protection Today and Some Trends." *Law/Technology*, 17, no. 1 (1984), pp. 3-12.

2622 Rimas, Vytas M. "Trade Secret Protection of Computer Software." *Computer/Law Journal*, 5, no. 1 (Summer 1984), pp. 77-99.

2623 Rines, Robert H. "Some Areas of Basic Difference Between United States Patent Law and That of the Rest of the World—and Why." *Idea*, 28, no. 1 (1987-88), pp. 5-12.

2624 Rines, Robert H., et al. "Computer Software: A New Proposal for Intellectual Property Protection." *Idea*, 29, no. 1 (1988-89), pp. 3-18.

2625 Risberg, Robert L., Jr. "Five Years Without Infringement Litigation Under the Semiconductor Chip Protection Act: Unmasking the Spectre of Chip Piracy in an Era of Diverse and Incompatible Process Technologies." *Wisconsin Law Review*, 1990, no. 1 (1990), pp. 241-77.

2626 Ritter, Jeffrey B. "Defining International Electronic Commerce." *Northwestern Journal of International Law and Business*, 13, no.1 (Spring/Summer 1992), pp. 3-30.

2627 Roache, Jerome Y. "Computer Crime Deterrence." *American Journal of Criminal Law*, 13, no. 3 (Summer 1986), pp. 391-416.

2628 Robbins, Richard L. "Keeping Your Computer System Safe." *Wisconsin Lawyer*, 64, no. 4 (Apr. 1991), pp. 33-34.

2629 Roberts, Charley. "Congress Approves Two Revisions in Laws of Software Piracy, Fair Use." *Los Angeles Daily Journal*, 105, no. 198 (12 Oct. 1992), p. 5.

2630 Roberts, Charley. "House Report Questions Justice Policy." *Los Angeles Daily Journal*, 105, no. 3 (6 Jan. 1992), p. 7.

2631 Roberts, R. J. "Protection of Semiconductor Chip Design Under Canadian Copyright Law: Will Canada Follow the Lead of the United States?" *The University of Western Ontario Law Review*, 23, no. 1 (1985), pp. 101-109.

2632 Robertson, Bernard. "Electronic Mail—Is It Safe to Use?" *Computers and Security*, 10, no. 1 (Feb. 1991), pp. 17-19.

2633 Robins, Gary. "When a Virus Strikes...." *Stores*, 72, no. 1 (Jan. 1990), pp. 78, 83-84.

2634 Robinson, Duncan. "Ruble Helps Fight Software Piracy in Former USSR." *Journal of Commerce and Commercial*, 391, no. 27696 (31 Mar. 1992), p. 10A.

2635 Robinson, Peter. "Legal Issues Raised by Transborder Data Flow." *Canada-United States Law Journal,* 11 (1986), pp. 295-316.

2636 Robotham, Rosemarie. "Robopsychology." *Omni,* 11, no. 2 (Nov. 1988), pp. 42-49, 92.

2637 Rodau, Andrew. "Computer Software: Does Article 2 of the Uniform Commercial Code Apply?" *Emory Law Journal,* 35, no. 4 (Fall 1986), pp. 853-920.

2638 Rodau, Andrew. "Computer Software Contracts: A Review of the Caselaw." *Software Law Journal,* 2, no. 1 (Winter 1987), pp. 77-100. (First published in Akron Law Review, 21, no. 1 [Summer 1987], pp. 45-66.)

2639 Rodau, Andrew G. "Protecting Computer Software: After *Apple Computer, Inc. v. Franklin Computer Corp.,* 714 F.2d 1240 (3d Cir. 1983), Does Copyright Provide the Best Protection?" *Intellectual Property Law Review,* 18 (1986), pp. 413-38. (First published in *Temple Law Quarterly,* 57, no. 3 [1984], pp. 527-52.)

2640 Roden, Adrian. "Computer Crime and the Law." *Criminal Law Journal,* 15, no. 6 (Dec. 1991), pp. 397-415.

2641 Roffe, Pedro. "UNCTAD: Code of Conduct on Transfer of Technology." *Journal of World Trade Law,* 19, no. 6 (Nov.-Dec. 1985), pp. 669-72.

2642 Rogers, Michael, and Bob Cohn. "Not Too Much of a Headache: But Beware the Next Round of Computer Viruses!" *Newsweek,* 119, no. 11 (16 Mar. 1992), p. 60.

2643 Rogers, Michael, and Carroll Bogert. "Red Hackers, Arise!" *Newsweek,* 113, no. 12 (20 Mar. 1989), pp. 58-59.

2644 Rohrlach, H.-J. "Protection of Privacy and Security Measures in Data-Processing." *International Social Security Review,* 39, no. 1 (1986), pp. 14-23.

2645 Ronne, George E. "Computer Security Plan Is a Vital Business Need." *National Underwriter-Property & Casualty/Risk & Benefits Management Edition,* 95, no. 7 (18 Feb. 1991), pp. 14, 37.

2646 Ronne, George E. "Data Security: The Best Insurance." *Best's Review-Life/Health Insurance Edition,* 91, no. 12 (Apr. 1991), pp. 72, 74, 76, 78.

2647 Rooney, Paula. "'Michelangelo' Virus Poised to Hit March 6." *PC Week,* 9, no. 7 (17 Feb. 1992), pp. 45-46.

2648 Rooney, Paula. "Michelangelo's Scourge Brings Healthy Revenue." *PC Week,* 9, no. 11 (16 Mar. 1992), p. 14.

2649 Rooney, Paula. "PC Users Brace for Outbreak of Maltese Computer Virus." *PC Week,* 9, no. 9 (2 Mar. 1992), p. 37.

2650 Rooney, Paula. "Symantec Anti-Virus Gains New GUI to Lure Mac Novices." *PC Week,* 9, no. 45 (9 Nov. 1992), p. 7.

2651 Rooney, Paula. "Symantec Boosts Norton AntiVirus' Detection Range." *PC Week,* 9, no. 2 (13 Jan. 1992), pp. 41-42.

2652 Rooney, Paula. "Virus Solution to Be Surveyed in NCSA Report." *PC Week,* 9, no. 27 (6 July 1992), p. 25.

2653 Rooney, Paula. "Western Digital Chip Set Designed to Detect Viruses." *PC Week,* 9, no. 46 (16 Nov. 1992), p. 28.

2654 Root, Howard. "Copyright Infringement of Computer Programs: A Modification of the Substantial Similarity Test." *Minnesota Law Review,* 68, no. 6 (June 1984), pp. 1264-302.

2655 Ropski, Gary M., and Michael J. Kline. "A Primer on Intellectual Property Rights: The Basics of Patents, Trademarks, Copyrights, Trade Secrets, and Related Rights." *Albany Law Review,* 50, no. 2 (Winter 1986), pp. 405-35.

2656 Rose, Lance. "End-User Licensees of Computer Programs—Are They Allowed to Compete with Their Licensors?" *Rutgers Computer and Technology Law Journal,* 13, no. 2 (1987), pp. 297-316.

2657 Rosenberg, Jim. "Combatting PC Viruses." *Editor and Publisher,* 122, no. 35 (2 Sept. 1989), pp. 11PC, 31PC.

2658 Rosenberg, Jim. "Coping with a PC Virus: How the Memphis Commercial Appeal Handled a Computer Infection." *Editor and Publisher,* 122, no. 35 (2 Sept. 1989), pp. 8PC, 10PC.

2659 Rosenblatt, Kenneth. "Criminal Law and the Information Age: Protecting Trade Secrets from Disclosure in Criminal Cases." *The Computer Lawyer,* 8, no. 1 (Jan. 1991), pp. 15-18.

2660 Rosenblatt, Kenneth. "Deterring Computer Crime." *Technology Review,* 93, no. 2 (Feb.-Mar. 1990), pp. 34-40.

2661 Rosenblum, Howard S. "Software Escrows: Legal Concerns." *Boston Bar Journal,* 29, no. 5 (Nov.-Dec. 1985), pp. 22-27.

2662 Rosenwasser, Ronald N. "Computer Viruses: How to Guard Against Them; with the Help of Qualified Legal Counsel, a Carefully Prepared Contract Protects User and Vendor Interests." *The Office,* 115, no. 2 (Feb. 1992), pp. 11, 18.

2663 Ross, Steven J. "Viruses, Worms and Other (Computer) Plagues." *The EDP Auditor Journal,* 3 (1988), pp. 21-23.

2664 Roth, Steve. "Software Groups to Deal with Piracy Issue." *Publishers Weekly,* 225, no. 26 (29 June 1984), p. 74.

2665 Rothfeder, Jeffrey, and Evan I. Schwartz. "Computer Anarchism Calls for a Tough Response." *Business Week,* no. 3172 (6 Aug. 1990), p. 72.

2666 Rothfeder, Jeffrey, Stephen Phillips, Dean Foust, Wanda Cantrell, Paula Dwyer, and Michele Galen. "Is Nothing Private?" *Business Week,* no. 3122 (4 Sept. 1989), pp. 74-77, 80-82.

2667 Rottinger, Moritz. "Copyright Protection of Computer Programs and Videogames in Austria." *Software Protection,* 8, no. 8 (Jan. 1990), pp. 8-10.

2668 Rottinger, Moritz. "Legal Protection of Computer Programs in Germany: Renunciation of Copyright?" *Software Protection,* 6, no. 4 (Sept. 1987), pp. 8-13.

2669 Rubenking, Neil. "Vi-Spy Finds and Destroys Known Viruses." *PC Magazine,* 9, no. 11 (12 June 1990), p. 49.

2670 Rubenking, Neil J. "Infection Protection." *PC Magazine,* 8, no. 8 (25 Apr. 1989), pp. 193-96.

2671 Rudnick, Rhoda L. "Window Dressing: Trademark Protection for Computer Screen Displays and Software." *Intellectual Property Law Review,* 24 (1992), pp. 299-329.

2672 Rudnick, Robert E. "*Manufacturers Technologies, Inc. v. Cams, Inc.*: A False Hope for Software Developers Seeking Copyright Protection for Their Generated Screen Displays." *Rutgers Computer and Technology Journal,* 17, no. 1 (1991), pp. 211-50.

2673 "Rulings in *Apple v. Microsoft* and *H-P.*" *The Computer Lawyer,* 8, no. 4 (Apr. 1991), pp. 36-37.

2674 Rush, Andrea. "A User-Friendly Guide to Copyright Protection for Computer Programs in Canada." *Journal of the Copyright Society of the U.S.A.,* 38 (1990-91), pp. 92-100.

2675 Rush, Andrea F. "Copyright Protection for Computer Software and Semiconductor Chips in Canada—A Canadian Perspective." *Journal of the Copyright Society of the U.S.A.,* 33 (Oct. 1985-July 1986), pp. 162-72.

2676 Russo, Jack. "Do 'Box-Top' Software Licenses Work?" *Software Protection,* 2, no. 7 (Mar.-Apr. 1984), pp. 1-11.

2677 Russo, Jack. "Further Developments in Copyright Protection of the 'Look and Feel' of Computer Software: Recent Copyright Office Regulations." *Software Protection,* 7, no. 1 (June 1988), pp. 1-2.

2678 Russo, Jack. "Recent Developments in the Copyright Protection of the 'Look and Feel' of Computer Software: *Apple Computer v. Microsoft and Hewlett-Packard.*" *Software Protection,* 6, no. 10 (Mar. 1988), pp. 1-3.

2679 Rutledge, Linda S., and Lance J. Hoffman. "A Survey of Issues in Computer Network Security." *Computers and Security*, 5 (1986), pp. 296-308.

2680 Ryan, Richard W. "Does Insurance Really Ensure Computer Security?" *Risk Management*, 36, no. 11 (Nov. 1989), pp. 28-30, 32.

2681 Ryan, Thomas J., Jr. "The 'Flexibility' Factor in Copyright, Trade Secret and Patent Law for Computer Software: The Aftermath of *Sony*." *Ohio Northern University Law Review*, 11, no. 2 (1984), pp. 333-63.

2682 Ryen, Jeffrey I. "The Return of the *Walter* Test: Patentability of Claims Containing Mathematical Algorithms After *In Re Grams*." *Cornell Law Review*, 76, no. 4 (May 1991), pp. 962-83.

2683 "SPA Escalates Campaign to Wipe Out Piracy." *PC Week*, 8, no. 12 (25 Mar. 1991), p. 115.

2684 Saari, Juhani. "Computer Crime — Numbers Lie." *Computers and Security*, 6 (1987), pp. 111-17.

2685 Sadler, Brent W. "Intellectual Property Protection Through International Trade." *Houston Journal of International Law*, 14, no. 2 (Winter 1992), pp. 393-423.

2686 "Safe Snooping." *The Bulletin of the Atomic Scientists*, 46, no. 8 (Oct. 1990), pp. 5-6.

2687 "Safeguards Take Bite Out of Michelangelo." *PC Week*, 9, no. 10 (9 Mar. 1992), pp. 1, 13.

2688 Saffo, Paul. "Desperately Seeking Cyberspace." *Personal Computing*, 13, no. 5 (May 1989), pp. 247-48.

2689 Safire, William. "Americans Need Sophisticated Protection from Snoops." *Los Angeles Daily Journal*, 105, no. 146 (28 July 1992), p. 6.

2690 Saidman, Perry J. "Patents: There Is Something New Under the Sun." *Barrister*, 14, no. 1 (Winter 1987), pp. 52-55.

2691 Saltzberg, Edward C. "Legal and Technical Protection Through Software Locks." *Computer/Law Journal*, 5, no. 2 (Fall 1984), pp. 163-76.

2692 Sampson, Karen L. "Computer Viruses: Not Fads, Not Funny." *The Office*, 110, no. 4 (Oct. 1989), pp. 56-57, 59, 61.

2693 Samuels, Alec. "Data Protection Registration: Layman's Guide." *Solicitors' Journal*, 130, no. 12 (21 Mar. 1986), pp. 212-13.

2694 Samuels, Alec, and Penelope Pearce. "Data Protection Act 1984." *Solicitors' Journal*, 128, no. 35 (31 Aug. 1984), pp. 587-90.

2695 Samuels, Dorothy J. "Privacy in 1984: The Dark Side of the Computer." *USA Today*, 112, no. 2466 (Mar. 1984), pp. 32-34.

2696 Samuels, Linda B., and Jeffrey M. Samuels. "New Developments in Copyright Protection of Computer Software." *International Journal of Legal Information*, 15, no. 5-6 (Oct.-Dec. 1987), pp. 195-200.

2697 Samuels, Linda B., and Jeffrey M. Samuels. "Semiconductor Chip Protection Act of 1984: An Analytical Commentary." *American Business Law Journal*, 23, no. 4 (Winter 1986), pp. 601-16.

2698 Samuels, Linda B., and Le Thi Cao. "Survey of the Opinion of Software Development Companies Concerning Intellectual Property Protection." *Idea*, 32, no. 4 (1992), pp. 343-59.

2699 Samuelson, Pamela. "Allocating Ownership Rights in Computer-Generated Works." *University of Pittsburgh Law Review*, 47, no. 4 (Summer 1986), pp. 1185-1228.

2700 Samuelson, Pamela. "*Benson* Revisited: The Case Against Patent Protection for Algorithms and Other Computer Program-Related Inventions." *Emory Law Journal*, 39, no. 4 (Fall 1990), pp. 1025-1154.

2701 Samuelson, Pamela. "CONTU Revisited: The Case Against Copyright Protection for Computer Programs in Machine-Readable Form." *Duke Law Journal*, 1984, no. 4 (Sept. 1984), pp. 663-769.

2702 Samuelson, Pamela. "Computer Programs, User Interfaces, and Section 102(b) of the Copyright Act of 1976: A Critique of *Lotus v. Paperback*." *High Technology Law Journal*, 6, no. 2 (Fall 1991), pp. 209-69. (A slight variation of this article was published under the same title in *Law and Contemporary Problems*, 55, no. 2 (Spring 1992), pp. 311-53.)

2703 Samuelson, Pamela. "Creating a New Kind of Intellectual Property: Applying the Lessons of the Chip Law to Computer Programs." *Minnesota Law Review*, 70, no. 2 (Dec. 1985), pp. 471-531.

2704 Samuelson, Pamela. "Digital Media and the Changing Face of Intellectual Property Law." *Rutgers Computer and Technology Law Journal*, 16, no. 2 (1990), pp. 323-40.

2705 Samuelson, Pamela. "Modifying Copyrighted Software: Adjusting Copyright Doctrine to Accommodate a Technology." *Jurimetrics Journal*, 28, no. 2 (Winter 1988), pp. 179-221.

2706 Samuelson, Pamela. "The Need for Reform of the Software Licensing Policy of the Department of Defense." *Jurimetrics Journal*, 27, no. 1 (Fall 1986), pp. 9-64.

2707 Samuelson, Pamela. "Reflections on the State of American Software Copyright Law and the Perils of Teaching It." *Columbia-VLA Journal of Law and the Arts*, 13, no. 1 (1988), pp. 61-75.

2708 Samuelson, Pamela. "Some New Kinds of Authorship Made Possible by Computers and Some Intellectual Property Questions They Raise." *University of Pittsburgh Law Review*, 53, no. 3 (Spring 1992), pp. 685-704.

2709 Samuelson, Pamela. "Survey on the Patent/Copyright Interface for Computer Programs." *AIPLA Quarterly Journal,* 17, no. 3 (1989), pp. 256-93.

2710 Samuelson, Pamela. "Understanding the Implications of Selling Rights in Software to the Defense Department: A Journey Through the Regulatory Maze." *Rutgers Computer and Technology Law Journal,* 13, no. 1 (1987), pp. 33-58.

2711 Samuelson, Pamela, and Robert J. Glushko. "Comparing the Views of Lawyers and User Interface Designers on the Software Copyright 'Look and Feel' Lawsuits." *Jurimetrics Journal,* 30, no. 1 (Fall 1989), pp. 121-40.

2712 Sandhu, Ravi S. "Lattice-Based Enforcement of Chinese Walls." *Computers and Security,* 11, no. 8 (Dec. 1992), pp. 753-63.

2713 Sandza, Richard. "The Night of the Hackers." *Newsweek,* 104, no. 20 (12 Nov. 1984), pp. 17-18.

2714 Sandza, Richard. "The Revenge of the Hackers." *Newsweek,* 104, no. 25 (10 Dec. 1984), p. 81.

2715 Sandza, Richard. "Spying Through Computers?" *Newsweek,* 105, no. 23 (10 June 1985), p. 39.

2716 Saunders, Derek. "The Antitrust Implications of Computer Reservations Systems (CRS's)." *The Journal of Air Law and Commerce,* 51, no. 1 (1985), pp. 157-239.

2717 Saunders, Mary Jane. "The Electronic Communications Privacy Act of 1986: Privacy Meets the Computer Age." *The Computer Lawyer,* 3, no. 8 (Aug. 1986), pp. 21-26.

2718 Savage, Diane W., and Douglas K. Brotz. "The Copyright Status of Typeface Software." *The Computer Lawyer,* 6, no. 10 (Oct. 1989), pp. 1-9.

2719 Savage, Diane Wilkins. "Performance Warranties in Computer Contracts." *The Computer Lawyer,* 8, no. 12 (Dec. 1991), pp. 32-39.

2720 Savage, Nigel, and Chris Edwards. "The Data Protection Act 1984." *The Journal of Business Law,* 1984 (1984), pp. 463-67.

2721 Savage, Nigel, and Chris Edwards. "The Legislative Control of Data Processing—The British Approach." *Computer/Law Journal,* 6, no. 1 (Summer 1985), pp. 143-56.

2722 Saxby, Stephen. "Software Copyright—The Outstanding Questions: A View from the U.K." *Software Protection,* 5, no. 7 (Dec. 1986), pp. 7-12.

2723 Schares, Gail. "A German Hackers' Club That Promotes Creative Chaos." *Business Week,* no. 3063 (1 Aug. 1988), p. 71.

2724 Schatz, James E., and Bradley W. Anderson, and Holly Garland Langworthy. "What's Mine Is Yours? The Dilemma of a Factual Compilation." *University of Dayton Law Review,* 17, no. 2 (Winter 1992), pp. 423-55.

2725 Schatz, Willie. "Putting on the Cuffs." *Datamation,* 32, no. 14 (15 July 1986), pp. 40-42.

2726 Scheier, Robert L. "Shareware: A Vital Part of the PC Industry." *PC Week,* 7, no. 6 (12 Feb. 1990), p. 62.

2727 Scheinfeld, Robert C., and Gary M. Butter. "Using Trade Secret Law to Protect Computer Software." *Rutgers Computer and Technology Law Journal,* 17, no. 2 (1991), pp. 381-419.

2728 Schiffres, Manuel. "The Shadowy World of Computer 'Hackers.'" *U.S. News and World Report,* 98, no. 21 (3 June 1985), pp. 58-60.

2729 Schiffres, Manuel. "The Struggle to Thwart Software Pirates." *U.S. News and World Report,* 98, no. 11 (25 Mar. 1985), p. 72.

2730 Schlack, Mark. "How to Keep Viruses Off Your LAN." *Datamation,* 37, no. 20 (15 Oct. 1991), pp. 87-88, 90.

2731 Schleifer, Liane A. "Damage Awards and Computer Systems—Trends." *Emory Law Journal,* 35, no. 1 (Winter 1986), pp. 255-90.

2732 Schlinsog, Allen C., Jr. "*Advent Systems Ltd. v. Unisys Corp.*: UCC Governs Software Transactions." *Software Law Journal,* 4, no. 4 (Dec. 1991), pp. 611-29.

2733 Schmemann, Serge. "Computer Buffs Tapped NASA Files." *The New York Times,* 136 (16 Sept. 1987), p. A12.

2734 Schmitt, Richard B. "Microsoft Sees Gain in Ruling on Apple's Suit." *The Wall Street Journal,* 213, no. 56 (22 Mar. 1989), p. B5.

2735 Schneider, Eugene C., and Gregory W. Therkalsen. "How Secure Are Your Systems?" *Best's Review—Property/Casualty Insurance Edition,* 91, no. 7 (Nov. 1990), pp. 68-70, 72.

2736 Schnell, Angelika, and Anna M. Freska. "On the Threshold of 1992 Europe Debates Software Protection: Report on the International Symposium on Reverse Engineering in West Berlin, March 1989." *Santa Clara Computer and High Technology Law Journal,* 6, no. 1 (Mar. 1990), pp. 59-74.

2737 Schrage, Michael. "Virus Vandalism Is a Prelude to Future Computer Crime." *Los Angeles Times* (12 Oct. 1989), pp. D1, D16.

2738 Schroeder, Erica. "Buyers Seek Simple But Thorough Antiviral Programs." *PC Week,* 8, no. 1 (7 Jan. 1991), pp. 93-97.

2739 Schroeder, Robert A. "Licensing of Rights to Intellectual Property." *Albany Law Review,* 50, no. 2 (Winter 1986), pp. 455-74.

2740 Schuman, Patricia. "Social Goals vs. Private Interests: Players in the Information Arena Clash." *Publishers Weekly,* 226, no. 21 (23 Nov. 1984), pp. 56-58.

2741 Schuyler, Michael. "Viri Again and Again and Again." *Computers in Libraries,* 12, no. 5 (May 1992), pp. 30-32.

2742 Schwartz, Evan. "These Viruses Won't Give You Headaches." *Business Week,* no. 3169 (16 July 1990), p. 158H.

2743 Schwartz, Evan I., Jeffrey Rothfeder, and Mark Lewyn. "Viruses? Who You Gonna Call? 'Hackerbusters': Computer Security Is a $3 Billion Industry—But Critics Say 'There Are Some Charlatans Out There.'" *Business Week,* no. 3172 (6 Aug. 1990), pp. 71-72.

2744 Schwartz, John. "The Hacker Dragnet." *Newsweek,* 115, no. 18 (30 Apr. 1990), p. 50.

2745 Schwartz, John. "Hackers of the World, Unite!" *Newsweek,* 116, no. 1 (2 July 1990), pp. 36-37.

2746 Schwartz, John, and Debra Rosenberg. "Computing the Cost of Copyright: Programmers Fight 'Look and Feel' Lawsuits." *Newsweek,* 116, no. 9 (27 Aug. 1990), p. 52.

2747 Schwartz, John, and Richard Sandza. "Big Bucks for Virus Killers." *Newsweek,* 112, no. 22 (28 Nov. 1988), p. 82.

2748 Schwartz, Lloyd. "House Passes Bill to Fight Computer, Credit Card Crime." *Electronic News,* 30, no. 1508 (30 July 1984), p. 16.

2749 Schwartz, Melvin. "Computer Security: Planning to Protect Corporate Assets." *Journal of Business Strategy,* 11, no. 1 (Jan.-Feb. 1990), pp. 38-41.

2750 Schwartz, Paul. "Data Processing and Government Administration: The Failure of the American Legal Response to the Computer." *Hastings Law Journal,* 43, no. 5 (July 1992), pp. 1321-89.

2751 Schwartz, Steven L. "Clients, Computers, and Contracts: A User-Friendly Approach." *Michigan Bar Journal,* 65, no. 3 (Mar. 1986), pp. 304-7.

2752 Schwarz, Michael. "Tear-Me-Open Software License Agreements: A Uniform Commercial Code Perspective on an Innovative Contract of Adhesion." *Computer/Law Journal,* 7, no. 2 (Fall 1986), pp. 261-88.

2753 Schweitzer, James A. "How Security Fits In—A Management View." *Computers and Security,* 6 (1987), pp. 129-32.

2754 "Scientific Application Group SCIA S. V. v. Koerhuis Software." *Software Protection,* 4, no. 9 (Feb. 1986), pp. 8-10.

2755 Sciglimpaglia, Robert J., Jr. "Computer Hacking: A Global Offense." *Pace Yearbook of International Law,* 3 (1991), pp. 199-266.

2756 "Score One for the Hackers of America." *Newsweek,* 116, no. 6 (6 Aug. 1990), p. 48.

2757 Scott, Michael D. "Computer Software Cases; the 'Look and Feel' Controversy." *Trial,* 25, no. 3 (Mar. 1989), pp. 48-55.

2758 Scott, Michael D. "Contemporary Issues in Domestic Transactions for Computer Goods and Services." *Software Law Journal,* 3, no. 4 (Apr. 1990), pp. 615-35.

2759 Scott, Michael D. "Copyright Protection of Software in Mexico and Its Impact on Proprietary Rights." *Software Protection,* 3, no. 7 (Dec. 1984), pp. 8-10.

2760 Scott, Michael D. "Copyright Transfers and Computer Software." *Software Protection,* 3, no. 8 (Jan. 1985), pp. 12-14.

2761 Scott, Michael D. "New Legislation to Prohibit Software Rentals, Leases and Lending." *Software Protection,* 3, no. 7 (Dec. 1984), pp. 10-13.

2762 Scott, Michael D. "A Pirates' Haven in Hong Kong: Although There Are Local Laws Protecting Computer Software, Few American Makers Have Tried to Fight the Illicit Trade." *The National Law Journal,* 10, no. 51 (29 Aug. 1988), p. 11.

2763 Scott, Michael D. "Software Patentability in the United Kingdom." *Software Protection,* 3, no. 8 (Jan. 1985), pp. 15-16.

2764 Scott, Michael D. "Software Protection — Prognosis of the Future." *Software Protection,* 2, no. 8 (May 1984), pp. 2-7.

2765 Scott, Michael D. "Software Protection Through Copyright — The U.S. Experience." *Software Protection,* 3, no. 5 (Oct. 1984), pp. 1-12.

2766 Scott, Michael D. "State Governments Immune from Copyright Infringement." *Software Protection,* 7, no. 5 (Oct. 1988), p. 8.

2767 Scott, Michael D. "Vault v. Quaid: 5th Circuit Sounds Death Knell for Louisiana Shrink-Wrap License Law." *Software Protection,* 7, no. 2 (July 1988), pp. 1-3.

2768 Scott, Michael D. "Worms, Booby Traps and Liability: A Personal Observation." *Software Protection,* 3, no. 6 (Nov. 1984), pp. 11-13.

2769 Scott, Sandra Davidson, and Elliot Jaspin. "Should Government Copyright Its Computer Software?" *Law/Technology,* 25, no. 1 (1992), pp. 1-24.

2770 "Screen Displays Are Proper Subject Matter for Copyright Protection." *University of Illinois Law Review,* 1988, no. 3 (1988), pp. 757-83.

2771 "Sealing the Computer Leaks: Skadden, Arps Case Is a Tough Lesson in Security." *ABA Journal,* 70 (Oct. 1984), pp. 25-27.

2772 "Security System Users Focus on Computer Crime." *National Underwriters — Property and Casualty Insurance Edition*, 90, no. 1 (3 Jan. 1986), pp. 3, 17.

2773 Seecof, Benjamin R. "Scanning Into the Future of Copyrightable Images: Computer-Based Image Processing Poses a Present Threat." *High Technology Law Journal*, 5, no. 2 (Fall 1990), pp. 371-400.

2774 "Sega Pays $43 Million in Patent Dispute." *The Computer Lawyer*, 9, no. 6 (June 1992), p. 37.

2775 Segundo, Gonzalo San. "The Cost of Computer Crime." *World Press Review*, 35, no. 6 (June 1988), p. 47.

2776 Seidel, Arthur H. "Copyright Protection for Computer Software." *The Practical Lawyer*, 32, no. 6 (Sept. 1986), pp. 31-36.

2777 "Selection of Communities in Cable Directory Is Protectable." *The Computer Lawyer*, 9, no. 7 (July 1992), p. 38.

2778 Seligman, Daniel. "The Devil in Direct Marketing." *Fortune*, 123, no. 5 (11 Mar. 1991), pp. 123-24.

2779 Seline, Christopher J. "Eavesdropping on the Compromising Emanations of Electronic Equipment: The Laws of England and the United States." *Case Western Reserve Journal of International Law*, 23, no. 2 (Spring 1991), pp. 359-98.

2780 Selinger, Jerry R. "Protecting Computer Software in the Business Environment: Patents, Copyrights and Trade Secrets." *Intellectual Property Law Review*, 16 (1984), pp. 31-56.

2781 Selvin, Paul. "Campus Hackers and the Pentagon." *The Nation*, 247, no. 16 (28 Nov. 1988), pp. 563-66.

2782 Selwitz, Robert. "Computer 'Virus' Can Put Hotel Communications at Risk." *Hotel and Motel Management*, 204, no. 12 (14 Aug. 1989), pp. 50-52.

2783 Selz, Michael. "Computer Vaccines or Snake Oil?" *The Wall Street Journal*, 214, no. 73 (13 Oct. 1989), pp. B1-B2.

2784 "Semiconductor Chip Design Protection — A New Intellectual Property Right." *Oregon Law Review*, 65, no. 4 (1986), pp. 789-808.

2785 "Semiconductor Chip Protection." *Maryland Journal of International Law and Trade*, 12, no. 1 (Fall 1987), pp. 83-102.

2786 "Senate Provides New Piracy Penalties." *The Computer Lawyer*, 9, no. 8 (Aug. 1992), p. 37.

2787 Sessions, William S. "Computer Crimes: An Escalating Crime Trend." *FBI Law Enforcement Bulletin*, 60, no. 2 (Feb. 1991), pp. 12-15.

2788 Seymour, Jim. "Be Glad That the SPA Isn't Auditing Your Company." *PC Week*, 7, no. 16 (23 Apr. 1990), p. 10.

2789 Seymour, Jim. "Lessons to Learn from the Virus That Wasn't." *PC Week*, 9, no. 12 (23 Mar. 1992), p. 77.

2790 Seymour, Jim. "Wheels of Justice Grind to a Halt in 'Worm' Case." *PC Week*, 7, no. 19 (14 May 1990), p. 16.

2791 Shackleford, Steve. "Computer-Related Crime: An International Problem in Need of an International Solution." *Texas International Law Journal*, 27, no. 2 (Spring 1992), pp. 479-505.

2792 Shain, M. "Security in Electronic Funds Transfer: Message Integrity in Money Transfer and Bond Settlements Through GE Information Services' Global Network." *Computers and Security*, 8, no. 3 (May 1989), pp. 209-21.

2793 Shalgi, Moshe. "Computer-Ware: Protection and Evidence, an Israeli Draft Bill." *Computer/Law Journal*, 9, no. 3 (Summer 1989), pp. 299-319.

2794 Shapiro, E. Donald, and Michelle L. Weinberg. "DNA Data Banking: The Dangerous Erosion of Privacy." *Cleveland State Law Review*, 38, no. 3 (1990), pp. 455-86.

2795 Shattuck, John. "In the Shadow of *1984*: National Identification Systems, Computer-Matching, and Privacy in the United States." *Hastings Law Journal*, 35, no. 6 (July 1984), pp. 991-1005.

2796 Sheils, Paul T., and Robert Penchina. "What's All the Fuss About *Feist*? The Sky Is Not Falling on the Intellectual Property Rights of Online Database Proprietors." *University of Dayton Law Review*, 17, no. 2 (Winter 1992), pp. 563-606.

2797 Sherizen, Sanford. "Criminological Concepts and Research Findings Relevant for Improving Computer Crime Control." *Computers and Security*, 9, no. 3 (May 1990), pp. 215-22.

2798 Sherizen, Sanford. "European Unification '92 Impacts on Information Security." *Computers and Security*, 10, no. 7 (Nov. 1991), pp. 601-10.

2799 Sherizen, Sanford. "Successful Security Relies on Corporate Awareness Training." *Data Management*, 22, no. 12 (Dec. 1984), pp. 10-12.

2800 Shih, Theodore. "The Semiconductor Chip Protection Act of 1984: Is Copyright Protection for Utilitarian Articles Desirable?" *Computer/Law Journal*, 7, no. 2 (Fall 1986), pp. 129-201.

2801 Sholkoff, Jack. "Breaking the Mold: Forging a New and Comprehensive Standard of Protection for Computer Software." *Computer/Law Journal*, 8, no. 4 (Fall 1988), pp. 389-453.

2802 Shoop, Julie Gannon. "Electronic Monitoring: Is Big Brother at the Office?" *Trial*, 28, no. 1 (Jan. 1992), pp. 13-15.

2803 Shoukang, Guo. "Some Opinions on the Legal Protection of Computer Software in China." *Software Protection,* 4, no. 6 (Nov. 1985), pp. 7-8.

2804 Shulman, Seth. "(Artificial) Germ Warfare." *Technology Review,* 94, no. 7 (Oct. 1991), pp. 18-19.

2805 Shulman, Seth. "'Virus-Proof' Computer Security System." *Nature,* 337, no. 6202 (5 Jan. 1989), p. 4.

2806 Sidel, Mark. "Copyright, Trademark and Patent Law in the People's Republic of China." *Texas International Law Journal,* 21, no. 2 (Spring 1986), pp. 259-89.

2807 Siegel, Daniel R., and Ronald S. Laurie. "Beyond Microcode: *Alloy v. Ultratek*—The First Attempt to Extend Copyright Protection to Computer Hardware." *The Computer Lawyer,* 6, no. 4 (Apr. 1989), pp. 1-16.

2808 Simitis, Spiros. "Data Protection—Experiences and Tendencies." *Law/Technology,* 18, no. 4 (1985), pp. 3-22.

2809 Simitis, Spiros. "Reviewing Privacy in an Information Society." *University of Pennsylvania Law Review,* 135, no. 3 (Mar. 1987), pp. 707-46.

2810 Singer, Arnold A. "Computer Vulnerability and Safeguards." *The EDP Auditor Journal,* 3 (1988), pp. 7-8.

2811 Sinnott, Timothy J. "Copyright in Operating System Software on Computer Chips: A Tale of Two Apples." *Intellectual Property Journal,* 3, no. 1 (Feb. 1987), pp. 1-48.

2812 "Site Licensing: It's All in the Implementation." *Software Protection,* 4, no. 1 (June 1985), pp. 12-14.

2813 Slind-Flor, Victoria. "High Tech, High Stakes: In High-Technology Intellectual Property, Litigation and Firms Continue to Blossom." *The National Law Journal,* 13, no. 46 (22 July 1991), pp. 1, 26.

2814 Slind-Flor, Victoria. "Lawyers, Programmers Interface." *The National Law Journal,* 14, no. 28 (16 Mar. 1992), pp. 3, 12.

2815 Slind-Flor, Victoria. "Will Ruling Impact Borland's Fall Trial?" *The National Law Journal,* 14, no. 45 (13 July 1992), pp. 19, 26.

2816 Slind-Flor, Victoria, and Claudia MacLachlan. "Law Firms Get 'Stoned' and 'Michelangelo'd.'" *The National Law Journal,* 14, no. 28 (16 Mar. 1992), p. 2.

2817 "Small Business Reliance on Computer Software: There Should Be Protection." *Computer/Law Journal,* 10, no. 4 (Dec. 1990), pp. 635-51.

2818 Smallwood, Christopher. "FCC Regulation of Computers." *The Computer Lawyer,* 9, no. 3 (Mar. 1992), pp. 25-31.

2819 Smedinghoff, Thomas J. "Critique of Trade Secret Approach to Protecting
      Computer Software — Part 1." *Software Protection*, 2, no. 5 (Jan. 1984),
      pp. 3-13.

2820 Smedinghoff, Thomas J. "Critique of Trade Secret Approach to Protecting
      Computer Software — Part 2." *Software Protection*, 2, no. 6 (Feb. 1984),
      pp. 1-11.

2821 Smedinghoff, Thomas J. "Developments in Software Copyright Law." *Soft-
      ware Law Journal*, 3, no. 4 (Apr. 1990), pp. 637-86.

2822 Smegal, Thomas F., Jr. "Legality of 'Interim Copying' Is Disputed." *The
      National Law Journal*, 14, no. 44 (6 July 1992), pp. 20, 24.

2823 Smith, Albert C., and Jared A. Slosberg. "Beware! Trade Secret Software
      May Be Patented by a Later Inventor." *The Computer Lawyer*, 7, no. 11
      (Nov. 1990), pp. 15-24.

2824 Smith, Albert C., and John Sullivan. "The Impact of U.S. Patents and
      Customs on Importations." *The Computer Lawyer*, 8, no. 10 (Oct. 1991),
      pp. 16-23.

2825 Smith, Anastasia Watson, and Aretha Jones. "Computerizing Medical
      Records: Legal and Administrative Changes Necessary." *HealthSpan*, 8,
      no. 11 (Dec. 1991), pp. 3-6.

2826 Smith, Diana. "Who Is Calling Your Computer Next? Hacker!" *Criminal
      Justice Journal*, 8, no. 1 (1985), pp. 89-114.

2827 Smith, Donna. "Copyright Protection for the Intellectual Property Rights
      to Recombinant Deoxyribonucleic Acid: A Proposal." *St. Mary's Law
      Journal*, 19, no. 4 (1988), pp. 1083-113.

2828 Smith, Emily T. "Have Computer Viruses Turned Into a Plague?" *Business
      Week*, no. 3217 (10 June 1991), p. 71.

2829 Smith, Frank G., III, and Martin J. Elgison. "*DCA v. SoftKlone*: The Con-
      tinuing Saga of Copyright, Computers, and Clones." *The Computer
      Lawyer*, 4, no. 4 (Apr. 1987), pp. 13-18.

2830 Smith, James M. "Patentability of Software. What Can and Cannot Be
      Patented." *Idea*, 31, no. 3 (1991), pp. 183-206.

2831 Smith, Kerry M. L. "Suing the Provider of Computer Software: How Courts
      Are Applying U.C.C. Article Two, Strict Tort Liability, and Professional
      Malpractice." *Williamette Law Review*, 24, no. 3 (Summer 1988), pp.
      743-65.

2832 Smith, Richard H. "Patenting Computer-Related Inventions." *Software
      Law Journal*, 1, no. 1 (Fall 1985), pp. 33-53.

2833 Smith, Richard H., E. Robert Yoches, and John F. Hornick. "Guide for the
      Perplexed: What Is the Problem and What Do We Do Until It Is Solved?"
      AIPLA Quarterly Journal, 17, no. 3 (1989), pp. 215-31.

2834 Smith, Timothy C. "Towards a Consistent Test for Substantial Similarity Regarding Infringement of Copyrighted Aspects of Computer Programs." *Golden Gate University Law Review*, 22, no. 2 (Spring 1992), pp. 431-53.

2835 Snowman, Stacy. "Preemption of the Louisiana Software Enforcement Act by Copyright Law (Or Suffocation by Shrink-Wrap)." *Comm/Ent*, 8, no. 2 (1985-86), pp. 163-256.

2836 Snyder, Phillip W. "Typeface Design After the Desktop Revolution: A New Case for Legal Protection." *Columbia-VLA Journal of Law and the Arts*, 16, no. 1 (Fall 1991), pp. 97-142.

2837 "Softright: A Legislative Solution to the Problem of Users' and Producers' Rights in Computer Software." *Louisiana Law Review*, 44 (1984), pp. 1413-83.

2838 "Software Copying Policies: The Next Step in Piracy Prevention?" *The Journal of Law and Technology*, 2, no. 1 (Winter 1987), pp. 43-68.

2839 "Software Copyright: Send in the Brits." *The Economist*, 317, no. 7679 (3 Nov. 1990), p. 77.

2840 "Software Copyright: Solomon Wanted." *The Economist*, 316, no. 7673 (22 Sept. 1990), pp. 74-75.

2841 "Software Copyright Law: The Enforceability Sham." *Loyola Law Review*, 35, no. 2 (Summer 1989), pp. 485-507.

2842 "Software Developer Allowed to Reject Executory Contract with Distributor." *The Computer Lawyer*, 4, no. 3 (Mar. 1987), p. 28.

2843 "Software Protection in South Africa: Current Legislative Activity." *Software Protection*, 10, no. 2 (July 1991), pp. 1-4.

2844 "Software Warranty Bill Introduced in Massachusetts." *The Computer Lawyer*, 4, no. 5 (May 1987), p. 37.

2845 Solarz, Artur. "Computer-Related Embezzlement." *Computers and Security*, 6, no. 1 (Feb. 1987), pp. 49-53.

2846 Solomon, Alan. "The Virus Authors Strike Back." *Computers and Security*, 11, no. 7 (Nov. 1992), pp. 602-6.

2847 Solomon, Robert H. "The Copyrightability of Computer Software Containing Trade Secrets." *Washington University Law Quarterly*, 63, no. 1 (Spring 1985), pp. 131-53.

2848 Solomon, Toby. "Personal Privacy and the '1984' Syndrome." *Western New England Law Review*, 7, no. 3 (1985), pp. 753-90.

2849 Soltysinski, Stanislaw. "Legal Protection for Computer Programs, Public Access to Information and Freedom of Competitive Research and Development Activities." *Rutgers Computer and Technology Law Journal*, 16, no. 2 (1990), pp. 447-74.

2850 Soma, John T., and B. F. Smith. "Software Trends: Who's Getting How Many of What? 1978 to 1987." *Journal of the Patent and Trademark Office Society,* 71, no. 5 (May 1989), pp. 415-32.

2851 Soma, John T., and Elizabeth J. Bedient. "Computer Security and the Protection of Sensitive but Not Classified Data: The Computer Security Act of 1987." *Air Force Law Review,* 30 (1989), pp. 135-46.

2852 Soma, John T., and Jay Batson. "The Legal Environment of Commercial Database Administration." *Jurimetrics Journal,* 27, no. 3 (Spring 1987), pp. 297-315.

2853 Soma, John T., and Lorna C. Youngs. "Confidential Communications and Information in a Computer Era." *Hofstra Law Review,* 12, no. 4 (Summer 1984), pp. 849-91.

2854 Soma, John T., Paula J. Smith, and Robert D. Sprague. "Legal Analysis of Electronic Bulletin Board Activities." *Western New England Law Review,* 7, no. 3 (1985), pp. 571-626.

2855 Soma, John T., Robert D. Sprague, M. Susan Lombardi, and Carolyn M. Lindh. "A Proposed Legal Advisor's Roadmap for Software Developers: On the Shoulders of Giants May No Breachers of Economic Relationships Nor Slavish Copiers Stand." *Denver University Law Review,* 68, no. 2 (1991), pp. 191-227.

2856 Soma, John T., and Stephen D. Shirey. "Computer and Software Law Audits." *Software Law Journal,* 1, no. 2 (Winter 1986), pp. 123-66.

2857 Song, Lu. "Computer Software Protection—New Development in the People's Republic of China." *Software Protection,* 10, no. 1 (June 1991), pp. 1-5.

2858 Sookman, Barry B. "Canadian Computer Litigation: Where We Are and Where We Are Going." *Software Protection,* 10, no. 11 (Apr. 1992), pp. 1-15.

2859 Sookman, Barry B. "Computer-Assisted Creation of Works Protection by Copyright." *Intellectual Property Journal,* 5, no. 2 (Jan. 1990), pp. 165-86.

2860 Sorokin, Leo T. "The Computerization of Government Information: Does It Circumvent Public Access Under the Freedom of Information Act and the Depository Library Program?" *Columbia Journal of Law and Social Problems,* 24, no. 2 (1991), pp. 267-98.

2861 Southard, C. Dennis, IV. "Individual Privacy and Governmental Efficiency: Technology's Effect on the Government's Ability to Gather, Store, and Distribute Information." *Computer/Law Journal,* 9, no. 3 (Summer 1989), pp. 359-74.

2862 Southard, Douglas K. "To Catch a Thief: Criminal Law Is Catching Up with High Tech's Information Thieves." *California Lawyer,* 6, no. 12 (Dec. 1986), pp. 23-25.

2863 Sowton, Elizabeth. "Attitude Problems." *The Banker,* 139, no. 766 (Dec. 1989), pp. 76-77.

2864 Spak, Michael I. "The Case to Be Made for Proposed Article 4A of the Uniform Commercial Code: What's a Trillion Dollars Between Friends?!" *Kentucky Law Journal,* 80, no. 1 (1991-92), pp. 167-223.

2865 Spaul, Barry. "Old-Fashioned Theft in a High-Tech Environment." *Accountancy,* 106, no. 1167 (Nov. 1990), pp. 120-21.

2866 Spaul, Barry J. "Protect and Survive." *Accountancy,* 103, no. 1148 (Apr. 1989), pp. 146-47.

2867 Speakman, Mark. "Patent Protection for Computer Software in Australia." *Software Protection,* 8, no. 12 (May 1990), pp. 9-16.

2868 Specht, Linda B., R. Clayton Trotter, Ronald M. Young, and Steve G. Sutton. "The Public Accounting Litigation Wars: Will Expert Systems Lead the Next Assault?" *Jurimetrics Journal,* 31, no. 2 (Winter 1991), pp. 247-57.

2869 Spector, Alfred Z. "Software, Interface, and Implementation." *Jurimetrics Journal,* 30, no. 1 (Fall 1989), pp. 79-90.

2870 Speer, Rebecca A. "Redefining the Limits of Copyright Law After *NEC v. INTEL.*" *Santa Clara Law Review,* 28, no. 3 (1988), pp. 683-708.

2871 Spiotta, Glenda D. "Local Government Compliance Issues: Minnesota's Open Meeting Law and Data Practices Act." *Hamline Journal of Public Law and Policy,* 12, no. 1 (Spring 1991), pp. 117-30.

2872. Spiram, Ram S. "Auditing Bank's Automated Teller Machines." *The EDP Auditor Journal,* 3 (1988), pp. 43-47.

2873 Spivack, Peter G. "Does Form Follow Function? The Idea/Expression Dichotomy in Copyright Protection of Computer Software." *UCLA Law Review,* 35, no. 4 (Apr. 1988), pp. 723-78.

2874 "Spoiling the Hacker's Fun." *Solicitors' Journal,* 133, no. 27 (7 July 1989), p. 855.

2875 Spoor, Jaap H. "Aspects of Copyright Protection of Computer Software." *Software Law Journal,* 1, no. 3 (Spring-Summer 1986), pp. 259-72.

2876 Spoor, Jaap H. "Protection of Computer Programs: General Report." *Software Law Journal,* 1, no. 3 (Spring-Summer 1986), pp. 457-70.

2877 Spoor, Jaap H. "Protection of Computer Software in the Netherlands." *Software Law Journal,* 1, no. 3 (Spring-Summer 1986), pp. 373-82.

2878 Sprague, Robert D. "Comment: Developing Theories of Legal Liability for Inaccurate Computer Information." *Law/Technology,* 24, no. 2 (1991), pp. 1-14.

2879 Sprague, Robert D. "Software Products Liability: Has Its Time Arrived?" *Western State University Law Review,* 19, no. 1 (Fall 1991), pp. 137-63.

2880 "Spreading a Virus: How Computer Science Was Caught Off Guard by One Young Hacker." *The Wall Street Journal,* 212, no. 90 (7 Nov. 1988), pp. A1, A6.

2881 Stabest, Sharon. "Kelly Programs." *The Wheat Journal of Technology,* 3 (1992), pp. 21-23.

2882 Stackhouse, Dale E. "Copyright Protection for U.S. Computer Software in Japan." *The Computer Lawyer,* 7, no. 4 (Apr. 1990), pp. 13-17.

2883 "Staff Paper on Intellectual Property Protection for Computer Software." *Software Protection,* 8, no. 10 (Mar. 1990), pp. 12-17.

2884 Staggs, H. Bradley. "Lessors of Computer Equipment: Do They Receive Fair Treatment Under the Bankruptcy Code?" *Rutgers Computer and Technology Law Journal,* 15, no. 1 (1989), pp. 81-101.

2885 Stallman, Richard. "Against Software Patents: The League for Programming Freedom." *Comm/Ent,* 14, no. 2 (Winter 1992), pp. 295-314.

2886 Stanley, Philip M. "Computer Crime Investigation and Investigators." *Computers and Security,* 5 (1986), pp. 309-13.

2887 Starke, J. G. "'Hacking' Into Computer Systems." *The Australian Law Journal,* 64 (Mar. 1990), pp. 105-7.

2888 Starke, J. G. "Privacy Protection and Transborder Data Flows." *The Australian Law Journal,* 65 (June 1991), pp. 354-56.

2889 Starke, J. G. "Restrictions on the Transborder Flows of Personal Data." *The Australian Law Journal,* 65 (Sept. 1991), pp. 560-62.

2890 Starkman, Robert D. "Computer Crime: The Federal vs State Approach to Solving the Problem." *Michigan Bar Journal,* 65, no. 3 (Mar. 1986), pp. 314-17.

2891 Starr, Barbara, Otis Port, Zachary Schiller, and Evert Clark. "Are Data Bases a Threat to National Security?" *Business Week,* no. 2975 (1 Dec. 1986), p. 39.

2892 Steele, David A. "Eavesdropping on Electromagnetic Radiation Emanating from Video Display Units: Legal and Self-Help Responses to New Form of Espionage." *The Criminal Law Quarterly,* 32. no. 2 (Mar. 1990), pp. 253-69.

2893 Stein, Henry. "Find the Biggest Danger to Your Computer System." *Electric Light and Power,* 67, no. 9 (Sept. 1989), p.24.

2894 Steinberg, Robert. "Microcode—Idea or Expression?" *Computer/Law Journal,* 9, no. 1 (Winter 1989), pp. 61-72.

2895 Steinberg, Robert. "*NEC v. INTEL*: The Battle Over Copyright Protection for Microcode." *Jurimetrics Journal,* 27, no. 2 (Winter 1987), pp. 173-99.

2896 Steinert-Threlkeld, Tom. "Computer-Protection Market Grows, Thrives on Fear." *The Washington Post,* 112, no. 169 (23 May 1989), pp. C1, C4.

2897 Stensaasen, Tarjei. "Legal Protection of Computer Software in the Nordic Countries." *Software Protection,* 8, no. 2 (July 1989), pp. 1-4.

2898 Stephens, Gene. "High-Tech Crime Fighting: The Threat to Civil Liberties." *The Futurist,* 24, no. 4 (July-Aug. 1990), pp. 20-25.

2899 Stephens, Keith. "Xerox Finally Wakes Up, But Is It Too Late?" *Santa Clara Computer and High Technology Law Journal,* 6 (1990-91), pp. 407-20.

2900 Stephens, Mark. "Clinton Team to Review Computer Security Policy." *InfoWorld,* 14, no. 49 (7 Dec. 1992), pp. 1, 135.

2901 Stephens, Mark. "DOS Virus Will Erase Disks on Columbus Day." *InfoWorld,* 11, no. 37 (11 Sept. 1989), p. 5.

2902 Stern, Akiba. "Software Piracy." *Brief,* 16, no. 4 (Summer 1987), pp. 28-33.

2903 Stern, Richard H. "The Bundle of Rights Suited to New Technology." *Intellectual Property Law Review,* 19 (1987), pp. 537-75. (First published in *University of Pittsburgh Law Review,* 47, no. 4 [Summer 1986], pp. 1229-67.)

2904 Stern, Richard H. "Copyright in Computer Programming Languages." *Rutgers Computer Technology Law Journal,* 17, no. 2 (1991), pp. 321-79.

2905 Stern, Richard H. "Copyright Infringement by Add-On Software: Going Beyond Deconstruction of the *Mona Lisa* Moustache Paradigm and Not Taking Video Game Cases Seriously." *Intellectual Property Law Review,* 24 (1992), pp. 429-46. (First published in *Jurimetrics Journal,* 31, no. 2 [Winter 1991], pp. 205-22.)

2906 Stern, Richard H. "Determining Liability for Infringement of Mask Work Rights Under the Semiconductor Chip Protection Act." *Minnesota Law Review,* 70, no. 2 (Dec. 1985), pp. 271-383.

2907 Stern, Richard H. "Legal Protection of Screen Displays and Other User Interfaces for Computers: A Problem in Balancing Incentives for Creation Against Need for Free Access to the Utilitarian." *Columbia-VLA Journal of Law and the Arts,* 14, no. 3 (1990), pp. 283-378.

2908 Stern, Richard H. "NEC v Intel—A New U.S. Approach to Reverse Engineering of Software?" *Software Protection,* 8, no. 6 (Nov. 1989), pp. 10-16.

2909 Stern, Richard H. "Shrink-Wrap Licenses of Mass Marketed Software: Enforceable Contracts or Whistling in the Dark?" *Rutgers Computer and Technology Law Journal*, 11, no. 1 (1985), pp. 51-92.

2910 Stern, Richard H. "Tales from the Algorithm War: *Benson* to *Iwahashi*, It's Deja Vu All Over Again." *AIPLA Quarterly Journal*, 18, no. 4 (1990), pp. 371-403.

2911 Stern, Steven. "Computer Software Protection After the 1984 Copyright Statutory Amendments." *The Australian Law Journal*, 60 (June 1986), pp. 333-44.

2912 Sterne, Robert Greene, and Perry J. Saidman. "Copying Mass-Marketed Software." *Byte*, 10, no. 2 (Feb. 1985), pp. 387-90.

2913 Stevens, Michael L. "Identifying and Charging Computer Crimes in the Military." *Military Law Review*, 110 (Fall 1985), pp. 59-94.

2914 Steward, Gillian. "Computer Sabotage." *Maclean's*, 97, no. 17 (23 Apr. 1984), pp. 59-60.

2915 Stieren, Carl. "Beating the Bugs: Viruses, Trojan Horses and Other Vermin." *Canadian Business*, 62, no. 8 (Aug. 1989), p. 67.

2916 Stiller, Wolfgang. "Protect Your Data with PCData, the Data Integrity ToolKit." *PC Magazine*, 9, no. 3 (13 Feb. 1990), pp. 263-83.

2917 Stim, Richard W. "The Medium Is the Message: *Apple Computer, Inc. v. Franklin Computer Corporation*." *University of San Francisco Law Review*, 18, no. 2 (Winter 1984), pp. 351-69.

2918 Stipp, David, and Paul B. Carroll. "One Mistake and 'Harmless' Mischief Brought Notoriety to Robert Morris Jr." *The Wall Street Journal*, 212, no. 90 (7 Nov. 1988), p. A6.

2919 Stokes, Michael D. "Copyright Law and Integrated Circuit Protection: When the Chips Are Down." *Computer/Law Journal*, 6, no. 3 (Winter 1986), pp. 543-69.

2920 Stoll, Cliff. "How Secure Are Computers in the U.S.A.?" *Computers and Security*, 7, no. 6 (Dec. 1988), pp. 543-47.

2921 Stork, Anita. "The Use of Arbitration in Copyright Disputes: *IBM v. Fujitsu*." *High Technology Law Journal*, 3, no. 2 (Fall 1988), pp. 241-65.

2922 Stover, Dawn. "Viruses, Worms, Trojans, and Bombs." *Popular Science*, 235, no. 3 (Sept. 1989), pp. 59-62, 104-8.

2923 Straub, Detmar W., Jr. "Organizational Structuring of the Computer Security Function." *Computers and Security*, 7, no. 2 (Apr. 1988), pp. 185-92.

2924 Strong, Donisa R. "The Computer Matching and Privacy Protection Act of 1988: Necessary Relief from the Erosion of the Privacy Act of 1974." *Software Law Journal*, 2, no. 3 (Summer 1988), pp. 391-422.

2925 Strong, Noel. "The Virus Threat Can Be Contained: How Does One Know If a System Is Infected? Watch for the Odd and Unusual Signs." *The Office*, 116, no. 5 (Nov. 1992), p. 64.

2926 "Student Symposium: A Survey of Software Copying Policy in Corporate America; Introduction." *The Journal of Law and Technology*, 2, no. 1 (Winter 1987), pp. 39-41.

2927 Stuller, Jay. "Computer Cops and Robbers." *Across the Board*, 26, no. 6 (June 1989), pp. 13-19.

2928 Styrcula, Keith A. "The Adequacy of Copyright Protection for Computer Software in the European Community 1992: A Critical Analysis of the EC's Draft Directive." *Jurimetrics Journal*, 31, no. 3 (Spring 1991), pp. 329-48.

2929 Sugiyama, Keiji, and Marcus Kosins, Jr. "The Japanese Solution to the Protection of Computer Programs." *Software Protection*, 4, no. 4 (Sept. 1985), pp. 11-14.

2930 Sullivan, Clare. "The Response of the Criminal Law in Australia to Computer Abuse." *Criminal Law Journal*, 12, no. 4 (Aug. 1988), pp. 228-50.

2931 Sullivan, Deidre. "Horizon System Protects Data Available by Modem." *American Banker*, 157, no. 225 (23 Nov. 1992), p. 3.

2932 Sullivan, Kristina B. "Central Point Program to Fight 400 Computer Viruses." *PC Week*, 8, no. 9 (4 Mar. 1991), pp. 14.

2933 Sullivan, Kristina B. "DOS-Based Package Takes Two-Pronged Approach to Viruses." *PC Week*, 8, no. 5 (4 Feb. 1991), p. 30.

2934 Sullivan, Kristina B. "Symantec's SAM 3.0 Simplifies Mac Virus Protection." *PC Week*, 8, no. 11 (18 Mar. 1991), p. 12.

2935 Sullivan, Kristina B. "Virus Policies Vary Widely—Study: 600-Plus Viruses Hit 63% of PCs." *PC Week*, 8, no. 49 (9 Dec. 1991), pp. 33, 36.

2936 Sullivan, Pamela J. "Legislative Surveys for the 1989 Rhode Island General Assembly: Computer Crime Act Amended to Include Computer Tampering, False Claims for Payment, and Civil Actions." *Suffolk University Law Review*, 24, no. 2 (1990), pp. 427-32.

2937 "Summary Judgment Denied on AMD's Licensing Defense in '287 Suit." *The Computer Lawyer*, 8, no. 8 (Aug. 1991), p. 31.

2938 Summers, Rita C., and Stanley A. Kurzban. "Potential Applications of Knowledge-bases Methods to Computer Security." *Computers and Security*, 7, no. 4 (Aug. 1988), pp. 373-85.

2939 Sumner, John P. "Computer Software Protection...." *Bench and Bar of Minnesota*, 41, no. 3 (Mar. 1984), pp. 15-17.

2940 Sumner, John P. "The Copyright/Patent Interface: Patent Protection for the Structure of Program Code." *Jurimetrics Journal,* 30, no. 1 (Fall 1989), pp. 107-19.

2941 Sumner, John P., and Dianne Plunkett. "Copyright, Patent, and Trade Secret Protection for Computer Software in Western Europe." *Computer/Law Journal,* 8, no. 4 (Fall 1988), pp. 327-73.

2942 Sumner, John P., and Stephen W. Buckingham. "Microcode Copyright Protection: A New Tool for Protecting Computer Products." *The Computer Lawyer,* 3, no. 10 (Oct. 1986), pp. 17-19.

2943 Sumner, John P., and Steven W. Lundberg. "Patentable Computer Program Features as Uncopyrightable Subject Matter." *AIPLA Quarterly Journal,* 17, no. 3 (1989), pp. 237-55.

2944 Sumner, John P., and Steven W. Lundberg. "Software Patents: Are They Here to Stay?" *The Computer Lawyer,* 8, no. 10 (Oct. 1991), pp. 8-15.

2945 Sundholm, Carl. "Computer Copyright Infringement: Beyond the Limits of the Iterative Test." *Santa Clara Computer and High-Technology Law Journal,* 3, no. 2 (1987), pp. 369-404.

2946 Sundholm, Carl. "Copyright Protection for Computer Programs Extends Beyond Literal Duplication to Structure, Sequence, and Organization. *Whelan Associates, Inc. v. Jaslow Dental Laboratory, Inc.*" *Santa Clara Computer and High-Technology Law Journal,* 3, no. 1 (Jan. 1987), pp. 221-30.

2947 Sundholm, Carl A. "High Technology Jurisprudence: In Defense of 'Look and Feel' Approaches to Copyright Protection." *Santa Clara Computer and High Technology Law Journal,* 8, no. 1 (May 1992), pp. 209-25.

2948 Surrel, Carol Ann. "The Treatment of Computer Software Works Made for Hire Under the Copyright Act of 1976." *Computer/Law Journal,* 5, no. 4 (Spring 1985), pp. 579-603.

2949 "Survey on Computer Crime May Serve as Basis for Legislation." *Journal of Accountancy,* 159, no. 5 (May 1985), p. 38.

2950 Sutton, Michael O. "Equities, Evidence, and the Elusive Scope of Copyright Protection for Computer Software." *Journal of the Patent and Trademark Office Society,* 69, no. 10 (Oct. 1987), pp. 551-66.

2951 Swernofsky, Steven A. "Expert Testimony in a Software Copyright Case." *Hamline Law Review,* 13, no. 2 (Spring 1990), pp. 333-51.

2952 Swinson, John. "Copyright Or Patent Or Both: An Algorithmic Approach to Computer Software Protection." *Harvard Journal of Law and Technology,* 5 (Fall 1991), pp. 145-214.

2953 Swinyard, W. R., H. Rinne, and A. Keng Kau. "The Morality of Software Piracy: A Cross-Cultural Analysis." *Journal of Business Ethics,* 9, no. 8 (Aug. 1990), pp. 655-64.

2954 "Symantec Boosts Protection in Mac Anti-Virus Software." *PC Week*, 7, no. 9 (5 Mar. 1990), p. 26.

2955 Syrowik, David. "Patent Protection for Software Technology—A Powerful New Form of Protection." *Michigan Bar Journal*, 67, no. 10 (Oct. 1988), pp. 968-74.

2956 Syrowik, David R. "Disclosing Computer Programs in an Application for a United States Patent—A Trap for the Unwary." *Jurimetrics Journal*, 26, no. 1 (Fall 1985), pp. 21-31. (Also published in *Software Law Journal*, 1, no. 1 [Fall 1985], pp. 55-65.)

2957 Syrowik, David R. "Intellectual Property Rights in Software—A Look at the Basics." *Michigan Bar Journal*, 56, no. 3 (Mar. 1986), pp. 292-97.

2958 Syrowik, David R. "International Software Protection." *Michigan Bar Journal*, 70, no. 7 (July 1991), pp. 656-62.

2959 Syrowik, David R. "Ownership of Intellectual Property Rights in Software—Trying to Cover All of the Bases." *Software Protection*, 5, no. 5 (Oct. 1986), pp. 9-19.

2960 Szibbo, Alec. "Copyright Reform in Canada: Phase One." *Software Protection*, 7, no. 3 (Aug. 1988), pp. 1-3.

2961 Szibbo, Alec, and Keith Spencer. "Sui Generis Semiconductor Chip Protection in Canada." *Software Protection*, 10, no. 3 (Aug. 1991), pp. 10-11.

2962 "TI Patent-Related Litigation Developments." *The Computer Lawyer*, 8, no. 1 (Jan. 1991), pp. 26-29.

2963 Tabbey, Kirk W. "Computer Crime: 'Preparing the Computer Specific Search Warrant.'" *Computers and Security*, 9, no. 2 (Apr. 1990), pp. 117-23.

2964 Tache, J. Rick. "Copyrightability of Computer Languages: Natural Expansion of Copyright Law or Destruction of the Copyright/Patent Distinction?" *Journal of the Patent and Trademark Office Society*, 72 (1990), pp. 564-76.

2965 "Taiwan Removed from Priority Lists." *The Computer Lawyer*, 9, no. 8 (Aug. 1992), p. 37.

2966 Takaishi, Yoshikazu. "The Perspective from Japan on Software Protection." *Software Law Journal*, 1, no. 2 (Winter 1986), pp. 187-215.

2967 Takenaka, Toshiko. "Extending the New Patent Misuse Limitation to Copyright: *Lasercomb America, Inc. v. Reynolds*." *Software Law Journal*, 5, no. 4 (Dec. 1992), pp. 739-70.

2968 Tan, Loke Khoon. "Understanding China's New Software Registration Scheme." *The Computer Lawyer*, 9, no. 8 (Aug. 1992), pp. 31-32.

2969 Tan, Loke Khoon. "U.S., China Sign Important Memorandum of Understanding." *The Computer Lawyer*, 9, no. 6 (June 1992), pp. 31-32.

2970 "Tandy's Suit Is Not a Breach." *The Computer Lawyer*, 9, no. 10 (Oct. 1992), p. 36.

2971 Tanenbaum, William A. "An Analysis and Guide to the Berne Convention Implementation Act: Amendments to the United States Copyright Act." *Hamline Law Review*, 13, no. 2 (Spring 1990), pp. 253-85.

2972 Tantum, Mark. "The Viper at Your Bosom." *Solicitors Journal*, 133, no. 24 (16 June 1989), pp. 772-74.

2973 Tao, Jerome T. "Theories of Computer Program Patentability." *Santa Clara Computer and High Technology Law Journal*, 7, no. 2 (Dec. 1991), pp. 291-319.

2974 Taphorn, J. B. "Software Protection in the International Marketplace." *North Carolina Journal of International Law and Commercial Regulation*, 10 (1985), pp. 617-31.

2975 Taphorn, Joseph B. "Hard Facts About Software Protection." *The Compleat Lawyer*, 2, no. 4 (Fall 1985), pp. 28-31, 54.

2976 Tapp, Stephen Kyle, and Daniel E. Wanat. "Computer Software Copyright Issues: Section 117 and Fair Use." *Memphis State University Law Review*, 22, no. 2 (Winter 1992), pp. 197-277.

2977 Tapper, Colin. "An Aspect of Copyright in Data Bases." *Northern Kentucky Law Review*, 14, no. 2 (1987), pp. 169-210.

2978 Tapper, Colin. "'Computer Crime': Scotch Mist?" *Criminal Law Review* (Jan. 1987), pp. 4-22.

2979 Tapper, Colin. "Copyright in Computer Programs: An International Perspective." *Santa Clara Computer and High- Technology Law Journal*, 1, no. 1 (Jan. 1985), pp. 13-25.

2980 Tapper, Colin. "New European Directions in Data Protection." *Journal of Law and Information Science*, 3, no. 1 (1992), pp. 9-24.

2981 "Tax Benefits to Plaintiff Resulting from Contract Are Irrelevant to Determination of Compensatory Damages for Defendant's Breach of Contract." *The Computer Lawyer*, 8, no. 1 (Jan. 1991), pp. 34-35.

2982 Taylor, Wendy. "How to Avoid the Threat of Virus-Infected Software." *PC Computing*, 4, no. 5 (May 1991), pp. 226-30.

2983 Taylor, Wendy. "Stung by Bum Software? Consider Legal Action." *PC Computing*, 4, no. 4 (Apr. 1991), pp. 218-20.

2984 Taylor, Wendy. "Virus Attacks: Fact or Fiction?" *PC Computing*, 5, no. 2 (Feb. 1992), pp. 260-63.

2985 Taylor, Wendy. "Virus-Proof Your PC." *PC Computing,* 5, no. 2 (Feb. 1992), pp. 122-26, 131-37.

2986 Taylor, Wm. David, III. "Copyright Protection for Computer Software After *Whelan Associates v. Jaslow Dental Laboratory." Missouri Law Review,* 54, no. 1 (Winter 1989), pp. 121-54.

2987 "Tech Tips: Fighting the Virus." *Black Enterprise,* 20, no. 6 (Jan. 1990), p. 39.

2988 "Telephone Company's White Pages Directory Not Copyrightable Compilation." *The Computer Lawyer,* 8, no. 4 (Apr. 1991), pp. 35-36.

2989 Tell, Lawrence J. "Software Copyrights: Keep Out the Pirates—But Let Innovators In." *Business Week,* no. 3014 (31 Aug. 1987), p. 31.

2990 Tellini, Mark P. "Uniform Copyright Protections for Computer Software in the EEC." *Boston College International and Comparative Law Review,* 13, no. 2 (Summer 1990), pp. 483-501.

2991 Tepper, Maury M., III. "Copyright Law: Integrating Successive Filtering Into the Bifurcated Substantial Similarity Inquiry in Software Copyright Infringement Cases: A Standard for Determining the Scope of Copyright Protection for Non-Literal Elements of Computer Programs." *Campbell Law Review,* 14, no. 1 (Winter 1991), pp. 1-67.

2992 "Terminal Case." *U.S. New and World Report,* 107, no. 6 (7 Aug. 1989), p. 11.

2993 "Terminal Madness." *Mother Jones,* 17, no. 3 (May-June 1992), p. 18.

2994 Terry, Chris. "Hardware and Software Keep Your PC Data Safe." *EDN,* 34, no. 18 (1 Sept. 1989), pp. 61-68.

2995 Tetterborn, Andrew. "Copyright in Computer Software—An Update." *Solicitors' Journal: Conveyancing Supplement 1985,* 1985 (19 Apr. 1985), p. 17.

2996 Thackeray, Gail. "Computer-Related Crimes: An Outline." *Jurimetrics Journal,* 25, no. 3 (Spring 1985), pp. 300-18.

2997 Thé, Lee. "Controlling Access to Your Data." *Personal Computing,* 9, no. 9 (Sept. 1985), pp. 60-71.

2998 Thibodeau, David J., and Michael van Bremen. "International Protection of Copyrightable Works Under the Berne Copyright Convention—What's a Hacker to Do?" *New Hampshire Bar Journal,* 30, no. 3 (Spring 1989), pp. 143-51.

2999 Thimbleby, Harold. "Can Viruses Ever Be Useful?" *Computers and Security,* 10, no. 2 (Apr. 1991), pp. 111-14.

3000 Thimbleby, Harold. "Thanks for Wiping the Memory." *New Scientist,* 126, no. 1717 (19 May 1990), p. 69.

3001 Thimbleby, Harold. "Turning Viruses to Good Use." *New Scientist,* 126, no. 1722 (23 June 1990), p. 72-73.

3002 "Think You Can Hack It?" *Time,* 134, no. 18 (30 Oct. 1989), p. 75.

3003 Thom, James A., and Peter G. Thorne. "Privacy Principles—Tacit Assumptions Under Threat." *Journal of Law and Information Science,* 2, no. 1 (1986), pp. 68-110.

3004 Thomas, Evan. "Moles Who Burrow for Microchips." *Time,* 125, no. 24 (17 June 1985), pp. 25-28.

3005 Thomas, Michael W. "Inbound Transfers of Japanese Technology Rights: Some Practical Considerations." *Santa Clara Computer and High Technology Law Journal,* 7, no. 2 (Dec. 1991), pp. 357-67.

3006 Thompson, Andrew. "The Potential Means of Protecting Computer Software in Scotland—Part 1." *The Journal of the Law Society of Scotland,* 29, no. 12 (Dec. 1984), pp. 480-82.

3007 Thompson, Andrew. "The Potential Means of Protecting Computer Software in Scotland—Part 2." *The Journal of the Law Society of Scotland,* 30, no. 1 (Jan. 1985), pp. 16-18.

3008 Thompson, Mark. "Call Interrupt: Prosecutors Fight Computer Criminals." *California Lawyer,* 8 (Sept. 1988), p. 28.

3009 Thompson, Mark. "Mac Attack on Software Rivals: Computer Giants Are Fighting Over Copyrights Again." *California Lawyer,* 8, no. 4 (May 1988), p. 17.

3010 Thompson, Mark. "Pursuing the Pirates: Ashton Tate's In-House Counsel Lead a Global Strike Force Against Computer Software Bootleggers." *California Lawyer,* 9, no. 11 (Nov. 1989), pp. 60-64, 136.

3011 Thompson, Mark. "When Bugs Bite: A Big Verdict Puts the Computer Industry on Notice That Glitches Can Be Costly." *California Lawyer,* 9, no. 6 (June 1989), p. 19.

3012 Thompson, Rosemary Simota. "Old Laws v. New Technology: Antediluvian Antitrust Tying Prohibitions and Operating System Software." *Software Law Journal,* 2, no. 2 (Spring 1988), pp. 221-41.

3013 Thompson, Terence W. "Bankruptcy Assignment of Software Licenses." *Commercial Law Journal,* 94, no. 3 (Fall 1989), pp. 344-57.

3014 Thompson, Terence W. "Software Supplier's Rights in the User's Bankruptcy." *Software Law Journal,* 3, no. 1 (Winter 1989), pp. 1-20.

3015 Thompson, Tom. "Information (Mis)management." *Byte: Macintosh Special Edition,* 14, no. 3 (Mar. 1989), p. MAC 2.

3016 Thomson, Warren R. "The Trademark Forum; Electronic Information in Trademark Practice." *The Trademark Reporter,* 74, no. 1 (Jan.-Feb. 1984), pp. 69-75.

3017 Thorne, Clive. "Shrink Wrap Package Licenses in Hong Kong." *Software Protection*, 4, no. 9 (Feb. 1986), pp.11-12.

3018 Thorne, Clive D. "Civil Remedies Against Software Piracy in Common Law Jurisdictions." *Software Protection*, 4, no. 3 (Aug. 1985), pp. 10-14.

3019 Thorne, Clive D. "'Hacking' in England: A Gap in the Law?" *Software Protection*, 6, no. 5 (Oct. 1987), pp. 18-19.

3020 "Thou Shalt Not Dupe." *Software Protection*, 4, no. 2 (July 1985), pp. 10-12.

3021 Thuraisingham, Bhavani, and Harvey H. Rubinovitz. "Multilevel Security Issues in Distributed Database Management Systems - III." *Computers and Security*, 11, no. 7 (Nov. 1992), pp. 661-74.

3022 Tierney, Daniel E. "The United States-Japan Semiconductor Controversy: A Strategic Guide to the Use of U.S. Trade Laws as a Legal and Political Instrument." *Albany Law Review*, 52, no. 1 (Fall 1987), pp. 363-403.

3023 Tigner, Brooks. "Pirates in the Dock." *International Management*, 46, no. 4 (May 1991), pp. 56-59.

3024 Tito, Celeste. "Broderbund Software, Inc. v. Unison World, Inc. 648 F.Supp. 1127 (1986)." *Computer/Law Journal*, 7, no. 4 (Fall 1987), pp. 535-42.

3025 Toedt, D. C. "*Bonito Boats* and the Primacy of the Patent System — Are There Implications for Software Functionality Copyrights?" *The Computer Lawyer*, 6, no. 1 (Jan. 1989), pp. 12-16.

3026 Toedt, D. C. "Reducing the Potential for Liability in the Dissemination of Computerized Information and Expertise." *The Computer Lawyer*, 6, no. 11 (Nov. 1989), pp. 1-12.

3027 Toedt, D. C., III. "Evidentiary Lessons from Recent Software Copyright Litigation." *The Computer Lawyer*, 4, no. 3 (Mar. 1987), pp. 19-22.

3028 Toedt, D. C., III. "The Model Software License Provisions: Precursor to a Gap-Filling Uniform License Statute?" *Rutgers Computer and Technology Law Journal*, 18, no. 2 (1992), pp. 521-679.

3029 Toedt, D. C., III. "Model Software Licensing Provisions." *The Computer Lawyer*, 8, no. 2 (Feb. 1991), pp. 16-33.

3030 Toedt, D. C., III. "Patents for Inventions Utilizing Computer Software: Some Practical Pointers." *The Computer Lawyer*, 9, no. 10 (Oct. 1992), pp. 12-17.

3031 Toedt, D. C., III. "Software Patent Controversies Lead to Different Outcomes in the Federal Circuit, PTO." *The Computer Lawyer*, 9, no. 7 (July 1992), pp. 18-20.

3032 Toedt, D. C., III. "Why Are We Re-Inventing the Wheel? Arguments Against Copyright Protection for Command-Driven Software Interfaces." *Software Law Journal,* 5, no. 2 (Apr. 1992), pp. 385-400.

3033 Tokars, Fredric W., and John C. Yates. "Legal Remedies for Computer Abuse." *Georgia State Bar Journal,* 21, no. 3 (Feb. 1985), pp. 100-6.

3034 Tomijima, Althea Uhlman. "A Discussion of Recent Amendments to the Japanese Copyright Law and Other Methods of Protecting Software in Japan." *Software Law Journal,* 1, no. 2 (Winter 1986), pp. 217-31.

3035 Tompkins, Frederick G., and Russell S. Rice. "Integrating Security Activities into the Software Development Life Cycle and the Software Quality Assurance Process." *Computers and Security,* 5 (1986), pp. 218-42.

3036 Tompkins, Joseph B., Jr., and Frederick S. Ansell. "Computer Crime: Keeping Up with High Tech Criminals." *Criminal Justice,* 1, no. 4 (Winter 1987), pp. 30-38.

3037 Tompkins, Joseph B., Jr., and Linda A. Mar. "An Analysis of the 1984 Federal Computer Crime Provisions." *Law/Technology,* 18, no. 2 (2nd Quarter 1985), pp. 1-34.

3038 Tompkins, Joseph B., Jr., and Linda A. Mar. "The 1984 Federal Computer Crime Statute: A Partial Answer to a Pervasive Problem." *Computer/Law Journal,* 6, no. 3 (Winter 1986), pp. 459-81.

3039 Toole, William W. "'Even If a Stranger Could Create Such a Work...' Software, Piracy, and Implications of the Implied Covenant of Good Faith: Has the *SAS* Court Gone Too Far?" *Computer/Law Journal,* 9, no. 2 (Spring 1989), pp. 145-62.

3040 Torczon, Richard L. "Copyright, Patent, and the Virtual Machine." *Computer/Law Journal,* 9, no. 3 (Summer 1989), pp. 321-57.

3041 Touponse, Marshall J. "The Application of Copyright Law to Computer Operating System Programs: *Apple Computer, Inc. v. Franklin Computer Corp.*" *Connecticut Law Review,* 17, no. 3 (Spring 1985), pp. 665-701.

3042 Tracy, Eleanor Johnson. "The Search for Copyproof Software." *Fortune,* 110, no. 5 (3 Sept. 1984), p. 83.

3043 Tracy, Eleanor Johnson. "Selling Software on the Honor System." *Fortune,* 110, no. 8 (15 Oct. 1984), p. 146.

3044 "Trade Secret Misappropriation Is Preempted." *The Computer Lawyer,* 9, no. 9 (Sept. 1992), p. 35.

3045 "Trade Secret Protection Extends to Manner in Which Non-Secret Utility Programs Are Arranged." *The Computer Lawyer,* 8, no. 2 (Feb. 1991), pp. 35-36.

3046 "Trade Secret Protection for Mass Market Computer Software: Old Solutions for New Problems." *Albany Law Review,* 51, no. 2 (Winter 1987), pp. 293-331.

3047 Tramontana, James. "Computer Viruses: Is There a Legal 'Antibiotic?'" *Rutgers Computer and Technology Law Journal,* 16, no. 1 (1990), pp. 253-84.

3048 Tremper, Charles R., and Mark A. Small. "Privacy Regulation of Computer-Assisted Testing and Instruction." *Washington Law Review,* 63, no. 4 (Oct. 1988), pp. 841-79.

3049 "Trial Court Ruling Rejects the Protection of 'Structure, Sequence and Organization' of Computer Programs." *Software Protection,* 10, no. 9 (Feb. 1992), pp. 1-3.

3050 Trubow, George B. "The European Harmonization of Data Protection Laws Threatens U.S. Participation in Trans Border Data Flow." *Northwestern Journal of International Law and Business,* 13, no. 1 (Spring/Summer 1992), pp. 159-76.

3051 Trubow, George B. "Information Law Overview." *The John Marshall Law Review,* 18, no. 4 (Summer 1985), pp. 815-28.

3052 Trubow, George B. "National Information Policy and the Management of Personal Records." *Software Law Journal,* 2, no. 1 (Winter 1987), pp. 101-12.

3053 Trubow, George B. "Protecting Informational Privacy in the Information Society." *Northern Illinois University Law Review,* 10, no. 2 (1990), pp. 521-42.

3054 "Trying to Cure Computer Viruses." *Modern Office Technology,* 34, no. 2 (Feb. 1989), pp. 35-36.

3055 Tucker, Greg. "Frontiers of Information Privacy in Australia." *Journal of Law and Information Science,* 3, no. 1 (1992), pp. 63-81.

3056 Tucker, Greg. "Privacy Protection and Transborder Data Flows." *The Australian Law Journal,* 65 (June 1991), pp. 354-56.

3057 Tucker, Greg. "Restrictions on the Transborder Flows of Personal Data." *The Australian Law Journal,* 65 (Sept. 1991), pp. 560-62.

3058 Tunick, David C. "Can the Purchaser of a Typewritten Copy of a Computer Program Authorize Another to Make a Disk Copy of the Program?" *Software Protection,* 8, no. 5 (Oct. 1989), pp. 1-5.

3059 Tunick, David C. "Legal Rights in Computer Software." *Santa Clara Computer and High Technology Law Journal,* 8, no. 2 (Aug. 1992), pp. 407-28.

3060 Tupman, W. A. "Ethics for Computer Technology and the Criminal Justice System." *Law, Computers and Artificial Intelligence*, 1, no. 1 (1992), pp. 133-48.

3061 Turkington, Richard C. "Legal Protection for the Confidentiality of Health Care Information in Pennsylvania: Patient and Client Access; Testimonial Privileges; Damage Recovery for Unauthorized Extra-Legal Disclosure." *Villanova Law Review*, 32, no. 2 (Apr. 1987), pp. 259-400.

3062 Turner, Clive. "Copyright and Parallel Importation: The Australian Experience and Recent Initiatives." *Intellectual Property Journal*, 7, no. 2 (Aug. 1992), pp. 149-86.

3063 Turner, Clive. "Copyright and the Parallel Importation of Goods into Australia—Two Recent Decisions." *The University of Queensland Law Journal*, 15, no. 1 (1988), pp. 85-89.

3064 Turner, Judith Axler. "A 75 Discrepancy Propels Astronomer Into a Maze of Computer Networks and Onto a Best-Seller List." *The Chronicles of Higher Education*, 36, no. 29 (4 Apr. 1990), p. A3.

3065 Turner, Paula F. "Computer Security: How to Protect Yours." *Legal Economics*, 13, no. 2 (Mar. 1987), pp. 49-50, 53.

3066 "2 Get Probation in Computer Crime." *The New York Times*, 138, no. 47876 (20 May 1989), p. 10.

3067 Tyde, Julia A. "Medical Computer Software: RX for Deadly Errors." *Software Law Journal*, 4, no. 1 (Oct. 1990), pp. 117-45.

3068 Tyner, Christopher L. "Building Fences for the Electronic Village." *Ethics: Easier Said Than Done*, 1991, no. 15 (1991), pp. 34-39.

3069 "UCC Inapplicable to Software Development Contract; Computer Programmer Held to Professional Liability Standard." *The Computer Lawyer*, 3, no. 9 (Sept. 1986), p. 30.

3070 "U.K. Moves to Amend Copyright Act to Cover Software." *Software Protection*, 3, no. 10 (Mar. 1985), pp. 15-16.

3071 "UK to Legislate on Intellectual Property." *Bulletin of Legal Developments*, 1987, no. 12 (3 July 1987), p. 126.

3072 "U.S. Raids Computer Pornography at Cornell." *The New York Times*, 142, no. 49156 (20 Nov. 1992), p. B4.

3073 "U.S. Trade Representative Expresses the 'U.S. Position' on the 'Reverse Engineering' Issue in the Proposed EC Software Directive." *Software Protection*, 8, no. 11 (Apr. 1990), pp. 10-13.

3074 Ugoretz, Jeffrey E. "Copyright—Computer Software—The Menu Command Structure of a Computer Program Is a Copyrightable Form of Expression. *Lotus Development Corp. v. Paperback Software Int'l*, 740

F.Supp. 37 (D. Mass. 1990)." *Rutgers Law Journal,* 22, no. 2 (Winter 1991), pp. 543-57.

3075 Ulanoff, Lance. "Virus Spread: Who's to Blame?" *PC Magazine,* 11, no. 17 (13 Oct. 1992), pp. 31-32.

3076 "Unauthorized Reproduction of Computer Program Is Criminal Offense Under New York Law." *The Computer Lawyer,* 3, no. 8 (Aug. 1986), p. 32.

3077 Uncapher, Willard. "Trouble in Cyberspace: Civil Liberties at Peril in the Information Age." *The Humanist,* 51, no. 5 (Sept.-Oct. 1991), pp. 5-14, 34.

3078 "Uniform Commercial Code: Disclaiming the Express Warranty in Computer Contracts—Taking the Byte Out of the UCC." *Oklahoma Law Review,* 40, no. 3 (Fall 1987), pp. 471-500.

3079 "United States v Zod." *The Economist,* 316, no. 7670 (1 Sept. 1990), pp. 23-24.

3080 "Unlucky for Some." *The Economist,* 313, no. 7624 (14 Oct. 1989), pp. 100-102.

3081 "Upward Departure from Criminal Sentencing Guidelines Deemed Appropriate." *The Computer Lawyer,* 9, no. 10 (Oct. 1992), pp. 37-38.

3082 Utter, Allan C. "The Four Essentials of Computer and Information Security." *Internal Auditor,* 46, no. 6 (Dec. 1989), pp. 44-50.

3083 "Vacating Invalidity Ruling May Be Harmful." *The Computer Lawyer,* 9, no. 9 (Sept. 1992), pp. 34-35.

3084 Valauskas, Edward J. "Copyright: Know Your Electronic Rights!" *Library Journal,* 117, no. 13 (Aug. 1992), pp. 40-43.

3085 Valeriano, Gary J. "Pitfalls in Insurance Coverage for 'Computer Crimes.'" *Defense Counsel Journal,* 59, no. 4 (Oct. 1992), pp. 511-23.

3086 Van Arsdale, Cory H. "Computer Programs and Other Faculty Writings Under the Work-for-Hire Doctrine: Who Owns the Intellectual's Property?" *Santa Clara Computer and High- Technology Law Journal,* 1, no. 1 (1985), pp. 141-67.

3087 Van Dam, M. Nicole. "The Scarlet Letter 'A': AIDS in a Computer Society." *Computer/Law Journal,* 10, no. 2 (Apr. 1990), pp. 233-64.

3088 van den Assem, Rene, and Willem-Jan van Elk. "A Chosen-Plaintext Attack on the Microsoft BASIC Protection." *Computers and Security,* 5, no. 1 (Mar. 1986), pp. 36-45.

3089 van der Lans, Rick F. "Data Security in a Relational Database Environment." *Computers and Security,* 5 (1986), pp. 128-34.

3090 van Heurck, Philippe. "TRASEC: Belgian Security System for Electronic Funds Transfers." *Computers and Security,* 6 (1987), pp. 261-68.

3091 Van Name, Mark L., and Bill Catchings. "Fear and Loathing on the Electronic Networking Frontier." *PC Week,* 8, no. 46 (18 Nov. 1991), p. 72.

3092 Van Name, Mark L., and Bill Catchings. "Security for Your Data Doesn't End in the Office." *PC Week,* 9, no. 39 (28 Sept. 1992), p. 79.

3093 van Wyk, Kenneth R. "The Lehigh Virus." *Computers and Security,* 8, no. 2 (Apr. 1989), pp. 107-10.

3094 Varadharajan, Vijay. "Verification of Network Security Protocols." *Computers and Security,* 8, no. 8 (Dec. 1989), pp. 693-708.

3095 Vasilyev, Dmitri, and Yevgeni Novikov. "Computer Viruses." *Soviet Life,* 1989, no. 7 (July 1989), pp. 37-38.

3096 "Vault Corporation v. Quaid Software Limited." *Software Protection,* 5, no. 12 (May 1987), pp. 11-19.

3097 "Vault Corporation v. Quaid Software Ltd." *Software Protection,* 7, no. 2 (July 1988), pp. 4-16.

3098 Venditto, Gus. "Pipeline." *PC Magazine,* 9, no. 4 (27 Feb. 1990), pp. 63-64.

3099 "Ven-Tel to Pay Hayes Attorneys' Fees and Expenses." *The Computer Lawyer,* 9, no. 12 (Dec. 1992), pp. 36-37.

3100 Verdesca, Joseph T., Jr. "Copyrighting the User Interface: Too Much Protection?" *Southwestern Law Journal,* 45, no. 2 (Fall 1991), pp. 1047-80.

3101 Vergari, James V. "Latent Legal Repercussions in Electronic Financial Services and Transactions." *Defense Law Journal,* 34, no. 4 (1985), pp. 539-74. (First published in *Computer/Law Journal,* 5, no. 2 [Fall 1984], pp. 177-215.)

3102 Verity, John. "The Market for Mainframes Will Never Be the Same." *Business Week,* no. 3019 (5 Oct. 1987), p. 62.

3103 Verity, John W. "Defense Against Pirates or Death to the Clones?: A Proposed EC Copyright Law Would Strengthen Computer Giants." *Business Week,* no. 3158 (7 May 1990), pp. 138-40.

3104 VerSteeg, Russ, and Paul K. Harrington. "Nonobviousness as an Element of Copyrightability? (Or, Is the Jewel in the Lotus a Cubic Zirconia?)." *U.C. Davis Law Review,* 25, no. 2 (Winter 1992), pp. 331-82.

3105 Verzola, Robert. "The West Is the Real Pirate." *World Press Review,* 39, no. 10 (Oct. 1992), p. 52.

3106 "Video Games A. Copyright 1. Copyright Infringement of Video Games: When the Chips Are Down." *Loyola Entertainment Law Journal,* 5 (1985), pp. 132-42

3107 "Video Games A. Copyright 2. Copyright Protection of Video Games: Pac-Man and Galaxian Granted Extended Play." *Loyola Entertainment Law Journal*, 5 (1985), pp. 143-48.

3108 Vines, James K. "Consumer Meets Computer: An Argument for Liberal Trademark Protection of Computer Hardware Configurations Under Section 43(a) of the Lanham Trademark Act." *Washington and Lee Law Review*, 44, no. 1 (Winter 1987), pp. 283-319.

3109 Vinje, Thomas C. "The Development of Interoperable Products Under the EC Software Directive." *The Computer Lawyer*, 8, no. 11 (Nov. 1991), pp. 1-12.

3110 Violano, Michael. "Are Employees Robbing Your Bank?" *Bankers Monthly*, 106, no. 4 (Apr. 1989), p. 42.

3111 "Virus Controller Chip Due from Western Digital." *PC Week*, 9, no. 45 (9 Nov. 1992), p. 3.

3112 "Virus Threat Exposes DP Weaknesses: When Data Travel, They're Open to Danger from Unknown Quarters." *ABA Banking Journal*, 82, no. 10 (Oct. 1990), pp. 98, 101, 103-104, 106.

3113 "Viruses: Limiting the Contagion." *Best's Review — Property/Casualty Insurance Edition*, 90, no. 10 (Feb. 1990), p. 42.

3114 Vitale, Joseph. "Electronic Mail: For Your Eyes Only?" *Channels of Communications*, 6, no. 2 (May 1986), p. 14.

3115 Vogel, Shawna. "Disease of the Year: Illness as Glitch." *Discover*, 10, no. 1 (Jan. 1989), pp. 64-66.

3116 von dem Hagen, Antoinette M. "Trade-Based Remedies for Copyright Infringement: Utilizing a 'Loss Preventative' Synthesis." *Comm/Ent*, 12, no. 1 (Fall 1989), pp. 99-152.

3117 von Hellfeld, Axel. "Protection of Inventions Comprising Computer Programs by the European and German Patent Offices — A Confrontation." *Idea*, 27, no. 3 (1987), pp. 163-82.

3118 von Solms, Sebastiaan, and David Naccache. "On Blind Signatures and Perfect Crimes." *Computers and Security*, 11, no. 6 (Oct. 1992), pp. 581-83.

3119 von Spakovsky, Hans A., Michael R. von Spakovsky, and Frank J. Graffeo. "The Limited Patenting of Computer Programs: A Proposed Statutory Approach." *Cumberland Law Review*, 16, no. 1 (1985-86), pp. 27-51.

3120 Voorhees, John J. "Price Discrimination and Software Licensing: Does the Robinson-Patman Act Fail to Accommodate Modern Technology?" *Washington University Law Quarterly*, 69, no. 1 (1991), pp. 317-36.

3121 Voss, Christopher. "The Legal Protection of Computer Programs in the European Economic Community." *Computer/Law Journal*, 11, no. 3 (Oct. 1992), pp. 441-59.

3122 Voydock, Victor L., and Stephen T. Kent. "Security in High-Level Network Protocols." *IEEE Communications Magazine*, 23, no. 7 (July 1985), pp. 12-24.

3123 Wadley, James B. "An Introduction to Copyright Protection of Computer Programs and the Semi-Conductor Chip Protection Act of 1984." *The Journal of the Kansas Bar Association*, 55, no. 5 (July 1986), pp. 8-13.

3124 Wagner, Amalia M. "The Challenge of Computer-Crime Legislation: How Should New York Respond?" *Buffalo Law Review*, 33, no. 3 (Fall 1984), pp. 777-814.

3125 Waite, Barbara L. "Electronic Mass Media and Copyright in Canada and the U.S." *Journal of the Patent and Trademark Office Society*, 71, no. 4 (Apr. 1989), pp. 269-309.

3126 Walden, I. N., and R. N. Savage. "Data Protection and Privacy Laws: Should Organisations Be Protected?" *International and Comparative Law Quarterly*, 37, no. 2 (Apr. 1988), pp. 337-47.

3127 Walden, Ian, and Nigel Savage. "The Legal Problems of Paperless Transactions." *The Journal of Business Law*, 1989 (Mar. 1989), pp. 102-12.

3128 Waldrop, M. Mitchell. "PARC Brings Adam Smith to Computing." *Science*, 244, no. 4901 (14 Apr. 1989), pp. 145-46.

3129 Walker, Craig M. "Computer and High Technology Product Liability in the 1980's." *Forum*, 19 (1983-84), pp. 684-93.

3130 Walker, Russell H. "Patent Law — *In re Iwahashi*: When Does an Algorithm Become a Machine?" *Memphis State University Law Review*, 21, no. 1 (Fall 1990), pp. 175-85.

3131 Wallace, N. W. P. "The Patentability of Software-Related Inventions Under the European Patent Convention." *Software Law Journal*, 1, no. 3 (Spring-Summer 1986), pp. 249-57.

3132 Wallich, Paul. "Digital Desperados: Hacker Indictments Raise Constitutional Questions." *Scientific American*, 263, no. 3 (Sept. 1990), pp. 34-38.

3133 Wallich, Paul. "Hostile Takeovers: How Can a Computer Network Welcome Only Friendly Users?" *Scientific American*, 260, no. 1 (Jan. 1989), pp. 22-26.

3134 Wallich, Paul. "Safe Bytes: What It Will Take to Keep Computers Secure." *Scientific American*, 264, no. 2 (Feb. 1991), pp. 28-29.

3135 Walpin, Gerald. "Computers: For Full Effectiveness, Limit Your Legal Risks." *Architectural Record*, 174 (Mar. 1986), pp. 41-43.

3136 Walpin, Gerald, and Michael V. P. Marks. "Buying a Computer? Here Are 10 Key Clauses to Get in Your Purchase Contract." *Architectural Record,* 174 (July 1986), pp. 35-37.

3137 Walsh, Michael J. "The Disclosure Requirements of 35 U. S. C. 112 and Software-Related Patent Applications: Debugging the System." *Intellectual Property Law Review,* 19 (1987), pp. 3-23. (First published in *Connecticut Law Review,* 18, no. 4 [Summer 1986], pp. 855-75.)

3138 Walter, Charles. "Defining the Scope of Software Copyright Protection for Maximum Public Benefit." *Rutgers Computer and Technology Law Journal,* 14, no. 1 (1988), pp. 1-158.

3139 Walter, Priscilla A. "Databases: Protecting an Asset; Avoiding a Liability." *The Computer Lawyer,* 8, no. 3 (Mar. 1991), pp. 10-20.

3140 Walter, Priscilla A. "Facts After *Feist*: A Copyright Conundrum." *The Practical Lawyer,* 37, no. 8 (Dec. 1991), pp. 67-81.

3141 Wang, Josephine. "Protection of Computer Software in Taiwan." *Software Protection,* 5, no. 11 (Apr. 1987), pp. 1-4.

3142 Wangerow, Ronald W., Stephen J. Foss, and Linda L. Malicki. "Summary of the Semiconductor Chip Protection Act of 1984." *Michigan Bar Journal,* 56, no. 3 (Mar. 1986), pp. 308-13.

3143 Wanke, Ronald L., Craig R. Culbertson, and Donald R. Cassling. "Protection Against Failing Vendors." *Software Law Journal,* 1, no. 4 (Fall 1987), pp. 523-39.

3144 Ware, Donald R. "Trade Secret Protection of Computer Software: The Common Law Encounters High Technology." *Boston Bar Journal,* 29, no. 5 (Nov.-Dec. 1985), pp. 6-11, 34.

3145 Ware, Willis H. "Emerging Privacy Issues." *Computers and Security,* 5 (1986), pp. 101-13.

3146 Warner, Paul D. "Taking a Stand Against Computer Viruses." *The CPA Journal,* 60, no. 4 (Apr. 1990), pp. 100-1.

3147 Warnot, James R. "Software Copyright Protection in the European Community: Existing Law and an Analysis of the Proposed Council Directive." *Santa Clara Computer and High Technology Law Journal,* 6, no. 2 (1990-91), pp. 355-76.

3148 Warren, Jennifer. "Hacker, 14, Accused of Credit Theft." *Los Angeles Times,* (18 Oct. 1989), p. A22.

3149 "Washington Report: Electronic Security: Some Hair-Raising Questions." *The Office,* 111, no. 5 (May 1990), p. 26.

3150 Wasik, Martin. "The Computer Misuse Act 1990." *The Criminal Law Review,* 1990 (Nov. 1990), pp. 767-79.

3151 Wasik, Martin. "Following in American Footsteps? Computer Crime Developments in Great Britain and Canada." *Northern Kentucky Law Review,* 14, no. 2 (1987), pp. 249-62.

3152 Wasik, Martin. "Law Reform Proposals on Computer Misuse." *The Criminal Law Review,* 1989 (Apr. 1989), pp. 257-70.

3153 Waters, Peter, and Peter G. Leonard. "A Whistle-Stop Tour of Practical Legal Considerations for U. S. Software Houses Doing Business in Australia." *Software Law Journal,* 5, no. 1 (Feb. 1992), pp. 127-51.

3154 Watson, Jack H., Jr. "Trade Secrets in the Computer Industry." *Georgia State Bar Journal,* 20, no. 4 (May 1984), pp. 210-15.

3155 Watts, Susan. "How to Avoid a Nasty Cold." *Management Today,* (Mar. 1989), p. 156.

3156 Watts, Susan, and Sharon Kingman. "Sloppy Software Was AIDS Disc's Achilles Heel." *New Scientist,* 125, no. 1698 (6 Jan. 1990), p. 34.

3157 Wayland, Tamara J. "Computer Technology—The National Stolen Property Act and Its Applicability to Property Rights in Computer Source Code—Do Rights Exist?—*United States v. Brown,* 925 F.2d 1301 (10th Cir. 1991)." *Temple Environmental Law and Technology Journal,* 11, no. 1 (Spring 1992), pp. 155-69.

3158 Wayner, Peter. "Goodbye, Mr. Chips." *Byte,* 14, no. 10 (Oct. 1989), p. 364.

3159 Wayner, Peter. "True Data." *Byte,* 16, no. 9 (Sept. 1991), pp. 122-28.

3160 Wayner, Peter. "Zero-Knowledge Proofs." *Byte,* 12, no. 11 (Oct. 1987), pp. 149-52.

3161 Waz, Joseph W., Jr. "Proposed Federal Supercomputer Network Highlights Policy Issues in Telecommunications, Copyright." *The Computer Lawyer,* 6, no. 10 (Oct. 1989), pp. 27-30.

3162 Webb, Ben. "Plan to Outlaw Hacking." *Nature,* 341, no. 6243 (19 Oct. 1989), p. 559.

3163 Webb, Jere M. "The Law of Trade Dress Infringement: A Survey of Recent Developments." *The Computer Lawyer,* 8, no. 9 (Sept. 1991), pp. 11-23.

3164 Webb, Jere M., and Lawrence A. Locke. "Intellectual Property Misuse: Developments in the Misuse Doctrine." *Harvard Journal of Law and Technology,* 4 (Spring 1991), pp. 237-67.

3165 Webb, Jeremy, and Barry Fox. "Michelangelo Disappoints the Virus Hunters." *New Scientist,* 133, no. 1812 (14 Mar. 1992), p. 10.

3166 Webber, Chris. "Recent Amendments to the Canadian Criminal Code Respecting Computer Abuse Offenses." *Santa Clara Computer and High-Technology Law Journal,* 3, no. 1 (Jan. 1987), pp. 165-90.

3167 Webber, Christopher. "Computer Crime or Jay-Walking on the Electronic Highway." *Criminal Law Quarterly*, 26, no. 2 (1984), pp. 217-50.

3168 Weber, Ellen Lauver. "Patenting Inventions That Embody Computer Programs Held as Trade Secrets—*White Consolidated Industries v. Vega Servo-Control*, 713 F.2d 788 (Fed. Cir. 1983)." *Washington Law Review*, 59, no. 3 (July 1984), pp. 601-15.

3169 Weber, Lori A. "Bad Bytes: The Application of Strict Products Liability to Computer Software." *St. John's Law Review*, 66, no. 2 (Spring 1992), pp. 469-85.

3170 Weber, Richard G. "Copyright Law—The Extension of Copyright Protection to Computer Operating Programs—*Apple Computer v. Franklin Computer* 714 F.2d 1240 (3d Cir. August 30, 1983)." *Western New England Law Review*, 7, no. 3 (1985), pp. 829-45.

3171 Weber, Robert. "Copyright in the Electronic Age." *Publishers Weekly*, 238, no. 14 (22 Mar. 1991), pp. 52-53.

3172 Weber, Ron. "Controls in Electronic Funds Transfer Systems: A Survey and Synthesis." *Computers and Security*, 8, no. 2 (Apr. 1989), pp. 123-37.

3173 Weberman, Ben. "Book-Entry Blues." *Forbes*, 137, no. 10 (5 May 1986), p. 104.

3174 Webster, Anne E. "University of Delaware and the Pakistani Computer Virus." *Computers and Security*, 8, no. 2 (Apr. 1989), pp. 103-105.

3175 Webster, Dan, and Tim Pryor. "Customs Administration of the High-Tech Copyright Protection Program." *Journal of the Patent and Trademark Office Society*, 73, no. 7 (July 1991), pp. 538-42.

3176 Webster, Jon O. "Copyright Protection of Systems Control Software Stored in Read Only Memory Chips: Into the World of Gulliver's Travels." *Buffalo Law Review*, 33, no. 1 (Winter 1984), pp. 193-224.

3177 Weichselbaum, Mindy J. "The EEC Directive on the Legal Protection of Computer Programs and U.S. Copyright Law: Should Copyright Law Permit Reverse Engineering of Computer Programs?" *Fordham International Law Journal*, 14, no. 4 (1990-91), pp. 1027-68.

3178 Weinberg, Steven M. "Overview of the Statutory Protection for Computer Programs and Chips (Part 1)." *The Practical Lawyer*, 34, no. 2 (Mar. 1988), pp. 41-60.

3179 Weinberg, Steven M. "Overview of the Statutory Protection for Computer Programs and Chips (Part 2)." *The Practical Lawyer*, 34, no. 3 (Apr. 1988), pp. 25-41.

3180 Weiner, Richard E. "A Practical Guide to Protecting Confidential Information Stored in a Company's Computer System." *Law/Technology*, 21, no. 2 (1988), pp. 1-19.

3181 Weingarten, Fred W. "Communications Technology: New Challenges to Privacy." *John Marshall Law Review,* 21, no. 4 (Summer 1988), pp. 735-53.

3182 Weinstein, Alvin S. "The Performance Audit: Minimizing Software Liability (Part 1)." *Idea,* 29, no. 2 (1988-89), pp. 127-35.

3183 Weintraub, William. "Teaching Computer Ethics in the Schools." *Education Digest,* 52, no. 6 (Feb. 1987), pp. 34-35.

3184 Weisman, Laurie E. "Copyright Law—Fifth Circuit Interprets Copyright Act to Allow Copying of Software for Any Legitimate Reason—*Vault Corp. v. Quaid Software Ltd.,* 847 F.2d 255 (5th Cir. 1988)." *Suffolk University Law Review,* 23, no. 3 (Fall 1989), pp. 905-12.

3185 Weiss, Kenneth P. "Controlling the Threat to Computer Security." *Management Review,* 79, no. 6 (June 1990), pp. 54-57.

3186 Weiss, Kenneth P. "Insecurity Spelled with Seven Es." *Management Review,* 79, no. 6 (June 1990), p. 57.

3187 Weitzman, Jeffrey. "Protecting the Look and Feel of Computer Programs." *Cardozo Law Review,* 10, no. 3 (Dec. 1988), pp. 561-92.

3188 Welch, Judith J., and Wayne L. Anderson. "Copyright Protection of Computer Software in Japan." *Computer/Law Journal,* 11, no. 2 (Apr. 1991), pp. 287-98.

3189 Wenig, Donald R. "Computer Transactions and Uniform Commercial Code Article 2A: Does 2A Fit?" *Software Law Journal,* 4, no. 3 (Oct. 1991), pp. 457-92.

3190 Wenskay, Donald L. "Neural Networks: A Prescription for Effective Protection." *The Computer Lawyer,* 8, no. 8 (Aug. 1991), pp. 12-23.

3191 Wernick, Alan S. "The Work Made for Hire and Joint Work Copyright Doctrines After *CCNV v. Reid*: 'What! You Mean I Don't Own It Even Though I Paid in Full for It?'" *Hamline Law Review,* 13, no. 2 (Spring 1990), pp. 287-95.

3192 Wesolowski, John S. "Copyright Infringement of Computer Programs: Preliminary Relief Granted Against an Alleged Infringer, Using the Iterative Test for Substantial Similarity." *Santa Clara Computer and High-Technology Law Journal,* 2, no. 2 (1986), pp. 417-23.

3193 Wessel, Milton R. "Introductory Comment on the Arizona State University LaST Frontier Conference on Copyright Protection of Computer Software." *Jurimetrics Journal,* 30, no. 1 (Fall 1989), pp. 1-9.

3194 Wessel, Milton R. "Substantial Similarity." *The Journal of Law and Technology,* 2, no. 1 (Winter 1987), pp. 35-38.

3195 Westermeier, J. T., and Philip D. Porter. "Computer Consultant's Liability." *Software Protection,* 7, no. 11-12 (Apr.-May 1989), pp. 1-3.

3196 Wetzel, James M. "Intellectual Property—Trademarks, Copyrights, and Unfair Competition." *The Compleat Lawyer,* 5, no. 3 (Summer 1988), pp. 53-56.

3197 Wharton, Leslie. "Legislative Issues in Computer Crime." *Harvard Journal on Legislation,* 21, no. 1 (Winter 1984), pp. 239-54.

3198 Wharton, Leslie. "Misuse and Copyright: A Legal Mismatch." *The Computer Lawyer,* 8, no. 3 (Mar. 1991), pp. 1-9.

3199 Wharton, Leslie. "Use and Expression: The Scope of Copyright Protection for Computer Programs." *Computer/Law Journal,* 5, no. 4 (Spring 1985), pp. 433-68.

3200 "What to Do About Computer Viruses." *Fortune,* 118, no. 13 (5 Dec. 1988), p. 16.

3201 *"Whelan Associates, Inc. v. Jaslow Dental Laboratory, Inc."* Software Protection, 5, no. 8 (Jan. 1987), pp. 2-19.

3202 *"Whelan Associates v. Jaslow Dental Laboratory*: Copyright Protection for the Structure and Sequence of Computer Programs." *Loyola of Los Angeles Law Review,* 21, no. 1 (Nov. 1987), pp. 255-303.

3203 *"Whelan v. Jaslow*: An Appraisal." *The Journal of Law and Technology,* 2, no. 1 (Winter 1987), pp. 1-3.

3204 White, Clinton, E., Jr. "Viruses and Worms: A Campus Under Attack." *Computers and Security,* 8, no. 4 (June 1989), pp. 283-90.

3205 "White Collar Crime: Survey of Law—Computer Crime." *American Criminal Law Review,* 23, no. 3 (Winter 1986), pp. 307-9.

3206 "White Collar Crime: Survey of Law—Computer Crime." *American Criminal Law Review,* 25, no. 3 (Winter 1988), pp. 367-70.

3207 "White-Collar Crime: Third Annual Survey of Law—Computer Crime." *American Criminal Law Review,* 22, no. 3 (Winter 1985), pp. 494-502.

3208 Whiting, Todd. "Understanding VAX/VMS Security." *Computers and Security,* 11, no. 8 (Dec. 1992), pp. 695-98.

3209 Whitmeyer, Randall M. "A Plea for Due Processes: Defining the Proper Scope of Patent Protection for Computer Software." *Northwestern University Law Review,* 85, no. 4 (Summer 1991), pp. 1103-38.

3210 Whitmyer, Claude F. "Computer Viruses: The Potential for Damage Exists." *The Office,* 110, no. 6 (Dec. 1989), p. 24.

3211 Whitmyer, Claude F. "Computer Viruses and How to Handle Them." *The Office,* 116, no. 5 (Nov. 1992), p. 30.

3212 Whitmyer, Claude F. "How to Beat the Attack of a Virus." *The Office,* 115, no. 6 (June 1992), p. 26.

3213 Whitmyer, Claude F. "How to Guard Against Software Loss? Protect It." *The Office*, 115, no. 5 (May 1992), p. 26.

3214 Whitmyer, Claude F. "More Protection Programs Than There Are Viruses." *The Office*, 110, no. 2 (Aug. 1989), p. 28.

3215 "The 'Whiz Kids': Hacking Away at Computer Crime." *Teen*, 28, no. 3 (Mar. 1984), p. 56.

3216 "Who Ya Gonna Call?" *The Economist*, 315, no. 7649 (7 Apr. 1990), p. 78.

3217 Wiegner, Kathleen. "The Trouble with E-Mail." *Working Woman*, (Apr. 1992), p. 46.

3218 Wiegner, Kathleen K. "Go Tell the Spartans." *Forbes*, 136, no. 16 (30 Dec. 1985), p. 91.

3219 Wiegner, Kathleen K. "Is Someone Listening to Your Computer?" *Forbes*, 145 (28 May 1990), pp. 342-43.

3220 Wiegner, Kathleen K. "When the Going Gets Tough, the Tough Go to Court." *Forbes*, 140, no. 14 (28 Dec. 1987), pp. 36-37.

3221 Wiegner, Kathleen K., and John Heins. "Can Las Vegas Sue Atlantic City?" *Forbes*, 143, no. 5 (6 Mar. 1989), pp. 130-33, 136-37.

3222 Wiener, Daniel P. "When a Virus Makes Your PC Sneeze." *U.S. News and World Report*, 108, no. 8 (26 Feb. 1990), p. 62.

3223 Wiggs, Blake R. "Canadian Copyright Protection for Computer Software — Recent Developments." *Software Protection*, 3, no. 12 (May 1985), pp. 8-18.

3224 Wilbur, Mary A. "Copyright Registration for Secret Computer Programs: Robbery of the Phoenix's Nest." *Jurimetrics Journal*, 24, no. 4 (Summer 1984), pp. 357-76.

3225 Wilder, Richard. "Computer Software in Europe and the United States: Is It Patentable Subject Matter?" *Idea*, 25, no. 2 (1984-85), pp. 51-60.

3226 Wiley, Richard E. "Report on Legal Developments in Electronic Publishing." *Jurimetrics Journal*, 27, no. 4 (Summer 1987), pp.403-22.

3227 Wiley, Richard E., and David E. Leibowitz. "Electronic Privacy Act Is Progress — But It Still Is Not a Panacea." *The National Law Journal*, 9, no. 18 (12 Jan. 1987), pp. 20-21.

3228 Wilf, Frederic M. "A Chip Off the Old Block: Copyright Law and the Semiconductor Chip Protection Act." *Computer/Law Journal*, 7, no. 2 (Fall 1986), pp. 245-60.

3229 Wilkes, Diana. "The Wiretap Statute: A Haven for Hackers." *Jurimetrics Journal*, 31, no. 4 (Summer 1990), pp. 415-27.

3230 Williams, Dennis A., and Richard Sandza. "Teaching Hackers Ethics." *Newsweek*, 105, no. 2 (14 Jan. 1985), p. 76.

3231 Williams, Gregg. "A Threat to Future Software." *Software Protection*, 4, no. 9 (Feb. 1986), pp.7-8.

3232 Williams, Kent M. "Immunizing the Electronic Office...." *Bench and Bar of Minnesota*, 49, no. 7 (Aug. 1992), pp. 23-24.

3233 Williams, L. K., Ray Pinner, and Gary Van Meter. "Computer Viruses and the CPA." *The CPA Journal*, 62, no. 1 (Jan. 1992), p. 78.

3234 Willick, Marshal S. "Professional Malpractice and the Unauthorized Practice of Professions: Some Legal and Ethical Aspects of the Use of Computers as Decision-Aids." *Rutgers Computer and Technology Law Journal*, 12, no. 1 (1986), pp. 1-32.

3235 Wilson, Darryl C. "Viewing Computer Crime: Where Does the Systems Error Really Exist?" *Computer/Law Journal*, 11, no. 2 (Apr. 1991), pp.265-85.

3236 Wilson, David I., and James A. LaBarre. "The Semiconductor Chip Protection Act of 1984: A Preliminary Analysis." *Journal of the Patent and Trademark Office Society*, 67, no. 2 (Feb. 1985), pp. 57-92.

3237 Wilson, Debra S. "Software Rental, Piracy, and Copyright Protection." *Computer/Law Journal*, 5, no. 1 (Summer 1984), pp. 125-41.

3238 Wilson, Katherine. "Privacy and Computer Law." *Law Institute Journal*, 65, no. 6 (June 1991), p. 461.

3239 Winans, Christopher. "As Computer Virus Fears Grow, Insurers Focus on the Coverage Question." *The Wall Street Journal*, 213, no. 106 (1 June 1989), p. A1.

3240 Winder, Robert. "Admissions of Guilt and Vulnerability." *American Banker*, 154, no. 39 (27 Feb. 1989), p. 14.

3241 Wines, Michael. "'Virus' Eliminated, Defense Aides Say." *The New York Times*, 138, no. 47680 (5 Nov. 1988), pp. 1, 7.

3242 Winters, Steven B. "Do Not Fold, Spindle or Mutilate: An Examination of Workplace Privacy in Electronic Mail." *Southern California Interdisciplinary Law Journal*, 1, no. 1 (Spring 1992), pp. 85-131.

3243 Winters, Vince. "Computer Usage and Invasion of Privacy: The Good, the Bad, and the Ugly." *Beverly Hills Bar Association Journal*, 22, no. 4 (Fall 1988), pp. 287-94.

3244 Wise, Ginger. "The Case of the Smiling Virus." *American Banker*, 154, no. 23 (2 Feb. 1989), p. 6.

3245 Wiseman, Simon. "Control of Confidentiality in Databases." *Computers and Security*, 9, no. 6 (Oct. 1990), pp. 529-37.

3246 Wiseman, Simon. "Preventing Viruses in Computer Systems." *Computers and Security,* 8, no. 5 (Aug. 1989), pp. 427-32.

3247 Witt, Lois R. "Terminally Nosy: Are Employers Free to Access Our Electronic Mail?" *Dickinson Law Review,* 96, no. 3 (Spring 1992), pp. 545-71.

3248 Wolf, Nora. "Greater Software Protection: New Bill in Congress Would Stiffen Penalties." *ABA Journal,* 72, no. 12 (Oct. 1986), p. 48.

3249 Wong, Ken. "Computer Fraud: An Ever Growing Threat." *Banker,* 135, no. 712 (June 1985), pp. 88-90.

3250 Wong, Kenneth K. "Computer-Related Fraud in the U.K." *EDPACS,* 11, no. 12 (June 1984), pp. 5-9.

3251 Wong, Russell T. "The Semiconductor Chip Protection Act: New Law for New Technology." *Journal of the Patent and Trademark Office Society,* 67, no. 10 (Oct. 1985), pp. 530-50.

3252 Wong, Wean Khing. "Protecting American Software in Japan." *Computer/Law Journal,* 8, no. 2 (Spring 1988), pp. 111-34.

3253 Wood, Charles Cresson. "Burning Computer Security, Privacy, and Freedom Issues." *Computers and Security,* 10, no. 6 (Oct. 1991), pp. 524-32.

3254 Wood, Charles Cresson. "A Context for Information Systems Security Planning." *Computers and Security,* 7, no. 5 (Oct. 1988), pp. 455-65.

3255 Wood, Charles Cresson. "Fifteen Major Forces Driving the Civilian Information Security Market." *Computers and Security,* 9, no. 8 (Dec. 1990), pp. 677-87.

3256 Wood, Charles Cresson. "Planning: A Means to Achieve Data Communications Security." *Computers and Security,* 8, no. 3 (May 1989), pp. 189-99.

3257 Wood, Charles Cresson, and Howard M. Zeidler. "Security Modules: Potent Information Security System Components." *Computers and Security,* 5 (1986), pp. 114-21.

3258 Wood, Chris. "Crime in the Computer Age." *Maclean's,* 101, no. 5 (25 Jan. 1988), pp. 28-30.

3259 Wood, Patrick. "Safe and Secure?" *Byte,* 14, no. 5 (May 1989), pp.253-58.

3260 Woods, William F. "Software Secrecy." *Brief,* 16, no. 4 (Summer 1987), pp. 34-37.

3261 Woodson, Wade, and Douglas C. Safreno. "The Semiconductor Chip Protection Act of 1984." *Santa Clara Computer and High-Technology Law Journal,* 1, no. 1 (1985), pp. 7-12.

3262 Work, Clemens P., Daniel P. Wiener, and Kenneth R. Sheets. "Yen to Match IBM Yields Japanese Competitor a Peep." *U.S. News and World Report*, 105, no. 23 (12 Dec. 1988), p. 76.

3263 "Worker Monitoring and Privacy." *The Futurist*, 22, no. 2 (Mar.- Apr. 1988), p. 51.

3264 "World-Wide Reports on Developments in Computer Security." *Computers and Security*, 7, no. 1 (Feb. 1988), pp. 97-100.

3265 "World-Wide Reports on Developments in Computer Security: Part II." *Computers and Security*, 7, no. 2 (Apr. 1988), pp. 207-209.

3266 Worthen, John D. "PC Protection." *Bank Management*, 68, no. 3 (Mar. 1992), pp. 57-58.

3267 Worthy, Clark H. "Determining the Scope of Copyright Protection for a Computer Program's Nonliteral Elements: Is It as Easy as 1*2*3*?*" *Washington and Lee Law Review*, 48, no. 3 (Summer 1991), pp. 1079-107.

3268 Wrenn, Gregory J. "Federal Intellectual Property Protection for Computer Software Audiovisual Look and Feel: The Lanham, Copyright, and Patent Acts." *High Technology Law Journal*, 4, no. 2 (Fall 1989), pp. 279-329.

3269 Wright, Benjamin. "Authenticating EDI: The Location of a Trusted Recordkeeper." *Software Law Journal*, 4, no. 2 (Apr. 1991), pp. 173-78.

3270 Wright, William H. "Litigation as a Mechanism for Inefficiency in Software Copyright Law." *UCLA Law Review*, 39, no. 2 (Dec. 1991), pp. 397-437.

3271 Wynn, Jack. "Meeting the Threat: Nearly 8,500 Sites in the Government's Financial Network Are Sensitive to Computer Viruses. They'll Be Shielded by Yearend." *American Banker*, 154, no. 23 (2 Feb. 1989), p. 8.

3272 "Xerox v. Apple: The Other Shoe Drops." *Software Protection*, 8, no. 7 (Dec. 1989), p. 4.

3273 "XTree Adds Virus Utility to Its Software Products." *PC Week*, 8, no. 42 (21 Oct. 1991), p. 69.

3274 Yamamoto, Takashi. "The Concept of 'Originality' and the Merger Doctrine in Japanese Copyright Law: The Meaning of the *System Science* Case." *Software Protection*, 9, no. 4 (Sept. 1990), pp. 1-8.

3275 Yanaga, Barron. "An Economic Analysis of Computer Software Copyright: A Welfare Model of Intellectual Property Rights." *Computer/Law Journal*, 11, no. 1 (Feb. 1991), pp. 173-96.

3276 Yates, John C., and Anthony E. DiResta. "Software Support and Hardware Maintenance Practices: Tying Considerations." *The Computer Lawyer*, 8, no. 6 (June 1991), pp. 17-32.

3277 Yates, John C., and Michael W. Mattox. "Intellectual Property." *Mercer Law Review*, 42, no. 1 (Fall 1990), pp. 295-345.

3278 Yee, Helen W. "Juvenile Computer Crime — Hacking: Criminal and Civil Liability." *Comm/Ent*, 7, no. 2 (1984-85), pp. 335-58.

3279 Yen, Elizabeth C. "Banking Decisions: Consumer Liability for Unauthorized ATM Transfers Cannot Be Enlarged by Contract Beyond the Liability Provisions of the Federal Electronic Fund Transfer Act." *The Banking Law Journal*, 106, no. 4 (July-Aug. 1989), pp. 377-80.

3280 Yoches, E. Robert. "Protection of Computer Software by Patents, Trade Secrets, and Trademarks." *Tort and Insurance Law Journal*, 22 (1986-87), pp. 334-87.

3281 York, Cynthia M. "Criminal Liability for the Misappropriation of Computer Software Trade Secrets." *University of Detroit Law Review*, 63, no. 3 (Spring 1986), pp. 481-98.

3282 Yuasa, Takashi. "Computer Data Base Protection — The Impact of Japanese Legislative Developments on United States and Japanese Copyright Laws." *Fordham International Law Journal*, 9, no. 2 (1985-86), pp. 191-212.

3283 Zacharia, Michael E., Michael A. Kvarme, and Christopher Chediak. "Export Controls in the Biotechnology Industry." *Santa Clara Computer and High-Technology Law Journal*, 3, no. 1 (Jan. 1987), pp. 141-64.

3284 Zajac, Bernard P., Jr. "Computer Viral Risks — How Bad Is the Threat." *Computers and Security*, 11, no. 1 (Mar. 1992), pp. 29-34.

3285 Zajac, Bernard P., Jr. "Computer Viruses: Can They Be Prevented?" *Computers and Security*, 9, no. 1 (Feb. 1990), pp. 25-31.

3286 Zajac, Bernard P, Jr. "Dial-Up Communication Lines: Can They Be Secured?" *Computers and Security*, 7, no. 1 (Feb. 1988), pp. 35-36.

3287 Zajac, Bernard P., Jr. "Distributed Data Processing: New Problems." *Computers and Security*, 7, no. 3 (June 1988), pp. 249-50.

3288 Zajac, Bernard P., Jr. "Interview with Clifford Stoll." *Computers and Security*, 9, no. 7 (Nov. 1990), pp. 601-3.

3289 Zajac, Bernard P., Jr. "Legal Options to Computer Viruses." *Computers and Security*, 8, no. 1 (Feb. 1989), pp. 25-27.

3290 Zajac, Bernard P., Jr. "The 1990s — What Will They Hold?" *Computers and Security*, 9, no. 6 (Oct. 1990), pp. 503-7.

3291 Zajac, Bernard P., Jr. "People: The 'Other' Side of Computer Security." *Computers and Security*, 9, no. 4 (June 1990), pp. 301-3.

3292 Zajac, Bernard P., Jr. "What to Do When You Have Reason to Believe Your Computer Has Been Compromised." *Computers and Security*, 5, no. 1 (Mar. 1986), pp. 11-16.

3293 Zammit, Joseph P. "Future Trends in Liability for Computer Usage." *New York State Bar Journal,* 59, no. 3 (Apr. 1987), pp. 26-28, 57.

3294 Zammit, Joseph P., and Linda K. Singer. "Trial Tactics in Computer-Related Litigation." *The Computer Lawyer,* 8, no. 12 (Dec. 1991), pp. 40-43.

3295 "Zeroing-In on Computer Crime." *Dun's Business Month,* 123, no. 4 (Apr. 1984), p. 15.

3296 Zhou, Xiao-Lin. "U.S.-China Trade Dispute and China's Intellectual Property Rights Protection." *New York University Journal of International Law and Politics,* 24, no. 3 (Spring 1992), pp. 1115-29.

3297 Zigelbaum, Debra M. "The Computer Software Protection Act: A Legislative Response to Software Piracy Through Software Rentals." *Software Law Journal,* 1, no. 1 (Fall 1985), pp. 67-93.

3298 Zimmerman, Joel S. "PC Security: So What's New?" *Datamation,* 31, no. 21 (1 Nov. 1985), pp. 86-92.

3299 Zimmerman, Michael R. "Drug Dealers Find Haven in On-Line Services." *PC Week,* 8, no. 9 (4 Mar. 1991), pp. 43, 49.

3300 Zimmerman, Michael R. "Hilgraeve Upgrade Offers Built-In Virus Detection." *PC Week,* 7, no. 18 (7 May 1990), p. 44.

3301 Zimmerman, Michael R. "Microcom Releases an MS-DOS Version of Virex Software." *PC Week,* 7, no. 19 (14 May 1990), p. 32.

3302 Zimmerman, Mitchell. "Substantial Similarity of Computer Programs After *Brown Bag.*" *The Computer Lawyer,* 9, no. 7 (July 1992), pp. 6-17.

3303 Zissu, Roger L. "The Past Revisited—The Copyright Act of 1976 at Mid Decade: *An Overview with Observations.*" *The Journal of the Copyright Society of the U.S.A.,* 34 (Oct. 1986-July 1987), pp. 4-28.

3304 Zorpette, Glenn. "Breaking the Enemy's Code: British Intelligence Deciphered Germany's Top Secret Military Communications with Colossus, an Early Vacuum-Tube Computer." *IEEE Spectrum,* 24, no. 9 (Sept. 1987), pp. 47-51.

Coauthor Index

Subject Index